Praise for A ROSE FOR HER GRAVE AND OTHER TRUE CASES
(Ann Rule's Crime Files: Vol. 1):

'Fascinating ... Each page is a gripper ... Ann Rule is truly a master crime writer in *A Rose for Her Grave and Other True Cases*, a book that breaks new ground in the true-crime field'
— *Real Crime Book Digest*

'[In] this chilling collection ... her unwavering voice presents even the most gruesome details rationally'
— *Publishers Weekly*

'Ann Rule ... has a great knack for horrific detail'
— *New York Daily News*

'Ann Rule is one of the best "true-crime" writers around ... The lady knows what she's talking and writing about'
— *Camden Courier-Post*

'The queen of the genre, Ann Rule, inaugurates a new series with *A Rose for Her Grave and Other True Cases*'
— *Philadelphia Enquirer*

Also by Ann Rule:

A ROSE FOR HER GRAVE AND OTHER TRUE CASES
(Ann Rule's Crime Files: Vol. 1)
THE STRANGER BESIDE ME
EVERYTHING SHE EVER WANTED
IF YOU REALLY LOVED ME
POSSESSION
SMALL SACRIFICES

Ann Rule is one of America's foremost true-crime writers, and the author of five bestsellers, including *A Rose for Her Grave*, volume one in this new series of true-crime stories; *If You Really Loved Me*, the chilling chronicle of a millionaire's murderous secret life; and *Everything She Ever Wanted*, the terrifying story of a sociopathic Georgia belle and her fatal allure. She is also the author of the bestselling *Small Sacrifices*, the horrific account of a woman's homicidal assault on her three young children; and *The Stranger Beside Me*, the fascinating tale of Rule's dawning horror as she realized her friend and co-worker Ted Bundy was a serial killer.

A former Seattle policewoman, she has published 1,400 articles and eight books on homicide cases. She lectures often to law enforcement professionals on serial murder, sadistic sociopaths and women who kill. She has testified before the US Senate and presented a seminar to the FBI Academy. She served on the US Justice Department task force setting up the Violent Criminal Apprehension Program (VI-CAP) now in use at FBI headquarters to track and trap serial killers. When she is not attending trials and researching new books, she makes her home near Seattle, Washington.

YOU BELONG TO ME
and Other True Cases

Ann Rule's Crime Files: Vol. 2

ANN RULE

WARNER BOOKS

A *Warner* Book

First published in the USA in 1994 by Pocket Books,
a division of Simon & Schuster, Inc.
First published in Great Britain in 1994 by Warner Books
Reprinted 1995

Copyright © 1994 by Ann Rule

The moral right of the author has been asserted.

The names of some individuals in this book have been changed.
Such names are indicated by an asterisk (*) the first time each
appears in the book.

All rights reserved.
No part of this publication may be reproduced,
stored in a retrieval system, or transmitted, in any
form or by any means, without the prior
permission in writing of the publisher, nor be
otherwise circulated in any form of binding or
cover other than that in which it is published and
without a similar condition including this
condition being imposed on the subsequent purchaser.

A CIP catalogue record for this book
is available from the British Library.

ISBN 0 7515 1140 4

Printed in England by Clays Ltd, St Ives plc

Warner Books
A Division of
Little, Brown and Company (UK)
Brettenham House
Lancaster Place
London WC2E 7EN

From the time my memory began I have believed that policemen are among the finest human beings on this earth. Nothing has ever changed my mind. My grandfather was a sheriff and then my uncle. At the age of 19 I became a law enforcement officer myself. With the wisdom and experience of almost four decades I have learned that there will always be a minute percentage of bad cops. But they are only a tiny blot on the bravery and dedication of the mass of men and women who protect us and uphold the law.

I dedicate *You Belong to Me* to the millions of good cops out there—to those who will, and too often *do*, lay down their lives for us.

I thank them and wish them Godspeed.

Acknowledgments

When a book is *true,* as this one is, I am totally dependent on facts, documentation, and the keen memories of other people. It is also a real challenge to gather photographs from dozens of sources, all of whom furnished them to me graciously and with trust that they would receive their precious *originals* back. I cannot say how much I appreciate that. And, too, I have my front-line critics, my "first" readers who point out little slips that my eyes can no longer detect. And sometimes they have enthusiastic comments, and that's even better. They play such an important part.

As always, the names that follow are in no particular order because their lives and mine tend to cross again and again in different places on this earth and for different reasons. I think they will all understand.

Thank you Don and Susan Dappen, Phil and Margie Williams, Sandy Harris, Jimm Redmond, Pat and Fred Wessendorf, Jodi Dombroski, Carol Worley, Kathy and Gary Jacobi, Charles Steadham, Gerry Brittingham, Verne Carver, Bob and Denise Evans, Maureen and Bill Woodcock, Lisa and Martin Woodcock, Donna Anders, Bill and Shirley Hickman, Lola Linstad, "Tex" and Gene Parsons, Fay Moss, Gail

Acknowledgments

DiRe, Diane Brace, Bobbi Bennett, Chuck Wright, Robert Keppel, and Greg Canova.

And thank you to John Hansen, Mark Ericks, Joe Sanford, John Boatman, Sonny Davis, Hank Gruber, Rudy Sutlovich, Don Cameron, Duane Homan, Jim Yoshida, John Henry Browne, Len Randall, Mike Baily, Ted Forrester, Joyce and Pierce Brooks, Rod Englert, Dr. Clyde Snow, Mike Tando, Craig VandePutte, Bob and Gen Lofgren, Jim Lane, Jim Swenson, Gary Svendson, Dennis Elder, Colleen and Scott Elder, Claude and Ernie Bailey, Millie Yoacham, Austin and Charlotte Seth, Erik Seth and Denise Watson, Nils and Judith Seth, and Roberta Yochim.

Thank you to Sudden Printing in Burien for living up to your name.

I am a most fortunate writer to have the backup team I do, and I appreciate them: my editors at Pocket Books, Julie Rubenstein and Bill Grose; their editorial assistants, Liate Stehlik and Joe Gram; my publicist, Cindy Ratzlaff; Pocket's sensational art director, Paolo Pepe, who always understands what I am trying to say; my gentle but determined expert in literary law, Emily Remes. And finally, my literary agents, Joan and Joe Foley; and my theatrical agents, Mary Alice Kier and Anna Cottle. Bless you all!

Contents

Author's Note

You Belong to Me, the second in my anthology series, contains one book-length new case—the title story— and five cases from my files. *You Belong to Me* took me about as far away from familiar places as I could get; I found myself on the Treasure Coast of Florida, re- searching what may well be one of the more bizarre cases I have encountered. While this is a case of the nineties, the emotions involved are ageless. The killer, however, was someone even I would not have sus- pected, which only serves to prove again, I suppose, that there is no room for preconceived ideas or haste when it comes to solving murders.

Anyone who has read my work probably has sensed that I become very involved in the lives of the people I write about. These are not simply "stories" to me; I know full well that I am writing about real people. For a time, when I have finished a book or an article, I move away from the people I have met, involved in some new project. But I always go back, and I never forget. In the five revisited cases in this book I found myself walking back into the lives of human beings I had known before. Some of them, of course, were already dead when I "met" them, and nothing has changed for them; others in their stories have gone on, as we all must in the face of tragedy. I was amazed how much I learned as I updated the five cases I once thought I knew thoroughly: "Black Christmas," "One Trick Pony," "The Computer Error and the Killer," "The Vanishing," and "The Last Letter."

If there is one thread that weaves itself through *You Belong to Me,* it is that each piece has an element of shocking revelation. Innocent people are totally unaware of the thoughts and plans of someone they know so well (or think they do) that they have no fear of him or her—*or* of someone who moves so dimly in the background of their lives that they never consider the danger there.

Some killers follow their targets with stealthy surveillance. They are like ghosts who betray their presence by the snapping of a twig or quiet breathing on the other end of a phone line. Others are omnipresent, as familiar as your own face in the mirror.

Several of the following cases, including the title story—"You Belong to Me"—deal with obsessed lovers, and yet the paths they took to snare their quarries are as diverse as the human beings involved.

Predictably, there are few happy endings.

Nor are there happy endings when a serial killer sets out to stalk—not those he has ties to, but absolute strangers who have the great misfortune to possess certain characteristics that trigger a murderer into violence.

As I look for parallels and differences I realize that almost every case in this book is about *power,* about a killer's need not only to control his own life, but to direct the lives of others. Oddly, I have never researched a killer who was *truly* powerful; every one of them was acting out of weakness. All of them were hollow and empty inside—empty enough that they went to tortuous and tragic lengths to seize power from their victims.

They are all different. They are all alike.

I suspect there are cases in this second volume of my true crime files that will astound you and catch you off guard just as they did me.

Ann Rule

You Belong to Me

All of us wonder how a murderer selects his victim or victims; I think about this often. What chaotic synchronicity brought them together? Sometimes they have known each other for half a century or more; sometimes they are strangers until the ill-fated instant they meet. Always I find myself thinking, "If only . . ." If the victim had left a little later or a little earlier. If it hadn't rained or traffic had been lighter or heavier. If the partners in a marriage had never met, never dated, never fallen in love and had chosen someone else entirely. If only time could be rewound and choices that turned out to be fatal could be revised.

But of course, real life does not allow second guessing.

In the title story of this second volume, "You Belong to Me," there were so many variables that might have changed the terrible ending. The victim was, perhaps, not the woman the killer believed she was. Perhaps. The killer was the last person in the world most of us would have suspected.

1

PART ONE

Sandy

1

The slender woman *lay on her stomach in the grove of pine trees, the hot sun baking the air; even though its rays were filtered into stripes by the pine branches above her, the sun was almost as intense in March as it would be in full summer. Where she rested her head the pines opened three or four hours a day, just enough for one steady golden ray to spotlight her cheek. Her skin was exposed, but her nakedness was hidden from the drivers and passengers riding in the trucks and cars that whooshed by on the freeway lanes that bracketed the pine grove. She was as good as invisible. The woman paid no heed to the noise of the engines or to the diesel fumes that drifted into the clean woodsy air.*

The I-95 Interstate snakes all along the eastern seaboard of the United States, beginning on the border between Maine and New Brunswick, Canada, and ending in Miami. Some who have reason to know say that parts of 95 are the most dangerous stretches of road in America. It is certainly one of the busiest freeways and one of the first ever laid down across the land. Down and down 95 plunges, from the icy winter in the north to the balmy tropical always-summer of Florida. From Bangor to Boston to New York it rushes, skirting Philadelphia, passing through the heart of Washington, D.C., before it curves south through Virginia and the Carolinas. I-95 picks up the Atlantic Ocean salt wind passing through Savannah, and then hugs the Florida coastline: Jacksonville to Melbourne, Fort Pierce, Fort Lauderdale, and on into Miami, close by the sea all the way.

Families travel I-95 as they head for Disney World in Orlando and come home with their cars full of stuffed Mickey Mouses and funny hats. "Snowbirds" flee northern blizzards—and then wait until the very last moment of gently balmy Florida weather, timing their departure so that they can enjoy northern springtime and escape the thick, muggy heat of southern summers. Drug runners cruise along I-95, some of them with millions of dollars worth of drugs cleverly hidden, and others as transparent and klutzy as Disney's Goofy. Many of the travelers drive straight through the 1200-plus miles from New York to Miami, senior citizens tending to drowse behind the wheel, young men fortifying themselves with alcohol, and truck drivers with No-Doz. All of them keep a wary eye out for local law enforcement and the highway patrol. Everybody's pushing a little too fast. Troopers will look the other way for five or so miles over the speed limit; after that, the ticket books come out.

Interstate 95 passes through some of the prettiest country in Florida as it bisects the eastern coastal counties in the central part of the state: Brevard, Indian River, and St. Lucie. The Indian River parallels the coast from Cape Canaveral to Port Salerno, separating the narrow coastal islands and reefs from the mainland. Here dolphins leap and the gentle giant manatees swim so ponderously that boats threaten their survival as a species. Here the land is as flat as a plain, but lush with trees and flowers that flourish in steamy heat. Orange groves and pines, crotons and palmettos. Oleanders and hibiscus. When it rains in Indian River County the hot drops literally pound the earth; when the hurricanes come they can quickly transform acres of land heavy with rows of new condominiums back into the reefs they once were.

In recent years Indian River County has been spared the more ferocious vagaries of nature. Hurricane Andrew devastated Miami, but left Sebastian, Winter Beach, and Vero Beach scarcely touched. The last hurricane to do real damage in Indian River County was Hurricane David in 1979.

Tourism is the major industry in coastal Florida, but it is still a civilized tourism in Indian River County. There is no sense of crowding or traffic jams in Vero Beach. Two Florida state troopers on each shift can handle the stretch of I-95 that passes through Indian River County. Of course, there are drugs here—there are drugs everywhere, and both the county and the local departments expect to deal with that. But a cop can still have a listed home phone number, and he doesn't have to wire his house with a burglar alarm or glance nervously over his shoulder all the time.

Although most of the travelers heading north and south on I-95 scarcely notice what goes on in Indian River County, thousands of people live out their days there, half hoping that their quality of life, weather, and natural beauty won't be "discovered," making their area a little Miami. They know one another, recognize obvious snowbirds, get married, have babies, go to the PTA, and get divorced, and some of them die there.

* * *

7

The Vero Beach Police Department is housed in a white stucco building with bright blue trim; the Indian River County Sheriff's Office is beige stucco, and they are both surrounded by flowering bushes and trees. The Florida Highway Patrol headquarters for the district is located on North 25th Street down in Fort Pierce. All three departments work together, their boundaries touching and intersecting. Some days, the biggest problems local cops have are the vagrants who migrate down to enjoy a warm winter, a number of whom are misfits and mental cases.

And some days, Indian River County has unspeakably horrendous crimes.

Just as in California, Oregon, and Washington, there are few natives along Florida's coastlines. Hardly anybody living there was actually *born* there. Fred and Pat Wessendorf moved down from Gloversville in upstate New York in the fifties. Fred's dad had a place in Fellsmere in Indian River County. They were young marrieds then and had a baby son, Martin. But they soon had three daughters: Kathy, Susan, and Sandra Lynn. Fred worked for the Vero Beach *Press Journal* in production and later became expert at the highly technical process of setting colored photographs. For years Fred and Pat added to their income with a paper route, stocking newspaper dispensing machines in the wee hours of the morning.

A taciturn man who listens far more than he speaks, Fred married a pretty woman who more than makes up for his quietness; Pat Wessendorf says what she thinks and what she believes to be right—whether it is tactful or not. She always has. She is very protective of her children, a fierce mother hen when she thinks they are being threatened. In the last analysis, it is probably Sandra Lynn—"Sandy"—who gets most of Pat's energy. Sandy is the baby.

The young Wessendorfs worked hard to raise their four children. They lived in the house that Fred's dad had owned, a relatively small house on a big lot full of trees and flowers. When the three girls were at an age when they needed more space and privacy, Fred built them a kind of "dormitory" out in back of the main house. The Wessendorf girls were all blond and pretty, but as different as three sisters could be. Funny that two of them would marry cops. Susan and Sandy. Even so, the men they married seemed to have nothing at all in common beyond their careers.

Although their son Martin moved back to New York, the Wessendorfs' daughters all stayed close to home. Kathy and her husband raised kids and exotic birds and pets. When she visited Kathy, Pat Wessendorf sometimes had to steel herself, wondering what might come wandering into the room. Sometimes it was an iguana, sometimes some critter she didn't even recognize. Susan worked at a bank, and Kathy and Sandy would eventually work for the same company in Vero Beach, a real estate and investment firm.

Every Thursday, without fail, Pat and her three girls tried to get together for lunch. The Wessendorfs and their grown children were the last family in the world who ever expected trouble. But then, what family ever does? They had problems, of course, the kind that everybody runs into from time to time, but not big, tragic, shocking trouble—not the kind that brings with it years of nightmares and bitter memories.

2

Fred **and Pat** Wessendorf's kids were all individuals and seemed more so by the late 1980s. In her early thirties, Susan Wessendorf Dappen was unarguably the *athletic* daughter. Her husband Don (Donny to his friends) was a lieutenant with the Vero Beach Police Department. Chief Jim Gabbard invited the spouses of his officers to use the fully equipped gym at headquarters. Susan was there several times a week after work. She and Don jogged, usually taking their dog, Casey, along, and swam in their own pool.

"None of us girls really ever got into cooking," Sue remarked matter-of-factly. "Not me or Sandy, at least."

Don Dappen has never minded. Sue concentrated on her very responsible job at the bank and was a great mother to their two kids. Moreover, Sue was absolutely fascinated with Don's career from the beginning. Being a policeman's wife is one of the hardest jobs in the world. Some wives don't want to know what happens on a day or night shift. Knowing makes them more frightened for their husbands. The job is easier for a policeman to handle when his wife cares, though. And Sue always did.

Don Dappen became a cop when he was twenty years old. Stocky and muscular, a friendly man—but one with a subtly unmistakable air of authority—he made detective at twenty-three.

A few years ago Don Dappen could easily have seen the end of his career—and his life—when he took a chance at foiling a major drug deal. A twenty-eight-year-old Fort Lauderdale man and his partner, a forty-eight-year-old New York resident and a licensed pilot, had loaded a twin-engine Piper Navajo plane with fifty-six bales of marijuana weighing 1,300 pounds and headed somewhat precariously north from Miami. They made the mistake of stopping at the Vero Beach Municipal Airport to refuel.

At 9 p.m. on a Thursday night the plane taxied past the Federal Aviation Administration's flight service center, and the air traffic controller noted that the numbers on the plane did not match the numbers the pilot had radioed to the tower on landing.

The controller notified the Vero Beach Police Department, and Don Dappen responded in an unmarked car. The Vero Beach dispatcher informed him that the plane currently being refueled had serial numbers N4469R—numbers that matched those of a Piper Navajo reported stolen out of a Miami airport.

Don Dappen, who would later shake his head when he remembered the incident, realizing in retrospect how it might have ended, watched as the white Navajo, loaded with two hundred gallons of fuel, began to taxi slowly down the runway. Dappen turned on his blue bubble lights, hit the siren, and he drove directly onto the airfield, deliberately cutting in front of the moving plane.

He expected it to stop, but the pilot didn't even slow down. Instead he revved up his engine. Don Dappen pulled ahead of the plane while a Vero Beach patrol car raced along beside it. The policemen intended to at least slow the stolen plane.

At that point they were going eighty miles an hour. "He came up behind me real fast," Don recalled. "He just kept going. He didn't have any intention of stopping. All I could see from the whole back of my car was his headlights. . . ."

Playing a dangerous game of near-misses, Dappen veered off the runway, and then back in front of the Navajo. The pilot became airborne—but barely—skipping over the top of Dappen's car at no more than fifteen feet.

Weighed down by the bales of marijuana, the pilot couldn't get high enough to clear a cabbage palm tree at the west end of the airport. His left wing slammed into the palm, and the plane spun so violently that it ripped apart and catapulted through the darkness into the thick undergrowth at the end of the main runway. It ended in a smoldering heap, leaking the gas it had just taken aboard. Don Dappen and his fellow officer, along with firefighters, pulled the wounded drug traffickers from the wreckage.

"It was pitch dark," Dappen said. "You couldn't see anything, and there was an odor of nothing but gasoline."

Miraculously, the wrecked $245,000 plane didn't catch fire. Just as miraculously, the pilot and his partner survived, although they needed a hospital stay to recuperate. They were charged with trafficking marijuana, aggravated assault, resisting arrest with violence, and grand theft.

"The chase didn't get to me until I got home," Don Dappen said. "Then I started to think about it. . . ."

Sandy Wessendorf met *her* cop when she was still in high school. She and Timothy Scott Harris came together like two people in a novel, their meeting as close to a woman's romantic fantasy as you can get. Sandy was only sixteen, and Tim was twenty-one, those five years a wide stretch at that point in their lives. Had they been even a few years older, no one would have raised an eyebrow. But Sandra Lynn Wessendorf was a junior in high school, and Tim Harris was already a police officer in Sebastian, Florida, the tiny hamlet where she lived.

Although Sandy didn't really approve, one of her best friends had a terrific crush on another policeman on the Sebastian force. "He was married, and he even had three kids—but he gave my friend a line that only a teenage girl would believe," Sandy recalled from the vantage point of maturity some years later. "She really thought he was going to divorce his wife and marry *her*. She wouldn't listen to reason."

Sandy's girlfriend needed an excuse to get out of the house—and Sandy was it. "I went along one night while she met this cop. He was working partners with a cop named Tim Harris. Cindy* went off in the police car with the guy she was crazy about, and Tim sat in my car, and we talked. I don't know what they were doing—not for sure—but I know that Tim and I just talked. I'm sure I noticed that he was handsome, but he seemed so much older. I wasn't really impressed. Not that first night."

The next time Sandy ran into Tim Harris it was different. She never forgot that night. It was Sunday, January 14, 1979, shortly after eleven p.m., when Sandy and Cindy were driving in Sebastian near the airport. The girls heard just the beginning trill of a siren, and Sandy saw the whirling blue bubble light in her rearview mirror. She panicked for a moment and then pulled over to the curb.

Sandy needn't have worried. The tall young police-

*The names of some individuals in this book have been changed. Such names are indicated by an asterisk (*) the first time each appears in the book.

man who walked up to her window was Tim Harris, and he was grinning. This time Sandy had to admit that he was probably the best-looking guy she had ever seen in her life. He had dark brown hair and eyes even greener than her own. Sandy Wessendorf was popular; she pretty much had her choice of boys to go out with, and she had never considered dating an "older" man. Now she did.

"Miss," Tim said in mock seriousness, "I'm afraid I'm going to have to arrest you. You've violated a municipal ordinance."

"What?" Sandy knew she hadn't been speeding. Her dad had pounded driving safety into her head.

"I'm sorry, but I'm going to have to write you up for violation of a 916.83."

"What's that?" Sandy still wasn't sure if he was serious or if he was teasing her.

"Resisting an officer." He was very businesslike as he filled out the complaint affidavit on his clipboard. Sandy answered his questions, giving her address on Victoria Drive in Sebastian, her height and weight: "Five feet, four . . . 110 pounds." She saw him write down "blond" for her hair, and his lips twitched a little as he filled in "Eyes—Pretty."

"I'm arresting you on probable cause, for being non-sociable," Tim told her. He tore a copy of the arrest form off and handed it to her. "You'll have to comply with the instructions there at the bottom."

Sandy read what Tim had written, and she began to smile. "Resisting this officer at the Seb. Airport. But will fix that on 1-15-79 at 7 p.m. at City Hall—This officer is off duty then and maybe Sandy would like to go somewhere, *without* Cindy."

Tim explained that she would have to report to headquarters, or the "arrest" would stay on her record. Even at the age of sixteen, Sandy Wessendorf was stubborn. She didn't report to the police station the next night.

Tim Harris wasn't about to give up so easily. He pulled her over about four days later as she drove through Sebastian. This time he refused to return Sandy's driver's license after he'd asked to see it. "I'll be writing reports later at the station," he said. "And you can come pick up your license, and we can talk."

If she wanted her driver's license back, Sandy had no choice but to go down to Sebastian police headquarters. She spent some time with Tim, talking, although she held back from accepting an actual date with him. He was too old. He was out of school, an adult—and she still had her senior year ahead of her, and all the fun that went with that last year of school. She wasn't nearly ready to be tied down.

It wasn't that Tim frightened her. Not at all. He was a local boy, or right next door to local. He told her he had graduated from high school in 1976 in Satellite Beach, a little town about twenty-five miles north of Sebastian, built on the reef that led into Patrick Air Force Base and Cape Canaveral. Tim Harris had been a track star at Satellite High School, excelling in both high hurdles and cross country. His parents were divorced now. All Sandy knew about his family was that it sounded as though his dad had some really important job at Cape Canaveral, and his mother had a good career, too.

Sandy Wessendorf must have said "no" to Tim Harris a half dozen times, but he kept turning up in her life. Every time she looked around, Tim seemed to be nearby. No female could resist Tim Harris when he wanted something, and he certainly seemed to want Sandy.

So that January night in 1979 was really the beginning for them. Almost fifteen years later that yellowing arrest form for "resisting an officer" was still in Sandy's mementos, a reminder of that first, happy time, a wonderfully romantic meeting that didn't foreshadow all the pain, the disappointment, and the tragedies that came later.

Sandy eventually stopped avoiding Tim and agreed to meet him on a quiet road in Sebastian. He was on duty, but she was to drive her car and park it behind his. Her parents certainly wouldn't have approved if they had known the details of their sixteen-year-old daughter's romance with a twenty-one-year-old cop. But Sandy was already a little bit in love, and every time she saw Tim that emotion deepened.

When Tim finally came to call on Sandy at her home he was very polite; he called her parents "Mr. and Mrs. Wessendorf." (He always would—even after he knew them well.) Fred Wessendorf liked Tim. (He always would.) Pat wasn't so quick to warm to Sandy's suitor. But that was Pat, feisty and protective as a lioness, and she always felt uneasy about Tim. She recalled the first time she met Sandy's new boyfriend.

"Tim was weird. He was always creeping around," she remembered. "I heard the doorbell ring, but when I went to answer it there was nobody there. Tim was hiding in the shrubbery beside the house. Sandy said it was because he was shy—but for heaven's sake, he was a grown man and a policeman, and it struck me as definitely odd that he would play games like that. He was always like that, creeping around, hiding, and jumping out at you. . . ."

It wasn't a joke. That's the way Tim Harris was. He didn't come out laughing. He would walk around the house with his head hung low, like a gawky kid.

Sandy fell more and more in love with Tim Harris. She was flattered by his persistence. He simply would not take "no" for an answer, and he left her no time or space to see any other male. Tim was incredibly handsome in his uniform; he made high school boys look like kids. Sandy recalled "falling head over heels in love with him—as only a sixteen-year-old girl can."

Even so, it almost seemed as though the moment Sandy showed her love for Tim, he changed. For the first weeks that she dated Tim Sandy believed that they were going steady, even though he tormented her by flirting with her girlfriends. "It was odd," she said. "He seemed so shy, but he was always coming on to my friends. That really hurt me—and embarrassed me—but he didn't seem to care."

Besides flirting with her friends, Tim Harris was a completely undependable date. Sometimes Tim showed up, sometimes he showed up hours late, and sometimes he didn't show up at all. "He would tell me he'd been out of town—that he'd gone to see his mother."

Sandy always waited for Tim, afraid to leave the phone in case he might call. "I guess I was fascinated because he was so elusive."

Her mother was only disgusted; Pat Wessendorf hated to see any man make her daughter so miserable. One time when Tim showed up late—playing his hiding-in-the-bushes game, as usual—Pat lied and told him that Sandy wasn't home. Sandy was horrified when she found out that her mother had sent Tim away without even telling her. He *had* kept his promise to come over—if belatedly—and Sandy could always rationalize and make excuses for him.

What Sandy Wessendorf hadn't realized was that Tim was dating another girl at least as often as he was seeing her. Tim's absences finally grew to a point where Sandy couldn't ignore the obvious any longer. Too many of Tim's excuses were totally implausible. She asked questions around Sebastian and learned that her rival was a pretty Melbourne Village girl named Michelle Schrader.* Michelle was attending college at Auburn up across the Alabama border. Sandy's hopes were completely dashed when Michelle called her and told her that she and Tim were going steady.

When Sandy confronted him, Tim grudgingly admitted that he *was* seeing someone else, but he explained that it wasn't anything serious—nothing for Sandy to give a second thought to. "We're having problems," he insisted. "I'm trying to break up with her."

Both young women were too deeply involved with the handsome policeman to simply walk away, and Tim seemed almost to enjoy the tug-of-war. It didn't take brilliant detective work for Sandy to discover that Tim was not only dating Michelle, he was engaged to her!

At one point, in the spring of 1979, Sandy and her sister, Susan, traveled up to see Michelle in Auburn, Alabama. Sandy still hoped that Michelle had been exaggerating her hold on Tim, but the visit only made seventeen-year-old Sandy Wessendorf feel worse. Michelle was wearing an engagement ring Tim had given her, and she showed Sandy and Susan her wedding gown and bragged about her wedding plans, "We're going to be married in August," she told Sandy. "I'm going to quit college to marry Tim."

Sandy was crushed. Michelle was only a few years older, but she was so much more sophisticated, and she seemed so sure of Tim.

Michelle kept talking as if she had no idea what Tim meant to Sandy, or maybe she was just rubbing Sandy's nose in *her* relationship to make a point. "I hope when we come down [to Sebastian] me and Tim can take you and one of your little boyfriends to dinner."

"Little boyfriend" indeed! The only boyfriend that Sandy had was Tim—the same man who was Michelle's fiancé. As it turned out, there was no wedding for Tim and Michelle in August, 1979, but the knowledge that Tim had been engaged and never told her made Sandy break off with him. Although it hurt her, she wouldn't talk to him or see him. What was the point? She could never trust him again.

And then on August 30, 1979, Hurricane David roared out of Cuba and Puerto Rico and headed straight for the east coast of Florida with winds predicted to peak at 150 miles an hour.

"I got a call from Tim," Pat Wessendorf recalled. "He didn't say who he was, but I knew his voice. He said, 'This is the Sebastian Police Department, ma'am. We're just checking to be sure you all know what shelter to go to if the hurricane hits us.'"

"Yes, we do, Tim," Pat answered, letting him know he hadn't fooled her. She wasn't very happy about what the phone call really meant. It meant that Tim Harris still cared about Sandy, and that he was worried about her safety as the violent hurricane roared up the Florida coast. Pat felt almost a premonition; although Sandy would be thrilled to know that Tim still thought about her, Pat wondered if having Tim back in their lives could lead to happiness for any of them. He was handsome, he had a good job, he came from good people—and yet there was something about him that made the hairs prickle along Pat's neck. He had lied to Sandy, he always had another woman in the background, and he sneaked around like some prowler. Pat had noted that Tim would never look her straight in the eye; he wouldn't look anyone in the eye. Nobody could be that bashful —and be a policeman.

Hurricane David left a thousand people dead in its wake, but it brought Sandy and Tim back together. The night Tim called the Wessendorfs to check on their family's safety he had phoned from his apartment. Michelle was staying there with him. She overheard that call, and she knew that Tim still cared about Sandy.

Later Tim called Sandy and told her he just had to be sure she and her folks were okay. It had been three months since she had talked to him, but Sandy had wanted so much for Tim to come back to her. It had just about broken her heart not to see him or be with him.

After Hurricane David Tim was with Sandy again. But then he was still with Michelle, too. He walked a tightwire between the two girls. Tim often had to think fast to keep Michelle from realizing how much Sandy was back in his life.

Not fast enough. During Christmas vacation, 1979, Michelle saw what was happening, and she dropped out of Auburn and moved back home and in with Tim. Keeping him was far more important to her than her education.

Sandy Wessendorf was devastated. She lost weight and played her tape of "Sad Eyes" over and over again. She would have done anything to make Tim happy. "I would have jumped off a building for him if he asked me to. . . ." And there was no doubt that she meant it.

"I wanted him back so much that I started seeing him with her [Michelle] living there—at least for a little while. He bought us both Christmas presents, and he told me he would get rid of her. He was mean to her. He'd have me over there while she was there. . . . One time she jumped me. Like a cat—scratching and pulling my hair. Then she went in the bathroom and took a bunch of pills in there with her. I was frightened. What's this girl going to do? Kill herself?"

It was a histrionic gesture. Tim Harris had both Sandy and Michelle madly in love with him, two beautiful young women. He hated confrontations, but he seemed to enjoy being the center of so much attention. He should have said good-bye to one or the other, but he didn't.

Michelle lived with Tim for six months, and then she moved out. She told her co-workers at a local hospital that it was almost a relief to be done with him. It probably was. Michelle had come to work marked with purpling bruises, but she would never talk about how she got them. When she was truly through with Tim she *did* seem to be a much happier person.

And she had no more bruises.

It was early 1980. Sandy had won in the battle for Tim Harris. In many ways, however, she had lost—and she didn't even know it.

All three of her daughters got on Pat for being nosy and interfering with their lives—most of all with Sandy's—and yet she believed she had to. She had life experience, and they didn't. Pat had been lucky in finding Fred. He was a good man and a gentle man. Sandy didn't know that all men weren't like her father. And yet even Pat couldn't put her finger on anything truly wrong about Tim. He was only twenty-two, and a lot of twenty-two-year-old men—boys, really—didn't know what they wanted in a wife. Fred liked Tim, and Fred Wessendorf could usually read people pretty well. Pat continued to feel uneasy.

When Tim Harris came back to Sandy she was older and more wary of him; he had betrayed her too many times. Still, she wanted to believe him when he asked her to forgive him. Sandy never carried a grudge, not in her whole life. If someone apologized, she would accept it in a minute—and it was over. She didn't stay mad. And she loved Tim so much.

If anything, Sandy Wessendorf was more beautiful than she had been when Tim first pulled her over with his police car. Her blond hair was very long, butterscotch-colored with natural sun streaks. She wore scarcely any makeup—she didn't need it. Actually, Sandy was the epitome of what Tim Harris had always wanted in a girlfriend. A long time later he showed her a picture of his girlfriend in high school, and she was shocked. "She looked just like me," Sandy told her mom. "Almost exactly like me. It was so weird looking at that picture. It could have been *my* picture."

From the time he was in junior high Tim Harris had always had a girlfriend, and he stayed with each girl, if not faithfully, for a year or two. All of Tim's women —save Michelle Schrader—had long blond hair. Michelle had short dark hair. Tim was always the one who initiated the breakups, moving on to the next girl he had picked out. Anyone knowing Tim well knew he would never let a woman reject *him*.

There would always be something of a paradox in the young policeman's view of women. While he

sought them out continually and charmed them totally, there was a part of him that felt they deserved no
respect at all. Men who knew Tim recognized a thinly
veiled contempt for females, and it puzzled them.

"He could be strange," another cop recalled. "We'd
be driving down the street, and he'd hang out the
window and call some woman a slut or make obscene
gestures at her. I mean, the guy was a cop, for Pete's
sake—"

3

Tim Harris was, indeed, a cop. He had always
wanted to be a policeman, and he had kept his eye
firmly on that goal. When his parents divorced he
lived with his father and stepmother so that he could
graduate from Satellite High and stay in the town
where he had more contacts that would help him get
started in law enforcement.

Tim had always been a hard worker; he really had
no choice. Although his father, George, had a good job
as a draftsman working in the space program, and his
mother, Virginia, worked as an executive secretary,
Tim was only one among six Harris kids. They grew
up near Washington, D.C., at 522 North Imboden
Street in Alexandria, Virginia. Paul was born in
January of 1957, Tim on April 26, 1958, Bethany Lea
in September, 1960, Dan in June, 1961, David in
June, 1963, and Sarah in July of 1964. They were all

extremely photogenic children with brown hair and bluish-green eyes. Six children in seven years must have been a handful and a strain on the budget for George and Virginia Harris.

In 1965 George and Virginia moved with their young family from Washington, D.C., to Satellite Beach, where George had accepted a job in the burgeoning space program.

Tim worked whenever there were summer vacations and school breaks, usually at Disney World in Orlando. The summer after he graduated from Satellite High he worked as a busboy for a restaurant in Disney World. That fall he began to take courses at Brevard Community College in subjects he hoped would help him get a job in police work. In January, 1977, he was sponsored by the Satellite Beach Police Department to take the Basic Police Training Course at Brevard Community College. Even though he was willing to pay for the training himself, Tim had to have a sponsor. He was relieved and elated when the chief of the Satellite Beach Police Department stepped in, recommending that he be accepted in the police courses.

Tim finished the basic police course in April of 1977. He couldn't find a police job right away, so he joined the U.S. Army Reserve on July 1 and attended Military Police School from then until October. He had reached his full height of six feet, two inches, but he only weighed 175 pounds. He looked like what he was, a tall, skinny, good-looking nineteen-year-old kid, unformed and a little gawky. But he had a passion for law enforcement, and he was going to make it happen.

His counselor at Brevard Community College, William McEntee, wrote a letter recommending Tim to the mayor of Melbourne Village, Florida, as a good candidate for their minuscule police force. How well McEntee really knew Tim Harris is questionable. His letter is couched in terms that allowed him an escape hatch if Tim didn't work out.

"Apparently he [Tim Harris] will prove to be reliable, patient, and conscientious in carrying out his obligations.

"He appears to be free of self-doubt and disillusionment. Probably he will be a good team member, a good listener, and a sincere worker.

"I am willing to recommend that he be given favorable consideration."

It *was* a rather odd recommendation. Few would-be cops are tested for "disillusionment." At any rate, in November, 1977, Tim Harris was hired as a police officer for the Melbourne Village Police Department. Melbourne Village was a tiny town in Brevard County with a police force of only two or three officers. There wasn't much to do there, but it was a step on the ladder up to where Tim wanted to go; he wanted to become a Florida Highway Patrolman.

He was only nineteen, and he was a cop. That was enough for the moment.

It was in Melbourne Village that Tim had met Michelle Schrader, the girl who would vie with Sandy for him. Michelle was a high school senior when she met Tim. She was seventeen then, about the same age Sandy Wessendorf was two years later when she became involved with the handsome policeman. Tim could be charming. Michelle's parents had even invited Tim to live with them for a few months after he left his father's and stepmother's home.

Tim was voted Melbourne Village Police Officer of the Year during his abbreviated career there. Actually, it was a little bit like Sheriff Andy Taylor of Mayberry. Andy and Deputy Barney Fife made up Mayberry's sheriff's department, and there weren't that many officers on the Melbourne Village force either. The award had to pass back and forth among the skeleton police force, and Tim Harris was the only one on the force who hadn't had the honor.

In truth, the police department was troubled by reports it received about Tim Harris. There were allegations that Tim was using his badge and his status to stop young women, sometimes taking their licenses so that they would have to meet him to get them back. The kid was young and interested in women—but he had no business chasing them on the job. Moreover, Tim had allegedly arrested a motorist for having an expired temporary tag when there was a valid tag in the car's backseat. Besides that, Tim drove his squad car like a bat out of hell.

Tim Harris was given three choices: Melbourne Village's Police Officer of the Year could resign, be fired, or be placed on probation. Tim chose to resign. He wrote a short letter of resignation on July 3, 1978.

"It is [*sic*] regret I hereby tender my resignation from the Melbourne Village Police Department to be effective this date."

Apparently there were no hard feelings. More likely it was the closing of ranks that often happens among policemen. The rest of the world gives them a hard time; unless an offense is egregious, law enforcement takes care of its own.

The following November, the police chief, Robert Segien, gave Tim a letter of recommendation.

To Whom It May Concern:
    Timothy S. Harris was employed by this department for a period of nine months. During this time,

Officer Harris' enthusiasm toward his duties gave him the extra motivations to perform his duties in an excellent manner. Officer Harris' willingness to accept any assignment, regardless how unpleasant, coupled with amiable attitude, proves him to be a definite asset to any department that would require his services. He is an individual who his superiors can rely on to get the job done with a professional attitude. He is trustworthy, intelligent and has a high sense of responsibility towards his profession as a police officer.

With each new job application thereafter, Tim Harris explained that he had resigned from the Melbourne Village department because he "was very unhappy with the department," explaining that it did not live up to the professional standards he had expected.

Tim was very young, and a lot of young cops mature and stop hitting on women and driving too fast. Since the Melbourne Village Police Department soon ceased to exist at all, whatever problems Tim Harris had had there were forgotten. He was moving on with a virtually clean slate.

Tim worked for a while installing aluminum doors and windows. He told his employer—VI-CO Aluminum—that he had no intention of staying with them for long. He was going to have a career in law enforcement.

And he did. In 1978 Tim Harris joined the Sebastian, Florida, police department.

The lawmen who watch over Indian River County almost all recognize one another. When Don Dappen passes a county deputy he honks and waves. When the

Florida Highway Patrolmen pass local cops they do the same.

Indian County Sheriff's Detective Phil Williams met Tim Harris for the first time in 1979. And he didn't like him much. It is fairly routine in any police jurisdiction in America for fellow officers to cut each other some slack in traffic violations. If a cop is blatantly speeding or driving recklessly, he's going to get a ticket like anybody else; if he's a few miles over the limit, one of his own probably isn't going to write him up. But when Phil Williams was on his way to a call, driving through Sebastian, he heard a siren and saw the blue lights behind him.

"I had just passed the Sebastian city limits—where the speed limit goes up—and this Sebastian cop—it was Tim Harris—pulled me over, and he actually pulls out his ticket book. I thought he was kidding. But he wasn't," Williams remembers. "I just told him what I thought. He was out of his jurisdiction. He couldn't come after me—not unless he was in hot pursuit, and he sure wasn't. I had not been speeding in his jurisdiction.

"His demeanor left much to be desired. He began, 'I know you're a cop, but I'll write you anyway.' I peeled out and left him standing there in my dust."

Over the next decade Tim Harris and Phil Williams saw each other on the road from time to time. They weren't friends. They weren't enemies.

Sandy Wessendorf was due to graduate from Sebastian High School in June of 1980, but she didn't have to attend school for the last six months because she already had enough credits. All the Wessendorf kids worked hard. They joined their parents in working paper routes; besides covering her route, Sandy worked at the Danish bakery in a Publix supermarket.

Sandy had a good head for figures, and she saved her money. She saw very soon that Tim was not a frugal person. He was a spender. He always seemed to have something he wanted to buy. Tim didn't smoke, and he didn't drink, and he certainly didn't do drugs, but he seemed in a tearing hurry to have *things*.

He wanted to own his own home, and that struck Sandy as kind of sweet. Since his folks had divorced, Tim had never really felt he belonged anywhere. Not in his mother's home nor in his father's. Every once in a while Tim let Sandy think that they might get married someday. She wanted to believe him, but she still didn't trust him. It had only been a month since Tim broke off completely with Michelle.

Things were going pretty well between Tim and Sandy. She knew he still flirted with other girls, and she suspected he sometimes did more than that, but Sandy Wessendorf loved Tim Harris. He was her first love. He was her only love, and if Tim had some wild oats to sow, she would wait for him. She just wanted to be part of his life—the biggest part of his life—the woman who would be there when all the others were gone.

It was a lucky thing Sandy had a philosophical attitude, because one day she was visiting Tim at his apartment when she answered a knock on the door. A hysterical young woman, a waitress in a local pizza restaurant, stomped in and declared that she was pregnant—and that Tim was the father.

Sandy said nothing, but she pointed toward the bedroom, where Tim was still in bed. When he saw the sobbing waitress headed his way he put the covers over his head and wouldn't come out.

When the woman finally left, Tim started to cry. He might have been taken by surprise—but Sandy hadn't been. "I already kind of knew. I went over to his apartment one morning after he'd left for work, and I found a note. It was from her, and it said, 'Last night was great. I care about you. I want to see you again'—things like that."

Sandy was barely eighteen, but she was growing up way too fast. While Tim sobbed, terrified that the pizza waitress might be pregnant, Sandy asked him some probing questions about just *when* he'd slept with the woman. For once he answered truthfully. And Sandy thought grimly that Tim obviously didn't know anything about the female reproductive system, pregnancy, or babies.

"Well," Sandy said, "she might be pregnant—but it's too soon for her to know it yet. She's just trying to scare you."

Tim was vastly relieved.

The waitress never came back. "I wasn't jumping all over him," Sandy said, "In fact, he was so scared that I actually felt sorry for him. But he could see I was upset and that he had to straighten up a little bit."

Tim Harris was a curious mixture of little boy and macho cop. On the job he was strong and confident; with Sandy he was like a kid hiding behind his mother's skirts, letting her figure out his budget and pay his bills. A more sophisticated woman might have foreseen problems ahead, but Sandy wasn't in the least sophisticated. She was only learning to take terrible blows to the heart and keep on smiling. And keep on loving Tim Harris.

Tim was the first man Sandy had ever had sex with, and he would be the only man who made love to her for many, many years. The first time she slept with him she was only seventeen and didn't know what to expect, but she was disappointed anyway. "I was scared—and surprised when he was suddenly on top of me."

There was no foreplay and no soft kisses or loving words. No words at all. There never would be. "He threw me on the bed and that was it."

She hoped that their sex life would get better, but she didn't dream of saying that to Tim.

It wasn't long before Tim began to talk in earnest about marrying Sandy in the summer of 1980. She wasn't ready, and she didn't relish the idea of marrying Tim exactly one year after he was supposed to have had a wedding with Michelle. Sandy dragged her feet. She wanted to be absolutely sure of him before she married Tim. Naïvely she believed that Tim *would* be faithful once they were married, but she didn't want to rush it. "I really thought that once we were married, everything would change—that Tim would never cheat on me again."

By the summer of 1980 there was no question that they were a couple or that they would get married someday soon. Not only was Tim dependent upon Sandy, but she was a strikingly beautiful girl. Any other man would call him a fool for cheating on her.

In the late summer of 1980 Tim found a small house in the 600 block of Mulberry Street in Sebastian Heights. It wasn't fancy, but it was new, with maybe 900 square feet of living space and an enclosed garage. Sandy looked at it and grimaced when she saw it was *all* brown. Brown siding, brown roof, brown everything. But she was thrilled at the thought that this would be their *own* house.

Tim was making only about $16,000 a year at the Sebastian Police Department, and he didn't have the down payment on the $46,000 asking price, but he was installing some cove lighting for the contractor and managed to figure out a way to buy the little house without a down payment. He got a mortgage with

Gulf Atlantic in August, 1980, and agreed to make payments of $476.00 a month. He soon had truck payments, too, to General Motors—$207.05 a month —and a Sears card, and a Mastercard.

Sandy stepped in. First she took over the management of his finances, and long before they were married she combined their money, sharing whatever she had with him. "From the time I was seventeen I was helping him to pay the mortgage."

Tim planted grass in the little yard on Mulberry Street, and Sandy added a few flowers and the ubiquitous pink flamingos of Florida landscaping. As long as Sandy made Tim's payments on time—as she always did—the house on Mulberry Street would be his in thirty years.

Tim soon grew disenchanted with his new house. It wasn't big enough, and it wasn't fancy enough. He was a man with a remarkably low boredom threshold. He wanted things so desperately until he got them, and then things and people and even animals began to lose their fascination for him.

He always needed something new and something more.

4

The woman lying in the grove of pine trees and palmettos near I-95 was still there. Ants stung her bare buttocks. Nightfall brought with it a chill breeze from the ocean. Each morning the early spring sun was *hotter than the morning before. And still she didn't move, nor did anyone find her there.*

In December of 1980 Tim and Sandy went together to a jeweler and picked out her engagement ring. Sandy picked a date in April, but now it was Tim who dragged his feet. "He said he wanted to wait until I was nineteen, and that would have been in October. But I was eighteen when we set our wedding date for July 25, 1981. I remember our invitations said, 'And Two Shall Become One . . .'

"I was still scared to get married. In a way it was the happiest day of my life—but in another way it wasn't."

Tim and Sandy's wedding song was Karen Carpenter's "We've Only Just Begun," and Sandy wore a traditional white gown with a high neck of sheer embroidered lace and a fingertip veil edged in lace. She carried a bouquet of yellow roses and Shasta daisies. She looked very, very young and very innocent. She wore no makeup at all. Tim wore a brown tuxedo with a ruffled Edwardian shirt and a brown velvet vest. He wore a yellow rosebud in his lapel. Sebastian Police Chief Cummings performed the wedding ceremony.

Sandy and Tim looked so happy in their informal wedding pictures, toasting each other with piña coladas.

Despite the fact that he was extremely handsome, Tim Harris always hated to have his picture taken. When Sandy insisted he would grudgingly submit and put his arm around her. He smiled for the camera, but behind her back he was pinching Sandy *hard* to let her know how he really felt.

Their sex life was no better after their marriage. "It was still 'an act'—there was no love there," Sandy said. "I used to just turn my head and cry because in the beginning I thought it should be more romantic. I always thought it was going to be. I kept hoping—but it never was. I had nine years of sex without love."

The newlyweds left on their honeymoon that Saturday evening. Tim's brother, Danny, was getting married in West Virginia the next Saturday, so Tim and Sandy drove up through Georgia and North Carolina for the ceremony. They saw the Smoky Mountains and Chimney Rock, and—except for the physical side of their marriage—they got along wonderfully. When they were alone, driving through the beautiful countryside, it seemed to Sandy Harris as if they really had a whole clean slate ahead of them. Tim would be faithful; they would have babies and spend the rest of their lives together.

They stayed with Tim's family in West Virginia, and Sandy felt uncomfortable. Tim's mother, Virginia, and one of his sisters had driven down to Florida for Tim and Sandy's wedding. Sandy met her new mother-in-law for the first time the day before her wedding. It was difficult to spend four days of her honeymoon with a family she barely knew. Danny and Debbie Harris's candid wedding shots show a very attractive, apparently very happy family. Sandy, a bride of only a week herself, sat among them trying to smile. Tim was beside her, handsome as ever but self-conscious looking. As he did in almost every photograph ever taken of him, he tilted his head up and thrust his jaw forward. "He always managed to look like Lurch, the butler in 'The Addams Family' television show, when he had his picture taken," Sandy laughed.

In the family wedding pictures Tim's right arm was behind Sandy.

He was pinching her, but the camera didn't show that.

Sandy had always thought it strange that she knew so little about Tim's family. He just didn't care to talk much about them. When he did he was derisive about both his mother and his stepmother, although he was especially bitter about his stepmother. He blamed his father for divorcing his mother. Tim had lived with his father and stepmother so that he could graduate from Satellite Beach High, but he apparently was no longer welcome in their home. His stepmother appeared to hold as much enmity toward him as he did toward her. The only time Sandy ever met Tim's father was at her wedding, even though he lived only an hour north of them on Merritt Island.

The only family members Tim seemed at all close to were his younger brothers, Danny and David.

Sandy and Tim returned from their honeymoon to their little brown house at 656 Mulberry Street. "We hardly had anything in the way of furniture," Sandy remembered. "We had a table and a bed, I think. But Tim insisted on buying a high-tech, expensive alarm system to guard the house. It cost a lot more than what we had *in* the house."

At that point in their lives together Tim could have done almost anything, and Sandy would still have been wildly in love with him. She believed that they were embarking on a wonderful new life together. She had been extraordinarily patient with him while he got other women out of his system, but now they were "grown-ups" and they were together, faithful, just as it had said in their wedding vows. "I was crazy about Tim. I guess you could say that I was to the point of being obsessed with him. I would still have done anything for him."

Tim was about to see one of his lifelong dreams come true. On February 5, 1982, seven months after his marriage to Sandy Wessendorf, with his wife's urging, he applied to the Florida Highway Patrol for a position as a trooper. If ever there was an applicant who *looked* like a recruiting poster for a state trooper, it was Timothy Scott Harris. At six feet, two, he weighed 205 pounds, and it was all compact muscle. He was very handsome—more so, it seemed, with each year. He parted his dark hair on the left side, and it swept across his forehead in one thick wave. His eyes were as green as the Atlantic Ocean sometimes turned just before a storm—and as impenetrable. Sometimes Tim wore a mustache. He was twenty-three, but he could seem older. He had cut his law enforcement teeth in Melbourne Village and Sebastian, and he was far from a gung-ho kid at this point. He knew the ropes. He knew what to say and how to act.

The Florida Highway Patrol put applicants through tortuous physical, intelligence, and psychological tests. Patiently Tim filled out forms asking about his whole life, his family, his former employment. The Highway Patrol did background checks on both Tim and his family, and they didn't find a blemish on anyone's record.

Computer checks with the Clerk of Circuit Courts, the Clerk of County Courts, N.C.I.C. (National Crime Information Center at F.B.I. headquarters in Quantico), F.C.I.C. (Florida Crime Information Center), and local, county, and city law enforcement records drew no hits on the name Timothy Scott Harris. Nor should they have; Tim had never been arrested.

Nor had Sandra Lynn Wessendorf Harris, George

G. Harris, his father, Virginia Ann Harris, his mother, nor Paul, Bethany Lea, Daniel, David, or Sarah.

FHP investigators talked with Sandy's and Tim's next door neighbors on both sides. All they got was "Very good neighbors" and "No problems."

Tim explained that his first police job in Melbourne Village had been a big disappointment to him because he found the department so unprofessional, and he presented the glowing letter of recommendation from Chief Segien. He had good evaluations from the Sebastian Police Department, and he had never been fired from any job. He didn't drink, smoke, do drugs —and he never had. He answered all the questions as honestly as he could. Yes, he *had* had his driver's license suspended a long time back—when he was a teenager. For reckless driving. He had sold his car to pay the fine, and he had never lost his license again.

Thanks to Sandy, Tim had an excellent credit record. He listed his debts as $34,000 to Gulf Atlantic Mortgage for his house, $250 to Sears, Roebuck, and $150 to Master Charge.

The guy wasn't a saint. Yes, Tim admitted, he had taken a "sick day" off work from time to time when he wasn't really sick. Yes, he had probably stolen a candy bar as a kid.

The FHP checked him all the way back to Surfside Elementary School in Satellite Beach, and Tim Harris was clean. He was smart; he had graduated from high school with a 3.7. He had college training in police work, he had four years of law enforcement experience, and he was active in a military police unit of the military reserve.

At the time of his application to the Florida Highway Patrol Tim had been promoted to corporal in the Sebastian Police Department, and that made him third in command in the twelve-man department.

Trooper Robert T. Weber, an applicant investigator, summed up his background check: "The field investigation has established that the applicant is well qualified for the position of Trooper. There is nothing questionable found in my investigation of his background. He is well spoken, gives a very professional impression in his uniform, and I believe would be an asset to our Department. I recommend that he be given further consideration for employment with our agency."

By May of 1982 Tim was almost through the morass of requirements he had to meet to be hired as a trooper. The hardest of all was the oral exam. Any working cop remembers what it was like to sit before a board of ranking brass and answer questions, sweating all the time and wondering if there *was* a right answer, or if they were throwing trick questions at him.

Tim Harris's ordeal was on May 5, 1982, in Lantana, Florida. He faced an FHP lieutenant, a major, two sergeants, and a superintendent. Stone-faced, they nodded and checked their grading sheets. He was rated on his appearance, enunciation, manner, emotional control, comprehension, logic, and coherency.

He passed. He didn't blow them away, but he didn't fall on his face either. The rating forms were checked right down the middle. He drew four "Recommended" ratings. He did not impress the board so much that any of them checked "Recommended with confidence" or "Recommended with enthusiasm," but then he didn't get any "Recommended with hesitance" either.

Only one of the oral board members had picked up on a side of Tim that might make him less than desirable as a member of the elite highway patrol. Sergeant K.D. Buckner checked a box that read

"Self-conscious, ill at ease or lacks restraint," and another: "Slow in grasping subtleties, requires explanations."

Buckner's reservations were certainly not enough to blackball Tim Harris. He was hired. He resigned from the Sebastian Police Department and prepared to attend the Florida Highway Patrol's 65th Recruit Training School, which would begin on May 31, 1982, and finish August 13th. That would mean leaving his bride alone for three months while he was up at the state capital in Tallahassee.

Tim was elated, and Sandy was proud of him. "He looked so wonderful in his uniform," she recalled. "I always loved the way he looked in his uniform."

That summer of 1982 may have been the most romantic period of Sandy and Tim Harris's married life. All the while he was living at the Highway Patrol Academy in Tallahassee, Sandy drove the sixteen-hour round trip to see him every other weekend. She had her job back in Indian River County, so she couldn't leave until Saturday morning, and she had to head home again on Sunday, but the long drive in the summer heat was worth it—just so they could be together for eight or ten hours.

"I missed him so much while he was up in Tallahassee," Sandy remembered. "I didn't mind the drive at all. It was worth it just to see him for a little while."

There were fifty-five recruits in the FHP's sixty-fifth class, including ten women. They went to class from eight to five, five days a week, and most of Saturday. The weeks were intense and packed with information that might save the recruits' lives—or someone else's life—when they were out on the road. Everything from First Aid to Human Behavior, from Arrest Techniques to Courtroom Demeanor, from Criminal

Law to Crimes Against Persons. They learned how to gather and preserve evidence, how to lift fingerprints, and how to interview and interrogate. There were radar and other speed measurement devices to master. Of course, there was accident investigation. Tim Harris's main interest in law enforcement had always been traffic, and the FHP was the place to work it. Tim did very well in *every* subject at the academy, however.

His highest grade was a 99 in defensive driving, and his lowest was a respectable 88—in firearms. He excelled in criminal investigation and criminal law. Overall, his grade-point average at the patrol academy was 92.58. The FHP Academy put on a banquet and a graduation ceremony in mid-August, and Sandy Harris was in the audience, tremendously proud of her young husband.

Things worked out really well for them, too, as far as Tim's duty assignment was concerned. Although he had indicated on his application that he would be willing to be assigned anywhere in Florida, and he had meant it, both Tim and Sandy had lived in Indian River County for so long that they hated the thought of leaving. At the Academy Tim had met Lt. Gary Morgan and Trooper Byron Sickman. They knew him by sight from court hearings in Vero Beach. Both men would one day become good friends of Tim's, and back in 1982 they did him a favor.

"We knew that Tim was going to be transferred to someplace around Lake Okeechobee," Morgan recalled. "And we knew there was an opening in our Fort Pierce District, which is actually right in Vero Beach. So we looked him up to see if he wanted . . . to stay in Vero Beach . . . let him know we would . . . help him any way we could . . . to get a position right back in Indian River County."

It worked out that way. Tim worked in Lake Okeechobee for a very short time before he came back home. For the next eight years Trooper Tim Harris would be working the roads of Indian River County—roads and freeways he knew the way he knew his own face when he was shaving.

Sandy didn't have to move away from Pat and Fred Wessendorf and her sisters Susan and Kathy. They kept their little brown house, and they planned for the day they could buy some acreage and build a house big enough to raise kids in.

From the very beginning Trooper Tim Harris garnered excellent annual evaluations from his superior officers. He was consistently above average. The Florida Highway Patrol had hired themselves a superlative trooper.

"Trooper Harris is fourth in the four count district in DUI [Driving Under the Influence] arrests, total arrests, and correction cards. . . . He is a steady, dependable employee who requires only minimal supervision."

". . . always displays a positive attitude . . . has aligned himself to the goals of the Department."

"He has one of the highest DUI enforcements in the District."

"Trooper Harris . . . has been quick to volunteer for difficult assignments and displays an enthusiasm for professional law enforcement well beyond that of his counterparts."

"Has very good relationship with local State Attorney's Office and judges. Cases well prepared and organized in advance."

And yet it was almost as if Tim Harris lived in two different worlds: his job and his marriage. Some things didn't change at all after Sandy and Tim were

41

married. He had always been something of a loner. He wasn't interested in socializing with other couples, and he didn't seem to have any friends of his own, nothing beyond casual acquaintances in the Patrol. He went fishing sometimes with another trooper, but it was the fishing that was Tim's passion—not male bonding.

"I guess I forced him to get along with my brother-in-law, Don. They were both cops; they should have had something in common," Sandy recalled. "We'd play cards with Don and Susan, but that's the only social thing we did."

Tim didn't drink; he had an almost pathological aversion to alcohol. Don Dappen remembers one evening he had made piña coladas.

"Sandy told Tim, 'Just have one.' Tim drank one, and he enjoyed it. But when I asked him if he wanted another one, he was short with me. 'No, no!' What it was was he was beginning to feel the alcohol a little bit, and he seemed just so afraid of losing control. . . . Tim never even drank beer. I never saw him with a beer in his hand."

Even when they were dating, Tim had used physical force to control Sandy. That continued into their marriage. "If I did or said something he didn't like, he'd take my arm and twist it behind my back. Or he'd pinch me at the tops of my thighs, between my legs, where it really hurt—but it wouldn't show. He wanted his way, no matter what."

Sandy had always known that Tim was extravagant and impractical. He was a man who *wanted*. He had to have the newest and best car, the biggest boat, the newest technology. He would beg Sandy to buy him whatever it was that had taken his fancy at the moment—as if she were the mom and he the spoiled child. And he was relentless, nagging at her, promising, "Just let me get this, and I'll never ask for another thing."

Sometimes Sandy gave in. Sometimes she couldn't. Sandy had managed their finances for so long that she knew what they could afford and what they couldn't. And she had been with Tim for three years; she knew he would grow bored with each new toy, and he *would* ask for something again.

Sometimes she wondered where it would all end. With them in the poorhouse, probably.

Sandy made $15,000 a year, and Tim made a little over $22,000. They couldn't afford a new car every six months, a new boat, a new house, *and* a new baby on their income. And they were going to have a baby. Sandy was pregnant, due to deliver in the late spring of 1983.

Tim seemed happy enough about the baby, but he refused to acknowledge that Sandy couldn't do everything she had done before—lifting, working, sex. "You can still do this," he would insist, when she was so tired that she could hardly lift her arm. Sometimes she just couldn't keep up with all Tim expected of her. And Tim was often annoyed with her.

There was no question about what they would name the baby. Tim had long ago decided that if he ever had a daughter, her name would be Jennifer Lynn, and a son would be Timothy Jr. If he had married Michelle, it would have been the same. Those were the names he had picked out for *his* children. He allowed Sandy no input at all.

Among the things that Sandy continued to do while she was pregnant was to work full-time as a secretary *and* to deliver the morning papers on her 2 a.m. route. She delivered 250 papers in the summer, and 600 in the winter when the snowbirds were in residence. Sandy worked an area where there were apartment houses, and she had to lug two heavy sacks of the *Press Journal,* walking the whole route. She threw half the papers up to the second floor of apartment buildings and condos. "I was exhausted all the time," she sighed, remembering.

On the morning before Jennifer's birth Sandy felt some vague discomfort in her back and belly, but she had never had a baby and didn't recognize labor pains. She did prevail upon Tim to drive her on her route. When they got home he was impatient with her because she didn't know whether she should go to the hospital or not.

"I don't know," Sandy told Tim. "I don't know what to do."

"Well, make up your mind," he snapped, "because either you're going to the hospital now, or I'm going back to bed."

By the time Sandy realized she *was* in labor, she was in agony and they left for the hospital. When they neared the emergency entrance she asked Tim to let her off. But he was still angry with her because she had been indecisive, and he drove right on by, headed for the far parking lot. Sandy remembered, "I was in major, major pain, but he said, 'No, I'm going to go park, and you're going to walk, bitch.'"

And walk Sandy did. But when the ER personnel saw her they ran for a wheelchair. Jennifer Lynn Harris was born five hours later.

Tim had refused to go into the labor room with Sandy, and he had laughed when she asked him to go to Lamaze classes with her, but he seemed pleased and proud when Jennifer was born.

Tim had always called Sandy terrible names when he was angry, "slut" and "bitch." They were the same names he called out to female strangers on the street.

There had never been any arguing with him; when Sandy tried to protest something he had said to her, he invariably turned on his heel and said, "Shut up, slut."

Still, she loved him. There never was and there never will be any explaining of why human beings love one another. Sandy felt bound to Tim. If she was no longer "obsessed" with him, she kept trying to please him. She figured there had to be some combination that would make him happy. She just had not come upon it yet. No one in her family had ever been divorced, and Sandy had married Tim, intending to be married forever.

For a long time Sandy was able to rationalize that Tim was different from other men. He didn't drink or smoke, and he worked hard. She knew women who were worse off.

She was sure she did.

Tim worked different shifts: 8 to 4 p.m., 4 to midnight, 11 to 7 a.m. Although Sandy had been jealous of other women before they were married, she didn't worry about that any longer. She would wait up for Tim and ask him about what had happened on his shift. "I was really interested," she remembered. "And most of the time there would have been some incident he told me about, so it seemed as though I was sharing in his life some."

Tim still flirted. "He had the eye—he had a way of looking at someone," Sandy said. "I don't think a grown woman would buy it, but I think a young girl—with the way he looked in his uniform and his green eyes . . ."

But Sandy believed that he was only flirting. He still said suggestive things to her girlfriends when they came over, but she thought that was because he resented their being there.

All in all, assuming that no marriage was perfect, Sandy Harris believed hers was about as good as anybody's. She adored her baby daughter, she loved her handsome husband, and she liked her life. She took some courses in bookkeeping at Indian River Community College so that she could get a better job, and she and Tim talked about when they would be building their new house—the house that would come up to Tim's specifications.

Tim's job with the FHP meant that they could think about selling the little house on Mulberry. They drove around Indian River County looking for land they could afford. One day Sandy found an acre lot in an area called Citrus Hideaway, the second lot from the corner off County Road 510. It was ten miles north of Vero Beach near the crossroads known as Wabbasso. There were no houses in the development yet—unless you counted the huge pseudo-plantation at the end of 75th Court: "O'Hara's Scarlett."

Sandy fell in love with the land; the acre she wanted had pine trees and palmettos and endless possibilities. It would take $15,000 to buy it, and she didn't see how they could afford it—unless *both* she and Tim agreed to tighten their belts and economize. She knew she could, but she doubted Tim would agree. Whenever she demurred at some new purchase he suggested, he got angry.

5

By the early 1980s, Phil Williams, the Indian River County deputy who had once roared away from one of Tim Harris's traffic stops, was moving up in the sheriff's office. Both Phil and Tim were men utterly consumed with their careers. They were also fairly close in age. But that was about all they had in common. Despite his protestations of poverty, Tim had grown up in relative affluence, while Phil was country all the way. When they passed each other on the road they half waved. Phil had never forgotten Tim's picayune excuse to pull him over, and he never cared much for Harris again. It didn't matter; the chance that they would ever work on the same case was remote. Phil's obsession was in solving crimes, and Tim's was catching drunk drivers.

Phil Williams was as solidly built as a linebacker, with a friendly, sometimes deceptively open face and a luxuriant mustache. His mother's folks came from Suwannee County up north near the Georgia border, where the biggest "city" was Live Oak. His father's people were from Vero Beach. "Coming up, we probably broke every fish and game law there was," Williams laughed as he remembered his boyhood. "We sure didn't have any of us in law enforcement. If I can say anything about my past and how it's helped me in investigations, I guess it's because I can figure how the bad guys are going to do something. . . . I think a person's education is not so much a piece of paper they've got hanging up on the wall, but the sum of the experiences they've lived through."

Phil's dad, Wallace Williams, worked at the power plant for the city of Vero Beach for thirty years. His mom, Audrey, worked for the First Union bank. He had two sisters, Arlene and Francine.

Growing up, Phil Williams went to elementary school with at least three future killers, a fact whose irony was not lost on him when he pondered it as an adult. "I remember Sylvan Bishop—we were in first grade together. Later he used to tell me that his number one wish was to be on the F.B.I.'s Most Wanted List. I didn't really think he meant it."

Sylvan almost made it. In September, 1970, when he was eighteen, Sylvan Bishop reported that he had discovered two decomposed bodies in a woods west of Vero Beach. The victims were eventually identified as Kathleen Phillips, nineteen, and her friend, Joanna Malandrino, twenty. They hadn't been reported missing because their families thought they were on a trip from their home in Hollywood, Florida, to see Joanna's grandmother up in New Jersey. They *had* traveled north on I-95, but they hadn't gone more than a hundred miles before they developed car trouble and stopped at a service station in Vero Beach in the wee hours of the morning of September 1.

Sylvan Bishop was the night attendant. Apparently working toward his life's ambition, Sylvan had already been to reform school in Okeechobee and Marianna, to jail in Appalachee, and in a state mental institution for six weeks. The naïve girls from Hollywood, Florida, thought he was being exceptionally kind when he offered to drive them into town at the end of his shift, and they waited until he got off duty at 6:30 a.m.

No one ever saw them alive after that. Sylvan Bishop had indeed made the "big time" in crime, and he was charged with two counts of first degree murder. When Phil Williams heard that, he recalled Sylvan's childhood goal and remembered the kid at the next desk in first grade. He realized then that killers weren't always strangers; a murderer could be someone who was so much a part of your own world that you might never suspect him—or her.

If experience counts, Williams had a doctorate in the painful side of real life, both his own and the cases he'd worked. Only one case would ever make him cry, though, and it wouldn't unfold until he was almost two decades into his career as a cop.

In the late sixties and early seventies in Vero Beach Phil Williams was a member of a rock band, playing guitar and singing. The group never made it big, although their forty-song repertoire made them much in demand at Indian River County dances and civic functions. The little band never quite made enough money to survive, perhaps because Williams refused to work bar gigs exclusively, and bands performing in church basements and fraternal lodges rarely made headlines.

When he was seventeen Phil Williams joined the army before they could draft him. He spent two and a half weeks at Fort Jackson in South Carolina, expecting to be shipped out any day for basic training. But the army didn't want him; he had an "H-3 hearing profile." That meant Williams had high-frequency hearing deafness, probably caused by his sitting in the middle of his rock band. In a time when young men were *looking* for excuses not to go to Vietnam, Phil

Williams was disappointed to find himself back home in twenty days with an honorable discharge. He could hear just fine, but the army doctors thought the noise of battle might aggravate his H-3 profile, and the service wouldn't take that responsibility. Fortunately for Florida citizens, Williams never had a problem passing police physicals.

Phil Williams got married in 1971 and became the father of a son in 1975. Two years later he and his first wife divorced. "The tremendous psychological pain that I experienced with the divorce in 1977 eventually subsided," Williams recalled, "and left in its place knowledge that would enable me to know and feel the intense emotions of others who were experiencing the same intense psychological trauma—allow me to have compassion towards others. You might say that divorce was the hardest school I ever attended."

Williams remembered trying to find the words to tell his little boy that he wouldn't be living with him anymore. "I told him I'd always be his daddy, and I'd always be there for him—but it tore me up. I didn't know how that particular experience would help me in an investigation a long time later."

When his reconstituted band showed no sign of going places, Phil Williams took a job with Piper Aircraft in Vero Beach as a mechanic. Three years later the gasoline shortage hit, and he could see that Piper was going to be hit hard. It was economics and not a passion for being a cop that made him apply to the Indian River County Sheriff's Office. He hired on in September, 1974. Williams was as surprised as anybody when he found he loved it and seemed to have a natural ability for law enforcement.

It sure wasn't the money. Indian River County was paying its deputies $8,000 a year. Williams was remarried, and he couldn't support a wife and pay child support on that, so he started his own landscaping business in his off-duty hours. Eventually he had twenty-five accounts and hired fellow officers to help out.

His interest in growing things continued. In his own back yard he grew mangoes, two varieties of grapes, two varieties of guavas, papayas, blackberries, loquats, pineapples, and nectarines. He once saved a huge old oak tree by filling a rotten cavity with 300 pounds of concrete. It's still standing.

In 1980 Williams asked for a transfer and became an agricultural detective, part of the Ranch and Groves Unit. At that time Indian River County was having agricultural thefts of more than $150,000 a year. Sometimes it was basic old-time cattle rustling, sometimes produce. On occasion agricultural detectives had to seek the source of chemical leakage that was poisoning the groundwater. The unit also investigated drug smugglers, an avocation that was growing tremendously in Florida in the seventies and eighties. "It was not unusual to find several bales of marijuana lying on a landing strip from a botched drug run the previous night," Williams said. "I learned the different airplane modifications that were common to drug-smuggling aircraft, as well as watercraft."

By infiltrating the agricultural stolen property network, Williams and his fellow Ranch and Grove detectives were able to keep the thieves so confused about who was a real buyer and who was an undercover detective that losses dropped from $150,000 to $12,000, a $138,000 savings for Indian River County farmers and orchardists.

There was one area of law enforcement that Phil Williams was destined for, whether he realized it or not. He was about to find himself in the eye of a grisly murder probe, and it would nearly destroy his faith in friendship and loyalty. Sylvan Bishop had been, he thought, an aberration—a funny kid who thought infamy was the same as fame.

The next connection to violent death hit Williams way too close to home. Before his first marriage Phil Williams had run with two close friends—"shirttail relatives," really: David Gore and Fred Waterfield. They hunted together, dated together, went all through school together. Fred had played in the band with Phil. "David Gore's mother introduced my parents to each other fifty years ago, and all of our families were close."

Phil hadn't been that surprised to learn that Sylvan Bishop had killed two girls. But he was poleaxed to find himself investigating a bloody crime involving men who had been like brothers to him.

"Indian River County . . . was experiencing a series of female disappearances. The suspicion fell squarely on . . . David Gore," Williams said quietly. "I just didn't believe him capable of committing the murders of five women, [but] I had long ago learned to respect the suspicions of my fellow law enforcement officers. I overheard radio traffic about a man chasing a naked woman near Gore's residence. . . . I responded and [along with several other officers] surrounded Gore's residence. I found the blood dripping from Gore's automobile trunk, and I assisted in exposing the dead female that was bound by rope inside the car trunk. There was no room for suspicion; Gore's guilt was evident."

Williams was ordered to go over to Fred Waterfield's house, so he wasn't around to see the capture of his former best friend, nor the rescue of a second woman David Gore had tied up in his attic.

Phil Williams continued to relate the incredible

story. "I went to Waterfield's, with whom I was equally friendly. Statements Waterfield made to me would help my department tie him into the kidnapping of the murdered girl in David Gore's vehicle, and in *six other serial murders . . .* and counting."

Phil Williams testified at the trials of both of his friends—for the prosecution. David Gore was sentenced to death, and Fred Waterfield to sixty-five years in prison. Acknowledging that he would never have suspected them, Williams was nonetheless fascinated by what secrets humans can hide behind smiling masks. "My interest in the psychology of the criminal mind—with a specific interest toward homicide—was born."

6

In 1988 Don Dappen would work alongside Phil Williams on a multi-agency task force formed to solve one of the most heinous multiple murder cases the Treasure Coast of Florida had ever known. Tommy Wyatt, twenty-six, and Michael Lovette, thirty-one—both escapees from a North Carolina prison roadgang—burst into a Domino's Pizza parlor in Vero Beach on May 18, 1988, allegedly intending only to rob it. But the Domino's safe was rigged so that it would not open for fifteen minutes.

Wyatt and Lovette decided to wait, but they didn't just *wait;* they terrorized their hapless captives. While Lovette held a gun on them, Wyatt raped twenty-eight-year-old Frances Edwards, the store manager's wife, while her husband was forced to watch. When Wyatt was finished he put a gun to the back of her head and calmly pulled the trigger. Then he spun and shot Billy Edwards, twenty-seven, in the chest. Terribly wounded but still fighting to protect his mortally injured wife, Edwards was no match for Wyatt. Wyatt put a .38-caliber Smith and Wesson pistol to the Domino's logo on Edwards's baseball cap and pulled the trigger.

Matt Bornoosh, also twenty-seven, a driver for Domino's, dropped to his knees and began to pray. Grinning, Wyatt fired at Bornoosh's head but only grazed his scalp. He shoved the barrel of the gun roughly into Bornoosh's ear and said softly, "If you listen *real close,* you'll hear it coming . . ."

And then he pulled the trigger. Incredibly, Matt Bornoosh lived for several hours, although he never regained consciousness.

Vero Beach Police Sergeant Pete Huber thought to grab his 35mm camera and take pictures of the scene even as ambulance sirens wailed in the distance. His pictures would play a most effective part in a trial three years later. So would the new forensic technique using DNA markers to correlate semen with blood types and tracing the results to a rapist.

The car the killers had stolen in Jacksonville two days earlier overheated and stalled as they were leaving Vero Beach. Lovette and Wyatt parked on a side road west of town, piled tissue paper on the front seat, and torched the car. They hitchhiked west on State Road 60 after they had stashed a briefcase full of money from the Domino's under a bridge.

In a bar in Seffner, Tommy Wyatt, chubby and baby-faced and a consummate con artist, picked up a trusting young woman named Cathy Nydegger.

Lovette and Wyatt headed back toward Vero Beach to retrieve their pizza loot. They found it and turned toward Tampa. Tommy Wyatt stopped the car along an isolated dirt road and signaled to Cathy Nydegger to come with him as he walked away into a field. Lovette heard some low talking and then a scuffle, and then a single shot sounded.

The two men dragged the girl's body to the bank of a canal.

Tommy Wyatt had left no witnesses behind. It would be almost three years before justice was meted out to the conscienceless killers, but justice *did* prevail. State Attorney Bruce Colton told a Sarasota jury that the task force of lawmen had gathered 82 witnesses and 155 pieces of physical evidence.

Both Tommy Wyatt and Michael Lovette were sentenced to death in Florida's electric chair. Lovette's appeal to avoid execution was successful in 1994.

The Domino's Pizza murders had every police officer along the Treasure Coast working almost round the clock in May of 1988 as they looked for suspects. This was the first time that Don Dappen saw Phil Williams in action—he noted that the county detective was like a bulldog. Phil wouldn't let go of anything until he found out what he needed to know. Dappen had no idea then how closely the two would be aligned in less than two years in a murder case that would shock both of them more, if possible, than the grotesquely cruel pizza executions.

Dappen could still laugh, though, when he recalled Phil Williams. "He *is* as down home as you can get. He isn't kidding you. He *is* a real old country boy. During the pizza manhunt we were down in some ditch looking for a gun, and I said, 'Let's go have lunch,' and Phil says, 'I'll stay right here for lunch,' and I thought he was kidding. But he took out his knife and sliced off some kind of a weed or something, and he started eating it."

Williams knew his vegetation all right, both from his boyhood and from his years as a landscaper. Given his choice, he would probably have taken a hamburger, but he could survive on the land if he had to. He was only half kidding.

During the early years of their marriages Sandy and Tim Harris and Don and Sue Dappen continued to play cards, and Pat Wessendorf and her three daughters still had lunch every Thursday. Still, Sandy was more likely to tell her sisters what was going on with her and Tim than to confide in her mother. If she found out Tim wasn't treating Sandy well, Pat would demand action, while Susan and Kathy would listen and nod sympathetically. *They* saw that Tim seemed to do things deliberately to make Sandy miserable. He even flirted with them, although he didn't get any encouragement. Susan told him to cut it out, and Kathy was embarrassed.

Sandy Harris kept hoping that things would improve. She loved him so much; she still believed he would realize it and return that love. They had so much history together—too much for her to give up on their marriage.

Don Dappen found Tim an odd kind of guy. They were friends first because they were married to sisters, and second because they were cops, but Dappen sensed that Tim was basically a loner. Tim loved to fish, and he loved boats, and he loved to catch drunk drivers. Outside of that, it was hard to find anything to talk to him about. One thing Dappen noticed early on was that Tim appeared to literally hate women.

"We'd be riding down the street, and he'd see a girl walking on the side of the road, and he'd slow up, roll down his window, and yell—I mean *yell*—at the top of his lungs, 'Hey, slut!' and then he'd flick his tongue in and out at the girl. I'd say, 'What's the matter with you? Are you crazy?' and he'd just laugh.

"Sometimes Tim would pull up on the bumper of a car being driven slowly by an old man or an old woman, and he'd just lay on his horn—I mean for forty-five seconds or so. I cringed. And one day we were up in Gifford—in the black section—and a black guy's just walking down the road. And Tim just pulled up beside this guy, rolls down his window, and yells at him, 'Hey, nigger! Where you headed?'"

Don Dappen was appalled. Tim was a state trooper, a grown man, and he was acting like a crude and cruel teenager. "I told him, 'Just let me out. Just pull over and let me out here.'"

Tim Harris, of course, called his wife names as derogatory as any he called other women. He showed no respect for anyone beyond his superiors on the Patrol. Sandy could not understand what motivated her husband. Sometimes it seemed as if he observed the world from an entirely different viewpoint than anyone she had ever met, as if he were looking through the wrong end of a spyglass and everything and everyone looked ugly to him.

When Tim came home after working a fatal accident Sandy saw that the tragedy of it didn't seem to touch him at all. She knew that Donny felt bad when he had to investigate fatalities, but Tim gave out tickets and pulled bodies out of wrecks with exactly the same ease.

"Sometimes he'd come home and say, 'We had a really good accident tonight,'" Sandy remembered. "He said, 'This guy flew one way out the window, and it sliced the top of his head off, and the other one flew out the door, and he made a real splat where he landed. It was neat.'"

One time Tim was called out on an accident near Fort Pierce where a little boy died, probably because he had not been wearing a seat belt. "Tim didn't care. The little boy was black," Sandy said. "And black people meant even less to him than everybody else. It was a *child,* but Tim didn't care."

Sometimes Tim and Sandy watched TV together in the evenings when he was working the day shift. Beyond sex, that was the extent of any marital togetherness. Outside of Tim's job and what happened when he was out on patrol, they never talked about anything except what Tim wanted to buy next. Still, Sandy kept trying.

"Tim was only really happy when he got something new," Sandy said. "But then he got bored with it so quickly. He had four new trucks in two years—a white Toyota pickup, a Blazer, a Chevy S-10, and a Dodge Ram."

But it wasn't just cars. Tim Harris wanted boats too. The first was a fairly modest eighteen-foot Sun Skiff. He traded up to a twenty-one-foot Well Craft.

"He always wanted a bigger, better boat than any of the other troopers had," Sandy said. "And he usually got it. He didn't have many weekends off, but when he did, the only family things we did were with the boat. We'd go down the river to the islands—either taking a picnic lunch or buying hamburgers. The kids liked that."

Sandy kept most of her marriage problems to herself. She was sure that it was *she* who was doing something wrong. And Tim liked everything to "look rosy" on the surface; he would have been very angry if she told anyone that they had problems.

In 1985 they bought the acre of land in Citrus Hideaway. They had hoped to use their equity in the Mulberry Street house to pay for the land, but when they finally sold the little brown house they didn't come out one penny ahead. Fred and Pat Wessendorf loaned them $15,000 to pay for the land. With that Sandy was able to negotiate a mortgage loan for $45,000 to build a home.

Tim sent away for the blueprints for the house he wanted, spending hundreds of dollars on the plans. He spread them out enthusiastically as he pointed out features to Sandy. She looked at the blueprints aghast. The house had 6,000 square feet! It even had a maid's room. "I was making $21,000 a year, and Tim was making $29,000. How were we ever going to pay for a house that big? Tim said that I wasn't counting on his Army Reserve pay—but that was only $160.00 more a month. He was just totally unrealistic."

They butted heads again, the dreamer and the practical bookkeeper. They had yet to pay off even one of Tim's trucks or boats before he turned them in on newer, more expensive models, and they were rapidly sinking deeper in debt.

Tim and Sandy fought over the new house plans—or rather, they came to the kind of impasse they always did when the stress level in their marriage rose too high. Tim called Sandy a slut and turned his back on her. They didn't speak for a couple of weeks.

Sandy couldn't understand why Tim chose gutter terms to call her when they had even the mildest of arguments. Sandy's fidelity was unblemished. She loved him. She never even looked at another man. Still, Tim always resorted to ugly names when he was angry with her. She hoped a home of their own would change their lives.

Finally Sandy found some house plans that she

thought might work. She combined them with drawings of her own and the features that Tim wanted and came up with enough to have blueprints drawn for a home they *could* afford. It was a compromise that both she and Tim could live with. They agreed that Tim would build the house for them, saving labor costs. He was very talented with his hands—if only he didn't get bored before he was finished. They could still have almost 3,000 square feet—four bedrooms and two bathrooms.

Tim Harris *was* skilled at building. He could do everything from carpentry to intricate tile work, and he was a strong and tireless worker. He saved them thousands of dollars by working on their new house himself. When Tim wasn't on duty he was working on the place in Citrus Hideaway. It would be the first house on 75th Court—although later the street would be built up with very expensive residences. It was a great investment, a solid foundation on which Tim and Sandy could build their financial future.

Originally Sandy, Tim, and Jennifer had planned to live in a little trailer on the Citrus Hideaway property while Tim built their house, but that wasn't really practical. They had no electricity, and the trailer was small. Besides, Sandy was pregnant again, and she could barely turn around in the tiny trailer. Tim and Sandy moved in with Pat and Fred Wessendorf in the interval between leaving their old house and moving into their new one.

Just as he did with every other area of his life, Tim operated from completely opposite and contradictory ends of the scale when he built his dream house. He was both an extremely talented and precise carpenter and a sloppy and careless worker. He spent way too much on some phases of their new home and cut

corners in other areas where it wasn't necessary. As he
set the framework for the white stucco house he put in
twice as many studs as the place needed. He had a
stud every six inches. Even Fred Wessendorf, who
usually kept his thoughts to himself, wondered aloud
if Tim needed *that* much wood in the frame. It was
almost a fortress, so heavy that no wind, no storm, not
even a hurricane could blow it away. Of course,
buying twice as much timber as the house plans
required sent their costs soaring. Tim did a beautiful
tile job in the bathrooms—but he left grout smears on
the tile when he finished. By the time Sandy discovered that, the grout had dried and was almost impossible to get off. She and Tim argued "almost every day"
until the house was done. "I thought he was wasting
money and material.

"But I loved that house," Sandy sighed. "It was
designed just like we wanted it—so everything was
convenient; there was a place for everything."

And it was beautiful besides. The little house on
Mulberry Street would have fit inside the double
garage of their new house. It was gleaming white
stucco, two-story, with a wide overhanging roof.
There was a bay window in the living room and a
stone fireplace with a raised hearth. The master
bedroom was huge, and there was a room for Jennifer
and a nursery for the new baby.

Tim worked long hours to finish up the house so
that they could move in in time for Christmas, 1985.
Their new baby was due around then, too.

A lot of young marriages get off to rocky starts. In
December of 1985 Sandy had just turned twenty, and
Tim was only five years older. On the positive side of
the ledger, they both had highly responsible jobs, and
they would soon have two children. With the new

house it looked as though things were going to turn out all right after all. The first thing Sandy did was hang their wedding pictures beside the stone fireplace.

Maybe, if they both gave everything they had to make this marriage work, they *could* succeed, and all their arguments would disappear. Sandy knew that other people—even her own sisters—wondered why she stayed with Tim. But nobody who hadn't been where she was could understand. When Tim was charming and sweet, no man could be sweeter. He could wipe away the bad times and make her believe in him again. Her heart still skipped beats when she saw him in his uniform. If he didn't care for her, would he have worn himself out building a house with his own hands?

And yet, despite Sandy's optimism, things were already falling apart. If it is ever possible to pinpoint an event or a moment in time when the seeds of tragedy silently take root, that Christmas season of 1985 would be the beginning of the falling down, down, and down for Tim and Sandy Harris.

7

It was December, 1985, when Trooper Tim Harris responded to an automobile accident near Vero Beach. It wasn't much more than a fender-bender. One of the passengers was a slender blond woman. Routinely Tim jotted down the names, addresses, and phone numbers of the passengers and witnesses. He had noticed the blond woman immediately, although he didn't give any indication that he had. She was probably in her early thirties, very attractive, and she stared hard at him as he went about his job.

Whether it was Tim Harris who called DeeLisa Davis* or *she* who called him—as he always claimed —an affair that would threaten his marriage began. Tim would always insist that he hadn't really thought about DeeLisa after he finished the accident report, but that she had called him at work and made it so obvious that she was available for a "fling" that he would have been crazy to refuse.

Sandy was hugely pregnant, and Tim was exhausted from driving his territory every night, building his house all day, and living with his in-laws. Most of all, he was bored.

When Tim Harris was bored he always did something to change his situation.

DeeLisa assured Tim she wanted nothing more than an interlude, and he believed her. If he had even the vaguest understanding of the female psyche, Tim Harris would have known that it is a rare woman who truly wants only a physical affair. DeeLisa was divorced, with small children, and she worked at the phone company.

She was about to fall totally in love with Tim Harris.

Tim had revealed very little about his private life to DeeLisa, and she had been careful not to ask questions. He wore a wedding ring, and she wasn't a fool. Still . . .

In early January, 1986, the house in Citrus Hideaway was finally ready for the Harrises to occupy. Sandy barely made it in time to get halfway settled before she gave birth to Timothy Scott Harris, Jr. He was born just a week after they moved in. With her second delivery Sandy had to have a caesarean, and she was in the hospital recovering for several days.

Tim brought DeeLisa to his new home, proudly showing off his handiwork. He took her into the master bedroom and drew her down with him on the bed he usually shared with Sandy. DeeLisa couldn't miss the signs that a woman lived in the house with Tim. She just had to know for sure, even though she didn't expect to like the answer. She finally asked, "A woman lives here. Probably your wife. Where *is* she?"

"She's in the hospital," Tim answered flatly. "She just had a baby."

DeeLisa drew in a sharp breath. If she had had the courage of her convictions, she would have left then. It was one thing to sleep with another woman's husband; it seemed so much more immoral to sleep with Tim in the bedroom that he shared with his wife—while that wife was in the hospital with his new baby. DeeLisa knew she should leave, but she couldn't.

She was already crazy about the man.

Sandy didn't know. She wouldn't know for a long, long, time. When she brought Timmy home from the hospital Tim was nice to her and even waited on her some while she recovered. He had wanted two girls, he had told her—and not a baby boy. But once he saw Tim Jr., he doted on his son.

They went on with their life. It was great having the new house, but its novelty soon wore off for Tim. He wasn't the least bit interested in putting in landscaping or in fixing anything that broke. It had been a new adventure for him, and now he was done with it. When one of the cupboard doors fell off its hinges Sandy asked Tim to fix it—but he never did. It hung there for years.

Tim put in Bahia grass that was easy to take care of, and he bought himself a riding lawn mower. He also bought a satellite dish.

Sandy couldn't stop him from buying one new "toy" after another. He bought a computer, but he tired of it in a few weeks and rarely used it again. He decided to build a greenhouse, and he bought several sheets of aluminum, worked on the greenhouse for a few hours, and, frustrated, threw the aluminum in a pile of junk in the backyard.

Sandy and Tim still had no friends—not the kind that they could invite over and go to parties with. They now had a house plenty big enough to have company, but Tim didn't want company.

"Tim was nice to people's faces," Sandy said. "But he called them 'those scumbags' behind their backs. He made obscene sounds at women. Everybody else's wife was a 'slut' to Tim. He hated everybody. He would never go to neighborhood barbecues. We hardly ever went to Patrol parties."

Tim didn't want Sandy to have girlfriends, either. After a while she simply stopped trying to have friends. It wasn't worth the fights or the effort. "My mom was my only friend—the only one I had to talk to."

Sandy hadn't the faintest hint that her husband was having an affair. He had, of course, the ideal profession for a marital cheat. Troopers kept their patrol cars at their own homes, and they went to work from home without ever having to report in to headquarters at the beginning of a shift. Often the radio dispatcher called them out from home when they were needed on the Interstate to help on an accident or a search.

Sandy never knew exactly where Tim was at any given time.

Sandy Harris had two babies, a job, and a house to

take care of. She loved Tim still, but sometimes he was almost like having a third child. She wanted to believe he loved their kids, but he wouldn't help with them. He never bathed them or fed them. "If I called him to ask him if he was going to pick them up from day care, he would never give me an answer. He would only say, 'I might, slut—and I might not.'"

She couldn't count on him; sometimes Sandy got there and Tim had already picked up the children. "Sometimes they were waiting for me, sometimes they were home already, but I always had to stop by the nursery to see if they were there. He picked them up if *he* felt like it—not to do a favor for me."

Except for her children, Sandy lived in an emotional vacuum. Tim didn't make it easy for her to work and be confident that her babies were taken care of, too.

Sandy still paid all the bills and kept their bank account balanced. She knew if she didn't that nothing would ever be paid. When Tim Harris wanted to buy something, "he begged and pleaded," and she usually gave in. It didn't do a bit of good for Sandy to show him the bills they already owed. "If Tim charged something and didn't tell me about it, I wouldn't find out until the bill came. If he wrote a check without telling me, I'll admit I'd blow up and yell at him. But Tim would never argue with me. He would call me a slut and walk away."

"'Just this one thing,' Tim always said. Like 'Just let me get the Dodge Ram truck and I'll never ask for another thing.'"

Sandy knew he would. But she always gave in in the end. Sandy would eventually take out a second—and then a *third*—mortgage on their new home so that they could buy the new trucks and the bigger boats for Tim. Each time she gave in to his demands he was cheerful and pleasant to be around for a while—but it never lasted.

"Why do you need something new all the time?" she asked him once.

"I never had anything when I was a kid," he told her. "Now it's my turn."

That was hard for her to believe. Tim's parents appeared to have had a lot more money than the Wessendorfs did. But Tim harbored tremendous resentment toward both of his parents. Sandy didn't know why—he wouldn't talk about it. He never sent his mother Christmas or birthday presents—not even cards—and he forbade Sandy to send any. Nevertheless, Virginia Harris always sent cards and presents, more when the babies were born.

Living as she was in a passive-aggressive marriage, Sandy Wessendorf Harris slowly began to change. The sweet, round-faced teenager who had loved the young policeman so blindly no longer existed. Her big dreams had been blasted away. Her marriage had no sound foundation, and she could never predict what Tim might do or not do. She had always trusted in the goodness of life, but now she grew wary.

Sandy took on a harder edge. Her parents and her sisters could see it, and it troubled them. It was the kind of brittle shell that people pulled on when they had been hurt too much, too many times.

"Sometimes," Sandy admitted, "I would almost wish he'd be killed out there on the highway—just to be rid of him and his meanness. I didn't want him to come home and demand sex. He'd be due home at midnight, and at five minutes to, I'd pretend to be asleep. It didn't do any good. It was always slam-bam-thank-you-ma'am, and I still cried after, in spite of myself."

She didn't know Tim was having an affair. She just

thought he hated her and his life with her. She no longer had any idea how to fix that.

The off-duty Tim Harris was alternately awkward and shy—and contemptuous around human beings. He trusted only the sea, and he trusted the man he became when he was in uniform behind the wheel of a powerful patrol car.

And he *was* good as a Florida State Trooper. On June 14, 1987, the *Miami Herald* featured Tim in a four-column spread about how drivers in his district were reacting to the raising of the speed limit to sixty-five miles an hour. The new law—affecting only certain regions—had gone into effect on April 27th. Tim and his fellow troopers working along the Treasure Coast on I-95 had issued 712 tickets to drivers during May. The year before they had given out 842.

Tim Harris said flatly, "Speeders will be speeders. There are just some people who are going to drive ten or twelve miles over the limit no matter what. And on top of that, you've still got your real high rollers who are going to be going ninety or better."

While *Herald* reporter Phil Long rode with Tim, he watched him hand out two tickets. One driver was going eighty-two, according to Tim's radar gun; the next was going seventy-six, both of them in the sixty-five-miles-per-hour zone. Long took pictures of Tim behind the wheel of his patrol car and as he lectured the drivers. He was still very handsome, although he looked more mature; he had put on some weight and had just a trace of jowls.

A month later the *Miami Herald* featured Tim Harris again. He explained a new technique the Patrol had implemented, one that would negate the effectiveness of radar detectors. The new speed trap, known as VASCAR Plus (Visual Average Speed Computer and Recorder), allowed the trooper to remain stationary and punch into a little black box the time it took a car to travel a pre-measured distance. The device also would enable a moving Patrol unit to measure the speed of a car traveling either in front of or behind him. "You know the time and the distance," Tim said. "So you come up with the speed."

Tim smiled as he said that about ninety percent of the drivers the Patrol was nabbing with VASCAR had Fuzzbusters and were unpleasantly surprised to be stopped—because the VASCAR had no beam and emitted no signal, so the radar detectors were useless.

Patrolmen were asked to put in ten overtime hours apiece each week. That would cost the Treasure Coast patrol area a lot of money, but the counties involved, which got a portion of the speeding fines, would do well. Speeding fines were $44 for traveling 56 to 65 mph, $74 for those going 66 to 79 mph. The real speeders, Tim's "high rollers," would pay $99 plus $2 for each additional mile per hour.

Tim was the law; he was the trooper picked by Captain Dean Sullivan in the Fort Pierce office of the Florida Highway Patrol to represent the department. Sandy was proud of all the articles written about Tim, and she cut them out for her scrapbook. If ever a woman was ambivalent about her man, it was Sandy Harris. Times like that, she was glad Tim was her husband.

Other times were bad. Tim still called her and other women "sluts" and "bitches." He still refused to make friends with other couples. He still pinched Sandy high up on the inside of her thighs where no one but he would see the blackish-purple bruises. He still twisted her arms behind her back when she made him angry.

And Sandy remained completely unaware of Tim's mistress, DeeLisa Davis.

8

The woman in the pine grove was still alone. She had been there so long now that even the little animals who lived and died there were no longer aware of her. The insects no longer stung her exposed flesh. She had become part of their environment, as inanimate as a fallen pine bough, as silent as the night sometimes grew when there was no wind at all off the river.

Right through his 1988 evaluation Tim Harris continued to "exceed" what was expected of a Florida State Trooper. His superiors checked off the top box in every category. Sure, he was a quiet kind of guy, but he would stop and shoot the breeze with any of his fellow troopers. He did his job, and he did it well. He was always where he was supposed to be, and when they called him out for extra duty he never complained.

In 1987 Tim had put in a request to work as a K-9 officer, to get a dog and to be sent to K-9 training at Fort Lauderdale. The FHP was adding some more dogs so that they could be trained for their drug interdiction program. Beyond catching drunk drivers, Tim Harris was most interested in cutting down on the swath drug dealers were ripping through Florida. He was excited when he was given orders to report to K-9 school.

Tim's dog was named Shadow. Shadow was a

beautiful male long-haired Alsatian who weighed ninety pounds. Tim spent weeks training with his dog, and when they came home to Indian River County the two were bonded inextricably. Tim built a chain-link pen for Shadow out beside the new house. Like most K-9s, Shadow was a gentle family pet with Sandy, Jennifer, and Timmy—but when he was working with Tim, he was ready to tear apart anyone who threatened his "partner." In fact, Shadow was exceptionally protective of Tim.

Tim was not averse to using Shadow to tease someone sadistically. It was the only kind of humor he understood. Sue Dappen happened to be afraid of dogs. One day Sue walked into her sister's house and didn't see Shadow sitting quietly in the foyer. Tim grinned and said softly, "Shadow, *watch her.*" The big dog immediately perked up his ears and started growling at Sue, and she froze in terror—as Tim had known she would. Don walked in behind Sue, saw what was going on, and said, "Tim! Cut it out!"

Tim did, but he laughed heartily.

For a while Tim was so caught up in Shadow that everything else paled. Even his enforcement percentage levels dropped, although his sergeant explained that was because he had been away at K-9 training school. "He and his canine are always available to call out."

Tim had even put his affair with DeeLisa on hold while he was down in Lauderdale training with Shadow, and neither she nor Sandy saw much of him when he came back and went to work with his dog.

Tim's actual duties didn't really change. He was still investigating accidents, arresting DUIs, and writing tickets for speeders, and he was in his old familiar district. The only difference was that from mid-1987 on, Tim had Shadow with him. The Patrol had promised to work both Tim and Shadow into a new felony program, focusing particularly on drug interdiction, but either there wasn't enough tax money to set up the program or the officials were dragging their feet, because two years went by and there was no upgrading of the felony program.

Tim Harris and Shadow made an impressive-looking pair when they stopped an errant driver: the tall trooper, made even taller in his campaign hat, and the dog who looked as though he'd like nothing better than to be released from the backseat to chomp off an arm and a leg or two. The Shadow who played with Sandy's and Tim's babies was a completely different dog than the Shadow on duty. In a way, Tim and Shadow shared that trait; each of them had two different and widely diverse personalities.

There was a brief respite of calm in the Harris's marriage after Tim got Shadow. But inevitably Tim got bored with Shadow, too. If he had been able to train Shadow to be a drug-sniffing dog and they could have worked felonies together—man and dog—as Tim wanted to do, it would have been different.

Tim took good care of Shadow at first, but then Sandy realized that he was locking his dog in his den for hours and hours when he was off-duty. She sighed. Just as with every other new toy he got, Tim no longer wanted to be bothered with Shadow, but Shadow was a living, feeling, creature, and he adored Tim. She felt sorry for the dog and tried to let him out to be with her and Jennifer and Timmy whenever she could.

Now that Tim's interest in Shadow had diminished, he grew bored again. He came to Sandy with a request that she could scarcely believe. "He wanted a helicopter! Can you *believe* that? He wanted his own helicopter. He was going to buy a kit and build it—he said it would only cost $28,000. I finally talked and talked and got him to think about getting a bigger boat instead."

A boat would be the lesser of two evils.

To make up for the lost helicopter it would have to be a really big boat. This time Tim bought a twenty-five-foot extra wide Cubby Proline 200 horsepower cabin cruiser that cost $45,000. That was when Sandy arranged for a third mortgage on their new house. Originally their monthly payment had been workable, and even the second mortgage wasn't too difficult to pay off as long as they were both working. Tim's $45,000 boat loan scared Sandy; she knew they could lose their precious acre in Citrus Hideaway so easily.

Sandy worked over their budget, and no matter how she added it up it always came out the same. The house payment was up to $1,094, the boat payment was $329, Tim's new truck was $350, and Tim drove the truck so much that their gasoline bill was usually over $250 a month. That meant that they owed $2,023 a month before they could even think about groceries, day care, utilities, or clothes. They had no entertainment costs because they never went anywhere. If Tim was home in the evening, they watched television. They never talked anymore.

Before taxes, Sandy and Tim together brought in only $3,900 a month. Sandy was scared to death they were going to go bankrupt.

Tim didn't care; he was wildly happy about his new boat. He bought $2,000 worth of scuba equipment. He bought a $1,200 cellular phone, and the first month's phone bill was $600.

Beyond being out there in the night cruising I-95 looking for speeders, drunks, and drug runners, or sitting quietly in the daytime in one of those hidden spots troopers always seem to know about where they can observe traffic unseen, Tim loved the water. He had grown up on the Indian River and all the little islands that seemed to drift along in it. Some of the islands he whizzed by were only lumps of land too tiny to have a name, but some had docks where he could moor the big, new boat.

The Indian River could take him out into the Atlantic Ocean if he chose. Tim had no fear of the water at all. He almost dared it to drown him, although he worried about Jennifer and Timmy when they played near the omnipresent streams, rivers, and inlets. Once, when Timmy was about two and a half, Sandy was watching the children wade in shallow water, and Timmy went under and swallowed some water before Sandy could grab him and tip him upside down.

Although Timmy was never in any real danger, Tim railed at her for months for being careless. "Remember," he would intone ominously, "when our son nearly drowned—"

That always made Sandy feel guilty, although she knew there were few kids who hadn't had a noseful or two of water when they were toddlers, and she always watched the kids like a hawk when they were wading.

Tim himself was like a dolphin in the water. Now that he owned the biggest boat of all the law enforcement officers in Indian River County, he occasionally invited them to go fishing or scuba diving with him. His brother-in-law, Don Dappen, often went along.

One time Tim took several officers out in his boat to scuba dive. He volunteered to stay with the anchor line while they dived. The first man popped up from the ocean's depths and was horrified to see that Tim's boat was hundreds of yards away and drifting further. His shouts drew no response, so he swam as hard as he could, barely reaching it before it disappeared over the horizon. Exhausted, he managed to pull himself aboard. Tim wasn't there, and the anchor sure wasn't doing its job. The cop had no choice but to cut the anchor loose completely and turn the boat back to where the signal flag floated. The other men would surface soon, exhausted, to find the Cubby cruiser was gone. He could only assume that Tim had gone over the side and drowned.

Gradually the other men popped up, grateful to find the boat waiting—but shocked to hear that Tim was missing. Don Dappen wondered how he was going to break the news to Sandy. And then, amazingly, Tim Harris burst from the water. Alive and well. He laughed at their concern for his safety, but he was angry that they had cut his anchor adrift. Tim couldn't get it through his head that they might all have drowned if the boat had gotten away.

Another time Don was along on a midnight dive for lobsters. It was the opening day of the season, and they had to descend to the Indian River's bottom carefully or the riptide heading for the vastness of the Atlantic Ocean could pull them off the rope like autumn leaves in a hurricane. Tim laughed at Don's warning and said he'd go down first and look around.

"When we got down," Don remembered, "we couldn't see him. It should have been easy, because all we had to do was turn off our lights and we would have seen Tim's. But he wasn't there."

They surfaced, once again sure that Tim had drowned. The ship's radio was crackling, and there was a call from the skipper of the last boat in a long line of pleasure craft anchored out toward the ocean. "We have a man named Tim on board," the man said. "Is he by any chance off your boat?"

Tim *had* been caught in the riptide, despite his assurances that he would descend with caution. When

Don put together the information from the boaters along the line he learned that Tim hadn't fought the tide at all, nor had he accepted help from the yachts he passed. He had lain back and floated as if he were home in his swimming pool while he passed dozens of boats whose owners stared in horror. At the final moment, as he drifted near the very last cruiser between himself and the open sea, the captain threw him a rope and pulled him aboard. Tim hadn't been frightened. It was almost as if he was completely unaware that he was headed for deadly undercurrents, sharks, and certain death.

It was almost as if he didn't care.

Lt. Gary Morgan, the FHP officer who had originally been responsible for helping Tim get assigned to Indian River County, became one of Tim's supervisors in 1989. Several troopers had mentioned to Morgan that Tim was very disappointed that there had been no follow-up on the promised development of the felony program. Morgan called Tim in and talked with him. Tim said he felt he just didn't have the time to train Shadow for the drug interdiction program. He wasn't getting a chance to use his dog for what Shadow had been bred for.

"I sat him down," Morgan recalled. "I promised him we would schedule a month ahead of time for him to train the dog. I would give him certain days, and I'd give him sometimes eight hours—the whole day— sometimes four hours to work his dog, take it to the different training grounds, and to take it to the vet and things like that. You know, I kind of let him have a free rein as far as doing what he wanted to do with the dog and working the dog on the Interstate with the drug interdiction program. I didn't use him to work wrecks except when I actually needed him—when all

the other troopers were tied up. . . . I would call on
him, and he would always go and never give me any
complaints about working the wrecks. . . . I'd give
him Indian River, Saint Lucie, and let him roam up
and down the Interstate, working the dog."

Shadow did good work, responding to Tim in their
expanded program, and man and dog spent more time
together. Shadow even made the Vero Beach *Press
Journal* himself in 1989. "The Shadow knows—and
proved it Thursday morning . . ."

Shadow and Tim had been instrumental in appre-
hending a suspect in a rash of auto thefts. The suspect
fled into a deep woods, and Shadow sniffed him out.
There Tim found the most recently stolen car, and
four more that were being stripped down.

Shadow continued to be the canine darling of the
media. He and Tim posed together under the headline
"Not Your Ordinary Puppy." Tim explained to the
reporter that Shadow was an *official* member of the
Florida Highway Patrol and had as much right as
human troopers to wear a badge—and Shadow did,
hanging from his collar.

Sometime in 1989 word came down that the FHP
was taking applications for troopers who were interested in going into newly beefed-up felony programs.
Trooper Tim Harris was one of those selected.

That wasn't surprising. He was a much-commended
trooper. On August 4, 1989, Assistant Florida State
Attorney Stuart A. Webb wrote to Patrol Major William Driggers and Colonel Randall Jones:

"The enclosed order is forwarded for your information and action. I must add that the defendant was
forced to enter a plea due to the excellent case
developed by your Trooper T.S. Harris. Although
there were only traces of marijuana found, he devoted
the extra time and effort to ensure success, and he

made my job very easy. Trooper Harris was outstanding at every phase of the case and is a credit to himself, your leadership, and the Florida Highway Patrol."

Trooper Harris, whose last evaluation said he was "highly competent" and required minimal supervision, that he was "flexible and adapts easily to change . . . a valuable asset to the Division," apparently did not see himself that way. He was an angry, morose, and miserable man.

Who knows what it takes to make a particular man happy? Timothy Scott Harris *should* have been happy in the late summer of 1989. He had a beautiful wife who loved him even though she sometimes wished she didn't, a beautiful mistress who also loved him and who also sometimes wished she didn't, two healthy, happy kids, a fine big house he had built with his own hands, a job he had always wanted, a chance to move up, and a loyal dog who loved him, too—without reservations. Tim was movie-star handsome, healthy, and his fellow troopers respected him.

But Tim Harris wasn't happy. He had secret sexual fantasies that neither of the women in his life fulfilled. He discussed his obsessions with no one. Never a man to talk much beyond casual conversation, he certainly would not reveal those things that snaked through his mind when he traced the dark ribbons of I-95 as they curled north to Melbourne and then south to Port St. Lucie.

PART TWO

Lorraine

9

Although Lorraine Marie Dombroski Boisseau
Hendricks and Sandra Lynn Wessendorf Harris were
never to meet, the two women might have liked each
other; they had a lot in common. Like Sandy Harris,
Lorraine was born in the first week of October.
Sandy's birthday was October 6th, and Lorraine's was
October 3rd. Lorraine, however, was sixteen years
older than Sandy, although she scarcely looked it. She
was very beautiful—movie-star beautiful. Model
beautiful. She could also look like a pixie when she
eschewed makeup and high-fashion clothes—as she
often did. At the age of forty-three Lorraine looked
perhaps thirty. She was five feet, six inches tall and
weighed under 125 pounds. Her chestnut-colored hair
was extremely thick, and her eyes were brown and
sparkling.

Probably the most memorable thing about Lorraine
was her ebullient love of life. She had a wonderful
smile and the energy of ten ordinary women.

Like Sandy Harris, Lorraine Hendricks had been
through some hard times, and like Sandy, she was a
woman who handled problems competently rather
than collapsing into tears. Neither woman had ever let

life's misfortunes get the better of her for long. Both Lorraine and Sandy had parents who were always there to back them up.

Lorraine was born in Stamford, Connecticut, in October of 1946 to Frank and Josephine "Jodi" Dombroski. Frank was a career army officer who served under General Dwight D. Eisenhower in the European Theater in World War II.

Like all service families, the Dombroskis and their son and daughter moved frequently. When Lorraine was five they were in Germany; they would have a second tour there. When she was seventeen they were at Fort Holabird in Baltimore. And there were many, many duty stations in between until Frank retired as a major in 1965. He had served his country for twenty-four and a half years. "The Major" was a strong, quiet-spoken man who adored his only daughter. Not surprisingly, Lorraine was raised to respect men in uniform. Her dad was a shining example for her.

Jodi Dombroski was a pretty woman, and Lorraine looked very much like her, although she was taller than her mother. They had the same smile, the same belief in the importance of the continuity of family. Lorraine kept a little plaque in her kitchen reminding the viewer that love and knowledge are handed down generation to generation.

The Dombroskis were strong Catholics, and for much of her life Jodi Dombroski worked as a volunteer—for the Red Cross, for hospitals, for her church—and she imbued Lorraine with the belief that those who were fortunate had an obligation to those who were not.

Lorraine was a natural athlete. She was a strong swimmer and earned her senior life saving badge when she was sixteen and her father was stationed at Fort Holabird. Her mother, wearing her Red Cross volunteer uniform, stood by, smiling proudly.

Lorraine Dombroski grew up to be an almost incandescently lovely teenager, although she herself didn't seem to realize it.

"When we were in Baltimore," Jodi said, "I remember how surprised Lorraine was when I suggested she enter a beauty pageant where the prize was a college wardrobe. She laughed and said she would never win—but she did win."

Lorraine went on to win many other beauty contests. She was Miss Stamford, Connecticut, in 1967, and then first runner-up to Miss Connecticut. In the talent contest she performed the history of drums—from jazz to rock and roll to African rhythm. "Lori" had brains, too, and she had a remarkable talent for languages. She attended the University of Connecticut. By the time she was an adult she was fluent in French, German, Spanish, and Polish. She was always especially proud of her Polish roots. When she went to classes to learn Polish she threw herself into the process, as she did in all her pursuits. In no time Lorraine was inviting the teacher home to meet her parents, to have a home-cooked Polish meal.

Although her hair would darken later, at eighteen Lorraine Dombroski was the very epitome of the lovely blonde with the perfect figure that most teenage girls long to emulate. If she hadn't been so nice, she might have aroused some jealousy. But she *was* nice. She was particularly drawn to little kids, old people, and, especially, animals.

She always would be.

Because of her tremendous kindness it would be easy to pigeonhole Lorraine as a "goody-goody"—too nice to be true. She was much more than that. There are people who seem to accept life as it comes, never swerving from whatever path they find themselves on. Not Lorraine Dombroski. She was curious and adventurous, and she was more than a bit of a daredevil. She would try anything once—as long as it didn't go against her own moral code. She was a drummer in a rock and roll band for a while, she climbed mountains and swung off them on ropes, and she tried parachuting.

When she was younger she didn't mind being called "Lori," although later she preferred her full name. To her best friend, Carol, she was usually "Lor."

Lori Dombroski was within a semester of graduating from college when she dropped out to marry John Boisseau in 1977. Carol Worley, her friend for more than a dozen years, perhaps her closest confidante, recalled, "She put him through the rest of his college. She was very, very much in love with John, and she loved her life with him. Sometimes her friends complained that Lori was working and John was just going to school—but *she* never said a word against him. She was so happy with him. They hiked, they canoed, they camped—they rode motorcycles through the wilds of the Everglades. She loved all those things they did."

Lori and John Boisseau were involved in motocross racing, and when she was in her early twenties Lori nearly died in a crash in a motorcycle race. She ended up in an intensive care unit and then underwent emergency surgery in which much of her liver and all of her gallbladder were removed. Aside from the scar left, she scarcely thought about her injuries once she was healed. It wasn't the first time she had been injured taking part in one sport or another, and it wouldn't be the last.

John's ambition was to be a professional musician, and they lived most of the decade they were together in the Miami area. For a time Lori modeled. Her long hair was bleached until it looked like shimmering wheat, her skin was golden tan, and she posed in white go-go boots and a minidress in an ad for the Florida Highway Patrol and the Governor's Highway Safety Commission. Smiling directly into the camera, Lorraine opened the first carton of 1971–72 Florida plates that all state motorists were asked to display on their vehicles.

The plates read, "Sunshine State—ARRIVE ALIVE—Florida."

Lori and John Boisseau were divorced after eleven years. It no longer matters what they fought about, but years later Lorraine would confide to Carol Worley that in retrospect she felt she had acted too hastily—that she had let her pride get in the way of what might have been mended with counseling. "I said good-bye too quickly," Lori sighed. "I could have forgiven him." Ironically, both of their careers blossomed after their divorce.

John, once leader of the rock trio "The Better Halves," moved up rapidly in the music world, but not only as a musician; he owned a sound stage and rented trucks, cables, every kind of musical equipment musical groups that came into the Miami area for concerts might need.

Lorraine was an idea woman, creative, enthusiastic, and sparkling. Her career choice was public relations, communications, and marketing. She was a natural at innovative advertising, and she handled people with tact and sensitivity.

More than that, Lorraine Hendricks was a woman who truly *liked* people and drew them to her like a magnet. More than one friend, searching for a word to describe her, finally came up with "magical."

"She *was* magic," one associate recalled. "You could see it in her eyes, in her smile—her *aura*, I guess you'd call it. When you walked into a room with

Lorraine, people wanted to talk to her. In no time they were her friends."

Not surprisingly, Lorraine's expertise and natural charm sent her rapidly up the ladder in her career. She spent fourteen years in the Fort Lauderdale area working for Jack Drury and Associates, The Communications Group, North Broward Hospital District Medical Centers, the Hospital Corporation of America, and Humana Hospitals. She had a fifteen-year association with Stubbs and Associates of Atlanta as a promotional marketing representative.

Lorraine tried skydiving, and she skied in Switzerland. She decided she wanted to learn ballet, but she refused to "go to some class with a bunch of uncoordinated women in tight leotards." Instead she took a beginning ballet class with twelve-year-olds, learning the basics. She didn't care a bit that she was taller than all the other students, that she was a grown-up and they were children. Carol Worley laughs, remembering. "Lorraine was actually in a *recital*—this big thirty-five-year-old woman with a bunch of twelve-year-old girls, and she wasn't in the least embarrassed."

When she was married to John, they taught classes in kung fu, and at one time Lorraine was nationally ranked as a black belt. Indeed, she was the first Caucasian female to reach the rank of black belt in kung fu karate in the United States. Her perfect, slender figure might have made her appear delicate. She was anything but.

Woe be unto any ordinary predatory male who looked on the exquisite and outwardly fragile beauty of Lorraine Boisseau and saw a woman who could not put up a fight. And win. Lorraine even taught self-defense to women, both those her own age and senior citizens. She was a champion of all women, but she

went out of her way to help those women who had
been bruised by life, women who no longer believed in
themselves. If she couldn't hire them herself, she
would see to it that they found jobs, and that they had
nice clothes to wear until they could afford to buy
their own.

Lorraine and Carol "just kind of hung out together," her best friend remembers. Carol Worley was a
physical therapist at the University Community Hospital in Fort Lauderdale when Lorraine was their
public information officer. They met for the first time
in November, 1978. Lorraine had had a skiing accident in Zermatt and had cartilage surgery on her
knee, and Carol had just come to work as a therapist
at University Community. Carol ran for exercise, but
only about two miles at a stretch.

"Would running help my knee heal?" Lorraine
asked.

That was a new one for Carol; most of her patients
favored their injured parts and moved them gingerly.
Nobody ever wanted to *run*. Lorraine did.

"Yes," Carol said slowly. "Yes, I guess it would—if
you don't push it."

And run Lorraine did. "And then," Carol recalls,
"Lorraine came to me and said, 'Carol, I'm going to
run in a *race*—7.2 miles!' She had this infectious
enthusiasm that you couldn't resist—and the next
thing I knew, I said, 'Well, I'm going to run with you
then!' I'd never run more than two miles in my life,
but Lorraine got a whole group of us from the hospital
to run. It wasn't long after that that she came to me
and said, 'Carol, I'm going to run a marathon!'"

And this time they both ran in a marathon. Carol
was ten years younger than Lorraine, but no one ever
guessed Lorraine's age correctly. "She and I ran 26.2

miles!" Carol says. "That's the way she did things. Afterward, these friends who took us asked, 'Well, are you going to run it again next year?' We took one look at each other and said, 'Not on your life!' But you know, the next year we did it again."

Whenever Carol Worley pictures Lorraine she sees her in her running clothes, with her long hair braided into pigtails, with no makeup, and with a triumphant grin on her face. "Or I *hear* her. She always wore high heels at work, and you'd hear this click-clickety-click coming down the hall, and you *knew* it had to be Lorraine—nobody else moved that fast."

Lorraine was the consummate animal lover. She found an old horse that nobody wanted, a gelding she described as having "one foot in the glue factory." Lorraine paid fifty dollars for him, adopted him, and kept his misnomer: Flicka. They were the same age— thirty. "Flicka was a big part of Lori's life for a long time," Carol remembers. "She would spend all night in the stable sitting up with that horse. She spent so much money when Flicka's hooves got infected after the pasture flooded. One time Flicka fell in the stable, and the people who owned the barn were so angry— because they thought they were going to have to take a wall down to get Flicka out. But Lori got friends and equipment, and they all went out there and hauled Flicka back up on his feet, and he lived another six or seven years!" Indeed, Flicka lived to be forty-two, an almost unheard-of age for a horse.

Lorraine visited Flicka twice a day and took care of him. "After she divorced John," Carol Worley says, "Lorraine used to say, 'Flicka's my best friend.'"

Lorraine had a birthday party for Flicka every year, and her friends brought apples and carrot cake and appropriate presents. One year Flicka made the local society pages for his birthday party, and his picture appeared. He, of course, wore a party hat. Another birthday was filmed for the eleven o'clock news in Miami.

One thing that Lorraine couldn't bear was to see dead animals left in the road. She was often late for appointments because she stopped and moved them to the grassy shoulder of the road and tried to find something to cover them. "She actually kept a shovel or something in her trunk," Carol recalls. "So she could lift them off the road and give them some dignity. If she saw an animal that had been hit in a neighborhood, she would go and knock on doors to try to find out who it belonged to and tell them so they wouldn't have to find it themselves."

Lorraine was single for two years after she divorced John Boisseau. Then she met Rick Hendricks, an executive with Eastern Airlines and a captain in the army reserve, in 1979. Lorraine quickly fell in love with Rick; they were married six weeks after they met. Their wedding was in the northwest, where Rick's best man lived, and they honeymooned at a ski resort.

Lorraine was in her early thirties by then, and she longed for a family. She was bitterly disappointed when she suffered a miscarriage. And then, when she was almost thirty-eight, Lorraine became pregnant again. On June 28, 1984, she gave birth to a baby girl by caesarean section: Katherine. Lorraine's own hair had darkened to brown, but Katherine had golden blond hair, just as her mother had once had. And as with her mother, there was a magical sense about Katherine. Lorraine adored her.

As much as her career meant to her, nothing was more important to Lorraine Hendricks than her baby girl. She took a sabbatical from work until Katherine was old enough to go to school. Six years away from such a competitive world was taking a chance—but Lorraine never considered doing otherwise.

Now, when Lorraine ran in marathons, Katherine was a part of it, too. She wore a tiny tank top with the same logo her mother's had, a little visor, athletic socks, and running shoes. In one race Lorraine actually *pushed* Katherine for 6.2 miles—not in a jogging stroller, but in a regular stroller. In a 9.2 race Lorraine was exhausted, but still she scooped up her baby toward the end so Katherine could share the joy of crossing the finish line.

Katherine Hendricks spoke Polish before she spoke English. Lorraine spoke to her baby girl in the language of her heritage, and so did the Dombroskis, knowing that it is much easier for very young children to learn a foreign language. By the time she was three or four Katherine spoke both English and Polish well. Lorraine laughed when one of Katherine's pre-school teachers called her in and said, with a perplexed look on her face, "Katherine is using words, teaching the other children—we're not sure what they are. We think they may be inappropriate—"

"Those are *Polish* words," Lorraine said. "I can assure you that they're not the least bit naughty."

Lorraine learned her grandmother's recipes for traditional Polish dishes and spent days each spring preparing an Easter feast identical to those that had graced tables in Poland a hundred years earlier. She worked with Polish families who had just immigrated and helped them set up households in America.

In 1988 Rick Hendricks was offered an excellent job as an executive with Blue Cross—but it meant a move from Fort Lauderdale to Jacksonville. It was a wrench for Lorraine Hendricks to leave her friends, but she didn't hesitate. The only thing she insisted on was that

Flicka would come along, too. It was going to cost a lot to transport a forty-two-year-old horse on a six-hour trip, but Lorraine and Flicka lucked out. A man who trained race horses offered Flicka a free luxury ride to Jacksonville in his empty top-of-the-line horse trailer. Flicka—along with their corgis, Amy and Si—moved to Jacksonville in 1988, too.

Lorraine and Rick Hendricks worked to keep their marriage together. They were both nice people, but they had little in common—beyond Katherine. Lorraine was a physical woman who craved the outdoor life and the exercise she was used to. In the beginning of their marriage they had done things together—Lorraine had even learned to rappel down cliffs with Rick's reserve unit. But now Rick tended to put his energy into his career, and he preferred to stay home on weekends. In Jacksonville, for the first time in her life, Lorraine put on weight. She wasn't bored—she was never bored—but she chafed at inactivity.

In the end, despite their hope that they could stay together for Katherine's sake, Rick and Lorraine had to acknowledge that they were living separate lives long before they finally filed for divorce. They didn't live together long after the move to Jacksonville. Rick reluctantly moved into his own apartment, but he was still a big part of his daughter's life.

When Katherine was almost six Lorraine opened her own public relations business in Jacksonville. She called it Lorelei Promotions, Ltd. Lorraine listed "communications, marketing and promotions, and special events" as the services her company offered.

Lorraine Hendricks knew the meaning of "Lorelei" in folk culture; in German mythology, the Lorelei was a siren of the Rhine River whose haunting songs lured sailors to shipwreck and death. But for her, the Lorelei rock was a special place in Germany that she had loved when she lived there as a little girl. "Lorelei" and "Lorraine" sounded somewhat alike, too, so she hoped it would be something prospective clients would remember.

Lorraine Hendricks herself was the exact opposite of a "Lorelei" personality. If anything, she gave too much of herself to help other people, spread herself way too thin.

From mid-1989 to the spring of 1990 Lorraine was incredibly busy as she re-entered the business world. Her Miami-Fort Lauderdale credentials opened doors in Jacksonville. She was especially talented at putting on conventions and festivals where huge numbers of people had to be transported, housed, fed, and entertained. She thrived on the myriad details and logistics that would have daunted most people. She and her friend and associate, Ruth Straley, working with the American Society of Military Comptrollers, brought 3,000 people into Jacksonville for their annual convention. It was the largest convention ever held in Jacksonville and a huge success.

Lorraine managed a Mature Life Expo, the first of its type for Jacksonville, and her ideas helped make the 1989 Gator Bowl memorable. Lorraine orchestrated the West Virginia pre-game pep rally and a sixties vintage sock hop featuring the one and only Chubby Checker doing "The Twist" and all of his other hits.

Lorraine didn't like to travel, because it meant being away from Katherine—but wherever she was, no matter how busy she was, Lorraine never failed to stop everything at Katherine's bedtime and call home to tuck her little girl in—at least verbally. One thing Katherine knew: her mother would always be there for her.

Lorraine met the man who would become one of

her dearest professional and personal friends in Jacksonville as she and Ruth Straley were working on the Military Comptrollers convention. They wanted a dynamite line-up of entertainers for the closing night of the convention and contacted Mike Raleigh,* who was—and is—one of the most successful entertainment agents and producers on the east coast. Based in New York, Raleigh often came to Florida to set up shows for conventions, clubs, posh hotels, and festivals, and he could pick up a phone and arrange for almost any celebrity a client might ask for. He had built shows around Red Skelton, Rich Little, Barbara Mandrell, Lee Greenwood, and scores of other stars.

It was May 26, 1989, when Lorraine met Mike Raleigh. They liked each other immediately. He could see that she had tremendous potential in the entertainment world, and he was supportive and encouraging, introducing her to celebrities like Joan Rivers, the Smothers Brothers, Frankie Avalon, and Jim Stafford. Raleigh could bring in country and western stars, Broadway stars, television and movie headliners. Like Lorraine, Mike Raleigh could be something of a workaholic, and they quickly developed a mutual respect.

Suddenly, in her early forties, Lorraine's whole life seemed to be changing for the better; doors were opening wide for her, and she was happier than she had ever imagined she could be. Although she hadn't expected to, didn't want to, and certainly had no time to, Lorraine Hendricks met a man with whom she would fall blindingly, irrevocably, impossibly in love. Given what was to come, his name no longer matters, and identifying him would only cause him pain. Still, he would one day remark that meeting Lorraine was the most "classically magic and romantic meeting that ever could be. . . . It came as close to undeniable true love at first sight as anything I've ever experienced."

Neither Lorraine nor the man knew if their relationship could continue as romantically as it had begun, and they moved cautiously, in awe of their feelings. In a sense, she was like a high school girl. She took her new love to Miami to introduce him to Carol Worley, and the moment she got home she called Carol and said, "Well, what do you think of him? Isn't he wonderful?"

Carol agreed that he was, indeed, wonderful. He was someone she would never have pictured with Lorraine, and yet they seemed to belong together. "But Lorraine was being careful. She had agonized over her divorce from Rick, wanting to do the right thing, and she was moving slowly, but I could tell they were so much in love."

In the meantime Lorraine plunged deeper into her growing business. Mike Raleigh helped her and Ruth Straley set up the program for the final night of their huge Jacksonville Conference. He arranged to have Gary Morris, whose operatic voice had thrilled New York audiences in *Les Misérables* and who starred on Broadway with Linda Ronstadt in *La Bohème,* headline the show. Morris is also famous for his crossover hit "Wind Beneath My Wings." The words to that song would always be special to Lorraine Hendricks.

For another event, the 1989 Night of the Stars, on New Year's Eve, Mike Raleigh and Lorraine put on a show with Jim Stafford, Joan Rivers, Danny Gans, the impressionist, and the Bill Allred Orchestra. Lorraine picked Joan Rivers up at the airport and escorted her back to the hotel before the show. Lorraine was never intimidated by celebrities; she treated them as she did everyone, with grace and warmth.

She worked on a fund-raiser starring the Smothers

Brothers for the Big Brothers and Big Sisters in Jacksonville. Mike Raleigh remembers seeing tiny Katherine Hendricks in June, 1989, sitting on the late Gamble Rogers's lap backstage, giggling while he "taught" her how to play his guitar. For Raleigh it is a bittersweet memory; the beloved folk singer and songwriter would die a hero soon after as Rogers tried to rescue a drowning victim.

Some of the evenings Lorraine planned *were* extravaganzas with major celebrities like Joan Rivers and the Smothers Brothers; others were more modest. Whichever, Lorraine was adept at judging what her clients needed and coordinating the host of details for an evening or a weekend that would be memorable for both the convention attendees and their spouses and children, something to make up for the sometimes dreary banquets and long-winded speeches that mark most business conventions.

Lorraine and Rick Hendricks had parted amicably —so amicably, in fact, that theirs was a "do-it-yourself" divorce, with their legal advice furnished by a divorce kit. Neither wanted to take advantage of the other.

Their divorce was to have been final by March 4, 1990, but the judge they appeared before had asked for a modification of their divorce papers. Under child support Lorraine and Rick had written "optional," and the judge said that was much too vague a term. Although neither could envision a time when Katherine would not come first, the divorce judge thought she would be better protected if an actual amount of support or schedule of escalating support payments was specified.

Rick Hendricks could see his point, and he agreed to specify Katherine's support, and also to allow a short delay until their divorce became final. Lorraine believed, on March 4, that her divorce *was* final. She said as much to her friend, Carol Worley: "It's over; it's a done deal."

Their marriage hadn't exploded—it had just wound down until there was nothing left. Lorraine was sad about that; she had expected to be married to only one man—and forever—but her life hadn't turned out that way.

Lorraine's parents had sold their house in Connecticut and moved to a condominium in Jacksonville so that they would be on hand to care for Katherine after school.

After so many years working on her career, and despite the half dozen years she had taken off to give Katherine a good start, everything Lorraine touched turned to gold. That didn't mean she would give up her volunteer work or her close ties with St. Joseph's Catholic Church. She still taught Spanish at the church school. Lorraine was an indefatigable woman who found time for everyone who needed her.

Lorraine Hendricks was always in a hurry; she tried to crowd so much into her life. Her business wasn't something that could be worked on a nine-to-five basis. Even though she dreaded raising her daughter alone, it was a challenge she was confident she could meet.

In her mind, that spring, there was no challenge she couldn't handle.

10

It was a watershed time then for two Florida couples in 1989. Two marriages—two marriages among thousands in Florida that year—were coming to a close.

Lorraine and Rick Hendricks had already agreed to divorce when Tim Harris invited Sandy out for dinner on September 27, 1989. Although she had been pleasantly surprised, it would turn out to be a meal Sandy would never forget, an evening that would haunt her for years. It was to have been a birthday celebration for Sandy, who would turn twenty-seven on October 6th. Tim would be working a night shift on her birthday, so he told her they would celebrate early.

It wasn't a fancy restaurant, but Sandy didn't mind. It was a rare thing for them to go out without the children.

Their food had just arrived when Tim ducked his head and blurted, "I think you should know. I'm seeing another woman."

Sandy stared at him, stunned. She was taken completely off guard. Yes, Tim had continued to flirt with her friends, her sisters, practically every woman he saw. But she had had absolutely no idea that he might be having an affair. They had promised to be faithful to each other when they got married, and she believed that they had both kept their vows. They argued, certainly. And Tim drove her crazy with worry about finances because of his "toys," but Sandy had never even suspected there was another woman.

She looked at Tim and saw that he was calmly eating his meal. He glanced up and said, "Go on—eat your food before it gets cold."

She couldn't swallow. She could scarcely breathe. How could he have told her something like that and not realize what it would do to her? From the way Tim was acting, he might just as well have said that it looked as if it was going to rain.

Sandy Harris had long since grown accustomed to that peculiar flatness in her husband's manner, as if the emotions that rocked other people to their bones only drifted over him like a slight breeze. But this was truly incomprehensible to her. Tim had just told her that he was seeing another woman, told her in the middle of what was to have been a celebration of her birthday, and he was sitting across from her chewing his food as if their whole world hadn't just shifted off center and threatened to crash.

Sandy peppered Tim with questions. He wouldn't tell her the woman's name. He wouldn't tell her what she did. "All he would say was that she was a 'professional' woman, and that could have meant anything."

"How long has this been going on?" Sandy asked.

"A couple of weeks, maybe."

"You're sleeping with her, aren't you?"

Tim shook his head. "No. I've never had sex with her. It's not what you think. We just talk."

"You *talk?*"

"I don't see why you're getting so bent out of shape. We just talk."

"Then why won't you tell me who she is?"

"It doesn't matter. I'm going to keep on talking to her."

Sick to her stomach, Sandy pushed her full plate away. Forever after, when her birthday came around, she would remember that terrible night, the first time she became aware that Tim wasn't just flirting with women to tease her, he was having an affair. And that he had chosen her birthday celebration to tell her. Sandy never believed for a moment that he was seeing some woman solely for conversation. How dumb did he think she was? She was no longer the naive sixteen-year-old that Tim once knew, but he seemed to feel he could tell her anything and she'd swallow it.

When he finally saw how upset Sandy was, Tim took her home. Quite probably he realized that he had made a terrible tactical mistake by telling her about the other woman. But it was too late.

They fought. Sandy demanded to know who her rival was, and Tim wouldn't answer. He turned away, ignoring her.

She was infuriated by his refusal to have a discussion with her. "You're just like your father."

For once in their marriage she had found words that would get a reaction out of Tim. He turned back, white-faced with rage. "No! No! I'm nothing at all like my father."

Perhaps he was; perhaps not. Sandy had seen the estrangement widen between her husband and his parents. He might look like them—those two classically handsome people—but he acted as though he were a changeling child dropped into a family he had never bonded with. Tim's brother David was the only one vaguely like Tim. David had been a cop, too, but he'd been fired from the force. What had happened while Tim was growing up to make him treat women like dirt? Sandy often wondered.

Tim, who had never been a man to grasp subtlety, was anything but subtle about his pursuit of another woman. A few days after Sandy's disastrous birthday "party" he told her he was going fishing. After he had left, Sandy discovered he hadn't even bothered to take his fishing poles.

After Tim broke his news to Sandy about his other woman he apparently expected their marriage to go on as before. Sandy's life had imploded, blown all to pieces, and she walked through the rubble, dazed. Always before she had forgiven Tim for everything. But this time she could not let it rest. She was as obsessed as every betrayed wife is, needing to know the details and yet dreading what she might learn. What Sandy did learn made her feel worse.

"I started asking questions and asking questions," Sandy said. "I finally got more information out of several different people, and everything started fitting together. Tim confessed everything to me. He'd been seeing her for four years!"

Sandy was as shocked to find out that Tim had been sneaking out to meet DeeLisa for more than four years as she had been to learn that he was unfaithful. "The only time he wasn't seeing her was when he was going through the dog training with Shadow."

This man, her husband, had been difficult to live with, but the one thing Sandy had been sure of was that he was as faithful to her as she had been to him. That commitment had been the glue that held their marriage together. It hadn't mattered what her family thought or what the neighbors thought. She and Tim had pledged their fidelity to each other, and at some point, Sandy had believed, Tim would grow up, and they would have a marriage that was an equal partnership.

Now that hope had ended. Tim Harris hadn't changed one iota from the overgrown boy he had been when Sandy herself was sixteen. Only now they had two babies and a house and cars and boats. She knew that they were going to lose everything, but worst of all, she had lost the love of her life.

Sandy found out that DeeLisa Davis was almost ten years older than Tim, divorced with young children, a woman with long bleached-blond hair, and with a slender figure not that different from Sandy's. *Why?* Sandy couldn't understand. She knew that *she* was prettier than DeeLisa, and she was certainly younger. Tim had always hated long hair—at least he said he did—and yet he had chosen to cheat with a woman who had hair very much like his wife's.

Sandy Harris tried to hide from her family the fact that her marriage was disintegrating, hoping still that there would be some way to salvage it. She knew that once she told her mother, Pat Wessendorf would never forgive Tim. And so she bided her time, but now Sandy was on the alert. Tim promised her that he wouldn't see DeeLisa anymore, but Sandy didn't believe him. Like any woman who learns she has been lied to for years, she was poised to prevent that from ever happening again.

Always before when Tim had been called out to work an accident, she had believed that that was where he was going when he roared away from their home in his patrol car. She no longer believed that. She found that Tim had often pretended that DeeLisa was a patrol dispatcher calling him out. He hadn't gone out on patrol business at all; he had simply driven over to DeeLisa's house to spend stolen hours with her.

"I took the mileage on his car, wrote it down," Sandy remembered. "One time he said he was working security down in West Palm Beach, moonlighting while they built the mall down there. Well, the odometer came out to exactly the mileage to DeeLisa's house and back."

Tim and Sandy tried marriage counseling in early November. Tim insisted that he was no longer seeing DeeLisa and that he wanted to make his marriage work. Tim was lying to both Sandy and the counselor. It didn't take Sandy long to find out that Tim was still seeing DeeLisa as much as ever.

One night Tim was called out by the "dispatcher," but his patrol car was being repaired. He told Sandy he was going to drive his truck to another trooper's house and borrow his patrol unit. Sandy waited a few minutes, then called the other trooper and asked to speak to Tim.

"Tim's not here," the trooper said, mystified. "I haven't seen Tim for weeks."

Sandy wasn't mystified. She knew Tim was with DeeLisa. Sandy finally gave up. She filed for divorce the next day. It was late November, 1989. One would expect that Tim would have been relieved. He had treated Sandy as an annoyance, an impediment, for years. Instead he was horrified. He was stunned and full of disbelief that Sandy would leave him. He pleaded with her to change her mind.

"I just want someone to care about me," he said.

"It's funny, I guess," Sandy Harris said. "He never said 'I love you,' or 'I don't want to lose you.' He just said, 'I want someone to care about *me.*'

"It wasn't so much that he didn't want to lose me," Sandy Harris said sadly. "It was that he didn't want anyone else to have me."

The day after the Harris divorce action notice appeared in the local newspaper, Sandy's phone rang at 2 a.m. The caller hung up without speaking. Sandy suspected it was DeeLisa. She didn't know where Tim was—but apparently he wasn't with DeeLisa either. The next morning, Tim phoned Sandy at work to say that DeeLisa had called him and said that if he didn't move out and stay with her, she would see that he was fired. Sandy didn't know whether DeeLisa had really said that, but Tim insisted that he didn't want DeeLisa; he wanted Sandy. "You're the only one I love," he promised.

Tim had so much of his salary tied up in payments on his boats, trucks, and cars, not to mention their third house mortgage, that he told Sandy he couldn't afford to pay rent on another place. Sandy felt sorry for him and said that he could stay in the house—but not as her husband—until they figured out some plan. She would live her life, and he would live his. The divorce was going through, she insisted, and his living in their home was only temporary.

Tim tried futilely to talk Sandy into dropping her divorce action. "He was out of control most of the time, breaking things around the house. He even broke his own expensive camera. He lost interest in everything," Sandy recalled. "I was afraid he would lose his job."

If Sandy was civil to him, Tim took her softness as a sign that she was going to drop the divorce. He saw things the way he wanted to. When he came home from seeing DeeLisa and Sandy let him know she knew where he had been, he thought that meant she cared. Sandy was resolute; her mind was made up, but Tim saw vacillation and indecision because he wanted to. He *needed* to. He was a dog in the manger, and no woman who had ever "belonged" to him had the right to leave him—not until *he* decided he wanted her gone.

In his view, Sandy belonged to him.

Sandy Harris was a beautiful woman. Suddenly Tim seemed to realize that. He was obsessed with maintaining control over her. Although *he* was free to come and go and to see DeeLisa, he didn't want Sandy going anywhere.

She wasn't *dating,* certainly; she had her hands full with her job and her two babies.

Tim railed against what he considered Sandy's family's interference in his marriage. Pat was vocal about her opinion that Sandy should get the divorce as soon as she could. In fact, when Sandy hadn't filed the moment she learned about DeeLisa Davis, Pat was furious with her daughter.

"My mom didn't even speak to me for a couple of weeks," Sandy recalled. "She thought I took too long to decide to leave Tim after I found out he was cheating."

That was Pat. She saw the world in black and white, and Tim had stepped miles over the line of what she would accept in a son-in-law.

Susan and Don Dappen knew the situation, of course. They tried to mind their own business, but the problem only grew more bizarre and more fraught with danger. Tim was jealous of Sandy, absolutely poleaxed when he realized that she was not going to take him back and that she intended to start a life without him as soon as their divorce was final.

Don Dappen had seen seemingly normal men turn into obsessive stalkers when their women left them. He had seen men who would rather have a woman dead than let her go. And he had never found Tim exactly "normal" to begin with. He was a loner whose behavior had always been unpredictable.

Dappen worried what Tim might do next. He hoped that Tim's career—which had always been so important to him—would keep him from doing anything crazy.

Tim had acknowledged to Don that he had "screwed up" when he started dating DeeLisa. He had first promised he would never see her again, but later he asked advice about how he could keep both his wife and his mistress in his life. Don had told him to make up his mind and make it up fast; he didn't tell Sandy, but he told Tim to clean up his act. When Tim realized Don hadn't said anything about it to Sandy, Tim would say later—and incorrectly—that Don "was neutral—he was fine. . . ."

On December 9, 1989, Tim's obsession with Sandy boiled over. Susan, knowing that Sandy needed desperately to get out for a while, had invited her sister to go to the UpTown Lounge in Vero Beach with her. It was a Saturday night, and Don had duty at the Vero Beach Police Department. They wouldn't be out late, and it was a hometown kind of place where the two sisters could go without being bothered.

Tim Harris—who had been a desultory father at best—had suddenly become generous in his offers to baby-sit his children. He had asked Sandy if he could watch the children on that Saturday evening. As he recalled it, "She said 'No,' that she was going to take them over to Nana's, and I said, 'You know, I can watch the kids. I don't care if . . . if you want to go out, that's fine, you know. I would appreciate it if you just didn't go out with other guys, until we're, you know, finally divorced.'"

The handsome state patrolman was nothing if not ambiguous. His recall is that he was understanding and accommodating. His wife told confidantes a different scenario.

"Tim would come up behind me and put his hands

105

around my neck and say, 'I could snap your neck and kill you right now.' One time I finally said, 'Go ahead and do it then.' He let go and walked away."

On the night of December 9th Tim Harris followed Sandy and Susan Dappen to the Vero Beach Police Department, where they stopped in to see Don Dappen before heading over to the UpTown. Dappen heard a commotion in the hallway and walked out to see his about-to-be-ex-brother-in-law staring strangely at Sandy. Tim began to shout at Sandy, apparently oblivious to the fact that he was in a police station hallway and that Don, in command that night, was listening.

Tim Harris was clearly out of control, blind with rage. Don had vowed to stay out of Sandy's marital troubles, but Tim had gone too far. "I always told myself that if Sandy or the kids were in *jeopardy,* all bets were off," Don said.

"Get out of here, Tim," Dappen said. "That's enough. Get out of the police department or you'll be sorry."

Tim Harris could see that Dappen meant business, and he stalked out of the Vero Beach Police Department, leapt into his truck, and burned rubber as he roared away.

Worried about his wife and sister-in-law, Dappen followed Susan's car to the parking lot behind the lounge. In moments he saw Tim running across the lot toward Sandy, shouting, "Sandy! Come home! You're supposed to be with me!"

Don Dappen jumped out of his car and started to say, "Tim—"

"Stay the fuck out of it!" Tim shouted furiously.

"No, I won't stay out of it," Dappen said firmly. "You're in a public place."

Tim Harris, who rarely swore, let loose a string of

vulgarities, turned his back on his brother-in-law, and followed Sandy into the club. If Sandy had had any hopes of sitting with her sister and having a quiet drink or two, they were dashed. Tim insisted that he had to talk with her, making such a spectacle that people turned around to stare at them.

Don Dappen could see that things were escalating. *He* didn't want to have to be the Vero Beach officer who arrested Tim—if it got to that point. More than that, he sensed that Tim *wanted* to get into a physical fight with him, and Dappen wasn't going to let that happen. He called in one of his officers and explained the situation, that it was a marital hassle, that Tim was a state trooper. He asked his officer to keep an eye on the situation and keep it as low profile as possible. "If we can solve this thing peacefully, then do it. If he crosses the line, then take him. Act as you would in any other situation where you didn't know the people involved."

The young cop did a good job. Tim left, but Don waited outside, out of sight, watching.

Tim came back not once, but twice. "The guy was popping up from out of the blue," Dappen remembered. "Sandy and Sue went in the bar, and all of a sudden Tim just raced into the bar."

It was a tough situation for Don Dappen. The bar was full of people; he didn't know what his brother-in-law might do. He decided to speak to the bouncers and ask them to keep an eye on Tim, and they said they would.

"It wasn't five minutes before Tim came out of the bar with Sandy. He had his arm over her shoulder, pinning her head against him—not applying any pressure that I could see, but she couldn't move away from him."

"Sandy," Don said, "where you going?"

Sandy had given up. "I'm going home with him. I don't want to cause any more problems. I don't want him to go to jail, Donny."

Don Dappen was frustrated, but he had never been a man to stick his nose in other people's business—if he could help it. "Sandy," he said firmly, "you don't have to do this. I want you to understand you have other options."

"No," she said. "I need to get out of here."

"O.K." Dappen watched as Tim led Sandy away in a headlock; he looked back at his brother-in-law with a triumphant grin, a grin that said, See, she belongs to me, and you can't do anything about it.

"I have to admit"—Dappen grimaced—"I really wanted a piece out of him, but I didn't say anything. It was their deal."

How odd, really, that Tim Harris, for whom fidelity was a foreign word, was convinced that his wife was cheating on him. If Sandy Harris thought her life had been hell before, she now began to see how bad things could be.

Don Dappen worried about his sister-in-law, and he was furious with Tim Harris for behaving like a foul-mouthed teenager, both in the Vero Beach police station and in the UpTown.

Dappen went back to his car and called his dispatcher, "Get me FHP. Get me whichever supervisor is on duty, and tell him I want to talk to him. He can come to my office, or I'll meet him someplace."

Within ten minutes Lieutenant Gary Morgan walked into Dappen's office. Dappen liked Morgan; he had known him for years.

"Gary," Dappen said. "I could have arrested Tim. You've got to take a good look at him. The guy's unbalanced; he shouldn't be out there stopping people on the Interstate."

Morgan knew about Tim's impending divorce, and he knew Tim had been acting out of character—or at least out of the character he had always presented to the Patrol. But Morgan wasn't Tim's primary supervisor; Tim's supervisor was stationed down in Lantana, sixty miles south. Both Dappen and Morgan talked to him by phone, and he asked for a written report.

Don Dappen wrote that report and left it at the desk of the Vero Beach Police Department for pickup by the Florida Highway Patrol the next day.

"I don't know what happened to it," Dappen said. "It mysteriously disappeared; it never made it into Tim's jacket. I don't know who picked it up—it wasn't Gary Morgan, I know that."

The Florida Highway Patrol at least had Dappen's phone call, and they knew that Tim Harris's job performance had dropped—but not nearly enough for them to deem him unfit for duty. Besides, the UpTown incident had occurred off duty, and it involved mainly a domestic dispute—part of Harris's private life. They decided to keep an eye on the situation, but they took no disciplinary action against Harris.

Police work—all police work—is hard on marriages. Every working cop knows that. There are so many factors involved. For one thing, uniforms attract some women like an aphrodisiac, and the opportunity to cheat is always there, far more than it might be for an accountant or an insurance salesman. Many officers want to leave the job at the station, refusing to talk with their wives about what they have seen during an eight-hour watch. Sometimes it's too ugly and tragic to share and to remember. The worse things get out on the street, the more officers want to keep their own loved ones sacrosanct. Even though their spouses protect them out of love and concern, wives—and,

with a growing number of female officers, *husbands*—
often feel cut off and unimportant.

Cops form a circle that shuts out the rest of the
world, and nobody who really understands blames
them. They are often targets of ridicule for "civilians." Together, they all speak the same language, a
language the rest of the population doesn't understand. No one who hasn't been there when the blood is
still warm and gunpowder laces the air can possibly
understand the stress, the pressure, the terrible sights,
noises, and smells that policemen deal with. A cop's
partner is often the closest human being in his life.
Closer, indeed, in terms of shared experience and
mutual heartache, than a cop's wife.

A lot of marriages crumble. A lot of cops are less
than proficient on the job for a while. The vast
majority of them emerge from divorce and are soon
up to speed again.

It was ironic that Tim's dream of working on the
felony program had finally come to pass just as his
marriage was ending. Tim and Trooper Dean Burrows
would both be working felonies under the supervision
of Lt. Gary Morgan.

Even before Don Dappen's call Morgan was aware
that Tim's work performance was faltering. It was
obvious to Tim's fellow troopers and to his superiors
that he was not the outstanding patrolman that he had
been. Tim Harris had been the most gung-ho trooper
in his district as he relentlessly followed and stopped
speeders and druggers. His averages had always been
way up there. They no longer were.

"His performance was definitely acceptable," Morgan hastened to point out. "But not what he was
normally capable of doing."

The Patrol was between a rock and a hard place.

They couldn't really take a man off active duty because his home life was chaotic, and he was still doing his job. As it turned out, their decision about the stability of Tim Harris was a tragically bad call.

Tim's unexplained absences from home were as transparent as cellophane, and Sandy, through necessity, was growing more crafty. She pushed "redial" when Tim had made a phone call before leaving the house. Invariably, DeeLisa's voice answered. And Tim's mileage *never* matched the distances he told Sandy he would be traveling.

Tim often deliberately provoked an argument with Sandy so he could storm out of the house and be gone all night. After one obvious altercation Sandy sighed and said, "Tim, I'm too tired to fight with you. If you want to visit your girlfriend, just go!"

He left, but he came back in no time. "It was no fun seeing DeeLisa," Sandy said. "Not if I knew he was there."

It didn't take a psychiatrist to see that Tim Harris was coming unglued. Twice in January, 1990, he asked for leaves of absence from the Patrol so he could work on his marriage. In all his years on the force he had rarely called in sick. Now he did—often.

By late January, 1990, Sandy Harris realized that she and Tim could no longer live in the same house. She suggested that they needed "two weeks apart" to get their heads straightened out. Maybe then they could talk together and figure out where they were going.

Reluctantly, Tim agreed to move out for two weeks. Secretly, Sandy hoped that Tim's leaving would be permanent. He seemed afraid to go it alone, and he probably would vacillate between two women until he was eighty if somebody didn't make him get off the dime. He couldn't give up DeeLisa, and he couldn't give up Sandy. Well, then, Sandy decided, let him live with DeeLisa. Sandy only wanted her freedom. She was weary of being lied to and uneasy when she sensed his car trailing behind her, feeling eyes watching her in the night.

Tim Harris's friends on the Florida Highway Patrol tried, in February, 1990, to help him get his life together. He had never been really close with any of them off-duty, and he had never talked about his private life. But all they had to do was look at him to see he was in bad shape. He had weighed about 230 pounds, and now he looked as if he had lost at least forty pounds. He had deep circles under his eyes and looked haggard. Tim's marital problems seemed to be an open secret; the formerly taciturn trooper talked of nothing but getting back together with his wife.

Lt. Gary Morgan saw that Tim was depressed. "I told him there was light at the end of the tunnel," Morgan recalled.

Over and over Tim admitted that he had "screwed up," but he had repented, he said, and all he cared about was his wife and his family. But his wife had a cold and unforgiving heart, he confided earnestly. Tim did not mention that he was still deeply involved with DeeLisa Davis.

Indeed, Tim's friends in the Florida Highway Patrol felt so sorry for him that they called Gary Morgan to see if he could find a spot where Tim could stay. Morgan owned a house on Seventh Place in Vero Beach, but he wasn't currently living there; he was temporarily working down in Palm Beach. Morgan already had a young trooper living in his house to keep an eye on it. Sure, he said, he would ask the other officer if he would mind if Tim—and, of course, Shadow, his dog—bunked there for two weeks.

Morgan let Tim know that he had a free place to stay, and that he would leave a key under the mat for him the following Friday.

But Tim didn't show up; Lt. Morgan was at his Vero Beach house all weekend, mowing the lawn and doing minor repairs, but he didn't hear from Tim Harris. When Gary Morgan came north the next weekend he saw that Tim had apparently moved in. Harris's personal belongings were in the spare bedroom and bathroom.

Actually, Tim Harris's presence in his lieutenant's house was wraithlike. Morgan didn't see *him.* He saw Tim's things and his dog. When the two weeks were up Tim called and asked Gary Morgan if he could stay longer. "I told him it kind of messed up my weekends," Morgan recalled, "because [with him there] I couldn't come home on weekends—so he said he would stay only during the week and be out of there by Friday night."

Tim was true to his word. He was gone the next Saturday when Morgan drove up, but Tim's dog, Shadow, was there, and Morgan gave the K-9 dog food and water.

The next weekend Tim's belongings were all gone, and so was his dog. He had left a note on the kitchen table thanking his lieutenant for letting him stay.

Tim had other places to stay. He was welcome to spend some nights at his brother's house, and sometimes he slept in his new truck at one of the rest stops along I-95, or on his new boat. And of course, he was always welcome to stay with DeeLisa. She would have liked him to be with her every night.

But now Tim Harris wanted only to spend his nights with the woman he had devised such elaborate plans to sneak away from.

When Sandy had found the acre lot in Citrus

Hideaway, its isolation and distance from other homes were part of its charm for her. Living there alone with her babies, aware that Tim might be out of the house physically, but that he still considered it, her, and the children totally his possessions, Sandy wished mightily for the sight of lit windows next door or across the street when dusk fell. Instead, the lots were so big that she could see only black beyond her windows.

If Tim wanted to get in, Sandy knew he could do it easily. Tim knew every inch of the house that had once been symbolic of a bright future for them. He should; he had built it himself. And now that he was banished from it—if only for two weeks—he began to let himself into the house while Sandy was at work or at her parents' house.

High up in the rafters Tim found a spot in the pink insulation and formed a depression there. Carefully he inserted a tape recorder, splicing wires so that the recorder would turn on automatically when the phone receiver was lifted. He hid a second tape recorder in the mechanism of a sofa bed. All of Sandy's calls—in or out—would now be recorded on tape, waiting for Tim to listen to them at his leisure.

She had no idea.

Tim didn't move in with DeeLisa. He stayed for a few weeks with his brother, David, and his wife, Melissa. But David's wife was expecting a baby, and it was crowded in their mobile home.

The first night Sandy heard noises against the side of the house where Tim had built a pen for Shadow, she was terrified. Jarred from her sleep, she lay rigid in bed and heard heavy footsteps moving around upstairs.

With her heart in her throat she tiptoed toward the

children's rooms. In Timmy's room she saw a shadow on the floor next to his bed.

It was Tim, sleeping there beside his son. If she hadn't been through so much anguish with her husband, Sandy might have thought it sad or even touching. Instead she sighed and went back to the master bedroom.

Tim broke in almost every night after that. Sandy would hear him as he balanced atop Shadow's pen and then when he stepped onto the roof. He didn't come near her, and he was usually gone in the morning. But if Sandy got a phone call, she often heard a soft click, and she knew that Tim had lifted the receiver of the upstairs extension, that he was listening, his huge hand over the mouthpiece of the phone upstairs so she couldn't hear him breathing.

Sometimes Tim didn't sneak into the second floor window. That didn't allow Sandy to sleep any easier. Looking out in the dusk, she often saw Tim sitting in his truck back in the pines.

Just watching her.

Even when she didn't see him, Sandy knew that Tim could very well be close by. And she remembered how many times he had told her he could snap her neck in two so easily.

11

In Jacksonville, 165 miles north of Vero Beach, Lorraine Hendricks's business was doing wonderfully. Lorelei Promotions was selected to handle the opening of the Carriage Club retirement village. The opulent residences for senior citizens demanded an equally elegant grand opening, and Lorraine didn't disappoint them. She had white horses, carriages, and everyone dressed as if they were attending a magnificent ball at the turn of the century. Lorraine herself wore a satin off-the-shoulder gown, long white gloves, and a triple strand of pearls, and her thick, gleaming hair was swept into a pompadour topped with a diamond tiara.

On February 10, 1990, Lorraine assisted the Heart Guild of Northeast Florida in producing a benefit during the week of Valentine's Day. She presented the heartthrob of the late fifties, Frankie Avalon, and once again she helped to carry off a night to remember, and one that brought a bonanza to heart research in Florida.

Blissfully in love, seeing the career that she had always longed for do so well, there was nothing more in the world that Lorraine Hendricks could ask for.

In February, 1990, Sandy Harris had no idea that a tape recorder whirred away up in the attic, keeping track of every call she received and every call she made. She didn't know that Tim broke into the house during the day, too, so that he could change the tapes in the recorder. Nor did Sandy know that Tim had taken her office key from her purse and had a duplicate made.

Valentine's Day—the day meant for lovers—was a nightmare for Sandy Harris. After midnight on February 13 Tim didn't break into his own house; instead he unlocked the office where Sandy worked, an office full of private financial records. Stealthily, carefully, he spent hours carrying out a surprise he had for Sandy.

By the time Sandy Harris got to work on Valentine's Day her job hung by a thread. Her boss was furious and upset that someone had crept around their offices during the night. Bewildered, Sandy walked into her office—or as far inside it as she could get. The room was filled with red and white balloons, and there was a huge box of chocolates on her desk. As Sandy tried to move around balloons were compressed against the wall or punctured by something sharp on her desk, and they popped loudly. Numbly, Sandy looked at the curious faces of her fellow employees staring at her, and then at her boss, and she burst into tears. Her life had been reduced to this. She had no place that was private. No haven at all.

Sobbing, she walked out of her office and drove home. He was the last person on earth she wanted to see, but Tim was there waiting, grinning in happy expectation—as if he thought she had rushed home to thank him for her wonderful Valentine's surprise. She looked at him, horrified. He actually *believed* that she would be pleased by what he had done.

Sandy brushed by him and headed for the bathroom, where she could lock the door and shut him away, if only for a few minutes. She saw a tape recorder there, a machine she had never seen before. Tim hadn't expected her to come home in the middle of the day, and he had apparently been listening to something on the tape.

Sandy turned it on. Puzzled, she heard her own voice, and then it dawned on her that somehow Tim had been taping her phone calls. But *how?* She listened to an innocuous conversation she had had with her sister and heard each of them hang up. The recorder rolled on, and another call began. But this time it wasn't her own voice that Sandy heard, but Tim's. Tim was talking to DeeLisa, and he was begging his mistress to let him come and visit. He sounded every bit as desperate to be with DeeLisa as he did when he beseeched Sandy to take him back.

My God, Sandy wondered, was he crazy? All the balloons and chocolate and sneaking in every night to be in the house with her, and here was his voice pleading with DeeLisa the same way he pleaded with her.

Grimly, Sandy turned the volume up until Tim could hear his own voice calling DeeLisa. Sandy heard the sound of his feet running toward her, and then he hit the door, pounding and yelling at her to let him in. The door buckled; Tim was clearly trying to break it down.

Sandy opened it and stepped back, clutching the tape in her hand. He lunged for her, and she twisted away and ran.

"He chased me around the house, trying to get the tape. I had never, *never* seen him that angry."

Tim Harris had secrets, his own secrets—and Sandy had stumbled on one. And with that he had lost any chance at all that she would ever take him back. He hadn't changed. He still lied. All of his determined courting wasn't worth anything now that she had the proof of his continued infidelity in her hand.

Even so, Sandy found Tim's anger out of all proportion to what had happened. It wasn't as though she hadn't caught him in lies about DeeLisa before—not once, but over and over and over. Stubbornly clinging to the tape, Sandy looked back at the man who had been her husband for almost nine years, and she scarcely recognized him. His face was red and contorted, and fury surrounded him like a miasmic cloud.

Sandy Harris was a realist; she had to be. She knew that Tim's own character flaws had led them to where they were in February, 1990—but she blamed DeeLisa Davis, too. DeeLisa Davis had done everything she could to break up Sandy's marriage. The two women had never met face-to-face, although Sandy knew DeeLisa's voice and had seen her from a distance.

She was about to see her close up. Sue Dappen and Sandy took their children to the skating rink in Vero Beach every Saturday. "One Saturday," Sandy remembered, "I saw DeeLisa there. Somehow, I knew it was her—and then Jennifer said, 'Look! There's DeeLisa!' and I realized that Tim had been taking our kids over to see his mistress."

Sandy stared curiously at the woman who was sitting on a bench taking off her skates. She was much older than Sandy was, and she was attractive, but not astoundingly so. Before Sue could stop her Sandy skated over to DeeLisa Davis and waited until DeeLisa looked up.

"I guess you know who I am, but I don't know who you are," Sandy said sarcastically.

"Don't talk in front of my kids," DeeLisa said.

119

"Well, *my* kids know all about you," Sandy said.

DeeLisa grabbed her skates and her children and ran out of the rink. "She couldn't get away fast enough," Sandy said bitterly. It really didn't matter to Sandy anymore, but she was remembering all those times Tim had lied to her about DeeLisa.

On Saturday night, March 3, 1990, one of Sandy's girlfriends got married, and Sandy was asked to be her matron of honor. A year earlier she would have asked Tim to go with her. Now she refused his offer to go along. She had a good time—for the first time in years. She didn't stay late; she wanted to be home with the kids. When one of the groomsmen called her later to ask her to join him for a drink, she laughed and talked to him for a few minutes. She forgot that her phone was probably still wired to one of Tim's damnable tape recorders.

Sandy refused the date, but it didn't matter. Tim retrieved that tape later that evening, and he was livid that Sandy had actually defied him and gone to the wedding without him. He was sure she must have come on to the guy who called her. Every time Sandy thought Tim couldn't get any angrier, he proved to her that he could. He had held in his rage for most of their marriage, showing it only by refusing to speak to her for days. He no longer repressed his anger. She wondered if he had had that cauldron of rage inside all those years.

If she hadn't been such a nervous wreck, the double standard Sandy was living under might have been laughable. She had no interest in other men. One day she talked to one of the troopers that Tim sometimes went fishing with. When Sandy argued that Tim had no right to be sobbing and whining and furious over their divorce—not after he had cheated on her for almost five years—the trooper blurted, "Well, what did you expect him to do when he was working third watch? Just hang around the house while you were working?"

"I just hung around the house while he was on duty nights. I didn't cheat on him."

"That's different."

Why? Sandy wondered. Why was it different when Tim cheated? Why should he be so bored and horny during the daytime when she was at work? She didn't believe a man was entitled to betray a marriage any more than a woman was.

Sandy Harris was frantically trying to juggle all the problems in her life. She realized in early March, 1990, that she could no longer continue paying the huge mortgage on the new house. Regretfully and quietly she put it up for sale. She agreed to let the realtor hold an open house on Sunday, March 4th.

Tim found out. Even though the realtor didn't have a car with her company's name on it, Tim knew. Of course he knew. He was monitoring every call in and out, every conversation that took place inside Sandy's house. He had backup tape recorders. It was only a day after Tim had been so angry about the wedding she attended alone; Sandy's selling their home was, to him, the most flagrant example of her shoving him out of her life, making decisions without him.

For the first time Sandy Harris had moments of fear. Real fear. She wondered if she would ever get away from Tim. She wondered if they would both die before he let her go. . . .

12

Since Lorraine Hendricks had lived in the Fort Lauderdale/Miami area for more than fifteen years and had lived in the Mandarin area of Jacksonville for only two, she often returned to her former home. Lorraine still drove down to Fort Lauderdale to see her physician and dentist, both family friends. The trip down I-95 was over two hundred miles, but she was used to it and drove it fairly often.

Lorraine Hendricks had a dental appointment with Dr. Joe Hilton in Fort Lauderdale on Monday, March 5, 1990. She had been having extensive dental work done with Hilton. She also was scheduled to meet with Mike Lutz of Tropical Realty at 6 p.m. on that Sunday night. Along with her parents, she owned a condo on Wimbleton Drive in Plantation, and they were considering selling it.

Most important of all, Carol Worley was about to move to Washington State, and Lorraine wanted to see her before she left. "She called me Saturday morning—March third," Carol recalled. "I can hear her saying, 'Don't think you're getting out of Florida without seeing me one more time!'"

Carol said she was busy cleaning her house, and that she would finish up Sunday morning. After that she would be around the corner at her brother's house. Her phone would be disconnected, but Carol gave Lorraine her brother's number.

Lorraine said she would be in Fort Lauderdale by one the next afternoon. Carol grinned to herself; she knew Lorraine, and she doubted seriously that Lorraine was going to get out of bed by five or six and hit the road on a Sunday morning. It was a good six-hour drive. She figured Lorraine would probably come rolling in about three and planned accordingly.

Around midnight on Saturday night Lorraine talked to Mike Raleigh. She promised to call him from Miami so they could talk about a project they were working on. As always, he warned her to be careful, and as always, she assured him she would be.

In truth, Lorraine left her home on Remler Drive in Jacksonville about 8 a.m. on Sunday, March 4th. She could take care of her real estate dealings, visit with Carol, and go to her dental appointment the next day. Lorraine's busy schedule occasionally led her to drive too fast as she coordinated the many different facets of her life. She was a woman who got things done, and she could be impatient to get on to the next task, the next appointment. In fact, she had had eight speeding tickets in the previous seven years. She had commented wryly to a friend that she couldn't afford another speeding ticket. That was for sure; she was right next door to having her license suspended. She tried to drive right at the speed limit or under.

But, as everyone else does, Lorraine would daydream about the man she had come to love, or some business problem, or what the future held for her, and her foot would involuntarily press down harder on the accelerator. And then, too, she always listened to tapes when she traveled, and a fast beat tended to be reflected on her speedometer.

What Lorraine didn't know as she left on her March 4th trip was that her license actually *had* already been suspended. Her notification was in the mail but would not be delivered for a few more days.

It wasn't that big a deal. She could get it back if she went through the steps the State of Florida listed. "Before your driving privilege may be reinstated, you must do the following: Contact the court and meet their requirements. Any fine must be sent or delivered to the Duval County Court Clerk's address listed below. *Do not mail fine to this department.* Written certification that you have complied must be obtained from the court clerk and presented to any Driver's License examining office. You will be required to pay a $25.00 service fee. . . ."

Frank and Jodi Dombroski arrived early that Sunday morning in March to look after Katherine until Rick arrived from his apartment to take over. He had promised to be there at eleven, and he was.

Lorraine was dressed casually. She wore stone-washed jeans and a reddish-brown blouse, and she slipped moccasins onto her feet. Her Honda Accord was a 1982 model, but it ran well—except for the fact that its gas gauge didn't work. Rick always warned her to watch that, because she could run out of gas someplace on the Interstate miles from nowhere if she wasn't careful. He advised her to reset the odometer every time she filled up with gas, and then figure out how many miles she could go on a tank. When she saw that number coming up she should pull off and buy gas. She usually checked the oil, too, because the eight-year-old car tended to run a quart or two low.

But March 4 was a sunny, warm day, and Lorraine wasn't worried. She knew the road well, and she enjoyed driving alone with her tape deck's volume turned up and her earphones on so that she could enjoy the stereo effect of the music.

Lorraine called her father from the road about 10 a.m. to ask how things were going, and to talk to Katherine and tell her she would be home the next day. She also asked her dad to look for a slip of paper with Carol Worley's brother's number—which she had forgotten to bring along—so she could call ahead and tell her friend she was running a little late.

After that there were no more calls from Lorraine.

Lorraine Hendricks did not arrive at her friend Carol's house in Fort Lauderdale that Sunday afternoon by 1 p.m., and she hadn't called ahead, either. Carol wasn't worried. She expected Lorraine to be late, and she had no phone in the house she was moving out of. By three she was at her brother's place, expecting to see the little gray Honda come down the street any moment.

"When she wasn't there by three," Carol admits, "I got kind of angry. I thought she could at least have let me know she would be that late—or that she wasn't coming. That wasn't like Lorraine."

Carol dug through the stuff she had already packed and found the number for the condo in Plantation Lorraine was trying to sell. "I kept calling and calling there, and no one answered. And then I tried to call her home in Jacksonville—but of course, no one answered there. And then Lorraine's mom—Jodi—called *me* about five o'clock to see if Lorraine was with me. Of course, she wasn't."

Lorraine's father had taken it upon himself to call every Highway Patrol office along the Interstate. He introduced himself as "Major Dombroski"—which he was. He didn't say he was an army major and not a Patrol major. He wanted information on where his daughter might be. None of the Patrol offices had any report on her.

"Rick Hendricks finally called me at midnight," Carol Worley remembers. "No one had heard from Lorraine."

Lorraine had not met with real estate agent Mike Lutz in Plantation, Florida, at six. Nor did Lorraine show up for her dental appointment on Monday morning. Her estranged husband and her parents kept calling everyone they could think of to see if they might have heard from her.

No one had.

In almost every state in America there is a twenty-four-hour waiting period between the time an adult does not show up where he or she is supposed to be and the time he or she is legally considered to be a missing person. By Monday, March 5, 1990, Lorraine Marie Hendricks was listed in every computer system in the State of Florida. Her physical description, the clothes she had worn, her birth date, and her home address were all noted. In the unemotional language of the teletype there were nevertheless words that chilled: "Missing Adult, Endangered . . . Good Mental Condition . . . Foul Play Suspected . . ."

Lorraine Hendricks's frantic relatives tried to tell themselves that nothing could have happened to Lorraine on a sunny Sunday afternoon. She would never have picked up a hitchhiker, and she had planned no stops—except to buy gas—between Jacksonville and Fort Lauderdale. If she had been in an accident, the Highway Patrol would know, and they would have notified her family. As it was, the Patrol had answered just enough of their questions to make them desperately worried. They had found Lorraine's car. Just that. They had not found any trace of Lorraine or her purse, wallet, or glasses.

Florida Highway Patrolman Mike Transue, whose

patrol district included the same long stretch of I-95 north and south through Indian River and St. Lucie counties that Tim Harris worked, was on the day shift on Monday, March 5th, and he had found her car. Shortly before noon he noted the 1982 silver Honda Accord parked on the right shoulder of southbound I-95, precisely at milepost 157.5.

Transue pulled in behind the Honda and walked around it. There was no one in the car, and he could see no one around it. It was a four-door model, and the front doors were unlocked. It was ripe for theft; he could see a number of items inside that might have tempted someone: a shiny red briefcase with miscellaneous papers inside, a 35mm camera, a blue and tan tote bag with expensive running shoes inside, a gray makeup bag, a Pulsar watch, headphones, a red suitcase, a pair of ankle weights, and a blue windbreaker jacket. With all that stuff still intact, he assumed the car hadn't been there long.

Transue called in a "Wants and Warrants" on Florida plate AKJ-65U and received word back that the last person known to be driving the Honda was a Jacksonville woman named Lorraine Hendricks, and that she had been reported missing. The Florida Highway Patrol dispatcher contacted the Duval County Sheriff's Office in Jacksonville, and Detective M.E. Hyde requested that the abandoned car be towed so that any evidence inside would be preserved.

The car was towed to the Courtesy Auto Service in Vero Beach. Transue put a hold on the vehicle until it could be processed by investigators.

After the car was towed away Transue sprayed red paint on the right shoulder of I-95 to mark the place where it had been.

Rick Hendricks, who was listed as co-owner of the

silver Honda, was at home, trying to explain to his little girl why her mother hadn't come back as she had promised.

No one knew where Lorraine Hendricks was. Something unexpected had to have happened to her to make her walk away from her car on I-95. Or maybe she hadn't even been *in* the car by that time. No, something had occurred between wherever she had stopped to make that last phone call to her father, Frank, and the lonely spot on the Interstate now marked with paint as red as blood.

Something. But what?

Phil Williams, the cop who might just as well have remained an airline mechanic or a rock musician or a landscaper, the cop who grew up with three guys who became brutal killers, the cop who had become a superb detective, was about to step into one of the most unbelievable and grotesque cases any detective —anywhere—has ever encountered.

Williams had a personal credo. "I've always been willing to do whatever is necessary . . . and I mean *whatever* is necessary to solve a case."

Early on, when he was attending the police academy, the local police authorities were trying to solve the murder of a small girl. They came to the academy and asked for volunteers from the soon-to-be policemen; they were looking for the knife used to kill the child, and they needed all the manpower they could get.

"The nastiest job of all," Williams remembers, "was to get down in the ditch and wade that canal and search that black, silty water for the weapon. That's the job I took."

The alligators and the critters in the canal didn't bother Williams. "Canals like that were my playgrounds when I was growing up," he says laconically. Later, of course, Phil Williams and Don Dappen would wallow through similar ditches and overgrown waterways as they searched for the Domino's Pizza killers.

What Phil Williams had on March 5, 1990, was a missing woman, a car abandoned along a busy freeway, no sign whatsoever of foul play—nothing concrete at all. In the beginning it didn't seem to be that unusual a case. He expected that Lorraine Hendricks was probably going to show up in a day or so with some kind of explanation about where she had been. He had seen too many "missing" adults not to believe that. People disappeared for reasons of their own and came back for other reasons.

They began with the car. Williams met Florida Department of Law Enforcement Agent Bruce McMann at Courtesy Auto in Vero Beach. It was almost eerie how normal the car looked; its owner might have just stepped away for a moment. Lorraine's briefcase was in the rear seat, and it had business papers in it. There were two unopened pieces of luggage. Nothing had been disturbed, and both back doors were locked. The windows were all rolled up.

The two investigators saw the blue jacket on the front passenger seat; it was folded carefully over a headphone set and sunglasses. A box of Kleenex sat on the floorboard of the passenger seat. Beside it were both plastic and paper drinking cups. If anyone had sat in the passenger seat, his—or *her*—feet would have crushed the items on the floor and probably smashed the sunglasses. No, it seemed clear that only one person had been in the car, and that had been the driver.

As far as they could tell at this point, nothing was missing but the car keys, and the missing woman's purse or wallet . . . and Lorraine Hendricks herself.

"The usual suspicion would be she had a boyfriend," Williams says. "That she intended to meet someone. But the thing of it is, why didn't she just go on down to the Wayfarer and leave her car in the restaurant parking lot? It was only a mile from where her car was. Why just park it out there on 95?"

Bruce McMann and Phil Williams began processing the car, dusting for fingerprints, vacuuming the interior for hairs and fibers—or infinitesimal bits of dirt or debris that might prove vital at some future time. (The fingerprints would prove to be useless. Three weeks later the Florida Department of Law Enforcement lab would report that all prints with enough points to identify them belonged to Lorraine Hendricks.)

Lorraine Hendricks's father and her estranged husband Rick had called to say they were on their way to Vero Beach. Rick had a spare key for the Honda, and he thought he might also be able to tell them if anything was missing.

Williams talked with Rick Hendricks. He noted that Hendricks did not seem as frantically worried as Lorraine's father, Frank Dombroski, was. He didn't think much of that; he had been a detective long enough to know that people showed their emotions in vastly different ways. Hendricks told him soon after they met that he and Lorraine were divorcing. No hard feelings. No animosity. "Lorraine and I have agreed in most of the financial settlements already," Hendricks added. He said they shared a most important common bond, Katherine.

Rick Hendricks said that Lorraine was dating someone else, a man she had met through her business.

Williams studied Hendricks's face; he detected no anger there over the other man. Apparently there was no *reason* for Lorraine to sneak around and meet some other man. She and Hendricks no longer lived together. This had all the signs of a friendly divorce, but he was taking nothing for granted until he checked it out.

As far as anything being missing from the Honda Rick said that Lorraine's purse was gone. She usu lly carried a brown purse with a zipper and kept her wallet inside.

They checked the oil level in the Honda, and it registered two to three quarts low—probably not enough to make the engine freeze up. It might have been enough to make the oil light come on. Williams wondered if she had pulled over to check her oil and if someone had come along and grabbed her.

The Honda's odometer read 57.9 miles.

That might be an important clue, Hendricks explained. He said that the fuel gauge didn't work, and that Lorraine would have set the odometer at zero the last time she got gas. Williams nodded. They should be able to trace her path north and find out where she had stopped for gas exactly 57.9 miles before her car ended up on the shoulder of I-95.

"Try it," Williams said to Rick Hendricks. "See if it turns over."

Rick Hendricks slipped his spare key into the ignition, and the engine cranked up easily. There seemed to be no mechanical problems at all. Almost as an afterthought, Hendricks opened the glove box and ran his hand along the bottom. "There's something else missing. The registration is gone, too."

Williams released the car to Hendricks and Frank Dombroski, who planned to drive it back to Jacksonville. They added oil to be sure Dombroski wouldn't have difficulty on the way home. Later Rick called Phil Williams from Jacksonville to say that he had had no car troubles at all on the drive.

Williams asked Rick Hendricks to drain three quarts of oil from the Honda and then to drive it and see if the oil light came on or if any other difficulties ensued. None did.

Retracing Lorraine Hendricks's drive exactly 57.9 miles brought easier answers than the rest of the probe would. Traveling 57.9 miles north from the red paint spot on the Interstate brought the investigators to Exit 50 off I-95.

There was an Amoco station there, and the missing woman's father thought she had probably gassed up there because she had an Amoco credit card. Detective Don Brown, with the Brevard County Sheriff's Office, checked with Amoco and found that Lorraine had, indeed, charged gas at the Amoco station at Exit 50 on the morning of March 4. The Sunshine Food and Fruits store was located there at 3580 Cheney Highway, and the manager remembered seeing Lorraine Hendricks there. She was a very attractive woman whom most men would remember. He also recalled that she had used the pay phone afterward.

The woman who had actually initialed Lorraine's gas charge slip remembered her, too. She was sure from looking at the slip that Lorraine Hendricks had been in the Amoco station between 9:45 and 10:00 that Sunday morning.

That fit. That would have been the call to her father in Jacksonville, and she might have tried to call Carol Worley in Fort Lauderdale at the same time.

Had she picked up a hitchhiker? If she had, it would have been completely against her normal pattern. Her relatives said Lorraine was too savvy to do that. Had she been *forced* to take a rider along? Maybe.

When Lorraine Hendricks was headed someplace she fixed her mind on her destination. That was one of the reasons her driving record was less than perfect. Looking over the computer printout he'd received from the Department of Highway Safety and Motor Vehicles, Phil Williams grimaced.

> 1-14-83: 65 MPH in a 45 zone
> 6-21-84: 59 MPH in a 40 zone
> 7-24-85: 57 MPH in a 40 zone
> 9-19-85: 41 MPH in a 25 zone
> 6-05-86: 49 MPH in a 30 zone
> 3-11-87: 56 MPH in a 35 zone
> 12-27-89: 60 MPH in a 45 zone
> 1-06-90: Careless or improper driving
> 2-06-90: 51 MPH in a 35 zone
> 2-16-90: Failed to pay traffic fine

Lorraine Hendricks had a lead foot.

"Who would Lorraine stop for?" Williams asked Rick Hendricks. He didn't want to mention the possibility of foul play yet. Maybe he would never have to. "Would she pick up a hitchhiker?"

Hendricks shook his head. "She stopped for turtles and cops. That's all."

"Turtles?"

"She loves animals. I've seen her pull over and go out in the road and carry a turtle out of the road so it wouldn't get hit."

"And I can see why she stopped for cops," Williams said. "She had no choice."

Hendricks shrugged. You couldn't argue with Lorraine's reputation as a speeder.

Turtles and cops. Turtles and cops.

Williams mulled over that odd combination in his mind and thought about "what ifs." What if Lorraine Hendricks had pulled over to rescue another turtle? She could have been out there in the middle of the Interstate and been hit, maybe killed. If the driver panicked, he might have thrown her in the back of his car—or truck—and taken off. Naaah. They would have some sign of a hit-and-run in the road. Blood, torn clothing, a shoe. Something.

Okay. Say she was rescuing a turtle and somebody came along, saw an astoundingly good-looking woman alone at the edge of the road, and grabbed her. That was a more likely scenario than the first. That would explain why she had left her front doors unlocked.

Whatever had happened to Lorraine Hendricks, the chance that she was alive and safe diminished with each passing hour.

Detective Phil Williams gave news releases to local newspapers so that her disappearance would be publicized by March 8th and the public might come forward with leads in a case where there were no leads at all. He had copies made of the two pictures of Lorraine that Rick Hendricks had given him—one of Lorraine with Rick and Katherine, and the other by herself. In the latter she wore a white blouse and a black jumper, and she smiled into the camera. The public certainly called in with tips and suggestions, but none that seemed to relate to Lorraine Hendricks. Nonetheless, every call was evaluated and logged.

"At that point we didn't know what was valuable and what was not," Williams explained. "We kept everything."

13

Duval County Detectives Roy Myers and Mike Robinson had now entered Lorraine Hendricks's name in the NCIC (National Crime Information Center) computers in Quantico, Virginia. If she surfaced anywhere in America, local cops would have the information in their computers.

Mike Raleigh, like all of Lorraine's friends, was stunned when he learned that she had disappeared. He told his fiancée, Alice,* that something had to have happened to her. The Lorraine he knew would never have walked away from her responsibilities on purpose. "I may have to leave," he explained. "I'm worried sick, and I might have to just go on down there, to do anything I can to help."

On Tuesday, March 6, Raleigh had a show in Orlando with Jim Stafford to oversee, but after the show he drove to Exit 50 off I-95—the last place anyone had heard from Lorraine. He arrived at 4 a.m. and got a motel room while he waited for dawn. He wasn't sure what he was going to do, but there had to be something. At first light Raleigh surveyed the businesses located at Exit 50; there was one of the south's ubiquitous Waffle House restaurants, several motels, and a couple of gas stations. He went first to the Amoco station and talked to employees who had worked the morning shift when Lorraine was there on Sunday. He carried her photograph and showed it to employees at the gas station, and then he moved on to the other businesses. He found two people who *did* remember seeing the woman in the photo.

But neither of them had noticed where Lorraine went or with whom she might have left.

Mike Raleigh contacted a detective in Brevard County and asked what more he could do. He was especially worried because the massive annual motor- cyclists' convention was taking place in Daytona Beach, thirty-five miles north of Exit 50, and Lorraine would have passed close to that area. Lorraine was still a motorcycle fan, and Raleigh was afraid she might have picked the wrong group to talk to.

The investigator studied Raleigh and finally said, "You can go home. There's nothing you can do that isn't already being done."

"I couldn't go home," Raleigh recalled four years later. "I kept driving south. I knew that her car was supposed to have been found some fifty-seven miles from there, and I spotted that red splotch of paint beside the road. That's where I met Phil Williams for the first time."

Raleigh didn't fool himself. He suspected that one of the detectives from further north had alerted Williams. "I drove up, and Phil was already sitting there in his car. He stepped out, and he didn't drop a beat. He just said, 'Hello, Mike. Let's talk.'"

Just as Raleigh wanted to know if detectives were doing everything they could to find Lorraine, Phil wanted to find out exactly who Mike Raleigh was— both to check on his whereabouts during the weekend Lorraine disappeared and to round out his own profile of the missing woman. He knew that Mike Raleigh was one of the people Lorraine had worked with in Northern Florida. He already knew Raleigh had no police record, and that no one had a bad word to say about him.

Raleigh struck Williams as a "gentleman" who looked more like a professor than an entertainment entrepreneur. He was tall and lanky and wore glasses. He looked to be in his early to mid-forties. He talked slowly and deliberately, weighing his words before he spoke.

Raleigh could easily reconstruct his own whereabouts on Sunday, March 4. He had been in his Florida office in Orlando from about two until five, and several of his employees verified that. Before that he had been with an attorney friend while they attempted to locate two lots they had purchased in High Springs. They had spoken to several residents in that area in their search for the overgrown lots.

"That evening?" Williams asked.

"I was out late in Orlando Sunday night to review a couple of acts I had working there at Pleasure Island." Raleigh said he had rented a Lincoln from Budget Rental at the Orlando Airport.

It all checked out. A witness put Raleigh at Disney World in Orlando from 8 p.m. until the wee hours. It would have been well nigh impossible for Raleigh to have been with Lorraine between eight a.m., on Sunday, March 4, when she left her home in Jacksonville, and noon the next day when Mike Transue tagged her abandoned car.

Beyond that, Williams believed that Raleigh was sincerely concerned for the safety of the woman he had worked with for less than a year. He was extremely eager to help in the investigation and tried to think of anyone who would want to harm her. Raleigh explained he had brought Lorraine along in the entertainment business and introduced her to many of the movers and shakers, feeling it was important for her to relate to the big names in the industry on a social level. Lorraine had paid her dues; she had worked for years in small cities' pageants and festivals with local talent. She was about to see her dream of working with big-time acts come true.

Raleigh listed some of the stellar names that Lorraine had booked for her benefits and festivals. He described her as a woman whose intelligence and friendliness let her fit into any situation. She was very beautiful, she dressed impeccably, and she could carry on a conversation with anyone; she was not dazzled by celebrities, and she fit into their world very well. Raleigh felt she had a real future in the entertainment world.

Phil threw out questions, "What ifs" and "What would she have done if—?" and "How would she have reacted if—?"

Raleigh explained that Lorraine was a talker. "She's a public relations person—that's what she does best. She's a salesperson, and she's a negotiator." If someone has abducted Lorraine, she is smart enough and savvy enough to be one step ahead of that person. "*If* she can keep them talking—"

Phil Williams was aware that he, too, had to pass muster. Mike Raleigh was clearly a man whose career demanded absolute attention to detail and who did nothing halfway. He searched Williams's face as they talked, as if he was judging him.

He was. "When I left that day," Raleigh recalled, "I felt absolutely that Phil would find Lorraine, that he would find out what had happened to her. I believed that. I knew it would take a very special man—one with fortitude, strength of character, and conviction —to do that. When Phil Williams assured me that he was never going to give up on finding Lorraine, that he wasn't going to drop the case, I believed him."

Phil Williams kept his promise, but the next two days passed with no sign whatsoever of Lorraine Hendricks.

Williams had to trace the movements of the new man in Lorraine's life, the man she had fallen in love with so rapidly. Just as he had found with Mike Raleigh, Williams discovered that Matthew,* a Jacksonville businessman, had been far away from Indian River County when Lorraine vanished. In fact, he had left on a plane headed for Europe early Saturday morning, March 3. Williams confirmed that the man had actually boarded the plane. His secretary had informed him of the tragedy, and he was already heading back to America.

Finally Phil Williams decided there was nothing to do but to start back at ground zero—the last place she had been seen. Back at the splotch of red paint beside I-95.

On March 8 the Brevard County Sheriff's Office helicopter had circled the area, making continual passes overhead. They flew in a spiral pattern while a spotter watched the trees and fields below. It wasn't easy to see beyond the morass of palmettos and pines. The helicopter search answered no questions for the investigators. If Lorraine Hendricks was down there someplace, she was not visible from the air.

The next day every law enforcement agency in the vicinity of where Lorraine's car had been found mobilized for a concentrated search of the area. She was either a thousand miles away or very close. If she was close, Phil Williams wanted to find her. "We went back out there and decided we were going to search up and down the shoulders on both sides of the Interstate."

Phil Williams and his fellow detectives Larry Smetzer, Mark Johnson, and Joe Bobrowskas and a number of Ranch and Groves deputies began on the shoulder of the Interstate where the gray Honda had been. They walked the shoulders and the median strip from State Road 512 to the thickly wooded portion of the median. The median there was about a mile from where Lorraine's car was found. At its widest point it was about three hundred feet across. There was a dirt road that cut through the center of the median, designed to give state troopers a place to turn around on the Interstate rather than having to go to the next off-ramp if they saw a vehicle going the other way that they needed to check out in a hurry.

Literally a step at a time the ground searchers had covered 3.1 miles, hoping to find something that might lead them to Lorraine Hendricks, missing now for five days. They didn't ask for much—maybe a button, one of her moccasins, her purse, some scrap of paper that they could tie to Lorraine. They found nothing at all.

State Trooper Mike Transue, working his regular shift along I-95, stopped by and talked casually with the Indian River County investigators. So did Tim Harris, who worked the same stretch of Interstate that Transue did. It had been Transue, of course, who had first located Lorraine Hendricks's car. The sheriff's men and the highway patrolmen talked about the baffling case, shaking their heads.

Tim Harris had Shadow in his car with him, and Williams looked over at the beautiful animal, who watched him suspiciously from his perch in the backseat of Tim's car. Shadow's teeth looked four inches long.

He turned to Tim Harris. "Your dog's a search dog, isn't he? Could we use him in looking for a body?"

Tim whirled around, and then he nodded. "Possibly. But he does better at night. It'd be a good idea, but we should wait until it cools down a little bit. Right now he'd burn out too quick in the woods. But sure, I'd be glad to help out."

Williams didn't know that much about K-9 dogs. Some dog handlers said that dogs smelled bodies up in the air and not on the ground at all. Different breeds worked in different ways. Bloodhounds were said to churn up ground scents with their long ears. The wind was whipping up pretty good, and Phil figured that Tim meant it would cool down the area by nightfall. If they hadn't found anything by evening, he would see if Harris could bring his dog out.

Tim Harris didn't mention to Phil Williams that the area they were searching was his patrol area; he probably assumed that Williams knew.

Shadow watched Williams more closely and began to bark and bare his teeth even more. The detective figured that *he* looked like a bad guy to Harris's dog.

"Call me if you need the dog later," Tim said.

While Williams talked to Tim Harris he got a call on his walkie-talkie from Deputy Joe Bobrowskas, who asked if Harris could give him a ride back to his patrol car, which was parked two miles away down underneath the bridge by the Wayfarer.

"Could you?" Williams asked Harris.

Tim Harris shook his head. "Not with my dog in there. The dog would become violent."

But Tim didn't want Bobrowskas to have to walk all that way in the heat. He drove down to where Bobrowskas was, got the deputy's keys, and said he would drive to the Wayfarer, park his unit (with Shadow locked inside) and then drive Bobrowskas's car to him "if you'll just take me back up to my patrol car." That was fine with Bobrowskas; it was steaming out.

Tim Harris was adamant that no one could ride along in his car—not with Shadow leaning over the backseat. Shadow would just as soon take a chunk out of a cop as a felon. Tim Harris said that his particular dog just didn't want anyone riding along with *his* trooper.

The sun rose higher in the sky, and the wind did nothing to cool the day. Phil Williams tried to put himself into the mind of some man whose face he had never seen. "If I were going to have sex with a girl," Williams said to Larry Smetzer, pointing to the thick clump of weeds and trees there in the wide median strip, "that's where I'd go."

The two Indian River County detectives split up, with Smetzer going one way into the median and Williams the other.

Following his hunch, Phil Williams worked his way deeper and deeper into the pine and palmetto woods that took up most of the widest part of the median between northbound and southbound I-95. He sniffed the air for the smell of death, an odor no detective ever forgets once he has smelled it.

He smelled nothing. Probably Tim Harris had been right. The wind was blowing too hard for even a dog to work the area on scent alone.

And then, as the trees behind him shut out where he had been, and the trees in front of him gave no clue to what lay ahead, as the sun-dried vegetation beneath his feet crackled too loudly, Phil Williams felt a prickling at the back of his neck. He smelled the faintest odor of death, so light on the air that he wasn't sure he smelled it at all.

But then he was sure. It was hot, but he felt cold.

He saw something but he didn't recognize what he saw. None of his senses—not smell, sight, or sound—helped. Straight ahead, just in front of a crooked pine tree, there was a long mound beneath the dried grasses and pine needles. Something dark showed at the end nearest Williams. Closer to him, he saw what looked like a woman's brown wig.

Phil Williams moved forward, his curiosity winning out over a very basic desire to go back and bring the other investigators with him. He had thought he was beyond being shocked or spooked. But here in the shadow of the trees he was definitely spooked. "I'd worked homicides—a lot of them—but there's something about finding a body out in the woods when you're alone and your buddy's looking in some other part of the area. I ran back to get Larry.

"We can call off the search," he said quietly. "She's in there."

"Dead?" The question was academic.

Williams nodded. It was almost impossible to realize that the dead woman in the pines was the same woman whose smile blazed from the pictures he had released to the press. "Yeah, dead."

She was there. She lay, they could both see now, under a thick heap of pine needles and boughs. Had he looked away for only an instant Phil Williams would have missed seeing her entirely. Someone had secreted her carefully, deep in the center of the median, and then buried her with the dried vegetation. The round dark part Williams had glimpsed first was a woman's denuded skull. The "wig" was her own hair; decomposition was far advanced, and little animals had detached the scalp and hair and pulled it about three feet away from the body.

Careful where they stepped, Phil Williams and

Larry Smetzer moved around the mound that hid a human body. They could see that the woman lay on her face.

But there was something bizarre here. Someone had positioned her naked body so that her legs extended on either side of the pine tree. The tree trunk rose like some grotesque phallic symbol between her buttocks. She would not have fallen that way; that would have been impossible. No, someone extremely strong would have had to grasp her feet and drag her backward until her genitals were tight against the tree.

Phil Williams took photographs of the body site. Deputy Johnson remained with the dead woman while Williams and Smetzer went to use a pay phone at the Wayfarer. They didn't want their request for Dr. Fred Hobin, the medical examiner, to go out over the police airways where anyone with a scanner— particularly the media—could pick it up. If, as they believed, this was Lorraine Hendricks, they didn't want her family to hear the news that way.

Ron Sinclair and Anthony Oliver, identification technicians with the Indian River County Sheriff's Office, arrived at 1:15 that Friday afternoon and set up a perimeter around the body with yellow "Crime Scene—Do Not Cross" tape.

When Dr. Hobin arrived they slowly removed the pine boughs and needles hiding the woman's body. She was completely nude; if she had been wearing jewelry, it was gone now. A Band-Aid wound around one of her big toes. Because of the destruction caused by heat and insect activity, it would be impossible to identify her without dental X rays.

Her clothing and purse were gone, although the detectives did find a gold hoop earring a short distance from the body. It was real gold, expensive and classic in design. The victim was removed from the median strip and taken to Dr. Hobin's facilities to await autopsy that evening.

At 7 p.m. Dr. Hobin began his careful examination while Phil Williams and Tony Oliver observed and bagged evidence. Despite the advanced decomposition in the victim's head and face, Hobin hoped to determine the manner and cause of the woman's death. "Autopsy" means literally "to see for one's self," and the pathologist would now follow the precise steps that would tell him much about this body on the table in front of him.

Time of death was compatible with the date—March 4—that Lorraine Hendricks had vanished. The hot, humid March weather of Florida had accelerated postmortem changes, but Hobin was used to that.

The woman measured five feet five and weighed 135 pounds. Her teeth were in excellent repair, and her hair was fine and dark brown. Her skin was covered with bites from insects and ants that had probably occurred after death. At some point in her life she had undergone major abdominal surgery, and X rays revealed surgical clips in the right hepatic region. Both the entire right lobe of her liver and her gallbladder had been removed surgically.

Dr. Hobin found no broken bones, no skull fracture. There was no evidence of preexisting disease of the internal organs. He *did* find a fracture of the thyroid cartilage in the neck, a concealed hemorrhage deep in the tissues of the neck, and what he felt was a contusion injury at the front of the left shoulder.

If he had to explain those injuries to a lay person, he would say they indicated that she had been strangled. Hobin also suspected—although he could not prove it absolutely—that the woman had been beaten around the head. Injured tissue decomposes more rapidly than the rest of a body, and this victim's head was nearly skeletal, while her torso, arms, and legs were fully intact.

Identifying the body was tragically easy. Detectives didn't have to look far for Lorraine Hendricks's dentist; she had missed an appointment with him only five days before, and Dr. Hilton furnished her dental X rays at once. They matched the victim's in every way.

So did Lorraine Hendricks's fingerprints.

The detectives learned about the motorcycle accident Lorraine had been in two decades earlier. She had been gravely injured and had had to undergo surgery to stop hemorrhaging from a lacerated liver. Much of her liver had been removed at that time. Although she would have been near death from her injuries, the liver has remarkable regenerative capability, and once the hemorrhaging had stopped it had healed completely.

A sex crime kit was produced, and fingernail scrapings, scalp and pubic hair samples, pubic hair combings, and smear and swab preparations were done of the oral, anal, and vaginal cavities. A vaginal washing sample was taken. It was unlikely that they could find seminal fluid at all at this point, much less identify it as to blood type. Lorraine Hendricks had lain in the baking woods for five days. Routine blood screening proved completely negative for marijuana, cocaine, opiates, barbiturates, antidepressants, and sleeping pills.

Phil Williams had little doubt that Lorraine Hendricks had been the victim of a sexual attack. The position in which her body had been left was unmistakably sexual. Her killer had gone to great effort to arrange her legs around the pine tree's trunk in a grotesque tableau that suggested anal sodomy.

It was, perhaps, a Freudian symbolism, a final act of rage by a killer who might well have proved impotent once he either lured, dragged, or forced his victim into the shadows of the pine grove.

Maybe one day Williams would be able to answer that question—if he ever found the murderer he now knew he was looking for.

Lorraine Hendricks hadn't walked away of her own volition. She hadn't met a lover and run off with him. Something had made her stop on the right shoulder of I-95, and she had not been able to drive away again.

Ever.

14

The news that a woman had been murdered, quite probably in broad daylight, on busy I-95 triggered unreasoning fear in the hearts of scores of women who routinely traveled that freeway in Indian River County. How could it have happened? Surely there was always enough traffic out there so that it should have been extremely difficult to force a woman off the Interstate and into the dense median woods. If it could happen to Lorraine Hendricks, that meant it could happen to any of them.

Sandy Harris was frightened, particularly since she now lived alone with her two small children only a few miles from where Lorraine had been found. But then she reasoned that she was being silly. She had spent hundreds of nights alone while Tim worked graveyard, or when he was called out to work an accident. Still, it was creepy to think that the woman they had all been looking for had been right there all the time, dead.

And so close, really, to the house in Citrus Hideaway.

Sandy wasn't sure where Tim was sleeping. Sometimes she still heard him creeping into Timmy's window upstairs. Despite their problems, having him there wasn't as scary as being in the house alone. When she heard the noises overhead now Sandy would call out, "Tim, I know you're up there!"

"I had lost all fear of him. After a while I figured if he was going to do something to me, he would do it. I couldn't be afraid of him forever."

Tim either called or visited Sandy every day. And he still wanted to come back to her. But she knew now that he was telling DeeLisa the same things he was telling her. He wanted both of them desperately, or so he said, but she suspected he didn't want either of them. He just wanted the power of having them.

When Lorraine Hendricks's picture appeared in local papers and the *Miami Herald* under the headlines reading "Missing Jacksonville Woman Found Murdered," Phil Williams's telephone lines lit up. Laymen cannot conceive of the number of tips that come into detectives in a high profile case. Scores. Hundreds. Sometimes even thousands. They are all welcome, and they all have to be checked out—sooner or later, depending on the manpower available.

At this point it seemed that everyone on the Treasure Coast had a suspect or a theory. One caller said that he and a friend had crossed under the C54 Canal on Sunday and noted a white "expensive-looking" car parked low on the bank off I-95. "At first we thought it was hunters—but then we figured the car looked too fancy for hunting. It had a chrome grille rounded in the front."

Not much help, really. No license numbers. No description of anyone around the white car.

There were no hits on the credit cards Lorraine had carried in her purse. That would have helped, but apparently her killer had taken her purse and wallet in a vain effort to delay identification rather than to use her credit cards fraudulently. That made Williams feel that she had been killed not in a robbery, but for other motives. His first instinctive reaction had been that her murder was a sex killing, and nothing so far had made him change his mind.

Rick Hendricks called Williams the next day and said that he had just received a letter from the St. Lucie County Sheriff's Office telling him that Lorraine's wallet had been recovered in that county. It had been found before Lorraine's body had, so the St. Lucie sheriff had sent it to the address inside in a routine manner, not realizing its importance. Phil Williams and I.D. Tech Tony Oliver went to the county just south of their own and talked with Detective Messina.

Messina said the wallet had been turned in by a female custodian at the Fort Pierce rest stop off I-95, about twenty miles south of where Lorraine Hendricks and her car were located. The custodian said she had found the wallet sitting on top of trash in a garbage can in the rear picnic area on the southbound side of the rest stop. She had seen no purse or any clothing, nor anyone around the area at the time she discovered the wallet.

Rick Hendricks said that Lorraine's credit cards were still inside the wallet when it was returned to him by the St. Lucie Sheriff's office, but that her driver's license and any cash she might have been carrying were missing. Fingerprint technicians could raise no identifiable prints on the wallet.

Statistically, in any given week along the east coast of Florida, law enforcement authorities expected a certain number of homicides. Phil Williams wanted to know about any of them that might have some connection to the murder of Lorraine Hendricks, and he put out his request on the police wires.

Detective Hartman of Delray, Florida, notified Williams on March 13th that he had arrested a huge and wild young man named Jack Criger.* Criger had stabbed both his aunt and his mother to death in Delray. The M.O. was nothing at all like Williams's case. However, Criger had been arrested in South Carolina on the same day that Lorraine Hendricks's body was found. He had been in South Carolina since Wednesday, March 7th. The reason Hartman was calling was that Jack Criger had traveled to South Carolina along I-95. He had left Delray on March 2—two days before Lorraine Hendricks disappeared—and had been driving a four-door white 1985 Buick sedan. Well, Williams thought, that matched the "expensive" white car.

But nothing else matched. Hartman said that Criger was a cocaine addict and that he had admitted killing his mother and aunt while he was under the influence of drugs. He insisted he had committed no other crimes. His name went back in the hopper, but he was no longer a prime suspect.

The tips continued to pour in: (1) Brevard County (just north of Indian River County) authorities advised that a young woman had been abducted from Merritt Island by two men driving a rust-red Camaro. They had subsequently dropped her off in Columbia

County, and the white male suspects had become involved in a high-speed chase that went through Jasper into Lowndes County, Georgia, where they were arrested (no M.O. similarity). (2) A woman said she was northbound on I-95 on Saturday, March 3, and saw what looked like a Rhode Island State Patrol car with three antennas swing across the median. (3) A preacher at a Wabbasso church called to say that he was suspicious of a local man who drove a small gray vehicle. (4) A man said he had driven on I-95 the weekend before Lorraine Hendricks's disappearance and had seen a yellow Oldsmobile with a white male driver following a female's car, and that he had even gotten off the Interstate behind her at an exit. (5) A woman said she had seen a light tan Chrysler turning across the median near the crime scene on Monday, March 5 at about 4 p.m.

The help from the public went on and on: "Caller said he was on I-95 Sunday, 3/4, and saw 4-wheel-drive truck with loud pipes pull out of wooded area where the cops were at on Friday following. Truck was speeding. Caller never caught up." "Caller advised WM [white male] with brown shaggy hair kept bothering him at Waffle House for a hamburger . . . Caller had a funny feeling . . . might be vagrant . . . was at Exit 50, I-95, 11 to 12 noon . . . had weird personality." "Caller claims witness saw Lorraine Hendricks (ID'd by picture in papers) at Waffle House for two hours Sunday afternoon . . . (witness proves to be possible *Mental*)." "Caller advised he saw a WM about 2 p.m. Sunday, 3/4, in the Northbound Lane of I-95, just south of Brevard Co. Line . . . exited from grayish color Pontiac 4Dr . . . Older WM was driving. WM 6'2", exited and ran across the median . . . wearing bright green shorts." "Caller is Corrections Officer . . . 8:15 a.m., 3/5, subject walking with hat pulled down over his face. Was at woods line where the body was found. Subject carrying large brown suitcase that appeared heavy . . . wearing a Khaki type jacket . . ."

Detective Don Brown of Brevard County said that one of their deputies had interviewed a man in their county at I-95 and Melbourne, a man with a rather bizarre avocation. He gave his name as Rodney Marcello Martino.* He was thirty-nine, a short, rather wispy man who drove a Dodge Coronet.

"Martino told our man that he drives I-95 every day from Fort Pierce to the 520 Exit—he claims his only mission in life is to help stranded motorists. Trouble is he had a pair of handcuffs in the glove box, and he's got a rap sheet for rape."

It was beginning to sound as if I-95 was an obstacle course for trusting tourists.

Dutifully Phil Williams typed page after page of tips into his computer and followed up the most likely. The trouble was that most of them were like trying to find a certain butterfly that had flown across I-95 on the Sunday that someone forced or persuaded Lorraine Hendricks out of her car.

Williams had calls from psychics—and from psychos. He had calls from professionals and from citizens. Memory is probably the most imprecise function in the human brain. Many of the callers weren't sure of the day or time they had seen suspicious people or vehicles. Phil Williams had to prioritize, to pick those that sounded plausible and dismiss the others.

Lorraine Hendricks had either gone with someone she knew and trusted or had been taken from her car by a stranger. The question was really, *where* had Lorraine met her killer? It was possible that someone had gotten in her car when she stopped for gas way back at Exit 50.

Detective Bobby Mutter of the Titusville Police Department called Williams to say that on Saturday night, March 3, Detective Dan Carter of his department had observed a white male approaching vehicles, wandering from convenience store to convenience store. One of them had been at the Amoco station where Lorraine Hendricks was known to have stopped the next morning. Carter had stopped the man and asked for ID. He didn't have any but gave the name Erik Marshall Litton,* DOB 5-22-52. He said he was traveling south from Connecticut. Litton had been about five feet eight, 160 pounds, and he was wearing a reddish plaid shirt, dirty blue jeans, cowboy boots, and a dirty baseball cap. He had a filet-type knife with a plastic handle in a sheath at his side. Carter checked and found no wants or warrants on Litton, but he had received an emergency call and had had to leave the Amoco station to respond. The Titusville Police had had no further contact with Litton.

He might well have been at the Amoco station the next morning when Lorraine drove in.

A woman named Liane Stark* called Phil Williams to report that she had been in that Amoco station the previous summer. "I used the telephone booth, and a man—a black man—pretended to use the other phone there, but he was watching me. When I went back to my car he tried to get into the backseat behind the driver's seat. I was able to run inside and get the attendant to come back out with me. The man was gone."

If nothing else, Williams was hearing how dangerous rest stops and exit areas could be for women traveling alone. In the time a woman left her car to use the phone or the rest room, or to buy a candy bar or pay for her gas, someone could get into the backseat of an unlocked car. It *was* quite possible that Lorraine Hendricks had driven away from Exit 50 with a passenger crouched in the backseat, that she had been unaware that she was no longer traveling alone. But would the rider have waited over *fifty-seven* miles to make his move? Probably not.

Detective Greenhaigh of St. John's County just south of Jacksonville called to say that she was working a case that had possible similarities to the Hendricks case. An attractive woman had traveled to Jacksonville's Mayo Clinic on Tuesday, March 6th, two days after Lorraine vanished. After her appointment the woman had spent the day shopping around the clinic. As she traveled south toward home she noticed a man in a large gray car following her. He was tall—or at least sat "tall in the seat" of his car. Just outside Duval County he began to try to get her to pull over. He flashed his lights and pulled alongside her car, pointing at it as though she had a flat tire or some other problem. She knew there was nothing wrong with her car and pulled ahead. She turned off on US 1 and headed toward St. Augustine.

The man had followed her. "He shot her car window out," Detective Greenhaigh said. "A man who we believe is the same suspect followed a *second* victim back to the Duval County line that same night, using the same techniques to try to get her to pull over."

The tall man in the gray sedan made the mistake of trying to force an off-duty female St. Augustine detective later that night, and Detective Mary Loveck got a tag number. She checked it through the Department of Motor Vehicles and it came back to a Patrick Phillips,* WM, DOB 2/21/42, who stood several inches over six feet. The female detectives in St.

Augustine and in St. John's County were checking him out thoroughly. At the moment Phillips hadn't proved to have connections further south than St. Augustine, but he was a definite threat to women traveling alone.

Greenhaigh's call was bolstered by one from a woman named Brenda Lacy.* She said she had stopped for gas at a station off I-95 outside Jacksonville, and a tall man with sandy blond hair, about six feet two, had pulled over when she did. Her car needed repairs, which had taken about two hours. Brenda, who described herself as a fifty-year-old woman and "good-looking," had been puzzled and a little alarmed that the man hung around all the while she was at the station. He bought gas and asked her to go with him to St. Augustine. She refused, but he followed her down I-95 for several miles.

When Roger Gainey of the Clay County Sheriff's Office (west of St. Augustine) called, Phil Williams began to wonder if he might be looking for a serial killer. Gainey said that his department had been working on a homicide that had occurred six weeks before Lorraine Hendricks died. The victim profile and the M.O. were too similar to be ignored. Carol Orcutt, a beautiful blonde who was five feet four and weighed a hundred pounds, and who was also a businesswoman, had disappeared within a ten-mile radius of where Lorraine Hendricks had last been seen alive. Carol Orcutt's car, a red Thunderbird, had been found—its engine still running—on State Road 21, but Carol was gone.

Carol herself was found two weeks later—on January 27th—down a little-traveled dirt road. She had been murdered, and her body had been left in a position eerily similar to Lorraine Hendricks's. On autopsy she was found to have injuries very similar to those suffered by Lorraine Hendricks. She, too, had been found nude, and her clothing was missing. Lorraine's earring had been found, and Carol Orcutt's jewelry was still on her body.

Phil Williams traveled to Clay County and conferred with Lt. Jimm Redmond, who was in charge of the investigation, and Detective Gainey. The men agreed that they had cases with too many matches to be ignored. Both women came out of the Jacksonville area just prior to their deaths; both left from within a ten-mile radius; both bodies were left in unusual and grotesque positions; and both were taken out of vehicles beside roads that were quite well traveled.

They agreed to keep in touch. But there were no quick answers for either case.

Williams and Oliver checked with tow trucks that had worked I-95 between March 4th and 9th, and with the Florida troopers who traveled the Interstate continually, their eyes out for suspicious circumstances. Mike Transue and Tim Harris had seen nothing that would help the investigation, and neither had any of the other troopers who worked other shifts along I-95.

A detective's nightmare is always that another victim will die before he can catch the killer. Phil Williams worried about that; if they were dealing with a serial killer roving between Jacksonville and Fort Pierce, there was every likelihood that he would kill again. If he was near the beginning of his obsessive fantasies, it might be months. If, like Ted Bundy, who had terrorized Florida a dozen years earlier, he was at the height of his addiction to murder, there would be another victim within days.

Phil Williams knew that the U.S. Department of Justice had set up a crime analysis program called VICAP (Violent Criminal Apprehension Program) with a computer matrix at F.B.I. headquarters in Quantico, Virginia. The program offered help to local detectives all over America who were working unsolved homicides, particularly those that involved abductions; that were—at least on the surface—random, motiveless, or sexually oriented; and that were known or suspected to be part of a series.

VICAP, the brainchild of one of the most respected detectives in America, Pierce Brooks, former captain of homicide of the Los Angeles Police Department and a chief of police in Oregon and Colorado cities, gives detectives a chance to compare their cases with similar cases around the country, and, if they request it, a profile of a what the killer might be like from Special Agents in the Behavioral Science Unit of the F.B.I.

VICAP's information forms are lengthy—fourteen pages and 188 questions, plus a narrative summary—but experts on serial murder have long since learned that seemingly trivial details of an unsolved crime may turn out to be the clues that track and trap a killer.

And Phil Williams was a detective who would try *any* route to find his man—or woman. On March 12, tediously and meticulously, he filled out the VICAP form with everything he knew about Indian River County Case 90-15640. Lorraine's case. He listed two possible related cases: the Carol Orcutt case in Clay County, 90-005374, and the St. John's County investigation of the male motorist who followed women on freeways, 90-65161.

If VICAP came up with some hits, Williams's case might be easier to solve than he expected it was going to be.

There were no hits—but he had given it a try.

In the end, Phil Williams and Larry Smetzer, who was assisting in gathering data, would check out fifty-five leads before they found the key to solving Lorraine Hendricks's murder.

Smetzer's assignment was to pick up all tickets, warnings, field interviews, and any other data from the Florida Highway Patrol and other police agencies that might reveal any unusual contacts on I-95. It was possible that Lorraine's killer had been stopped or had come into contact with police on March 4.

It was, Williams and Smetzer admitted, a ten thousand-to-one long shot.

When they took their fifty-sixth call they would open a Pandora's box with dark secrets they would have chosen never to know. The answers to their questions would bring heartbreak to many more families.

15

Tim Harris stopped by to see Sandy on Saturday, March 10th, the morning that the headlines screamed that a woman's body had been found and that she had been identified as Lorraine Hendricks of Jacksonville.

Sandy read the article and breathed, "Oh, my God! I can't believe that someone actually did this."

"And she was really pretty, too," Tim said.

Sandy studied the tiny postage-stamp-sized picture that accompanied the story. It was difficult to see what the dead woman actually looked like. She wondered how Tim could tell if she had been pretty or not, and then Sandy felt a sick roiling in her stomach, and a kind of premonition that she didn't want to acknowledge. She shook her head and took a deep breath, and the feeling went away.

While the whole county was caught up with the mystery behind Lorraine Hendricks's murder, Sandy Harris still had to cope with her own hopelessly entangled marital problems. The decision to divorce Tim had been hard. Her decision to put the house up for sale was hard. Forcing Tim out of the house had been harder. *Keeping* him out was proving to be impossible. There wasn't a day that Tim didn't come by or call—or both. Now that she was lost to him, she had become utterly desirable.

Sandy still heard Tim in the night, clambering up what had once been Shadow's pen, creaking across the roof, and then sliding through Timmy's bedroom window. It was almost creepier when she *didn't* hear him come in. Sometimes she would be talking on the phone, suddenly hear a soft click, and realize that he was in the house, and that he was listening to her conversations.

Sandy had found one tape recorder, and she and Tim had had a major confrontation over it, but she didn't delude herself into believing that he didn't have others stashed here and there. He knew too much about her comings and goings; sometimes he would give himself away, and she knew he still had devices where he could listen to her calls when he wasn't in the house. Although she certainly wasn't involved with any other man, she hated the thought that her every outgoing call was being taped. She began to fight Tim on his own level. When she got home at night she dialed the number of some business that she knew was closed and had no answering machine. Then she let the phone ring for an hour.

When Tim came during the day to retrieve his hidden tapes, all he would have would be a tape full of the sounds of an endlessly ringing phone. That frustrated him tremendously, but it didn't stop him from surveilling Sandy constantly.

He was quite open now about his tape recorders. He would deliberately pull one out of the sofa or from some other hiding place and start playing it back in front of Sandy. He liked to taunt her: "If you only knew how many nights I've spent in this house when you didn't know I was here, you might be surprised."

He wrote Sandy letters and left them behind each day, proclaiming his devotion to her. "I love you. I always will. Why can't you see that and know how happy we can be again?"

Tim also taped messages to Sandy about how much he loved her, repeating the same phrases over and over, and then left the tapes for her to play. It was as though if he said it often enough, it would be true—and all the years of cheating and abuse would vanish.

But they wouldn't. They couldn't—not for Sandy any longer.

Lt. Gary Morgan talked with Tim and tried to make him face reality. "I told him that it had been . . . six months . . . since they'd been having problems, and I thought it was about time that he got himself pulled together and went on with his life and forgot about Sandy because there was no way he was gonna make her love him if she didn't want him back. . . . I didn't realize how hard it was hitting him until I saw him sitting in front of me that day. . . . He told me he wanted to give up the felony program. . . . I told him it was something he'd worked real hard for. Working the dog—the dog was one of the better dogs . . . I told him, 'I don't think it's something you want to give up, and then six months down the road you're gonna regret giving it up . . . because it's something you're not gonna be able to get back into.' . . . I thought the best thing for him to do was to get his marriage over with, life straightened out, and to keep his current position, because that's what made him happy before the problems, and I thought it would make him happy after. . . ."

But Tim was phasing out of the felony squad despite what his superiors advised. They felt sorry for him. But of course they had heard only one side. They didn't know he was *still* seeing DeeLisa.

On March 15 Tim gave up Shadow. Sandy begged him to let her keep the dog. She and the kids loved Shadow, and they sure would feel a lot safer having him with them at night, but Tim said the Patrol wouldn't consider that. That part was true; Shadow was a working dog, and he had cost the Patrol thousands of dollars.

Tim wrote to Bobby R. Burkett, director of the Fort Pierce Division of the Florida Highway Patrol:

I am requesting for re-assignment from Felony Canine Handler to Trooper I, Indian River County. Recent events concerning my family have prevented me from giving 100% to the program. I have been very satisfied with the program but I think in the best interest of the Florida Highway Patrol I give up my Canine Handler position. The additional duties have added to the stress to the point that I cannot give my best to the program.

I am requesting that K-9 Shadow be donated to me if he cannot be re-trained to another Trooper. I

will assist in any way that I can for the K-9 to be
re-trained to another handler.

It is with my deep regret that I request for
re-assignment.

Tim's request for transfer was granted. Tim would
be working traffic again and was no longer involved in
any way in the investigation into Lorraine Hendricks's murder. He never really had been—nothing
more than that day when Phil Williams asked to use
Shadow to try to find her body, and Tim had said it
was too hot and too windy.

One of Tim's lieutenants, Andy Morris, had agreed
that Tim's personal life and problems had gotten the
best of him, and he assisted him in getting professional help. Morris noted that Shadow was only four years
old, and that he could still bond and train with
another trooper. Sandy and the kids really missed
Shadow when he was reassigned to another trooper.

At the urging of the Florida Highway Patrol Tim
had seen a counselor in early March. He had always
refused to do so before, but he went, and he told Pat
Wessendorf that he was sure he could pull his marriage back together. Pat didn't think so. If he had truly
regretted cheating on Sandy and had never seen
DeeLisa Davis again, she would have forgiven her
son-in-law, too. But she knew he was still playing
games with Sandy's heart. She had seen him driving
down the street with DeeLisa with her own eyes.

She thought he was acting peculiar besides. Pat was
trying to help Sandy get the Citrus Hideaway house
fixed up to sell. Tim had let the yard go for a long time.
Pat had brought some plants out to spruce it up, and
she was just beginning to work when Tim drove up. "I
hadn't even started to put out the plants—I mean,
they were all still in the containers—and Tim drives

up and tells me how wonderful the yard looked. I stared at him, and he just seemed to be out of it—like he was sleepwalking."

Sandy Harris made tentative stabs at having a social life as a single woman. It wasn't easy. She had loved Tim since she was sixteen; now she was almost a dozen years older, and her self-esteem had suffered mightily in the interim. Sometimes she went out with her sisters, Sue and Kathy. She still had lunch on Thursdays with her mom and both her sisters. As far as she knew, Tim was living with DeeLisa—if you could call it that. During March, 1990, Tim was upstairs in *Sandy's* house almost every night. He never came near Sandy's bed, but he couldn't have been in DeeLisa's either.

Sandy wondered why DeeLisa put up with it.

And Pat Wessendorf wondered why Sandy put up with Tim's constant interference with her life. But in truth, Pat was beginning to be afraid of him. Of course, Pat didn't know about the times Tim had put his hands around Sandy's neck and threatened to choke the life out of her. She didn't know how bad things were.

Phil Williams made two more trips up to Jacksonville. Like all instinctive detectives, he knew that he would have to learn more about the victim than he knew about his own closest friends. Somewhere in Lorraine's life there had to have been something that made her temporarily vulnerable to her killer. The problem was that Williams didn't yet know what it was.

Sometimes he repeated to himself a funny little litany: "Cops and turtles—turtles and cops." When he saw turtles making their ponderous journeys across the baking hot surface of I-95 he thought of the dead woman in the woods, so compassionate that she would have stopped to save even those ugly creatures. It seemed a bitter irony that someone had destroyed *her* and left her in the slash pines alone.

On March 16 Rick Hendricks called Phil Williams at home and said that his bank had sent him a letter advising that a check for $100 on Lorraine's account had bounced. He wanted to go and get it, but Williams suggested that Hendricks wait, since he was coming up to Jacksonville in two days; he would check with the bank. It might prove to be just the lead they needed.

It wasn't. The signature was Lorraine's, and it was a check she had cashed before she left for her trip on March 4. Had she lived, she would long since have made a payroll deposit to cover it. No other checks came in, nor were there any credit card charges.

As Phil Williams worked the baffling murder case in his county the homicide rate in Florida scarcely diminished. Lou Sessa of the Palm Beach Sheriff's Office called Williams to say that they were working a murder investigation in the death of a 14-year-old girl who had been sexually assaulted and suffocated around March 18th. Williams considered it, but the M.O. was very different from the Hendricks and Orcutt cases. The Palm Beach victim was clothed, she wasn't a sophisticated businesswoman, she hadn't been left in a bizarre sexual position, and she had been found in a highly populated area rather than a quiet, lonely place.

Phil Williams still couldn't shake the "cops and turtles" image. He spoke with Bruce McMann of the Florida Department of Law Enforcement. *Could* there be police involvement? Could they possibly be looking for a rogue cop—or someone dressed like a cop? Ted Bundy had used that technique with deadly effectiveness. He had often identified himself as a policeman before he lured his victims away from shopping malls or campuses. All it had taken was the flash of a fake badge that anyone could buy through a magazine ad.

There were elements in this case that hinted that a *real* policeman or an ex-cop might be the killer. For one thing, the turnaround road through the pine woods median on I-95 was used almost exclusively by cops; few civilians even knew it was there. For another, Lorraine Hendricks's license and registration were missing. To a civilian, her credit cards surely would have been more interesting and rewarding. But a driver's license and vehicle registration were the first things every cop asked for.

But if Lorraine had been stopped by a policeman, there was no record of it. McMann ran all the available data they had through the NCIC and FCIC computers; he determined that the only time Lorraine Hendricks's car tag had been run through the system was when Trooper Mike Transue entered it at the time he found her abandoned car on March 5.

Nevertheless, Phil Williams agreed to set up a meet with the Highway Patrol brass in Fort Pierce to explore the cop theory.

And then Detective Helfer of the St. Lucie County Sheriff's Office called to say that he had been following the Hendricks case in the paper. "I want you to know that one of our detectives is working a case involving an ex-cop. He raped a woman. The interesting thing is that he grabbed her by the throat when he picked her up."

Helfer said he would try to get more specific information and call back. Oddly, Phil Williams received an anonymous letter that same day in which the writer suggested that Lorraine Hendricks might have been killed by a "deranged cop." The letter was signed "Concerned Citizen."

Phil Williams carefully carried the letter to Tony Oliver for processing. It could very well be a "catch me" letter. It wouldn't be the first time a killer couldn't wait for detectives to work through the puzzles he had left behind. Sometimes they got impatient to see their faces on the nightly news. Sometimes it was a "catch me if you can, you stupid cops" letter, a game that some murderers enjoyed.

It was the first day of spring. March 21, 1990. Phil Williams scarcely noticed.

The Indian River County Sheriff's investigators were exploring every avenue possible, no matter how ridiculous it might seem on the surface. Phil Williams and Larry Smetzer and Tony Oliver made up the main team, and Lt. Mary Hogan handled the yeoman's job of holding the press and the public at bay. This was the kind of case where reporters begged for details—and she could give them so few without jeopardizing the investigation. This was the kind of case that frightened the citizens of Indian River County, and they wanted to be assured that *they* were not in danger. Hogan walked a narrow line, always smiling, never letting the demands ruffle her. In the meantime she made sure the Hendricks case detectives received the financial wherewithal and the time they needed, unhampered by either the tight county budget or reporters. She managed somehow to assign other open cases to detectives who weren't under such intense pressure.

Phil Williams believed in listening to everyone who had a theory. "That was something I learned in my old band days. Don't ever be a one-man band; you can never have too many people. One more man may be just the one that makes the band work. That belief carried over into law enforcement for me."

The file on Lorraine Hendricks's murder was getting thicker every day.

Detective Larry Smetzer kept tracking down a number of documents from the Florida State Patrol and other agencies, including warning tickets and information about stops that troopers had made on Sunday, March 4th. Sergeant Coates of the FHP helped Smetzer with his search. It wasn't easy. Although city and county officers were required to call their dispatchers whenever they stopped a motorist, state troopers were not. Any stops the state officers might have made where they had not given out tickets or warning slips were virtually untraceable. Troopers were fairly autonomous. They kept their patrol units at their homes, they didn't report in to their headquarters at the beginning of their shifts, and they roamed their territory looking for speeders and drivers in need of help wherever they determined the traffic was heaviest.

The more people the investigators could find who had driven down I-95 on the day Lorraine Hendricks disappeared, the more likely they were to find an eyewitness—or an almost-eyewitness.

Among the warning tickets turned in to the Florida Highway Patrol was one that Trooper Tim Harris had written to a Diane Lonergan* at 10:48 a.m. on March 4th at State Road 9, not far from where Lorraine Hendricks's car had been located a day later by Trooper Mike Transue. Phil Williams was not, however, very excited about this information, as Patrol records also showed that Harris had made an actual arrest an hour later on March 4 that tended to take him out of the suspect or witness category. It was during the critical time period when Lorraine would have been driving into Indian River County, had she pursued her original plans, and it was many miles away from the wooded median.

Phil Williams also checked out the location of personnel in his own department on March 4 between 10:30 a.m. and 1 p.m. in the area along I-95. If Lorraine Hendricks had been stopped by someone she trusted because he *was* a cop—or because he was impersonating a cop—Williams couldn't avoid looking at the men who worked alongside him, as onerous a task as that might be. He was relieved to find that the area was so isolated, and "business" so slow that morning, that there had been no sheriff's cars along the Interstate within those parameters. He didn't want to find out that the cop theory was true, and most of all, he didn't want to discover that anyone working for the Indian River County Sheriff's Office was a sex killer. He had been through that before when he learned his friends were murderers. Enough pain there to last him a whole lifetime.

The contacts and calls that Phil Williams logged continued to add up. Call 53 came into the Indian River Sheriff's Office on March 24. A resident of Columbia County called to say he had read about a dead girl who was found in the back of a van. Williams contacted him for details. Nothing matched.

Call 54 was from a woman who said a gray van had tried to run her off the road on I-95.

Call 55 was from Detective Winker of the Cocoa Police Department across from Merritt Island. "A while back we had a black male driver who attempted to pull a woman over by using a blue light on his

Camaro. She stopped—but she drove off when she saw he wasn't in uniform."

Call 56 came from Sergeant Carroll Boyd, and it was in reference to Sandy Harris, the wife of Florida Highway Patrolman Tim Harris.

16

Early on the evening of Friday, March 23, Sandy met her sister Susan at the UpTown for a drink after work. Tim followed her there, as he seemed to be following her everywhere. Although she didn't see him, he hid behind a post and listened as she chatted with a girlfriend in the club. She didn't dance with anyone, and she left the bar early.

Pat Wessendorf was at the house in Citrus Hideaway with Timmy and Jennifer. She was standing in the yard when Tim suddenly roared around the corner in his latest vehicle—a brand-new 1990 red Camaro. He pulled into the driveway and slid over into the yard at full speed.

"I was afraid of him," Pat recalled. "I ran into the house. Sandy could still stand up to him, but he scared me. He was screaming at Sandy that she was a barfly and a tramp. He was getting out of control."

Tim had followed Sandy home from the UpTown. He had something to give her; it was a tape he had made telling her how much he loved her, how they could be happy together again if she would only take him back. Sandy walked around the shiny new Camaro, stunned. It had only been a short time since Tim had bought his truck. "Tim," she asked in amazement, "now how are you going to pull your boat?"

"I'll buy another truck," he snapped. "Don't worry about it."

When Tim Harris left that night he had scarcely turned off of 75th onto Highway 510 when he was involved in an accident. His new Camaro's fender was crumpled, and Tim was taken to the emergency room in Vero Beach. He had a blood alcohol reading of .01. He was far from legally impaired, but for Tim Harris it was astounding that he had any alcohol in his system at all. Tim didn't drink, and he didn't smoke. Or rather, he hadn't until now.

The E.R. called, and Sandy went to pick him up, wondering why he hadn't had them call DeeLisa. They drove to a park on the way home; she thought maybe she could get through to him somehow, just *talk* to him. Tim wasn't hurt badly. It was his mind that scared her; he could not grasp that she had come to get him because there had been no one else to do it. It didn't mean she loved him or that she wanted him back.

Tim scared Sandy. She could not even make a gesture of human decency without his assuming that she had forgotten all of his betrayals over the past eleven years. He talked over her, refusing to let her tell him, for the umpteenth time, that she was going ahead with the divorce. He acted as though they were as good as reconciled.

Tim Harris was building toward some cataclysm. Sandy had no idea what he might be capable of. He had given up his goal of being in the felony unit. He had given up Shadow. His work evaluations were slipping. He was a teetotaler who had suddenly begun to drink. He had sold his new truck—which he could at least sleep in—for an expensive sports car that he couldn't afford and which he had already banged up with his wild driving. He was rocketing around Indian River and St. Lucie counties like a crazy man, sleeping in rest stops, or at his brother's, or at DeeLisa's—but mostly upstairs in Sandy's house.

Sandy felt the way she did when they were on hurricane watch. The air was heavy with danger, an ominous sense of impending catastrophe.

On Sunday night, March 24, Sandy Harris was visiting in her living room with her next-door neighbors, the Rodney Tillmans. They had been very supportive of Sandy, and they were fully aware of how scary her dealings with Tim had become. They knew she was frightened, but Sandy was a woman who fought to appear capable. Even her mother had never seen her cry during this whole divorce fiasco, and her neighbors had never seen her let down and admit how rough things were. She still got up and went to work at her bookkeeping job every day, still took care of the children, still pasted on a smile to make it look as if everything was all right.

It was dark, shortly after nine, when the trio heard a loud thump on the second floor. Both the Tillmans jumped, but Sandy only sighed. "Tim's here. It's only Tim. I know he's up there."

While her neighbors waited, half embarrassed and half alarmed, Sandy ran up the stairs calling, "Tim? Tim, are you up there?"

"He was hiding behind the bathroom door, and he had my purse," Sandy recalled. "He'd taken it from my bedroom, and I saw it open on the bathroom counter. I said, 'Tim, I know you're behind the door—I *know* you're there.' And he finally came out. I said, 'Why don't you just be normal and come downstairs? Our neighbors are here.'"

Tim Harris edged out from behind the bathroom door and followed Sandy downstairs. But he wouldn't join in the conversation. "He just sat there staring— like a zombie. Then he got up and went in his study and sat there, ignoring everyone."

The Tillmans tried to make small talk, but it was an agonizingly embarrassing situation. It was clear Tim wanted them out of there. They made excuses and left.

As soon as he was sure their neighbors were out of earshot Tim grabbed Sandy roughly and dragged her across the room, muttering, "I have a present for you in my bag."

Tim outweighed Sandy by seventy pounds or more, and there was little point in fighting him. Jennifer and Timmy were in bed, and she didn't want to wake them. This wasn't the first time Tim had been physical with her, and she let him pull her along as she frantically tried to form a plan to get free of him.

Tim wrestled Sandy up the stairs and into the master bedroom and slammed the door behind him. He reached for a shiny black vinyl bag and pulled out a pair of handcuffs. They weren't flex cuffs; they were heavy metal cuffs.

And then Tim switched off the lights.

Tim reached out for her, and this time Sandy fought. He had never done anything like this before, and she was frightened. He slipped one cuff on, but Sandy kicked and twisted so that he couldn't latch the second cuff. It seemed like forever as they tumbled around on the bedroom floor, but it was probably closer to ten minutes. Helpless against Tim's strength, Sandy ended up on the floor next to the door.

"You're going to take me back," Tim growled into her ear, repeating that phrase over and over.

"I am going to divorce you," Sandy gasped stubbornly.

"You are going to take me back," he said again, as if he hadn't even heard her. He promised her that if she didn't take him back, they were both going to die. "You are going to take me back," he said again.

"No, I am not," she said through gritted teeth. "I am going to divorce you."

Tim Harris had threatened Sandy before, and he had placed his hands around her neck and told her how easily he could break it, but he had never truly *hurt* her. He was hurting her now. The wrist in the handcuff ached as he yanked on the cuffs, trying to completely immobilize her. She had rug burns and scrapes, and she knew that Tim was deadly serious.

Sandy began to scream, even though she knew all the windows were shut.

Tim was on top of her, straddling her. She turned her face away from his, and then she saw the gun. It was a handgun, and he held it right next to her head. She had no idea if it was loaded. He beat his huge fist on the floor right next to her face, and she was afraid to look to see if he still held the gun. "This could be your face," he breathed. "Think what I could do to your *face.*"

Sandy didn't doubt for a moment that Tim meant what he was saying.

Sandy's screams had awakened four-year-old Timmy, and he was banging on the door, asking her if she needed help. She didn't want her little boy to see this, and she told him it was all right—that he should go back to bed. Timmy tried to get in, but the door was locked. He started throwing things at the door, trying to save his mother.

At some point Sandy gave in. She fully believed that Tim was about to rape her and then kill her, and she feared for Timmy and Jennifer. With dull shock she knew that she had finally come to a place where she was afraid for her life. Not of being hurt. Not even of being forced to submit to sex. But of dying.

"Okay," Sandy gasped. "I'll take you back."

She didn't think Tim would believe her. "No way was he going to believe that I suddenly changed my mind like that, not after the way I had fought him."

But he did. Tim Harris actually believed that he had accomplished the reconciliation that he wanted. He was still on top of Sandy, but he wasn't hurting her. She called out to Timmy that everything was okay—that he should go back to bed.

She was very cautious, afraid Tim would flip out again. Sandy talked very slowly, very softly, as if she were calming a child. "Tomorrow we'll have a little ceremony—and we'll put our wedding rings back on," she said.

"Why don't we do it tonight?" Tim asked.

"No," Sandy stalled. "No, let's start off tomorrow—a whole new start." Slowly Tim lifted his weight off of her. She asked him if they could go downstairs so she could get a drink of water, because her throat hurt from screaming. He nodded agreeably. The back of her neck prickled as he followed her down the stairs.

Tim unlocked the cuff on Sandy's wrist. She could see that her skin was already purpling from broken blood vessels, and she knew she would have massive bruises there.

"He let me get a drink of water. He seemed to be almost back to normal, and I thought that I would be able to get him to leave. He walked into the living room and sat down, wanting to talk, trying to convince me again that we should get back together that night."

Tim was not in uniform. He was wearing a sports shirt and a pair of blue corduroy jeans. He stood up from the couch, and Sandy's heart sank. He unzipped his pants and took them off. What she saw gave her the biggest shock of her life.

Tim was wearing pantyhose and women's black lace panties with a sheer panel in the front.

"Before I go," he suggested, "why don't we do something kinky?"

"I freaked. I thought, Oh my, God! I had never, ever seen him in women's underclothes."

Sandy's veins felt icy with shock. Her huge, handsome, macho husband was standing there in women's lingerie. The panties weren't hers, and she didn't think the pantyhose were either. She never wore that color. Fighting hysteria, Sandy wondered where he had gotten them. Had he always had this fetish, and she'd never known? She kept her voice calm, although she didn't know how. Sandy watched as Tim took off the women's lingerie. He was half naked now, and wanting her to go back to the bedroom with him. But somehow she convinced him that they should put off having sex until they had their "little ceremony" and exchanged rings again. He seemed to agree with her, and she held her breath while he put his corduroy pants back on.

"Let me walk you to the door," she said, and amazingly, he went.

"Kiss me good-bye," Tim urged.

"I didn't want to. But I didn't want him to get out of control again, so I did," Sandy remembered. "I could hardly bear it, but I actually kissed him on the lips, and I turned around and walked upstairs as he left, acting as normal as I could, pretending like I was going to bed. I didn't want him to know how freaked out I was. Everything in me told me to grab the kids and run, but I didn't dare go anywhere that night, and I didn't dare call anyone for help either. There was no way of knowing how many tapes and bugs he had planted on my phones. We had that whole acre, and he always used to park out back, and I couldn't tell if he was out there or not, watching."

Sandy Harris was about to spend the longest night of her life.

"I stayed in my bed, awake, all night long, listening for Tim to crawl up the dog pen and come back in. But it was quiet. I don't know where he went."

Sandy had scheduled another open house with the realtor the next day. The woman had the key to get in. Sandy didn't wait. She grabbed her children and whatever clothes she could, and she drove to Susan and Don Dappen's house. "I was scared to death of Tim. I didn't know if I could ever go home again."

Don Dappen had tried for years to get along with his brother-in-law, but he'd been fed up with him since the scene in the Vero Beach Police Department in December. Dappen's complaint to Tim's superiors in the Patrol over that fiasco had driven the two men even further apart, though Tim had never been disciplined.

When Sandy and her children walked in that Sunday morning, Don knew what he had to do, even if it sounded cold. "Sandy," he said flatly, "you can turn right around and go back home—unless you're willing to file a complaint against Tim with the sheriff's department."

Sandy Harris did the same review in her mind that every battered wife has ever done. "I realized that the minute I did that, Tim would lose his job. How would I pay the bills and support myself and the children? I knew Don was right, though. My life was in jeopardy, and that was far more important than money. If Tim killed me, my children would be without a mother and a father."

She agreed that Don should call the sheriff, and she called her own lawyer. She wanted a restraining order so that she could go home again, although she doubted that a piece of paper would keep Tim away. She eventually got the restraining order, although her lawyer was patronizing. "Come on, Sandy," he soothed. "Your life can't be that bad."

Dappen sheltered his sister-in-law, niece, and nephew in his home. Everybody tried to pretend that life was normal, but they all knew it wasn't. Even the kids were nervous. They had an outdoor barbecue that night, and Dappen found himself glancing over his shoulder to be sure they had no unwanted company.

"I went outside later—at dusk—to shut the sprinklers off," Dappen recalled. "I caught a glimpse of 'this person' peering over our privacy fence beyond the pool, looking toward our living room. I yelled and took off after him—barefoot through the sand spurs."

Don Dappen knew it was Tim he was chasing. He ran back to the house and called the Sebastian police. They found Tim hiding on the golf course near Dappen's home. He was given a "Trespass after Warning" ticket.

Don Dappen filed another complaint against Tim with the Florida Highway Patrol. Tim Harris talked to Patrol Lt. Andy Morris. Morris had supervised Tim since he had come into the Felony Special Response Team in late 1989, four months earlier. Morris had been aware of Don Dappen's first complaint about Tim in December. That scuffle had been deemed a marital spat, and Tim was off-duty at the time. Tim's performance, while not a hundred percent in Morris's eyes, had been at least ninety percent during the past difficult months. Later Morris had given Tim time off to work out his problems with Sandy.

Morris had seen other troopers go through divorces that were far more strife-ridden than what he had seen in Tim Harris's. The psychologist Tim had been referred to had reported that he saw no signs of violence in Harris. Tim still had his job, although the Patrol made plans to take him off road duty and put him in an office until things settled down.

Tim promised to stay away from Don Dappen's house. He explained that he only wanted to see his children, and that Sandy was keeping them away from him. Sebastian police had a "Keep Watch" order on Dappen's home in case Tim showed up.

Tim didn't keep his promise. He didn't stay away from Sandy. When he saw her driving down the road the next morning he raced alongside her and then veered in front of her and forced her off the road. Don Dappen was following a little way behind her to be sure she got to work safely.

Tim was enraged at Dappen's interference. He came eyeball-to-eyeball with his brother-in-law, yelling, "Go ahead! Hit me! Hit me!"

Dappen came close; he wanted nothing more than to sock Tim until his teeth rattled. But then he backed off, knowing that that was what Tim wanted him to do. "Naw, I'm not going to hit you. But listen real close. If you bother Sandy or come near her or the kids again, or my family, I'm going to kill you. You know I'm not threatening you. I *will* literally blow your head off and not think twice about it."

"I'm going to call your chief!" Tim shouted.

"I'll give you his phone number, Tim," Dappen

said evenly. "But you know I'll do it, and if you come near us again, I'm going to kill you."

Tim Harris turned and got back in his car. He didn't like Don Dappen, but he respected him, and he knew Dappen meant every word he said. He gunned his Camaro and disappeared in a haze of road dust.

Don Dappen was a man who was slow to anger, but he felt in his gut that his family was in danger. He would not allow anything to happen to them.

As Phil Williams had sifted through the pile of leads and information the investigative team had gathered so far he had come upon the ticket written to Diane Lonergan. Initially it had seemed a useless bit of documentation. But then Williams had discovered that Tim Harris had no alibi at all for the time period following that stop. When the detective called to verify that it *was* Harris who had been booking a prisoner into jail shortly after he had stopped Diane Lonergan at 10:48 a.m. on March 4th, Williams was told that Tim Harris had a *new* serial number; another trooper had been assigned the number used on the booking slip. It was the *other* trooper who had made the arrest around 11:30 on Sunday morning. Tim might very well have remained on the Interstate near the median strip. And then again, he might have been miles away when Lorraine Hendricks crossed the border into Indian River County.

Phil Williams was curious about why Harris had stopped Diane Lonergan for going only five miles over the speed limit. He located Diane at her home near Miami and called to ask her if she remembered her encounter with Trooper Tim Harris. She did indeed.

"He stopped me for speeding, and I knew I wasn't speeding. I had my Cobra radar detector on, and it had not activated. He insisted I was going six miles over the limit. I knew I was only going about sixty-four miles an hour."

Williams made arrangements to talk with Diane and her husband again. A lot of people claim they weren't speeding, but there was something hinky that bothered Williams.

It was that very night that tip 56 came in. Sergeant Carroll Boyd called Williams about Sandy Harris's problems—not because Williams was assigned to the Hendricks murder case, but because he happened to be the detective on call on March 26th.

"I just wanted to advise you," Boyd began, "that Donny Dappen says his brother-in-law is behaving like an idiot. Tim Harris has apparently been prowling around Dappen's house and threatening his wife, Sandy."

Boyd said that they were going to arrest Tim Harris if they found him.

"No," Williams said. *"Don't* arrest him. If you find him, tell him that I'm investigating whether or not he's threatening Sandy."

Phil Williams wanted very much to open a dialogue with Tim Harris. If Harris suspected that Williams was interested in talking to him about Lorraine Hendricks's murder, he was likely to be on the defensive. If he thought Williams was only investigating a domestic dispute, it would be easier.

It would be a way in for Phil Williams.

Phil Williams arranged first to meet with Sandy Harris. He didn't want to go to Dappen's house; he knew that Tim was creeping around there. And he didn't want to go to Tim and Sandy's house in Citrus Hideaway. He didn't want Tim Harris to know that he was talking to Sandy. Sandy agreed to meet Williams and Tony Oliver in the parking lot of a high school.

Sandy already suspected that Tim might be a killer. She hadn't voiced her dread to anyone, and she tried not to think about it. Her complaint to the Indian River County Sheriff's Office about Tim's attack on her on Saturday night was officially logged as battery. Sandy was frightened by what Tim had done to her, but she was sick at heart about a deeper fear, a niggling suspicion that Tim had done something horrible, more horrible than she could ever have imagined.

By the time Phil Williams and Tony Oliver met with Sandy on Monday, March 26, the bruises on her right wrist had blossomed red and purple, and they photographed them as evidence. When she said that she had been brutally handcuffed, they believed her. They didn't want to plant any ideas about Tim's involvement in Lorraine Hendricks's death in her mind, and they were careful as they questioned her.

But she *knew.* Sandy had come to know every facet of Tim's personality. She had seen the violence, and she had heard the sweet talk. She, of all people, knew what he was capable of.

She wished mightily that she did not.

Sandy told Williams and Oliver that Tim had threatened to rape her several times while he had her pinned to the floor and partially handcuffed—that he had also threatened to kill both of them with a gun if she didn't come back to him. And she had to tell them about the women's undergarments, too, embarrassing as it was.

Phil Williams had no doubt that he was listening to a woman who had been utterly terrorized.

Tim Harris hadn't been thinking straight—especially for a cop who was well aware of the value of physical evidence. He had left the lacy black panties and the pantyhose behind.

"These aren't yours?" Williams asked Sandy.

She shook her head. "I've never seen them before. I always cut the tags off my underwear, and I don't wear brown pantyhose."

Phil Williams asked Sandy about her estranged husband's sexual preferences. Embarrassed, she revealed that Tim often asked for oral sex, something that turned her off. He also wanted to photograph her in positions that humiliated her. But his wearing the women's underwear was something new. She had been shocked.

The two detectives bagged the lingerie into evidence. They didn't know what kind of underwear Lorraine Hendricks had worn. All they had ever located of Lorraine's missing possessions were her wallet from the Fort Pierce rest stop and the single golden hoop earring near her body.

It didn't seem possible that even the kinkiest killer would put on the underwear of his victim and attempt to rape his own wife. But then it hardly seemed possible that a respected Florida State trooper with a jacket full of commendations could be the predatory killer they were looking for either. Phil Williams had to face the fact that Tim Harris merited further investigation.

Maybe he wasn't involved. They sincerely hoped he wasn't. One dirty cop blackens the reputation of all cops everywhere. But Williams and Oliver had to agree that Tim Harris seemed to be losing it. His behavior was becoming more and more bizarre, and they had to either find the evidence to convict him or look elsewhere and hope the guy got into some serious therapy.

Sandy Harris agreed to have a tape recorder attached to her phone at her office so that Tim's phone calls to her would be recorded. It was ironic; he had taped her calls for months. It probably would never occur to him that *he* was being taped surreptitiously.

She got her restraining order against Tim and moved back into her house. Every police agency in the area—city, county, and state—knew that she was afraid of Tim. That in itself might be enough protection for her.

Sandy didn't really think that Tim would hurt Jennifer or Timmy; they were his own children, and he begged to see them. There were no orders preventing Tim from seeing them, and on Monday, March 26, she let him take them out to dinner. He brought them back on time and sent a note in, thanking her for letting him spend time with his children. Sandy was cautious; she had seen him behave sweetly before—but only for a little while.

Wednesday night, March 28, Tim asked to take them overnight. Sandy said no. It was a school night, and Tim had no place, really, to take them. She didn't want them over at DeeLisa's, and there wasn't room at David and Melissa's house. Sandy asked her mother, Pat, to pick Jennifer and Timmy up after school and not to let Tim take them.

For all the times that Tim had *not* been there to pick up the children when he promised, he was there this day, and he followed his petrified mother-in-law, his red Camaro right on the bumper of her car. Pat was afraid he would take the children out of state where their mother could never find them. It was a moot point. Both Jennifer and Timmy cried when Tim tried to take them away with him, and he drove off without them.

17

A **detective** works a homicide case a little like someone untangling a seemingly impossible jumble of knots. First he must find the easiest knot and loosen that—just to find a way to get at the rest of them. Once he does that, each knot is a little bit easier than the one before. Williams had been trying and eliminating "knots" for three weeks, and now he had one that looked as though it was going to give. He had a place to focus his expertise and his energy.

He thought he had eliminated Tim Harris as a suspect early in his investigation when his serial number showed Tim had been making an arrest many miles away from where Lorraine Hendricks was killed. Now he knew that wasn't so. Another trooper had made the arrest attributed to Tim.

At this point Phil Williams knew that Harris had been acting weird, and there was nothing to show that he had ever moved from his original radar position on March 4th, a position close to where the gray Honda was found.

Phil Williams called Diane Lonergan again. She said that the trooper who stopped her had had a dog with him—an aggressive German shepherd-type dog. She had been annoyed when the officer directed her to step out of her car and walk back toward his vehicle. But when she got out his attitude had changed. "I'm pregnant—*very* pregnant now—and it was certainly

184

obvious that I was four weeks ago. He might not have noticed that when I was in the car, but he couldn't have missed it when I stepped out."

The trooper told her that he had clocked her speed at seventy-one miles an hour, and he wrote her a warning ticket. That had irritated her, and he had said, oddly, "You can just throw that away. It doesn't mean anything."

"Were you traveling alone?" Williams asked.

"Yes. All alone." She confided that she had been suspicious of the way the officer behaved, although he had been polite and professional on a surface level. But there was something about him that made her uneasy, and she had been upset by the encounter. She knew she wasn't speeding. And the trooper had to have known that, too.

Phil Williams couldn't help but wonder if Diane Lonergan's pregnancy had saved her life. It sounded as though she *had* been stopped when she wasn't speeding, and that Harris had only told her to tear up the ticket *after* he had her out of the car and could see she was pregnant.

Stan Lonergan wasn't eager to drive his wife up to Vero Beach so that she could point out the location where she had been stopped—not until Williams said, "You're a very lucky man, you know. There's another family who have lost their wife, mother, daughter. She came driving along that same stretch of Interstate about an hour after your wife did. We think maybe she got stopped for speeding, too. . . ."

Lonergan cleared his throat, and Williams could almost hear his thoughts as the brutal truth hit him. "We'll be up," he said. "Anytime you say."

The time had come to talk to Tim Harris. Phil Williams knew him, of course. He had never known him in the context of detective and suspect, or, in a way, cat and mouse. Tim Harris was smart, he knew all the ins and outs of police work, and he would be far more savvy than the average man on the street when it came to self-incrimination.

Conveniently, Tim Harris had heard that Phil Williams was investigating the incident with Sandy. Phil didn't have to call Tim. Tim called *him* and, after a short discussion, agreed to meet with Williams at Mama Mia's restaurant in Vero Beach. He expected Williams to question him about his problems with Sandy. He had been telling everyone who would listen how broken up he was about Sandy's throwing him out. It was quite possible that he viewed Williams as another listening ear for his love problems.

It is legal in Florida to tape surreptitiously. Certainly, Tim Harris had been using tapes to follow every breath his estranged wife took. Phil Williams knew Tim had been taping Sandy, and he smiled grimly as he fit a tiny tape recorder in a hollow below his armpit and adjusted his sports jacket. There would be a kind of poetic justice if Tim Harris implicated himself in the murder of Lorraine Hendricks on tape.

They set 2 p.m. on March 27th as the time for their meeting. Phil wasn't wasting any time; it was only a day after Sandy had talked with them about Tim's bizarre attack on her.

When Tim arrived in his red Camaro Phil saw that he had brought DeeLisa Davis with him. Phil had graduated from high school with DeeLisa back in 1971. He sighed. Sometimes he wondered if it would be easier to be a cop in a big city. It seemed as though he had had to arrest or interrogate so many people who had been his friends.

Phil Williams was a master interrogator, the deceptively casual country boy who had learned a long time back that every suspect had to be treated like a human being, no matter how heinous his—or her—crime might have been. Above all, Williams had to avoid any appearance of sitting in judgment. The worse the crime, the more careful he had to be to betray no shock and no disgust. He had to put the picture of Lorraine Hendricks's body lying abandoned in the woods completely out of his mind.

That wasn't going to be easy.

Phil Williams was in no hurry. He was going to take a sympathetic approach with Harris. Tim apparently had no recollection at all of the time, years ago now, when Phil had raced away from him and his ticket book when Tim was a gung-ho young Sebastian cop.

Every word of their conversation would be recorded by the little tape whirring beneath Williams's arm.

"How are you doing?" Williams greeted Tim Harris as Tim slid into Williams's car. He saw the trooper had dark circles etched beneath his eyes and that he was thin, almost gaunt.

"Not good at all. I'm telling you, not good."

"I think you're going through hell, ain't you?"

"It's worse than hell . . . and it's not helping with the relatives. The relatives are killing me."

"Is that DeeLisa?" Williams inclined his head toward the pretty woman who waited with one of her children in the Camaro.

"Yeah."

"I went to school with her . . . nice girl, nice girl."

"She's helped out a lot," Harris said.

"Yeah. Well, at least you got somebody standing by you, right?"

Tim said he wanted to tell Phil Williams the whole story, and for an instant Williams thought it was going to be almost too easy. It wasn't. For Tim, the "whole story" was about how badly he was being treated in his divorce wars by Sandy and her mother and sisters.

And now, Tim complained, it wasn't just the women in Sandy's family. Don Dappen had turned against him. Sandy and their children had been spending all their time at Don and Sue's house. "Donny answers [the phone] and says, 'Don't ever call her again. . . .' "

"The reason why she's staying there, Tim," Phil explained, "is that she says she's scared to death to stay at home."

Tim knew what Phil was talking about—the night Sandy claimed she had been handcuffed and almost raped. But Tim insisted that was all a misunderstanding. He said that Sandy had asked him to come over, and he had refused because she and the neighbors were drinking wine coolers and he didn't drink. He had called back a few hours later, and the neighbors were still there, and Sandy had urged him to come over. "She said, 'Well, why don't you just come on over? Maybe they will get the hint when you walk in the door.' "

Tim Harris's version of the night of March 24th was diametrically opposed to Sandy's. He insisted that Sandy had wanted a back rub, and that she had enjoyed wrestling and playing around with the handcuffs.

"I didn't put them all the way on her. . . . As a matter of fact, when she started crying and said it really hurt I took the things off. . . . I mean, I don't like talking about our sex life."

He ducked his head and wouldn't meet Williams's eyes, but Tim Harris continued to discuss in the most intimate detail his personal relationship with Sandy. According to his version, it had been Sandy who had kept luring him back to their home; it had been Sandy who couldn't make up her mind what she wanted. It had been Sandy who had suggested a number of sexual acts that she wanted to try. Tim explained that he would do anything to get Sandy back. Back rubs. Cuddling. Patting her with baby powder. Oral sex. Whatever she wanted.

Williams nodded sympathetically, but he wondered how the man before him could be so deluded or such a liar. Tim was the one with a girlfriend waiting in his Camaro, his backup woman whom he had kept on a string for five years. Tim seemed completely oblivious to any pain he might be causing DeeLisa.

Tim denied that he had brought any women's underwear to Sandy's house.

"I wonder where she got them from," Williams said mildly.

"Those are hers . . . they're all hers."

"You know, that's the only thing that worries me about her . . . making up shit, I mean, you know—" Phil began.

"I don't know what to tell you," Tim said earnestly. "You know, she's putting her panties on me . . ."

"Yeah."

"You know the sex and all that . . ."

"Yeah."

"But she didn't want sex that night, and she made it clear she didn't want it," Tim admitted. "As a matter of fact, when she started crying as far as the handcuffs go . . ."

"Ummm hmm."

Tim Harris's voice was earnest as he explained that Sandy had never been afraid of him, and that he had always agreed to do whatever she wanted. If she didn't want to be kissed on the mouth, he said "No problem" and kissed her on the cheek. If she didn't want him to stay overnight, he always left.

Phil Williams kept his face bland and friendly. Tim

seemed to brighten up. "You know," he said, "this is all going to end, and, you know, things are going to work out."

"Well, what's the chance of you staying away from Don?"

"I don't have any problem with that," Tim agreed, although he said that it was Don Dappen who was mostly causing the trouble with Sandy.

"I'm the one that is kind of monitoring that situation," Phil Williams said. He knew Sandy had a restraining order, and that she was panicked at the thought that Tim might take Jennifer and Timmy away—even for an hour.

Tim Harris's conversation went in predictable circles, always coming back to his great love for Sandy, to their wonderful sex life, to his belief that they would be back together if not for her interfering family, to the "tiny little thread" he still clung to that he believed bound him to Sandy. Phil Williams wasn't lying when he said he had been through the pain of divorce himself, that he could empathize. That was true, and that was all Tim Harris chose to hear. He quickly came to view Williams as a listening ear, a fellow cop who would understand.

And yet there was an undercurrent—Tim's reticence and his body language—that told Williams Tim Harris was directing the flow of conversation away from something as dangerous to him as an alligator waiting beneath the surface of a seemingly calm ditch.

Tim admitted that the Patrol had taken his gun away. Things weren't good. Not good at all. He admitted that he knew it would break DeeLisa's heart if he went back to Sandy. But he couldn't help it if DeeLisa wanted to stick with him.

DeeLisa had been waiting for Tim for a long time, out in the hot sun—and finally Phil Williams saw her and her child get out and head toward Phil's car, where he and Tim sat talking.

Tim Harris appeared to think almost exclusively of himself and of his own feelings. He confided that he was afraid he would lose his job if he was arrested for battery. He said he appreciated Phil Williams's taking the time to talk with him about his problems.

Phil offered to be available anytime. "Just give me a call," he said easily.

They had talked for hours. Neither of them had so much as touched on the subject of the dead woman out in the pines and palmettos.

Williams wondered if Tim was for real. He seemed to be a man with the narrowest of tunnel vision. He didn't seem worried about anything beyond his obsessive struggle to win his wife back. He was concerned about the possibility of the battery charge because that would mean his job. He *was* haggard and gaunt, but men suffering unrequited love often are.

But then, of course, Phil Williams had never once mentioned Lorraine Hendricks's name. If he had, would that have made Tim Harris sweat?

Maybe next time. Williams was certain there would be a next time.

Phil Williams fully expected to maintain his dialogue with Tim Harris; he felt that sooner or later Harris was going to open the curtain that hid dark fantasies waiting somewhere behind his clear and earnest green eyes. But in order to keep his position as the sympathetic listener, Williams was going to have to have a designated "bad guy."

And that man was going to have to be Donny Dappen.

Phil Williams went to see Don Dappen. They had known each other for years, one as an Indian River

County detective, one as a Vero Beach city detective. They had clambered through ditches and sloughs and fields together in the pizza murders. That was easy compared to this.

"Donny," Phil said slowly, "I want to ask you something. Would Tim be capable of killing someone?"

"You suspect him on the I-95, don't you?"

Williams just stared at Dappen, and Dappen nodded. "Yeah—yeah, I think he would be."

"Sandy has to understand that she can't tell anyone that we suspect Tim," Williams warned. "Can she do it?"

"I think so. None of us knew how bad it was for her until recently. She keeps things inside."

"And Donny," Williams continued, "I need a fall guy. I don't want to have Tim arrested on the battery charges—I have to get into a little better position with him, open him up more. To do that I have to make you the bad guy when I'm talking to him. Can you handle that?"

Dappen grinned. He knew that his brother-in-law already hated his guts. If it would help the investigation, he told Williams he didn't care what Phil said about him.

"Go ahead. Paint me as black as you want. I'll be your bad guy. I blew the whistle on him in the first place."

If Tim was guilty, he would have to be arrested. Dappen was in no hurry to have the detectives' suspicions about Tim become public. Things were ugly enough already. If Williams's hunch was right, what was going to come down would mean that their whole family would be spread all over the front page.

* * *

In the meantime Williams worked to connect Tim Harris to Lorraine Hendricks with physical evidence. It wasn't going to be easy. He doubted that Harris had ever seen Lorraine until that day she had the great misfortune to round the curve on I-95 and enter the trooper's line of sight. It would have had to have been a random thing. If she had not stopped for gas, or if she had stopped for gas and stayed five minutes longer on the phone, or if she had only left home later . . .

It didn't matter now.

Williams checked with Lorraine Hendricks's friends and her estranged husband to see what kind of lingerie she usually wore. He found that Lorraine had preferred delicate, frothy things—and that she often wore black lace panties. But no one of them could identify the black panties left in Sandy Harris's home as absolutely belonging to Lorraine. They were her size, although they were stretched out now from being worn by a two-hundred-pound man. As for pantyhose, who could say? Sandy knew they were not hers. But one pair of pantyhose looked pretty much like another.

The Lonergans drove to Vero Beach in the same car Diane Lonergan had been driving on March 4th. They accompanied Phil Williams north of town until Diane pointed out the area in the southbound lane of I-95 where she had been stopped on that vital Sunday. "I remember the sign that said how many miles it was to the Fort Pierce Outlet Malls," Diane explained.

The wooded median strip where Lorraine Hendricks's body had lain was a stone's throw away. Diane Lonergan pointed to a spot on the shoulder of I-95 where the trooper's unit had been sitting, facing traffic, when she first observed him. Phil Williams moved to that viewpoint and realized that Tim Harris had been able to see clearly who was in the cars as oncoming traffic approached. Diane Lonergan's car had slightly tinted windows, but it would have been quite possible for Tim Harris—from his vantage point—to see that she was a very pretty woman, and that she was alone.

It was only after Tim Harris had asked Diane to exit her car and walk back to his patrol car that he would have seen she was eight months pregnant.

Phil Williams knew now that in all likelihood Tim Harris had been in the area of the median on the Interstate when Lorraine Hendricks approached it.

If *he* hadn't done anything to her, Williams thought grimly, *somebody* had pulled off a murder right under his nose. . . .

18

Sandy Harris gave her consent for Phil Williams and Tony Oliver and Lt. Greg Edwards of the Florida Highway Patrol to search her home. They found a tape recorder that she had no idea was there—the Florida Highway Patrol–issue recorder that Tim had secreted beneath the pink insulation in the attic and spliced into the phone wires. In this first sweep of the home they also found drivers' licenses and ID papers for both men and women, but none for Lorraine Hendricks.

The tape in the attic recorder had recognizable voices on it: Sandy, DeeLisa, and Don Dappen. When Williams asked them if they had known they were being recorded during those particular conversations, none of them said they had, although Sandy, at least, wasn't surprised.

The attic tape recorder indicated that Tim had continued to break into the house in Citrus Hideaway even after Sandy had fled to Sue and Don's. Williams listened as he heard Tim talk to DeeLisa, and he wondered why the woman was so steadfastly sticking by Harris. The guy was deceiving her about his feelings for her, and at the same time he was rubbing her nose in his obsessive "love" for Sandy.

"Where are you?" DeeLisa's voice asked.

"Out." Tim said.

"Are you at a pay phone?"

"Sort of."

"Where are you?"

"Just don't ask me where I am, okay? I'm not with anybody, okay?"

"Timothy?"

"What, babe?"

"Is there anything you want to tell me?"

"What?"

"About the other night? . . . You were up there with her [Sandy]. Is there anything you want to tell me?"

"Like what?"

"Did you tell me anything wrong, or did you leave anything out?"

"As in what?"

"I'm asking if you had any physical contact with her . . . if you in any way hit her or roughed her up."

"I didn't hit her, and I didn't rough her up."

Tim Harris would have known the conversation was being recorded, Williams figured, but he probably didn't think anyone would ever find the tape recorder under the insulation. Even so, he was being cagey with DeeLisa.

"I want to know what happened the other night," DeeLisa pressed.

"I came up here to talk to her."

"And . . .?"

"She asked me to come upstairs and give her a powder, and I did—"

"Give her a *powder?*"

"Yeah, it's when you lay on the bed and you put powder on her back and rub her. Do you want me to continue?"

DeeLisa had to be a glutton for emotional pain. It was obvious to everyone that she adored Harris, and yet she asked him just what he had done with Sandy. Tim repeated to her exactly the story he had told Phil Williams—all the wrestling, hugging, kissing, the "accidental" bruising with the handcuffs. "I was just talking to her about letting me come back, and she agreed; she kissed me at the door, and I left."

DeeLisa wasn't buying the story any more than Phil Williams had.

Her voice was both hurt and angry. "It's really amazing how she's gone from someone who doesn't like sex to someone who's now saying, 'Give me a powder,' and accepting oral sex. . . . Every hour that goes by, almost, I keep hearing things that absolutely astound me."

Tim's voice was alarmed. *"Who* did you hear it from?"

"It's just a clue—it's just something I've been feeling and I thought I'd just ask."

"I'm *asking* you who did you talk to?"

"Nobody."

Tim continued to deny that he was in Sandy's

house. DeeLisa tricked him. Her job had taught her everything about phones. She used her three-way call system to call him on his call waiting, and he fell for it. "Hold on a second, the phone's ringing. Don't say anything right now," he told her.

After a pause he said, "Are you still there?"

"Yeah. I was just calling you, Timothy."

"Who was on the phone?"

"Me."

"Who?"

"Me," DeeLisa said, with a trace of sad smugness. "I used my three-way calling and called you." She had fooled him by putting him on hold. She knew now that Tim was at the Citrus Hideaway house.

"You think you're smart."

"Well, I'm getting smarter."

"That wasn't very nice."

"Really? Well, I'm sick and tired of being lied to, Timothy."

Tim denied that he was lying to her about anything and insisted that he hadn't wanted any physical relationship with Sandy. "It didn't happen because I wanted it—and it didn't happen because she wanted it," he finished lamely.

"Oh, you're just both prisoners, huh? Some alien made you lay down and do it. When I asked you what happened the other night you told me that you went there and that you argued."

"We argued."

"And then, when you left, she put her arms around you and said, 'I love you'?"

"That's what she did."

"Okay. You just happened to leave out a few details."

DeeLisa hung up on Tim, and the dial tone buzzed on the slowly revolving tape.

Williams labeled the tape and recorder and placed them in an evidence bag. Tim Harris was juggling too many stories, too many women, and all the time, Williams believed, he was hiding the biggest lie of all. Phil wondered how long he could keep it up. He suggested that they leave another FHP recorder in its place, but Tim's fellow troopers didn't want to do that. Despite the case that seemed to be building against him, he was still one of their own.

Williams sighed. He had had a plan to shake Tim Harris up a little. If a recorder was still there in the pink insulation, he could have staged a phone call to Sandy, saying that he had three eyewitnesses who had "seen" Tim pull Lorraine Hendricks over on March 4th. That would have made the hairs stand up on Tim's neck the next time he checked what he *thought* was his tape recorder.

Florida State Attorney General's Investigator Rick McIlwain had come aboard the investigative team, and he agreed that they must proceed with extreme delicacy. McIlwain was a polygraphist. But like most excellent lie-detector men, he knew that often the suspect never even needed to be hooked up to the leads on the lie box. The interrogation that came first, the threat of how much the polygraph might reveal, was enough to bring forth a confession.

The man they were tracking was no civilian; he knew the game, he knew the rules of evidence, and he knew how not to get caught. And he also knew how devastatingly accurate a polygraph readout could be as it traced a subject's respiration, galvanic skin responses, blood pressure, heartbeat. McIlwain figured the lie detector would alarm Tim Harris even more than it did most civilian suspects.

Despite the plethora of items the investigators had

carefully bagged and labeled, they had not come up with one scintilla—not even a hair or fiber—that could help them prove that Tim Harris had ever been near Lorraine Hendricks.

A dog hair found in the headliner of Lorraine's Honda, viewed under a scanning electron microscope, seemed to match her pet corgi at home far more than Shadow's coat. Besides, animal hair is very, very difficult to differentiate. Dog hair is nowhere near as damning evidence as human hair might be.

When Phil Williams had asked Tim Harris if he would furnish a pubic hair sample, Tim had responded by reaching down the front of his uniform trousers and plucking the sample right then and there. The hairs matched those found in the black lace panties, but that didn't help. Tim had admitted to wearing the panties, and his were the *only* hairs found caught in the mesh of either the panties or the pantyhose.

Sandy had once found Jennifer playing with a woman's purse in the garage of their house, but it wasn't Lorraine's purse. There was no way to prove whose it was; Tim said it had been turned in as lost, and he kept it only after he had exhausted all efforts to locate the owner.

True, Tim Harris was under extreme pressure, but it might take him a long, long time to break. When it seemed prudent it was agreed that McIlwain would become Williams's partner in interviewing Tim Harris. None of them expected Harris to give it all up at once. Their technique would be to build their case against him as solid as a brick wall. Each admission would be set in mortar and dried hard so that Harris couldn't go back, and each new change in his story would build on that.

And during all that time he must never realize how high the wall was growing.

On April 2 Tim Harris called Phil Williams. He wanted to talk about Sandy. "I had problems this weekend. I went to Don's house with a court order to take the kids for two days, and they refused to turn them over. . . . She said she was gonna press charges and all that good stuff, so I was just checking to see if anything was going on."

Tim added that the HIghway Patrol had taken him off the road and put him on administrative duties.

"What's that mean?" Williams asked, although he already knew.

"Paperwork."

"They got you like on a suspension-type thing?"

"Well, it's not really a suspension—it's just administrative duties."

Tim Harris said he'd like to have lunch with Phil and talk some more. Phil Williams picked him up at the Florida Highway Patrol station, and they drove along I-95. This time Phil was going to push harder; he was going to bring up Lorraine Hendricks's murder. He began by talking about Sunday, March 4th.

Yes, Tim said he remembered stopping a pregnant woman that Sunday. He hadn't mentioned it before because he hadn't considered it unusual.

On March 4, Tim said, he had spent most of his shift down in St. Lucie County. He might have stayed near the wooded median for a very short time after stopping the pregnant woman.

"How long?"

"Probably half hour, forty-five minutes . . ."

"Then the whole thing is, Tim," Phil commented, "that you had to see *something*."

"I didn't see anything . . . out of the ordinary."

"If I found one witness that said that they saw you pull her car over?"

"The girl I stopped?"

"No, the other girl."

"You mean the girl that's dead?"

"Um-hmm."

"It wasn't me."

Williams backed off and tried another angle. He explained that he just wanted something solid from Tim so that he could absolutely clear him, get all of this over and done with.

Tim thought about the pregnant woman's claim that she hadn't been speeding and said he thought her Fuzzbuster was probably broken.

"This one works. We tested it out six different ways."

"Did you talk to her?" Tim was suddenly alert.

"I must have," Phil answered obliquely. "I'm telling you a lot of things, ain't I?"

Asked if he would take a polygraph, Tim Harris said he would. Knowing that Tim knew all the polygraphers in the area, Phil asked him to pick which one he would like to have administer his lie detector test. Tim hedged, and Phil eased off. Tim Harris had already given him permission to search his squad car; he didn't want to push him too hard too fast.

"Well, the only thing I want to know is . . . is when this investigation is over," Phil Williams said carefully. "I want to know whether you had any involvement or not and whether I'm looking at the right person or even should be looking at you at all. Okay?"

His tone of voice was easy, but his words were blunt enough.

"I'm not a murderer, Phil. I'm not out to kill

people. . . . I understand where you're coming from, but I'm not out there killing people."

"And things you're doing." Phil probed deeper. "Weird shit, okay?"

Tim thought Phil was referring to his peeking in the windows at Don and Susan's house. He said he had only wanted to see his children.

"Weird shit, too, is wearing women's pantyhose and women's underwear," Phil continued.

Tim blamed that on Sandy. All the kinky sex stuff had been Sandy's idea. Aware of how terrified Sandy had become, how she was afraid even in her own home, Phil Williams doubted that Sandy had been the instigator of all the erotica, the cross-dressing, and the bondage. He did not, however, say as much.

Phil did hit Tim with the discovery of the tape player in the attic insulation and repeated Tim's conversation with DeeLisa. Tim grew quiet. *That* surprised him; he hadn't known that Phil knew about the hidden recorder. And he surely didn't know that Williams had been recording every word of *their* current conversations from the beginning—that even now the tiny recorder secreted in Phil's armpit was rolling along.

They went round and round again. Whenever Phil Williams got too close to Lorraine Hendricks's murder Tim dug in his heels. "I didn't kill her. . . . I didn't stop her, and I didn't see her."

He recalled he had spent most of that Sunday "profiling"—looking for cars with black or Hispanic males, the types he had come to suspect as drug runners. One thing was sure: Tim said he certainly hadn't been out there looking for single women to stop.

Phil Williams regretted once again that he and

Larry Smetzer and Tony Oliver had come up with exactly zip in the way of physical evidence; they had found nothing at all connecting Tim Harris to Lorraine Hendricks. They had a gold hoop earring from the palmetto grove that Rick Hendricks had identified as Lorraine's, they had the tissue, fluid, and hair and fiber samples from the autopsy (all of which had proved useless as evidence), the vacuumings from the victim's car and the possessions she had left behind, and they had also searched Tim Harris's car—with his permission—Sandy and Tim Harris's house, Tim's brother David's house, and the patrol cars of every Florida trooper who worked the I-95 corridor.

And still they had nothing they could use for probable cause for an arrest.

Phil Williams took a chance and told Tim that they had found red fibers not unlike the fibers from the carpet in Tim's new Camaro in the black lace panties and pantyhose. The crime lab *had* found several red synthetic carpet fibers as well as several dog hairs in the pantyhose Tim wore to Sandy's house the night he terrorized her. But the red fibers really didn't match Tim's Camaro's carpet. Williams didn't tell Tim that. He was fishing, dangling some bait for Tim to jump at.

And jump he did. At that point Tim Harris suddenly remembered that he had gone through Sandy's drawers some weeks ago, taken many of her nightgowns and panties, and carried them away in his car. He didn't say why he'd done that, and Williams didn't ask him— because he didn't believe him. But his ploy had worked. Tim Harris admitted readily that he *had* worn the black panties. He said he had stolen Sandy's panties, and then he had worn them back. That would explain the red carpet fibers clinging to them.

Only they weren't the right red fibers.

Phil Williams had caught Tim Harris in a lie. The first lie. Williams turned the key in his ignition, and they pulled out onto I-95.

That was enough for this day. Let the mortar dry a bit in the wall they were building around Tim Harris.

Phil turned toward Tim, explaining in his most casual voice that he needed to clear Tim so he could get on with catching the real killer. "It's muddying up the waters as far as my investigation. . . . Like the underwear . . . I mean the things have obviously had a man in them. . . . It looks pretty doggone obvious to me that you were lying to me. Well, my question is, *Why would Tim lie to me?"*

They headed back toward Vero Beach in silence.

It was only a day later when Tim Harris called and left his phone number on Phil Williams's pager.

"Can you tell me what's going on?" Harris asked when Williams called him back.

"Just getting the polygraph set up. Looks like this afternoon at five. What time you get off?"

"About five o'clock." Harris's voice was more closed off than Williams had ever heard it.

"You mind doing that this afternoon?" Williams asked.

"I'd like to, and I told you I would," Tim said, and Phil Williams's heart sank; Harris was backing off. "Because you told me that, you know, in your mind that would help you," Tim finished in the same earnest voice that really meant "No way."

"Um-hmm."

"But I've talked to an attorney, and he suggested I don't—and not because I have anything to hide from anybody. He said, 'That's the first thing people are going to think is you're trying to hide something'. . . .

But he also said it [the polygraph] can screw you over and unfairly screw you over."

Phil Williams didn't argue with Tim Harris. "It's entirely up to you. . . . It's just a chance to prove yourself innocent before God and the world."

Tim assured Phil that he was trying to cooperate, but the lie detector thing—well, he wasn't sure how accurate it would be. He was as anxious as anybody could be to get away from pushing papers and to get back on the road, but he just wasn't sure what to do.

"Well, like I said, Tim," Williams said easily, "if you could take the polygraph and pass, then I think that everything would be alleviated. If you'd take it and fail, we're right back where we are now."

"We're *nowhere*. . . . I think for right now I just don't want to take it."

"Okay. Well, let me call everybody and call it off, then."

Tim Harris's decision not to take the polygraph was almost as damning in Phil Williams's mind as if he *had* taken it and failed.

But there was something else. Tim Harris's reactions were too flat, and they were all wrong. He wasn't angry. He wasn't outraged. He didn't sound one bit like an innocent man who was indignant at being called a suspect. He should have been mad as hell. But he wasn't.

Tim sounded only like a very nervous, hesitant man.

The next day Tim Harris called Phil Williams again and asked him to come down to the Patrol office. Odd; he had to know that Williams was walking one step behind him, and yet he clung to him like a drowning man. Tim said he was getting really worried about losing his job. Lt. Greg Edwards from the Patrol was coming up from headquarters to investigate his case further. Tim wanted Phil Williams to tell him that everything was okay. But he was passive-aggressive, too; he was angry that Phil had caught him on tape on the attic recorder.

"Tim, you told *me* a lot of things," Phil said. "You bullshitted *me*. Now, you don't think that I'm going to possibly be able to set you up for a homicide, do you? I mean, what am I going to do?"

"I don't see how you can," Tim acknowledged, "because I haven't done anything."

Phil Williams had seen men about to break before, and now, even over the phone, he could hear Tim Harris beginning to come apart. They were both cops. He had used that before to explain his stubborn pursuit of the truth to Tim, and he used it now.

"You know, as far as putting the tape player back up in the attic—yeah, I wanted to see if you would go back to it. No big deal. . . . It's just as typical a tactic as when you sit beside the road and run radar. People slip into your trap. . . . You're a cop, you know what the deal is. At some point you gotta go sit down and give an official statement. You were at least in the area that day."

"There's no doubt that I was," Tim agreed.

"I don't like telephone interviews," Phil said. "We've talked casually beside the road; we've never had a sit-down—"

They were about to have their "sit-down." Tim Harris said he was ready to give a statement in person. Keeping his voice as calm as possible, Phil Williams suggested they meet at the State Attorney's Office. Tim said he would check with his captain, and if it was all right with him, he would come in. He would be there shortly before noon.

It had taken many contacts to get Tim Harris to a

place where he would give an official statement. Williams called Rick McIlwain at the State Attorney's Office and told him it was about to happen. It had to happen. If Tim Harris didn't confess to strangling Lorraine Hendricks, there was every likelihood he was going to walk away. Without a confession they had nothing. Even *with* a confession conviction might not be a sure thing. It works on television, but in real life any prosecutor will choose hard physical evidence over a confession or an eyewitness.

There was always the gnawing possibility that ate at Phil Williams. Maybe Tim Harris wasn't guilty. Just because the guy treated the women in his life as if they were his property, as if their feelings were negligible, just because he liked to dress up in ladies' lingerie, just because he liked to take photos of his sex partners, just because he happened to be in the area of the murder at the time of the murder, just because he had stopped a pregnant woman and then let her go when he saw her condition—

There were an awful lot of "just becauses."

The circumstantial stuff was piling up. The search of Tim Harris's patrol car, his papers, and his possessions had revealed a man preoccupied with sex—a man with the power that his uniform and his position gave him over both the women he knew and the women he encountered out on the freeways.

Phil Williams and Tony Oliver had found the carbon copies of Tim Harris's tickets and seen where he had jotted down notes on the back of some of the thin yellow sheets: comments on female drivers' measurements, their breasts, their legs, their sexiness. And hidden among his possessions where he must never have expected anyone to find them Tim kept two cartoons. One looked as though it had been mimeographed to be passed around among good old boys and draw raucous chortles, the kind of dirty joke that junior high school boys circulated.

The other was drawn in pencil on a sheet of a yellow legal tablet, and it looked like it could well have been drawn by the same hand that drew cartoons for Tim's children—entirely different kinds of cartoons. Both of the drawings Tim Harris kept hidden involved a state trooper stopping a sports car with a pretty female driver. Both involved the woman's giving oral sex to the trooper, who stood grinning while the woman knelt and serviced him.

In the cartoon on the yellow tablet the dialogue in the balloons was personal. The naked woman kneeling at the state patrolman's feet asked, "Trooper Harris, are you sure I'm doing this right?"

The trooper, drawn wearing dark glasses, answers, "Yes. This is the new breathalyzer test."

If Tim Harris was not a murderer, Phil Williams thought he most assuredly had no business out there on the I-95 Interstate, sighting down on women as they turned a curve and came into his view. It wasn't that the average cop—himself included—didn't appreciate an attractive woman. But Tim Harris gave Williams a hinky feeling. Harris just plain didn't *like* women; he used them for his own purposes, and when one had finally had the guts to walk away from him, he became darkly obsessive about getting her back.

Sandy Harris had, Williams thought, come perilously close to death the night Tim sat astride her and held a gun close by her head. If she hadn't kept her head and lied that she would take him back, she might never have seen the next morning.

Alone with a woman, Tim would have been a formidable threat. He was such a big man to begin with. And then he had Shadow, who responded to his master's bidding without question. The power of Shadow's jaws was evident in Tim's patrol unit. When the Indian River investigators searched the car they saw where Shadow had literally "eaten" huge chunks out of the upholstery on the door panels. Maybe he had been bored at being left alone in the patrol car for a time; maybe he had been trying to chew his way through the door at some time to get to Tim.

19

Tim Harris arrived at the State Attorney's Office as he had promised. It was early in the afternoon of Friday, April 6th, four weeks almost to the minute from when Phil Williams had discovered Lorraine Hendricks's body. Phil now ushered Tim into a conference room. There was a long table there surrounded by seven white leather swivel chairs, and the walls were lined with bookcases full of law books. It was very quiet, an inner sanctum in a busy office.

Williams told Tim that Rick McIlwain from the State Attorney's Office might be joining them, and Harris didn't demur.

They began at an innocuous place. What hours had Tim worked on March 4th? Second watch. "Eight to four."

As Tim recalled, he was driving Unit 444, his regular canine unit. Shadow was with him. He started running traffic on I-95, moving his radar between the

Indian River County north border and State Road 60 to the south.

Harris mostly answered Williams's questions with one-syllable answers: "Yes." "No." "Okay."

Tim said he had seen no one walking on the median, no one parked. It had just been a slow, ordinary Sunday.

At this point the door opened, and Rick McIlwain walked in smiling, extending his hand. "Hey, there," he said.

"How ya doing?" Tim responded, shaking McIlwain's hand firmly.

It was still very low key. Phil introduced the two men and continued his questioning. McIlwain listened but said nothing.

Tim recalled that he had set up his stationary radar near the wooded median strip that Sunday. He guessed it would have been between 10 and 11 a.m. He recalled that one of his fellow troopers, Carlin Parker, had come by, and they had talked for twenty minutes to half an hour.

"The warning ticket," Williams said. "Was Carlin there before that ticket—or after it?"

"I believe he was there before."

Tim denied that he had ever gone down into the woods in the median. "Not that day. . . . I've gone through there many times. . . . I take the dog through there and break him out and let him run out, doing tracks, in and out of there."

Williams asked if Tim had been in a particularly bad mood that day—feeling even more depressed and angry than he usually did, considering how he felt about his impending divorce.

"I'm probably in my worst mood right now, because of what's going on right now."

"Was there anything going on that Sunday—other than the normal?"

"I was probably better off back then, because I was still talking to Sandy, and we were still trying to get things together—back and forth."

On that Sunday, March 4, Tim said he'd just been sitting there "profiling" drivers. He could see inside the cars coming at him enough to see how many people were inside, if they were black or white, male or female, if they had tinted glass in their windows. That sort of thing. He was using an NT8 stationary radar unit, not the newer VASCAR technique. No, he would not have had the capability with the NT8 to lock in the seventy miles per hour that he said Diane Lonergan had been traveling and show the reading to her.

Tim remembered her, the "pregnant chick," remembered thinking that she might have been a policeman's wife, or maybe knew a policeman—from the way she spoke. "She was talking about the dog."

"Was she afraid of the dog?"

"I don't think she was afraid. She took note of it, because he was beating up against the window . . . and barking."

After he had written the warning ticket for Diane Lonergan Tim Harris thought he'd remained with his radar set up on the shoulder at the median for another fifteen or twenty minutes. He'd heard on the radio that Carlin Parker had made an arrest and was headed toward the jail. (It was Carlin who had been given Tim's old serial number; that arrest was the one originally attributed to Tim—the mistake that had given him a solid alibi in the beginning of the investigation.)

Tim Harris said he had left the median strip area

and headed south toward St. Lucie. He hadn't eaten a real lunch, only picked up a Big Gulp and a candy bar at the Seven-Eleven on the way. The only ticket he had given that day was to a black male who was "hitting the high nineties. . . . It took a little bit to catch up with him," Tim recalled.

Tim said he had turned back north toward his brother David's house at the end of his shift. He slept there that night. He had the next two days off.

"Okay, Tim," Williams said. "Do you remember if you went into any rest areas down that way?"

"I've gone through the St. Lucie rest area—"

"Let's go back to whenever you was sleeping in there."

Tim Harris laughed. "I was in a Ram Charger—uh—the truck I used to own before I traded it in for the Camaro."

Williams skillfully wound the conversation back to the polygraph, and Tim said he just didn't want to take it. He had taken one eight years before when he applied for the Patrol, and it had shown he was being deceptive about a time he'd been stopped by a policeman. He'd been telling the truth; the polygrapher had his driving record right there in front of him, but oddly Tim's answer had come up that he was hiding something. He hadn't trusted the machines since.

They had been talking for almost an hour, and Williams began to bear down, but only a little. "Just give me—in your own words—why you don't want to take one."

"Somehow," Tim began, "I have to convince you that I'm not involved in this—"

"How you going to do that?" Rick McIlwain asked bluntly. He wasn't smiling.

"I don't know. You seem to think that my problems with Sandy or the things that stemmed from that are involved in this, and they're maybe partially involved, but they're not. I'm not out there killing people."

McIlwain questioned Tim about his law enforcement career. Gradually he had become the lead questioner in this session, asking an innocuous question, slipping in a more dangerous one, and then dropping back. He asked Tim about his experience in conducting investigations.

"You know what needs to be done. You know the things that need to be looked at. Okay?"

"I understand," Tim said.

"And here you have a homicide," McIlwain pushed ahead. "Okay—you have a woman that left Jacksonville and was coming south on I-95. We know that she was in this area around eleven—eleven-thirty. We know that would have been the approximate time when she'd been coming through on I-95. *You* know you were in this area at about the time she was coming through."

"That's correct."

"Okay. And you're a police officer. And you are a witness in this case—"

"*If* I saw something."

"You're still a witness. You know what a witness is. You know why we have witnesses, why we have people going into court. . . . You're a witness any way you look at it because you were in the area. You were working. You were running radar. You stopped somebody and gave them a warning within a time frame that would put you still right there even after you got done writing that ticket. And here's her car, sitting on a road, not a half mile south of where you saw this one woman southward bound. And here the woman's body is found back up in the area of the turnaround place. . . . You have a dog?"

"Yes, sir."

"What is your dog trained to do?"

"Narcotics—search for people."

"Okay. This lady was reported missing on Monday, the day after you finished your last day shift. The car was found sometime Monday, just south of where you were running radar. You have a dog. Did you ever take your dog back up to there? Did anyone notify you and say, 'Hey, Tim, some girl's come up missing after she left Cocoa. Monday, her car was found right here on 95 in our area'?"

Tim shook his head slowly. "No, I believe I ran into Phil that week—Wednesday, or it might have been Thursday. . . . He was walking up and down the interstate—"

"It was Friday," Phil said quietly.

Tim insisted that no one had ever told him about the missing woman. He had found out about it only after reading something in the paper. The investigation hadn't been his responsibility, and he had paid little attention to it.

For all the hours they had talked Phil Williams had let Tim see him as a buddy, a commiserater about the woes women can bring, a fellow cop. McIlwain's questioning style was entirely different. He was jabbing hard at Tim, incredulous that a working trooper, a K-9 and felony officer, would not have been aware and very interested and involved in the search for a missing woman smack dab in the middle of his regular territory.

Tim stonewalled. "You're asking me about something that I don't know anything about."

"Hey," McIlwain said. "I'm just asking—"

"Killing someone's not normal," Tim said flatly.

"True . . . it's definitely not normal." McIlwain paused for a moment. "To *think* about committing a crime is not a crime, is it?"

"But who's thinking about committing one?" Tim countered.

"You *never* thought about committing a crime?"

"No, I haven't."

"Never have? Nothing's ever gone through your mind—you never picked up the paper and read about how somebody turned around and committed a bank robbery, or committed some kind of crime, and they got caught for it . . . and you thought, 'No, *damn*, if I was going to do something like that, I wouldn't have done it that way. I'd'a turned around and done it some other way.' You never thought about anything like that? Most normal people do."

"I must not be normal, then," Tim said mildly.

There was no time in this room, cosseted and isolated by the thick barrier of law books along its walls. The three men sat there, conversing in a deceptively mild way, as if two were not hunters and one was not their quarry. No bead of sweat marked Tim Harris's forehead; he stretched his long legs out comfortably on the carpeted floor. To a casual observer they might only have been three lawmen having a friendly conversation. And yet Rick McIlwain's questions were narrowing more and more into one channel, the channel that led straight back to the murder of Lorraine Hendricks.

Tim reminded Rick McIlwain and Phil Williams that he had been cooperative with all their requests for searches. "I've done everything that you asked me to do . . . short of finding the person who killed her."

Phil Williams recalled that Tim had refused the lie box.

Phil posed a question to Tim that only a cop would understand. "If you found narcotics in a vehicle, and there's somebody in the backseat . . . does that person know there's narcotics in the front seat?"

The question gave Tim Harris a chance to admit he was peripherally involved in Lorraine Hendricks's murder, but not the man they were looking for.

"Maybe," Tim Harris said inscrutably.

He showed no distress, no tension, but he was getting a little annoyed. Tim insisted they were focusing on him only because of the battery charges Sandy had filed against him and all the other marital troubles he had been going through. "I'm not the only one going through a divorce right now."

Tim wanted to know if he was still a "witness," or had he become a "suspect"?

He was still a witness, they assured him, but he clearly didn't believe them. He reminded them that he had come in against his attorney's advice—because "I don't have anything to hide from you."

On and on they talked in circles, widening circles and then tight, cautious circles, but they always came back to the black underwear Tim insisted was Sandy's, and the fact that Tim had been working I-95 when someone took Lorraine out of her car and that he *should* have seen something.

Tim Harris continued to blame his wife for all of his problems. Sandy, he said, knew full well that the black lace panties were her own. It was *Sandy* who should be put on the polygraph, not him.

But it was *Tim* that Rick McIlwain and Phil Williams wanted to hook up to the polygraph; his growing resistance to it fascinated them. They used that resistance to nudge him off his stolid position of both innocence and ignorance concerning Lorraine Hendricks's murder.

"So people that take them [polygraphs] are automatically guilty . . . that's what you're assuming right now," Tim challenged McIlwain.

"I'm not assuming anything," McIlwain said tight-ly. "If you assume something, what do you do, buddy? You make an ass out of you and me. A-S-S-U-M-E . . . I'm just saying I've done cops and cops. Cops are nothing. Cops are some of the best people in the world because they know the difference between right and wrong, and when they come in there and they haven't done it there's not a damn thing for them to worry about. They could give a shit less, you know. 'Ask me what you want.'"

Phil Williams pointed out once again that the first thing a guilty man always said was "I didn't do it."

"I know you're a cop, but just in this particular incident, just you saying 'I didn't do it' does not eliminate you."

"How long are you going to keep thinking that I did?" Tim asked.

"Until you prove you didn't."

It had been more than two hours, and they had reached a kind of impasse. Rick McIlwain cleared his throat and suggested another scenario to the tall trooper in front of him. "Is there a chance you stopped her, and you let her go, and you either gave her a verbal warning or something of that nature? And you're concerned now because she was found dead, and here you're saying, 'My God . . . I stopped this woman, and I let the woman go . . . and I didn't write nothing out, and if I turn around and tell them, "Yeah, I stopped her," I'm screwed?'"

"I've never stopped that lady before."

"Do you still take your dog up there [the median crime scene] to run?"

"Not anymore, I don't."

"Why?"

"Because of the crime scene."

"It's over now," McIlwain said.

"It's not over with until you find somebody."

Tim Harris was far from stupid. He detected that the climate in the room had changed. McIlwain was at his throat, and he wasn't about to back off. Phil was still more understanding, but Phil was pressing him, too, wanting more, more, *more* proof.

Tim was puzzled, though, that Phil hadn't already arrested him for wiretapping in Sandy's attic. Phil could have thrown him in jail for that, and investigated Lorraine Hendricks's murder at his leisure.

Tim asked Phil why he hadn't arrested him for tapping Sandy's phone.

"What's your feelings on that?" Phil asked.

"I assumed you had stopped it [an arrest] because you didn't want me to be put in jail."

Williams nodded. "I don't like to see cops go down. But neither do I like having the suspicion on my mind that a cop killed someone either."

"How do you think I feel walking around that station," Tim countered, "knowing that people think something?"

When the questions got too pointed, when he must have begun to panic inside—although he never betrayed it externally—Tim Harris's stance was always to suggest the investigators go to Sandy. Sandy would explain that the panties were hers. They could not know how true to form he was. He had *always* run to Sandy for comfort and shelter and for someone to clean up the messes he had made in his life. She had been only sixteen when he met her, and now she was twenty-seven and he was thirty-two. Sandy had always been able to smooth things over before; she had always forgiven him or borrowed more money or bought him the newest "toy" he needed to make his life happy. She had been his buffer against the world.

And now Sandy was gone from him. He had thrown

her away a number of times. This time she was not coming back. He didn't seem to know that, as he continually turned the conversation that had long since become an interrogation back to Sandy. "And I think if you talk to Sandy, and really let her know what's going on—" Tim said earnestly.

Successful interrogations are by their very nature lengthy, repetitive, and circuitous. This one certainly was. Phil Williams wondered why Tim didn't just get up and leave. Nobody was stopping him. From time to time Phil offered him a cold drink. When Tim accepted, Phil went to get the soda and took the opportunity to change the tape in his hidden recorder. He had used up three hours' worth now, and Harris was making no move to leave. Williams couldn't figure out if it was because Tim believed he was snowing them completely or because he had some subconscious need to tell them, to get the crime out of his head where it had to have been eating at him like acid for more than a month.

The calls that Tim had made to Sandy had all been taped, and he hadn't made one slip—nothing that would tie him to Lorraine Hendricks's murder. There was still always the chance that the guy was innocent —that he just happened to be a womanizer, a wife batterer, and a guy who liked to wear lady's underwear. He wouldn't be the first.

A small chance.

Tim asked how much longer they wanted to talk with him.

"Until you say 'I got to go,'" Williams answered.

"Are we going to beat a dead horse?"

Again they told him he was free to go at any time.

Tim Harris made no move to leave. He wanted something from them. He wanted them to tell him he was no longer a suspect. He wanted to go back out on the road, to have everyone forget he had ever been a suspect in a murder.

And that was something neither McIlwain nor Williams would give him. He had danced around every important question they had asked him. In three hours they had made only minuscule advances.

And yet there was a growing tension in the room. Rick McIlwain had become far more accusing and sarcastic.

"You're the good guy," Tim said suddenly, looking at Phil Williams, "and you're the bad guy," to McIlwain. It was an age-old interrogation technique. Mutt and Jeff. Good guy, bad guy.

"No, no," McIlwain disagreed. "We're not doing good guy, bad guy shit. . . . I've listened to you and listened to you and listened to you, and he's been as nice and polite as can be, and I'm a little edgy on it because I don't really know. He knows you better than I do."

Rick McIlwain and Phil Williams were closer than they realized to a break. Suddenly there was a subtle change in Tim Harris's answers, as if he was daring them to make something of the bits and pieces he revealed.

"If you got a problem, I think you better get it off your chest," McIlwain began again.

"Problem such as what?"

"Such as killing the woman."

"I told you I didn't kill her."

"Did you *stop* her?" Phillips shot out.

"What if I did? Would you think different?"

"Would that help us out?" McIlwain asked. "Yeah, it would—that would at least tell us she was in the area—"

"Suppose I had sex with her." Tim Harris said. "Would it make a difference?"

They were on the edge of something. The two interrogators scarcely breathed, but their faces betrayed nothing.

"What if you did?" Phil asked.

"Would it make a difference?"

"You got a bush bond, it would at least show what kind of lady she is," McIlwain said quietly.

"I know this girl's character, Tim," Phil Williams cut in. "One of the first things I do is character-line this person. . . . Her mother and father paint her as a nice little girl. . . ."

"Sandy's mom paints her as a nice little girl, too," Tim said bitterly.

Williams eased Tim Harris into what he sensed was coming next. He knew he could not betray even a trace of revulsion at whatever he was about to hear. If he exhibited a judgmental attitude, he would shut Harris down.

"What kind of situation was it?" McIlwain asked.

Tim began by talking in a roundabout way. They let him.

"Maybe it was perfectly normal—maybe not department policy, but maybe it was normal," Tim mused. "You leave. You think that maybe she leaves. . . . How do you think I'd feel if something like that happened and she ended up dead? Don't you think I'd feel guilty that I had a part in it?"

"Sure do," Phil said calmly. "And I think that would cause you to be worried on a polygraph."

Tim was ultimately concerned about being "normal." He had mentioned it many times over the past hours. It was a trait both McIlwain and Williams had seen before in murderers and sex offenders. No matter

ANN RULE

how heinous the crime, they didn't want to be seen as "abnormal" or "crazy."

Tim continued, almost talking to himself. "Having sex with someone that's a consenting person that is not resisting you. It's not against the law. Maybe it's not morally right—but killing somebody is. . . . I'm telling you I *didn't* kill her."

"What *did* you do?" McIlwain asked.

"I'll leave it at that."

Tim Harris had led his questioners to the edge of a precipice and then backed off. They could not, would not, drop it at this point, no matter how hard Harris dug his heels in. They were afraid he was going to leave, but he sat without moving a muscle.

"Come on, Tim." Williams urged.

"You're looking for a murderer, someone that's killed somebody. I'm not the one that did it."

"Did you stop the girl?" McIlwain pressed. "Did you have a conversation with her? Did you have a bush bond with her and let her go on down into St. Lucie County? What did you do?"

"There were bikers in that area," Tim said. "I didn't kill her. . . . I'm telling you I didn't kill her. I didn't have anything to do with that."

"Do you know who did?"

"No, I don't."

"What *do* you know?" McIlwain asked.

"Where was she when you last saw her?" Williams said.

The room crackled with tension. They were on the brink. Each of them felt it. The questions and the answers now came after agonizingly long pauses, as if each of them was feeling his way along that precipice, aware that one misstep would tumble the whole thing down. The very air in the room seemed thicker somehow. Phil Williams stole a sideways glance at

Tim and noted that his forehead was free of perspiration. He watched a bead of moisture slide down Tim's empty Coke can and waited for the answer that he knew would be the key, the way in they had been looking for for weeks.

"If I talk to you about it," Tim finally said, "you're going to think I did it."

Rick McIlwain kept his voice as emotionless as he could. "Not necessarily."

Phil Williams was blunt. "I'm thinking that now, Tim."

"I know you are." For the first time Tim—who rarely looked anyone straight in the eye—was staring directly into Williams's eyes so intensely that his gaze almost burned.

"You want to tell me something?" Williams asked.

Tim Harris's answers were convoluted. "I guess people try to tell somebody something when they feel responsible for it indirectly—not actually did it."

"*How* do you feel responsible 'indirectly'?" McIlwain asked.

"I'm telling you I didn't kill her, though."

Phil Williams glanced at his watch. *Damn.* He knew his tape was just about to run out. It was the worst of all possible times to have to break the mood in the room, but if Tim was about to confess to some culpability in Lorraine Hendricks's murder, Phil wanted it on tape. They had come a long way in the four and a half hours they had spent in this room. In the beginning Tim had not even admitted to any knowledge of the case. Now he had as much as conceded he knew what had happened.

Williams signaled to McIlwain. If Tim thought it peculiar that they were pausing at this point to freshen their Cokes, he gave no sign. Phil Williams left the room, removed Tape 7, and inserted Tape 8, side A. Then he grabbed a couple of soft drinks and walked back into the conference room.

They had to backtrack from where they had been until they had once again reached the point where Tim would talk about Lorraine Hendricks. They still had not the vaguest notion of a motive for Tim Harris, whose job as a Florida Trooper was his *life,* to kill a woman driving down his sector of the Interstate. They *did* know that Tim was totally obsessed with winning back Sandy, and that he harbored tremendous rage because she no longer wanted him.

Were the two parts of his life so entangled and obsessive that they had ignited murderous fury?

Rick McIlwain mused on what might have happened, giving Tim Harris a chance to add or change details. "It could have been an accident. Maybe somebody stops to park, she's on the side of the road—somebody else came up on her. They're talking. Maybe she said something that pissed them off—"

"What would she have said to somebody to piss them off?" Tim asked.

"I don't know . . . your wife ever piss you off?"

"Many times."

"You ever hit her?"

"No."

"Struggle with her?"

"I've struggled with her."

"You ever slap her around?"

Tim would not acknowledge slapping Sandy. He had held on to her arms, her shoulders. Yes, he had put his hands around Sandy's neck, put bruises on her. "But that doesn't make me a killer."

McIlwain switched to Lorraine Hendricks. Was it possible that a cop had stopped her and she told him

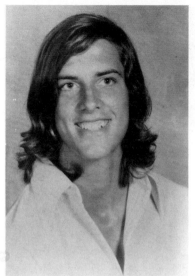

Tim as a handsome young student at Satellite High School in the mid-1970s. He was a track star, and he yearned to become a policeman.

Tim as a young Sebastian, Florida, cop in 1979. This is how he looked when he stopped Sandy Wessendorf's car and gave her an intriguing "ticket." She was 16 and he was 21.

Sandy and Tim at their wedding reception, July 25, 1981. Yellow rosebuds and daisies and piña coladas and great hope for a wonderful life together.

Sandy early in her marriage. Tim said he hated her long hair, but his mistress's hair was the same. Sandy had no idea he *had* a mistress.

Shadow, Tim's attack dog, adored his master/
trainer, and he was a loving family pet around the
Harris home. But if anyone had threatened Tim,
Shadow would have torn him to pieces.

The house that Tim built with his own hands in Citrus
Hideaway. Shadow's pen was in the back of the house. After
Sandy asked Tim to move out, he would sneak back in at night
by standing on Shadow's fence and then crawling up onto the
lower roof.

Sandy in 1993. She smiled for the camera, but she was desperately trying to pick up the shattered pieces of her life.

Tim sent this expensive angel doll to Sandy for Christmas, 1992, while he was in prison. The doll had a single "tear" seeping from her right eye. Tim sent nothing for his children that Christmas. He has never been able to set Sandy free of his possessive love.

Lorraine, 21, when she was selected "Miss Stamford" in the mid-1960s. "Lori" could have done almost anything for her talent segment, but she played the drums, giving a history of the instrument from Africa to rock 'n' roll.

In 1972 the young model posed for a safety campaign picture, sponsored by the Florida Highway Patrol and the Governor's Highway Safety Commission. The "Arrive Alive" plates, available to the public, were a sadly ironic commentary on what would happen to Lori two decades later.

Lorraine, at 33, in a 10-K marathon. She began running marathons to strengthen a knee she had injured while skiing in Switzerland. She would often carry her baby girl, Katherine, across the finish line.

Lorraine, Rick and toddler Katherine in happier days. Lorraine had longed for a good marriage and a baby. Even so, she and Rick parted as friends, and shared their love for Katherine.

Lorraine, around 40. This photo appeared in papers all over Florida after she vanished in March, 1990. Several people called sheriff's detectives to report having seen her. Tragically, they were mistaken.

The palmetto and pine woods that flourished on the median between north- and south-bound lanes of Interstate 95. Detective Phil Williams made a terrible discovery here on March 9, 1990.

Phil Williams came across this drawing and a similar cartoon among the trooper's possessions when he carried out a search warrant.

Florida Highway Patrolman Tim Harris, October, 1984. The years had changed the lean young trooper into a somewhat jowly but powerfully muscled man. He was highly regarded for his successful campaign against speeders and drug-runners on I-95. But underneath his professional exterior, Tim had bizarre fantasies.

The investigative team responsible for Tim's arrest. From left: Larry Smetzer, Tony Oliver, Rick McIlwain, Margy Hogan, Phil Williams and Bruce Colton.

Indian River County Detective Phil Williams in 1993. He now heads the sheriff's Internal Affairs Unit and administers lie-detector examinations.

BLACK CHRISTMAS

Derek Goldmark (left), 12, and Colin, 10. They were fatally injured on Christmas Eve, 1985, at the hands of a man who stalked the wrong family for the wrong reasons.

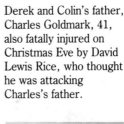

Derek and Colin's father, Charles Goldmark, 41, also fatally injured on Christmas Eve by David Lewis Rice, who thought he was attacking Charles's father.

David Lewis Rice, 27, stalked the Charles Goldmark family, believing he was wiping out communists. He had the wrong generation and the wrong information.

ONE TRICK PONY

Donna Bennett, around 1950, a few years before she met her future husband, Noyes "Russ" Howard. Her sister felt they had little in common, but Russ's charisma caught Donna, and she forgot her dreams of marrying a cowboy. She married him, knowing she was taking a chance on love. (Bobbi Bennett)

The Bennett sisters in the early 1950s. They were as close as sisters could be. Donna is on the left, and Bobbi is on the right. (Bobbi Bennett)

ONE TRICK PONY

This is how Russ Howard said he had found Donna after he'd returned from town with warm doughnuts and a new mailbox. Note the "paintbrush" swipes of blood just above her left elbow. Lt. Rod Englert, nationally renowned blood-spatter expert, said these were made as someone repositioned Donna's body, not by medium-velocity blood spatter from a horse-kick wound. Donna's shirt and jeans are pulled up as if she had been dragged by her boots.

Noyes "Russ" Howard on trial in 1986 for the murder of his wife, Donna, a dozen years after her death. The years since Russ met Donna are etched on his face.

Washington State Senior Assistant Attorney General Greg Canova, who successfully prosecuted Russ Howard for the murder of Donna Howard.

Bob Keppel, investigator for the Washington State Attorney General's Office, who would not quit until he uncovered what *really* happened to Donna Howard.

THE COMPUTER ERROR AND THE KILLER

Vonnie Stuth as a teenager.

Vonnie and her mother, Lola Linstad, on Vonnie's wedding day in May, 1974. Although Lola could not save her own daughter, she went on to co-found "Families and Friends of Victims of Violent Crimes and Missing Persons" to help other families.

THE COMPUTER ERROR AND THE KILLER

When Vonnie was a little girl, shown here holding her dog and with her sisters, Gary Addison Taylor was already roving the Detroit area searching out women to rape and bludgeon.

Gary Addison Taylor, convicted killer of Vonnie Stuth, confessed to the murders of a number of other females from Michigan to Texas. In the early 1970s he was supposed to be reporting, for counseling and medication, to a Michigan clinic for criminally insane felons. Through a tragic oversight he was never listed as a parole violator. He was free to roam America because the "wanted" information on him was not entered into law enforcement computers until it was far too late for Vonnie and his other victims.

THE VANISHING

On July 9, 1979, Stacy Sparks vanished from the I-5 freeway north of Seattle. The answer to what happened to her didn't come until September 14, 1981, and the truth was the one possibility no one had considered.

Detectives in Washington State circulated this picture of a Plymouth Arrow, a car just like the one Stacy had last been seen driving. Her car wasn't found until she herself was found.

Jackie and Bill Brand. He pursued her for years, but when he won her for himself he still wasn't happy.

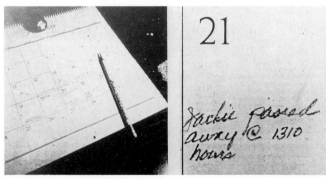

Bill Brand was nothing if not precise. He noted the minute of Jackie's death in military time.

she couldn't take another ticket, and that she had offered a bribe? "I'll give you a little piece if you let me off this one"?

"I've had it done before," Tim said cautiously.

"Have you ever taken them up on it? . . . *What* have you done to them?"

"Sent them on down the road with their ticket in their hand," Tim answered.

Rick McIlwain tried another tack. He told Tim Harris that he was almost beginning to believe that Tim had not killed Lorraine. "We're looking at a murder, and maybe it's not even a damn murder."

"It's a murder," Tim said firmly. "I can guarantee you that."

Why would he have said that? Williams turned to stare at Tim in amazement. Rick had given him a window to escape, and he hadn't taken it.

But it was hard to make sense of what Tim Harris was saying. Over and over he continued to insist that *he* had not killed Lorraine Hendricks, but he hinted that he knew more.

"I've known you for a long time, Tim," Phil Williams said. "I don't think you have the potential for killing somebody—"

"I didn't." (Odd tense. Not "I don't," but *"I didn't."*)

"But I do think," Williams continued, "you do have the potential for getting bush bonds. What cop doesn't?"

"The thing is," Tim said slowly, "if it went down that way and I walked away and she was still alive, and now she's dead."

Tim Harris was telling them that he had had sex with Lorraine Hendricks and that someone else must have killed her. They played along, throwing out possibilities. Tim Harris was ready to open up.

Whether he was willing to tell them everything was another matter.

"People have gone to jail for less things," Harris said. "I can sit here and tell you that I stopped her, and we had a conversation. She's going through a divorce, I'm going through a divorce. Things hit off real well, and we ended up in the median strip, no force involved . . . and I leave . . . and she ended up dead. Why do you think I feel the way I feel? I'm involved with some girl—I don't know her."

Again they asked him if he would take a polygraph test—just on what he had told them.

No.

Tim Harris had said he had seen no one else around the victim's car, nobody hitchhiking, no white van.

Again and again McIlwain hit on the theory that Tim was only a witness, not a suspect. A "witness" shouldn't be so leery of a polygraph.

But Tim Harris was. He was inflexible on that. No lie detector test. And no written statements with his signature on the bottom.

"Tim," Phil said, "if I was you, if I was you, I'd follow this thing through and let us go ahead and see who *did* kill her."

"You telling me *I* didn't?"

"I believe you," Williams said. "Okay?"

Rick McIlwain eased back in his chair; he had done his job. Now he would let Phil Williams build on the rapport he had established with Tim Harris.

"I might have stopped her, and I might have seen her, and I might have talked to her," Harris began tentatively.

"I know you talked to her. . . . What kind of girl was she?"

"She was a nice girl."

"Did you look at her picture?" Phil asked.

"She's a lot younger—a lot younger; she didn't look her age."

"Did she tell you she could speak Spanish and all those languages?"

"No. She had a little girl, Phil. How could I kill someone that's got a little girl?"

"She tell you she could not afford another ticket?"

"She wasn't stopped for speeding."

"Why then?"

"She was wearing headphones."

Bingo! No one but the investigative team knew that Lorraine Hendricks routinely listened to music through headphones while she drove. No one else knew they had found her headphones in her car. That information had never been published in any paper.

No murder victim ever gets to tell her—or his—side of the story. Only physical evidence, prior reputation, and holes in a suspect's story can speak for them. Now Tim Harris, whose disdain for women was legendary, told Rick McIlwain and Phil Williams that Lorraine Hendricks had been so starved for sex that she had offered to have both intercourse and oral sex with him, "because she hadn't had any for a while because of her divorce."

Tim Harris's version of his meeting with Lorraine seemed like nothing so much as those letters college boys write to *Playboy* and *Penthouse*. "I stopped her for the headphones, figured it would be an easy warning."

"Did she agree to go down there where you were?"

"She did. She was in a hurry, though." Harris explained that the woman had been headed toward Fort Lauderdale to see her little girl. "She had a time frame. She said she had to be down in Fort Lauderdale, I believe by six. She knew about my divorce. I talked to her about it. She was going through what she had done as far as her divorce—talking about the kids. I hate to say it, but I think she felt sorry for me."

"She was a compassionate person," Williams offered.

"Beg your pardon?"

"She was a compassionate person?"

"She seemed to be."

Lorraine had, Harris said, been interested in Shadow and asked about him. I'll bet she did, Williams thought. Shadow, with his fangs bared as they always were when someone approached Tim, was as scary an animal as he had ever seen.

"Where did the sex occur—in your car or her car?"

"In the palmettos." They had both backed their cars in there, behind a tree.

Harris described Lorraine Hendricks's clothing as long pants, a red outfit, a shirt—"some kind of university type—and loafer-type shoes."

Phil Williams held out a drawing of the turnaround and asked Tim to point out where he had had sex with Lorraine Hendricks.

"When you left, which way did you go?"

"I came out toward the west and then went south, and I assumed she was right behind me."

Phil held out an 8 x 10 photograph he had taken of the median and the Interstate. "Did you ever see her pull down into this area here, turn around or anything? . . . Did you ever look in your rearview mirror to see if she was coming out?"

"There were other cars coming. I just assumed she was right behind me—"

"Any possibility she could have gotten stuck?"

"She was worried about going across the median strip the first time when we crossed, and I told her to follow me."

At the very least, Trooper Tim Harris had been no

gentleman. If his story of consensual sex was true—which Williams doubted—Tim had not paused to see that Lorraine was safely out of the woods and the median strip and headed south before he cleared out.

Tim said he had no idea why Lorraine's driver's license and registration were missing. He had given them back to her right after he glanced at them.

"What kind of panties was she wearing?" Williams asked.

"Cotton . . . they weren't fancy ones, nothing sexy or anything."

Asked about what had happened to Lorraine's warning ticket, Tim said he had thrown all copies away—the white original, the driver's pink copy, and the yellow carbon copy. He insisted he hadn't done it to keep from being connected to her; she already knew his name from his nameplate. They had even discussed seeing each other when she returned from Fort Lauderdale.

Phil Williams and Rick McIlwain asked Tim a dozen times if he felt comfortable about taking a polygraph now that he had gotten the "truth" out.

He did not.

Rick McIlwain held the pictures of how Lorraine Hendricks had looked when she was found five days after she died. Both he and Williams noted how violently opposed Tim Harris was to looking at them. He had been a trooper for eight years, he had worked horrible fatal accidents and seen things that would make normal men vomit and pass out.

But he turned his head firmly away from the photographs.

"I've got to live with it for the rest of my life, knowing that I've done something with this girl, and now she's dead. Maybe I could have prevented that if maybe I'd stayed there and waited, or turned around and gone back and maybe seen if she really did get out of there. I could just imagine what that picture looks like that you want to show me, and I don't want to see it."

"These pictures are the result of what happened."

"I'm fixing to walk out this door in about two seconds," Tim threatened.

He would not look at the photographs in McIlwain's hand. He was as agitated as he had been in the entire five hours they had been closeted in this room together.

"That's the result of what happened when she died," McIlwain began.

Tim Harris was on his feet, knocking the white leather chair back, and in two strides he was out of the room. The door banged behind him.

Rick McIlwain turned to Phil Williams. "I say he doesn't want to see those pictures. . . . He's got a guilty conscience because of what happened."

Phil Williams nodded, pulled out his tape recorder, and turned it off. He had five hours of interrogation on the fragile brown ribbons of tape, five hours that chronicled a masterful police interrogation. The man who had just bolted from the room had begun the session intending to tell them nothing, and he had ended on the verge of a complete confession.

They were so close now.

20

Rick McIlwain and Phil Williams knew that they could not let Tim Harris cool off overnight. They still had too many unanswered questions. It just didn't make sense that Lorraine Hendricks's gray Honda should end up back on the shoulder of I-95 in the exact spot where Tim Harris said he had pulled her over. They didn't believe that she had ever driven it down into the wooded median. They suspected she had been taken down there under some kind of duress—whether Tim Harris had used his dog to frighten her into submission or his gun (as he had with Sandy two weeks after Lorraine's murder), or simply the authority his position and uniform gave him.

They gave Tim thirty minutes. They were sure he would head for DeeLisa's house. As much as he seemed to despise women, he always went to them for comfort, and they knew Sandy wasn't about to let him in. DeeLisa was standing by him, figuratively and literally holding his hand.

They were right. Tim was at DeeLisa's, and they asked him if he was ready to continue the interview he had left so precipitously. No, he didn't want to. "I'd rather not talk to you anymore right now," Harris said.

There was nothing they could do. They couldn't force him to talk. The guy was about ready to blow and spill everything. They knew it, but they couldn't hurry it, and they couldn't make it happen.

If there was one person Tim Harris respected, it was his captain, Dean Sullivan. Sullivan was advised of the situation and said he would be willing to speak with Tim if he came back in. He would do the best he could for his trooper. If Tim was guilty of murder, he would have to continue talking to the investigators. If he was innocent, he needed to cooperate with them to clear himself.

An hour and a half after their first visit to DeeLisa Davis's house Williams and McIlwain returned. DeeLisa had just come back from Gainesville, where her young son had had surgery earlier in the day. She probably had not had a worse day in a decade. She looked exhausted and apprehensive. She greeted Phil Williams, her old classmate, and apprehensively agreed to get Tim.

"Tim," Phil said, "you need to come on back down there and finish talking with us."

Not surprisingly, Tim didn't want to go. He changed his mind when he learned that Captain Sullivan had come in to talk with him and was waiting.

"Are you going to let me come home after I talk to you?" Tim asked.

"You take your car up there. It still stands the same way. You want to leave, you leave," McIlwain said.

But Tim Harris knew. Even as he headed back down to the State Attorney's Office he took DeeLisa with him. If he could not drive his car home, if he should be arrested, she could drive it home for him. And Tim wanted DeeLisa with him when he spoke to his captain. The trio remained behind closed doors for half an hour or more.

When they emerged it was obvious that this was a

different Tim Harris. The proud stance of the trooper was gone, and he seemed utterly deflated. He was ready, finally, to talk in detail about Sunday, March 4. He had only one request. He wanted someone to send for Sandy.

He needed Sandy.

DeeLisa's face was a sad mask. She obviously loved Tim Harris, no matter what he had done, no matter that he had humiliated her once again—this time in front of a room full of detectives and state attorneys. No one watching doubted that she would have held Tim's hand all through his upcoming session with State Attorney Bruce Colton if Tim needed her.

Bruce Colton was in charge of the State Attorney's Office in Florida's 19th Judicial District; that included Martin, St. Lucie, Okeechobee, and Indian River Counties. Tim had made it clear he no longer wanted to talk with Phil Williams and Rick McIlwain. They had winnowed the truth from his protestations of innocence, and he was sick of the sight of their faces and the sound of their voices.

Besides, Tim wanted somebody as high up on the state judicial ladder as he could get. If he gave a full confession to someone as powerful as Bruce Colton, Tim Harris obviously harbored the hope that he might make a deal.

Colton had agreed to come in to take an official statement from Tim.

When the door had closed behind Tim and Colton, Phil Williams asked DeeLisa what Tim had told her, and she said she had asked Tim if Lorraine's death had been an accident. "And he said 'no.' I asked him if he had done it, and he said it wasn't the Tim Harris I knew who did it—not Tim Harris, the trooper. . . ."

* * *

Phil Williams had alerted Don Dappen earlier that evening that something big was probably going to come down. Don knew they were grilling Tim. "I think Sandy half believed that Tim was guilty in Lorraine Hendricks's murder," Dappen recalls. "But she didn't *want* to believe it was true. Phil called up and said he had a favor to ask of me. He said that Tim had agreed to tell everything that had happened—but he wanted to talk to Sandy first. Just one more time."

Dappen groaned when he heard that. He figured Tim Harris wanted to leave something with Sandy, some horror that she would never forget—or some guilt she would carry for the rest of her life. But he promised Williams that he would talk to Sandy and call back. She might not be willing to come in; she had been through so much already.

Don Dappen talked to Sandy, explaining that he felt Tim was going to pull something—that he would not let her walk away without feeling that somehow she shared his guilt. "It's up to you if you want to go down or not."

Sandy said nothing for a long time, and then she looked up. "I'll go."

Dappen called Phil Williams and told him that he and Sandy would be there in about fifteen minutes.

It was April 7, very early now on Saturday morning, but it was still warm. Even so, Sandy's arms were covered with goose bumps. As much as she had tried to prepare herself for what she had feared would come, she was not ready. There was no way she would ever be ready.

Tim sat alone now in Bruce Colton's office, facing the state attorney. It was smaller than the conference room where Tim had spent the whole afternoon with

Phil and Rick. There was only Colton's desk with a phone, a jug of sharpened pencils, a Scotch tape dispenser, and two pictures of the state attorney's family. There was a typewriter and a little table with a lamp whose base looked like a globe. Incongruously, two stuffed animals—a tiger and a white Scottie dog—sat beside the lamp. There were no pictures on the wall, nothing for Tim Harris to look at except Bruce Colton's eyes.

As Bruce Colton entered the room Phil Williams shoved a microrecorder into Colton's suit jacket.

Tim sat in one of the two black leather chairs in front of the desk, his head down.

"Phil called," Colton began, "and Sandy's coming. Okay? He hasn't explained a whole lot to her, just that you're here and you want to talk to her."

"Can I talk to her?"

"If that's what you wanted me to do."

"I appreciate it."

Before they even touched on the subject that lay between them like a sleeping lion, before they roused all the ugliness and tragedy that had to be in Tim Harris's brain, Colton made it impeccably clear that he could promise Tim nothing at all. "I don't even want you to tell me anything because you're thinking that 'Sure he's telling me he can't promise me this— but I know if I tell him, that he will do this or that for me.'"

"I know what your job is," Tim said. "I know what you're expected to do."

Tim had been asked again if he wanted Phil or Rick or Captain Sullivan in the room while he gave his statement to Colton, and he shook his head when Colton asked him again.

"I don't want them."

"All right."

"They treated me right. I don't have any hard feelings toward them."

It was time.

None of the detectives, none of the state attorney's men, had been able to understand *why* this heretofore "perfect" state trooper had turned killer, although they all believed that he had. He had had everything a man could want, and he had systematically thrown it all away. Hell, a lot of cops—a lot of *men,* period— had tossed out perfectly good marriages when they went out chasing women. That part wasn't hard to figure out. But until now the investigators had no motive at all for Lorraine Hendricks's murder.

They knew Tim had stopped Lorraine for wearing headphones while she was driving. Only her killer would have known about the headphones. They had heard Tim's story that she offered him sex in exchange for tearing up her ticket, that she had willingly turned her car off a busy freeway into the green darkness of the pine and palmetto grove in the median. They had listened and avoided commenting or arguing with him about that—no matter their strong belief that it had not happened that way at all.

Tim had finally made some oblique reference to *why* he committed murder in his preliminary conversation with Bruce Colton. He had mentioned how much Lorraine had resembled Sandy.

Bruce Colton began his formal questioning at that point. "Did you tell her that she reminded you of Sandy?"

"I think I *called* her Sandy several times."

"Did she seem puzzled by that?"

"Yes."

"Did there ever get to be a point where it appeared to you that she was afraid of you?"

"Yes."

"Was that before you had sex?"

"After."

"Do you think it was a look in your eye—or did you say something to her that caused her to suddenly become afraid?"

"Don't think so."

"Did she try to run when she got afraid?"

"No. She was laying down."

Tim explained that he had been on top of Lorraine. "I told her I didn't want to hurt her."

"But something happened then, right?"

"I lost it."

"Did you choke her with your hands? Or was it like a chop to her neck, or did you like grab her around the neck? I know this is the part that's hardest to say, Tim."

"Mr. Colton, I'm going to think about this for the rest of my life."

"I know, and you have got to deal with it. How did that part happen? I'm not asking you why that part happened. I'm not asking you to give me an explanation. I'm asking *physically* how did that part happen?"

Tim Harris began to cry.

"Tim?" Colton urged.

"I don't want to remember."

"What is upsetting you is that you *do* remember. . . . Does it hurt you more to say it even than it hurts to remember it?"

"It hurts deep inside."

Tim Harris, the muscular man who loved arresting speeders and druggers, who controlled one of the most vicious dogs in the K-9 Unit, who had punched and pinched and choked and tormented women who loved him, cried like a child—like a spoiled child who had been called into the principal's office to explain why he had been naughty.

Bruce Colton waited, and the tape recorder catching this confession rolled on silently for a long time. Finally Harris's tears ebbed, and he was ready to answer more questions.

"You two were both still on the ground. She was completely undressed, right?" Colton asked.

Tim said he had his pants down and so did his victim, and that her blouse was pulled up.

"You had taken your holster, your gun belt off?"

"Yes."

"Did she get scared because you forced her to have sex?"

"No," Tim insisted. "There was no forcing the sex."

"Okay. Was there part of the sex that she agreed to, and then did you want to do something she didn't agree to? Is that what scared her?"

"No."

"When she died, Tim, was it fast?"

There was no sound at all in the room, save for the mechanical clickings of the air conditioning system. The two men sat frozen for what seemed like an hour.

Finally Tim spoke. "No . . . I wanted to stop it . . . I just couldn't stop, you know."

Tim Harris resisted giving details, no matter how Bruce Colton phrased his questions. "You're at the hardest part right now, Tim. Don't hold back."

"It's not quite that I'm gonna feel good about it."

"I'm not saying that you're going to feel good about it . . . you're going to feel better if you can tell me what happened."

"Am I crazy, Mr. Colton," Tim asked, "or am I just losing it?"

Bruce Colton explained again that it was not his

place to say what was or was not wrong with Tim Harris. "The medical examiner can tell us the cause of death [of Lorraine], but *you're* the one that has to fill in the details. . . . We can't just leave that to speculation."

They sat silent again for minutes. Finally Tim Harris heaved a great sigh and said, "I think I killed her with her own underwear. Put it around her neck."

"You mean like her underpants or her bra or what?"

"Her underpants."

"Did you put it around her neck and then pull on it . . . tighten it, squeezing it?"

This was like pulling teeth for Bruce Colton. Tim Harris would either not talk at all or would nod or shake his head. He finally acknowledged that after oral sex he had told Lorraine to remove her panties.

"At that point was she already getting afraid, do you think?"

"She didn't understand what was going on, I don't think."

"Did you ever pull a gun on her?"

"No."

"How about the dog? Did you ever threaten her with the dog?"

"No . . . I just asked her to take her clothes off."

"Okay. Well, after she took her pants off, did you immediately start to choke her, or was there much conversation first?"

"She rolled over on her stomach."

"Did you tell her to?"

"Yes."

"Did you have sex with her that way? Or did you attempt to?"

Again there was a long, long pause.

"Did you attempt to, Tim?"

"I rubbed up against her. I was on top of her."

"At that point do you feel that she had started to become frightened yet?"

Tim nodded.

"*Why* do you think that was—that she started to become frightened? Do you think you were becoming more aggressive or more forceful in telling her things?"

"I was talking to her like I was talking to Sandy. I kept calling her 'Sandy.' "

"Okay. When you say you were talking to her like you were talking to Sandy, was it as though you were angry at Sandy?"

"I asked her why she was divorcing me."

"What did this girl say?"

"She said, 'I know that you're hurt.' [She said] that she's not the girl I think she is."

"This girl said, 'I'm not the girl that you think I am'?" . . . And did that just kind of set you off? Or did you just more and more—in your mind think this was Sandy?"

"I think that's what I thought. . . I know she wasn't."

"Was she then laying on her stomach when you put the pants around her neck . . . and then how did you do it? Did you like sit on her or what?"

The tape rolled silent again.

"Come on, Tim," Colton urged.

"I wish you could read my mind."

"I know. But I can't. I can only depend on you to tell me what happened."

Tim Harris either could not or would not speak. Possibly the enormity of his crime had finally hit him. More likely he was weighing what a full confession would do to him. For thirty-three years his whole focus had been on himself. He knew his career was gone. He didn't want to go to prison. He had spent so many hours in court as a witness for the prosecution; he knew how much difference intent and time elapsed and mental capabilities could make in the length of a sentence.

"Were you still laying on her when you were pulling the pants around her neck, or had you sat up or gotten on your knees or what?"

"I was sitting up."

"On top of her still?"

"Yeah."

"By the time that you stopped choking her, were you sure she had stopped breathing?"

"No."

"Did you choke her for a long time, though? I mean until she stopped struggling and moving around?"

"Yes."

"What did you do then, Tim?"

Again Tim just stopped speaking. He seemed to be in a world of his own, his eyes averted from Colton's, his hands limp in his lap as if they had no part of him, and certainly no part of strangling the life from a beautiful, vibrant woman who had tried in vain to make him understand that she was not Sandy; she was not the woman he said had deserted him. The woman had shown compassion for him—a man who didn't know the meaning of the word.

"So what did you do?" Colton asked again.

"Stared . . ."

"After you realized that she had stopped breathing, what did you do next?"

"Went to help her . . . I couldn't do anything for her. . . . I couldn't do anything for her."

"You realized that she was dead?"

"Think she was . . . I didn't know what to do."

"What *did* you do, though?"

"Covered her up."

"With what?"

"Pine needles."

"What about her clothes?"

"I took her clothes off."

"Why . . . what were you thinking about that?"

"I don't know."

Tim Harris insisted through intensive questioning that he had no idea where Lorraine Hendricks's clothes were. He thought he must have taken them away in his patrol car, but he didn't know what he had done with them after that. He admitted that he had moved Lorraine's body.

"I moved her probably ten or fifteen feet from where we were doing things."

He recalled a "bunch of trees," but he could not remember what position he had left her in, whether she was face up or face down. "I couldn't look at her face anymore. . . . I didn't want to hurt that girl. I didn't want to hurt her."

The investigators knew that Tim had switched from his regular patrol car to a Mustang around the time of Lorraine Hendricks's murder. They also knew that someone had broken into that Mustang in the police garage, but Tim denied doing it. He didn't know where the clothes were. Yes, he had thrown Lorraine's wallet in the trash dumpster at the Fort Pierce rest area. He had put her driver's license and registration back in her purse, and he didn't know where her purse was.

Bruce Colton was fascinated with Tim's insistence that he had confused Lorraine Hendricks with Sandy. "It was when you started seeing her as Sandy that the problem occurred. . . . Was it almost from the time you were with her that she was reminding you of Sandy?"

"She looked a little bit like her. She doesn't have the same color hair, but the way she acted."

"But as you got into having sex with her, she more and more reminded you of Sandy?"

"I don't hate Sandy. I don't know why."

Tim insisted he had not gone back through the turnaround in the days before Lorraine was found. "I didn't go anywhere near it."

"Have you tried to confide in anybody else?" Colton asked.

"I tried to tell DeeLisa, but I can't talk about it."

Bruce Colton reminded Tim that there was another trooper in the area that Sunday morning.

"He's not involved," Tim said firmly.

That wasn't what Colton meant. "How did you know that he wouldn't ride up on you when this was occurring?"

"I didn't."

"Well, you knew he went to take a prisoner to the jail. . . . You heard that on the radio?"

Tim acknowledged that that was true. He had known exactly where Carlin Parker was.

"Have you ever had sex with anybody on the job before? I'm not saying that you forced them to, but has anyone voluntarily done it before?"

"That's how I met DeeLisa."

But Tim insisted there had been no other women; none of the beautiful women he had stopped over the past eight years had ever been sex partners—willing or unwilling.

Lorraine Hendricks was dead. She could not refute Tim Harris's words as he talked more freely now, soiling her reputation, describing her as a woman who willingly offered him sex to save herself a traffic ticket. Tim Harris didn't know that Phil Williams had already established Lorraine's pattern of behavior when she was stopped for speeding. She had taken her tickets sometimes quietly, sometimes a little sullenly. But she had never, never offered to exchange sex for a pass on a traffic ticket. All of her life Lorraine had had respect for a uniform—ever since she first saw her beloved father in his.

Interestingly, the trooper who kept cartoons and drawings of pretty girls performing fellatio on "Trooper Harris" as part of the "new breathalyzer test" insisted that he had "happened" to come upon just such a woman.

No, and no, and no, Tim Harris insisted to Bruce Colton. The girl in the Honda had not been afraid, and it was she who had initiated the idea of sex. She had performed fellatio upon him not once but twice, quite willingly. She had submitted to intercourse voluntarily. He was sure of that.

If Lorraine had been so willing to have sex with a complete stranger she had met on the Interstate, why had there been a strong indication on autopsy that she had been beaten around the face and head? Dr. Fred Hobin had told the investigators that the very rapid decomposition of her head—compared to the rest of her body—suggested that the victim had suffered severe trauma, probably from some kind of blows to her face. The investigators all wondered if Tim Harris hadn't slugged Lorraine to make her do what he wanted.

But Tim Harris insisted to Bruce Colton that the "girl" had become frightened only when he had her pinned to the ground on her face in the pine needles and when he began to call her by his wife's name.

"What did you say you asked her—thinking of Sandy?"

"Why she was divorcing me."

"And what did the girl say?"

"She said she wasn't Sandy."

"Was there any more talk between you before you started choking her—in other words, was the last thing she said, 'I'm not Sandy,' or was there anything after that?"

"No."

"Was it because you were choking her and she couldn't? Are you saying yes, Tim?"

"Yes."

And that was, tragically, when Tim Harris had "lost it." He had sat on Lorraine Hendricks's back, pinning her arms with his knees, and tightened her panties around her neck until she died. And then he had stripped her of her clothing, dragged her against the tree trunk (although he would not admit that part), and covered her with pine boughs and needles.

And returned to patrolling his district.

Sandy Harris waited outside the interview room. Bruce Colton asked Tim if he still wanted to see his estranged wife.

"Yes, I'm not going to hurt her."

"I'm not concerned about that. I just don't want you to feel that I'm forcing her on you."

"I want to see her, and I'm going to tell her I love her."

Sandy Harris would rather have been anywhere else. She stood in the doorway looking at the man who had terrorized *her* so recently. "Tim," she said softly. "Do you want to talk to me?"

"Can you hold me for a few minutes?" He threw his arms around her waist and tried to pull her close to him.

"Tim—" She stood rigid. Sandy didn't want to touch Tim. She couldn't believe he wanted her to, but then she remembered he had always been like this. He had believed her instantly when she told him she'd take him back, even though he had her handcuffed and forced to the floor with a gun next to her head. He would always believe what he wanted to.

"Are you going to talk to me?" she asked.

"Can you hold me for a few minutes?" he asked again.

"Please. Tim, *don't*. Tim, it's hard on me, too. I can't believe it—"

"Where's Timmy and Jennifer?" he asked.

"They're at Don's house right now. Tim, do you want to talk to me at all?"

"Can't you put your arms around me for a long time?"

Tim wouldn't speak to her with Bruce Colton in the room, and he asked to be alone with Sandy. There was no way Colton could risk that, not after hearing what he had heard in Tim's confession. Sandy had just learned that Tim had called the dying woman by *her* name, that his rage at her divorcing him had apparently sent him out looking for her "image" to destroy.

"Tim," Sandy implored. "Why did you do it? Whatever got into you to do that anyway, Tim . . . did you tell her it was me, and that's what you were trying to do to me? Do you wish it was me? Is that why you did it, Tim?"

"No."

"You kept telling me that you could do that to me, and you did it to someone else."

"You were my world," he said softly. "And I lost it."

"Tim, you threw it away, and you know it. You cheated on me for four years, and you sit there and tell me about it."

"I don't want to. I belong to you."

"You lost it a long time ago, Tim."

"I'm trying to put it back together."

Sandy Harris was shocked and frightened and angry. Tim had never played by other people's rules—only his own. Even now, even when he had just confessed to a terrible murder, he was sitting there and telling her that he was trying to put things back together.

"No," Sandy said. "Why did you do that to her, Tim? Why did you kill her?"

"The person that loves you didn't kill her. I need help. You were always there when I needed you, you know that. I won't have to call you anymore. . . . Don't think bad of me. I wish I could change it."

"Tim," Sandy said, with more awful possibilities dawning in her mind, "you didn't hurt anybody else, did you? Did you do it to anybody else?"

"No. I'm trying to get help."

"You don't do things like that when you need help, Tim. You've been threatening me for months. Like why didn't you get it [help] before then? Because back *months* ago—why didn't you do something before?"

"I thought I could control it."

"I gotta go, Tim." Her voice was washed of all feeling.

And Sandy Harris walked out of the room and out of Tim Harris's life. He had expected her to fix this, too, just as she had always fixed things for him. She had forgiven him a hundred times over. She no longer could.

Tim asked Bruce Colton if he could go, too. He knew it meant to jail. "I wish I were dead," he cried.

He didn't want his mother or father to know what he had done. He wanted to go someplace where "I can get help."

"Please don't let me go somewhere and rot," he said to Colton.

There was a grim irony in Tim Harris's request. That was exactly what he had meted out to his victim. He didn't know it, nor would he probably have cared, but the woman he left in the woods had cared so much for every living creature that she could not even leave a dog or cat dead in the road. It was as if the most unselfish human in Florida had, through a terrible synchronicity, crossed the path of the most selfish.

Sandy and Don Dappen still waited outside Colton's office. Dappen looked around at the men who waited with him. They were lawmen and attorneys whom he had known for almost two decades. And it was his own brother-in-law who had just confessed to one of the most heinous crimes he himself had ever encountered. They waited in awkward silence.

"They brought Tim by to go to the bathroom. He looked at Sandy and he looked at me," Dappen recalls. "A few minutes later he comes back by. You understand, by that time I *hated* the guy, but he was about to get me one more time. He stopped. He looked me right in the eye, and he leaned over and he whispered in my ear, *'Please take care of my kids.'* He walked away, and I busted out crying. Here I am—in front of all these guys I've worked with. And the guy got me. One last time."

It was the kids. Don Dappen realized in that one moment that this was all real, and that it was going to be the kids who would hurt the most. Not just Jennifer and Timmy, but Don's own kids, Chris and Charlene; Kathy's kids, Gary Jr., Freddie, and Michael; and even the sisters' niece and nephew, April Rose and Ryan, Martin's children in New York.

Most of all, Katherine Hendricks's whole life would be diminished; her mother, who had loved her so, was dead because of Tim Harris.

Phil Williams had written the arrest affidavit, and he served it on Tim Harris at 2:20 a.m. Although it was akin to bringing coals to Newcastle, Phil read Tim his Miranda rights. Tim answered after each sentence that he did, indeed, understand. Anything he said *could* be used against him in a court of law, and he did have the right to an attorney, and if he didn't have money to afford one, one would be appointed for him. It was almost psychedelic—reading a veteran cop his rights. But it was the law.

On the way to the Indian River County Jail, with Indian River County Sheriff's deputy Pete Lenz accompanying them, Phil asked Tim a question that had been nibbling at his mind ever since he had discovered Lorraine in that single heart-stopping moment.

"You remember, Tim, how she was," Phil began. "The way you dragged her and put her legs around the tree?"

Tim looked straight ahead, silent.

"Why?" Phil asked. "Could you tell me why you left her that way?"

"No reason."

"You got to admit that was a strange position. Did it mean something to you? Was there a reason?"

"I don't know."

When Phil Williams walked Tim Harris into jail to book him for murder the jailers' mouths fell open. At first they almost thought it was a joke. They had seen Tim, the tall, handsome trooper in uniform, as he ushered hundreds of prisoners in to be booked. He had waved at them, stopped to talk with them, been

one of the massive team that was law enforcement in
Indian River County. He had been one of them. And
now it was Tim himself who wore the handcuffs.

It was no joke, and Phil Williams felt no sense of
triumph. He was glad it was over, relieved that Tim
was no longer free to rove the freeways, but he didn't
feel like shouting and clapping his team of investigators on the back. None of them did. Instead tears
stung his eyes. One dirty cop sullies the reputation of
thousands of good cops. Beyond that, there was so
much pain for innocent people. Donny Dappen was a
tough cop, but he had cried, and Phil felt his own eyes
fill with tears.

And this was only the beginning of the pain. Phil
hoped they could block the details of Tim's confession
from the media for a little while at least. This was
going to hit the wire services with a bang, and he knew
they could expect a circus. Mary Hogan could only
hold reporters at bay for so long.

21

During the previous week Don Dappen had taken
Sandy and Susan and all their kids to Disney World in
Orlando for an overnight trip, not so much to keep
Tim from harassing them or trying to take Jennifer
and Timmy away, but just to help them forget for a
little while. He was glad he had; there would be no
forgetting now. Not for weeks, months, years—not
for the rest of their lives.

Tim's family was shocked and devastated. Phil Williams called David Harris Saturday morning to let him know that his brother had been arrested. David and Melissa were out, so he had no choice but to leave a message on their answering machine. Melissa watched her husband's face as he walked into the living room after playing his messages.

"David didn't believe it. . . . We didn't know what the problem was. We thought it had to do with Sandy. . . . We tried Sandy's house, and there was no answer."

Both David and Melissa had gone over to the jail to visit with Tim. David went in to see his brother, and Tim clung to him and sobbed, "Don't leave me."

Melissa remembered that David walked out in "total shock. He just kept saying, 'I can't believe it, I can't believe it,' and he was crying hysterically when he walked out."

Tim's mother flew down on Sunday to see him. She sat in her son's cell, holding him for fifteen or twenty minutes, neither of them saying a word. Tim's father came to Vero Beach, too, but he balked at going in to see his son. According to family members, the two men had not spoken for a half dozen years; Tim and his stepmother were engaged in a feud. At length Tim's father turned around and went home, saying that he refused to go to the jail and see his son in that position.

David Harris tried to explain that to Phil Williams. "My dad doesn't have anything to do with us."

Tim Harris was being held without bond and in isolation. There were reasons for the latter; cops don't always fare well when they find themselves on the other side of the bars. And *no* woman killer is respected in prison. Tim was both. For his own protection Tim was placed well away from the other prisoners. Jailers logged his behavior and movements every fifteen minutes.

The press found out about Tim Harris's arrest quickly; they had been watching the activity around the sheriff's office avidly, and they picked up on the tension. It was too big to keep under wraps. Harris's case was headlined in the *Miami Herald* and the Vero Beach *Press Journal* on Sunday, April 8, 1990. Columns and columns of details emerged, whetting the appetites of the tabloid television world.

The *Orlando Sentinel* headline read, "A Woman Is Slain, a Trooper Confesses, a Fear Festers"; the *Miami Herald's:* "Descent into Darkness—From Success to Suspect in Murder: State Trooper 'Snapped'".

Two women came forward after reading about Tim Harris's arrest and told Rick McIlwain that they didn't believe he had suddenly snapped. They had had the misfortune to deal with him months before, in July, 1989, and they characterized Harris as a "walking time bomb."

"He acted like he hated woman," said forty-seven-year-old Sandy Horne. She recalled that she and twenty-three-year-old Mary Turney had been southbound on I-95 about three in the afternoon when Tim Harris had come speeding up behind them near the Okeechobee Road exit in Fort Pierce. They saw no lights and heard no siren, and they began to pass the car in front of their truck. At that point Tim Harris had turned on his blue bubble lights and pulled them over. He didn't ask for their licenses or registration; he was obviously furious about something.

"He said, 'You're in my way, and I was in a hurry,'" Sandy Horne said. When the women began to protest he shouted at them. Horne said she had figured there was something wrong with the trooper—his rage was out of all proportion to the situation—and she slid her eyes down to read his name tag. He caught her looking at it, and he was enraged.

"He went wild," she said simply. He said he could cite her for littering because a plastic milk jug had flown out of the back of her pickup truck a half mile down the road near some woods.

"I went to get out of my truck to see if it had blown out," Horne said, "and I had one leg out, and he leaned against the door, and it caught my leg. He said, 'Where are you going?'"

She had explained that she wanted to check the back of her truck to be sure the three milk jugs she had were still there. Tim Harris would not allow it. Instead he ordered her to walk back along the Interstate and then down into the wooded median and retrieve the jug he said had flown out.

"I said I wasn't going down in the woods, and he said that six times at least." But she wouldn't go. The woods were dark and "spooky."

Horne said she had come forward because she was tired of reading in the papers that Tim Harris had just "snapped" recently.

"He had a bad temper a long time ago," she said. "We've never been treated so rudely in all our lives . . . I thought, 'God, I'm going to jail over a milk jug.' But he was a walking time bomb that day. I'm glad I didn't go [into the woods]."

There were several aspects to Tim Harris's confession that rankled Phil Williams. Tim had been so insistent that Lorraine Hendricks had readily agreed to have sex with him—what Florida lawmen referred to irreverently as a "bush bond." Everything that Phil had learned about Lorraine in his five weeks of investigation warred with that. To begin with, Phil had talked to several of the officers who had given her speeding tickets earlier, asking them about how she had acted—what kind of woman she seemed to be.

One thing she definitely was not was a flirt, according to the other officers, and she appeared anything but "easy." She had been businesslike with one Jacksonville policeman, and she had been annoyed and downright snappish with another. Why then would she have been so compliant with Tim Harris? It just didn't make sense.

A lot of things didn't make sense. Tim said that Lorraine had driven her car across the Interstate and down into the median strip—as had he—where they would be hidden in the trees. If that was true, Williams figured he and Larry Smetzer and Tony Oliver would have found some signs that two cars had been parked down in there. More than that, when Lorraine's car was processed they would have found weeds, pine twigs, palmetto leaves, and other debris from the median in the undercarriage of her Honda when they put it up on the rack. But they hadn't. The bottom of her car looked like that of a car driven on main roads and freeways.

If Tim Harris was telling the truth, he would have had to drive Lorraine's Honda back to where he had first pulled it over, park it on the Interstate, and then *walk* a mile along I-95 to get back to his patrol car. A tall trooper in uniform walking along the Interstate would certainly have drawn attention. Someone would have remembered seeing him. Phil didn't believe Tim would have taken that chance.

Lorraine's car had been found with both front doors unlocked and her belongings still inside, including her briefcase with important business papers. Everyone Phil Williams talked to said she had been a cautious woman—a woman who never would have left her car unlocked for more than a moment or two, and certainly not with her things inside.

The only way Lorraine would have walked away from her unlocked car would have been if Tim Harris had asked her to step back to his patrol car for a moment. This is a fairly standard procedure in Florida and elsewhere. Officers have the driver sit in the patrol unit while they have their dispatcher check "Wants and Warrants," and while they write tickets.

Lorraine might very well have complied with that request, thinking she would be back in her car in a few minutes. Common sense said that she would never have left her car unlocked and willingly accompanied a perfect stranger down into the darkening wood for sex.

Lorraine hadn't been hard up for sex; she had a lover. Williams knew Lorraine so well by this time; he had talked to almost everyone who had ever cared about her. She was a loving, passionate woman when she was in a permanent relationship. She had never, ever engaged in casual sex.

Her friend Carol Worley recalled Lorraine as modest—so modest she didn't even undress in front of other women in a health club locker room. Asked if Lorraine would have offered sex to get out of a speeding ticket, Carol's eyes flashed. "Never. *Never*. There is just no way. That was not Lorraine. . . . At one time Lorraine could have had a huge promotion —an executive came to her hotel room at midnight and suggested they could be more than friends. She was shocked, and she was mad. She sent him away. She didn't care how it might hurt her career."

No, Phil Williams believed that Lorraine Hendricks had been thinking about getting to Fort Lauderdale as quickly as she could to see her friend, get her dental work done, and take care of her real estate business so she could get back to her little girl in Jacksonville.

She did have a lousy driving record, but she didn't even know that her license had been suspended, and she could have gotten it reinstated by paying a fine or two. A woman with her class and her commitment to her child wouldn't be likely to barter sex for a free pass on a ticket. The women in Tim's *cartoons* would, and Phil Williams believed those women had taken over Tim's imagination so much that he had written his own scenario, filling in Lorraine's response so that it fit.

The dog. Shadow was quite possibly a part of Tim's power. Don Dappen thought about that, too. He would remember how Tim had said, "Watch her, Shadow," to torment Susan. Once Lorraine Hendricks had entered Tim's car, or even *approached* Tim's car, if Tim had said, "Watch her" to Shadow, Lorraine would have been as helpless as if the trooper held her in his gun sights. It wouldn't have mattered that she had a black belt in kung fu. How could she have stood off both a trained attack dog and a 200-pound state trooper? It was ironic for a woman who loved animals so much that a dog—a good dog under the control of a deranged master—might have helped hold her captive.

Williams knew that killers confess in diverse ways; some tell the straight truth, but more often they tend to slide over the parts of their crimes that either eat at their consciences the most or make them seem most guilty. The result is a self-serving confabulation.

Phil had no doubt that Tim Harris had stopped Lorraine or that he had talked with her. He knew too much about her. He knew she was getting a divorce, he knew she was headed toward Fort Lauderdale, and he knew she had a little girl. Tim had said repeatedly that she was going to *see* her little girl, while in reality she had left Katherine at home. It was possible that Lorraine had even said she was hurrying toward Katherine so that he would let her go.

It was highly unlikely that Lorraine Hendricks had agreed voluntarily to have sex with Tim Harris. However, once he had forced her into the woods and cuffed her around to demonstrate his strength, she would have realized that she might very well die if she didn't obey the trooper's commands. At that point she might have stopped struggling. She was, above all, a mother, and mothers down through the ages have sacrificed themselves, done whatever they had to for their children. Katherine was Lorraine's whole life. If she had to submit to the hulking trooper so that she could get back to Katherine, she probably would have done so. From what Phil Williams had learned about her character and her personality, he figured that was the way it had happened. Lorraine Hendricks, already bruised and injured, had believed Harris would release her after he was finished with her.

Too late, Lorraine must have realized that the trooper had trapped her and that he never intended to let her go. When she heard him calling her by another woman's name she had cried out, "I'm not the woman you think I am! *I'm* not Sandy!" *That* statement from Harris had the ring of truth.

There would be one slight comfort that Phil Williams could give Lorraine's family and friends. Death by strangulation is almost always very rapid. Once the carotid arteries leading to the brain are shut down with a ligature, unconsciousness follows almost immediately. In his rage Tim Harris might have continued to choke Lorraine Hendricks, but she would not have felt it or known. She would already have been in a safe place, a place fitting for a woman who had spent her whole life helping large and small creatures and making other people's lives richer.

A public defender was appointed to represent Tim Harris. Assistant Public Defender Clifford Barnes would defend him on charges of first-degree murder. The State of Florida was seeking the death penalty. Assistant State Attorney David Morgan said that he was not even considering a plea bargain that would keep Harris from joining the long roster of prisoners at the Florida State Penitentiary in Starke, Florida, who were awaiting their fatal moment in the electric chair.

"We're definitely pursuing first-degree murder," Morgan said, explaining that the state would rely on two aggravating circumstances that would make the first-degree charges stick—even if the defense could prove that Tim's crime wasn't premeditated.

In jail Tim Harris continued to cry much of the time. He was monitored by the closed-circuit television camera, although jail authorities did not consider it a suicide watch. DeeLisa Davis visited him faithfully, but Sandy did not. She was trying to cope with telling her children where their father was and to protect them from the teasing of their friends. She had to go to work every day and face her friends and co-workers. Vero Beach and Sebastian were basically small towns, and there were no secrets.

Major Frank and Jodi Dombroski tried to accept that their wonderful daughter was gone from them forever. Rick Hendricks had a little six-year-old daughter who would never again see her mother. Mike Raleigh had lost the business associate he'd found so brilliant. The man Lorraine had come to love had lost her before he really found her; he would remember her the rest of his life.

For Tim Harris it was as if Lorraine Hendricks's death was old business, something that had happened in the past, something that was not nearly as important in his mind as winning Sandy back. He was crying because he had lost Sandy, and for himself because he was locked up in a cell that he told visitors was filthy and disgusting.

Sandy was the one thing that had been denied Tim in his adult life, and he would not accept that she was gone. He wrote to her constantly, in pencil on lined jail-issue paper.

Tim sat in jail and sobbed as he wrote to Sandy, a letter carefully constructed to make her feel guilty and miss him and come back to him. But when it came to human feelings and compassion or even to understanding life from someone else's point of view, he just didn't get it.

Looking at the letter Tim sent in the last week of April is akin to viewing the same situation from both sides of the looking glass. Sandy had been so embarrassed when Tim broke into her office the night before Valentine's Day that she had gone home in tears. Tim had reconstructed that day in his memory, and it came out completely changed.

"I just wanted you to know," Tim began, "last night I cried myself to sleep. . . . It's dumb, I know, but I was thinking about Valentine's Day. Did you ever think to ask DeeLisa what I did for *her* on that day? Nothing. I think about those balloons, and how many trips it took me from my truck to inside, wondering if I was going to get caught. I kinda impressed myself. . . ."

He mused that he had thought about buying her some sexy outfit, but that Sandy knew he could never do that on his own—he had always had to have his daughter or some of the guys at his reserve camp with him.

"I don't ever want to see another Valentine's Day again," he wrote. "And to think you never even said, Thank you. *I love you. . . ."*

Tim Harris had received a fan letter from a woman who had read about his arrest, and he wrote to Sandy about that. "I figure if some lady that doesn't know me can write, why can't my wife? Maybe you don't want to be my wife? Wife and Husband are suppose to stand up for each other. . . . I want you to come see me every week. I want you to write me. I want the kids to write. I want you to love me. I want you to care about what happens to me. . . . Since you may not testify, why don't you sit with me in court? If you were in trouble—no matter how mad I was at you—I'd be there. . . ."

"I want . . ."

Again Tim Harris begged Sandy to take him back, to put his ring on her finger.

In May Tim sent Sandy a Mother's Day card. She had not written to him, and he didn't understand why. He seemed truly unable to grasp *what* might have happened to send her fleeing from him.

"I still can't figure out why you won't come to see me or write. You don't break a eight and a half year marriage off just like that. I can assure you that if we end up in a divorce, it will be because you wanted it. . . . Pretending I don't exist doesn't help. I never thought *you* were that type of girl. Your emotions . . . are hurt, so are mine. . . ."

Although one wondered how Tim thought he was going to escape his present legal troubles, he wrote to Sandy as if he were in jail for nothing more serious than a traffic violation. "I think I might want to move after this. Are you interested in coming with me?"

Tim sent Sandy articles condemning divorce. He sent her Robert Fulghum's *All I Ever Really Needed to Know I Learned in Kindergarten*. He quoted an article called "It's Never Too Late." The sentiments were meaningful and on target—except for the fact that Tim Harris was completely avoiding the huge black chasm that separated him from Sandy, the chasm that held infidelity, brutality, and murder.

Painstakingly Tim Harris drew pictures for Sandy and Jenny and Timmy. A single red rose, a Snoopy dog, and every letter ended with "Love Always" and his signature in a flourishing sweep of his pencil.

Sandy had to sell everything to keep going—Tim's boat, his car, their house. She was shocked to find that Tim had signed his income tax refund over to DeeLisa. And still his letters poured in, full of his undying love and his terrible fear that Sandy might date other men, and that his children would forget him. He warned her not to let them see his picture in the paper when he went to court.

Tim's letters had a stultifying sameness. Before Sandy opened them she knew what they would say. He still loved her. They should be together. He loved the children, and he wanted to hear from all of them, have visits from all of them. When he didn't hear from Sandy he suspected the jail was keeping her letters from him. He simply would not accept that she was through with him, that in some instances it *was* too late. Sandy read the letters, refolded them, and put them back into their envelopes. She didn't throw them away, and she didn't know why.

Finally she found a buyer for the house on 75th Court. Her family helped Sandy move out of what had once been her dream house. While Don Dappen was helping Sandy clear some stuff out of her house he checked all the closets for things she might have missed. Far back in a closet he found several pairs of nylons—with their feet cut off. They were not Sandy's, and they had been pushed back behind other clothes on the top shelf of a closet. Sandy had never seen them. For whatever reason, Tim must have put them there.

Sandy was able to build a much smaller place for herself and the children. She stayed in Indian River County, although there were times she thought of moving someplace far away, someplace where no one had ever heard of Tim or of her. But she had a good job, she had her family close by, and people were kind to her. Nobody was rubbing her nose in the scandal.

It might get worse when Tim was actually on trial, when all the details were spread across the papers again. But Sandy stayed. Her kids had their Uncle Don and their Grandpa Fred, and she had her mother and her sisters, Susan and Kathy.

22

Tim Harris's trial on charges of first-degree murder was set for October 9, 1990. The week before, Sandy would have her twenty-eighth birthday, and Lorraine Hendricks would have had her forty-fourth. Only a year earlier Tim himself had started the tumbling down of his life when he took Sandy out for her "birthday dinner" and told her bluntly that he was seeing another woman.

If he ever thought of that, it didn't matter now. It was a year later, and he stood a good chance of going to the electric chair. On September 19 the defense lost on a major point. Clifford Barnes's main defense stratagem was that Tim had been coerced and tricked into confessing. More than anything he wanted to keep Tim's taped statements to Phil Williams and Rick McIlwain and his confession to State Attorney Bruce Colton kept out of his trial.

This hearing was vital. If Judge Vocelle left the tapes in, Clifford Barnes would have little recourse but to try to convince a jury that his client was guilty of second-degree murder or manslaughter—but not of first-degree murder. "It doesn't look like the insanity defense will work," Barnes admitted. His interviews with his client had shown him a man eminently sane who had probably been sane at the time of the crime.

There was always the far-out possibility that if Judge Vocelle suppressed the tapes, the whole case could be thrown out, and Tim Harris would walk free. That seemed incredible, but State Attorney Bruce Colton testified that if Tim Harris had not confessed to the Hendricks murder, "I didn't feel we had enough probable cause to arrest him for murder."

Public Defender Barnes insisted that Tim had been taped under oppressive circumstances. "They constantly fostered his fear of being arrested," he said. "This was a masterpiece of psychological coercion. They did a heck of a job of breaking him down. The fact that he's a cop doesn't mean he doesn't have constitutional rights."

It was a risky stance at best. Tim Harris had carried a Miranda Warning card in his wallet for eight years;

he probably had read those rights aloud to thousands of motorists. He knew all along that he didn't have to talk with Phil Williams or Rick McIlwain or Bruce Colton. Indeed, Phil Williams had him on tape saying "I can walk out that door and tell you to drop dead and not talk to you anymore." And Bruce Colton had Tim on tape saying "I'm here because I want to [be]" as he made his official confession.

The courtroom was hushed as the tapes made on April 6th and 7th were played. Tim Harris's voice was clotted with tears as he described the murder of Lorraine Hendricks and his confusion over whether he had been strangling Lorraine or his wife, Sandy.

The real Tim Harris—the one in the courtroom— was stone-faced as he listened, his arms folded in front of him on the oak defense table. Photographers waited to catch some trace of emotion on his face, but they were disappointed. He had not talked to reporters in the five months since his arrest, and he was not about to give the photographers a good shot. Occasionally he shut his eyes, as if by doing so he could shut out the ugly details of Lorraine's death.

Wearing red jail coveralls, Tim Harris looked as if he had lost weight, but all of the media shots the lensmen *did* get showed a man handsome enough to be playing the *role* of a murder defendant in a movie or on television. An errant lock of his thick black hair fell over his forehead.

After a tense waiting period Circuit Judge L. B. Vocelle commented, "We're not dealing with a novice." He remarked that Tim Harris's eleven years of experience in law enforcement and extensive training were "obviously items the Court should take into consideration."

The tapes were in. Jurors in Tim's trial would hear

both the interrogation of the afternoon of April 7 and his confession.

Harris showed no disappointment. He had not expected the tape to be thrown out. As a working cop he knew that he had been legally "Mirandized." He had known what he was doing when he talked to Williams and the two men from the State Attorney's Office.

Barnes said he expected the worst. "It's a first-degree murder charge. It's a terrible crime. It's a small town, and it's an extremely complex issue." He was confident, however, that an appellate court would disagree with Judge Vocelle and said he planned to appeal the ruling after the first trial if Harris should be convicted.

Phil Williams remarked that even if Tim Harris had continued to deny killing Lorraine Hendricks on that long day of interrogation back in April, he would not have given up. "I would have taken him on a fishing trip," Williams said. "Nobody but me and him and the tape recorder."

As it turned out, there would be no murder trial for Timothy Scott Harris. On Friday, September 28, 1990, Tim broke his silence. Lorraine Hendricks's parents, alerted by Assistant State Attorney David Morgan, were present in Judge Vocelle's courtroom to hear Tim Harris admit that he had killed their only daughter. Major Frank Dombroski was stoic, and Jodi Dombroski fought to hold back tears.

Dressed in red jail coveralls, with his hands cuffed to his belt, Tim Harris entered the courtroom. He would not plead guilty to murder, but he would plead no contest to the first-degree murder charges. That would save him from the electric chair.

Harris stood before Judge Vocelle, his face blank. "I'm not going to be able to forget what happened," he said. "And I know there's nothing I can say to make things change. . . . I am truly sorry for her family and friends and the hurt I caused. I've hurt a lot of people, and I won't forget it. . . . I don't deserve to live."

Referring to Lorraine Hendricks's family, he said, "I wish they could forgive me. In time, I hope they will."

The Dombroskis stared at Harris, as if he were speaking in another language.

Tim talked of how much pride he had taken in his career as a policeman; he had never expected to find himself standing before a judge as a defendant. "I just hope law enforcement is not tarnished by what I've done, because law enforcement's not that way."

Judge Vocelle heard Tim Harris out, and then he sentenced him to life in prison.

For Lorraine's parents it was a tragically light sentence. They would have preferred to have known that Tim Harris was going to die himself for what he had done to Lorraine. Still, there was a closure now to all they had been through. "We'd just like to have a finality to the situation," Major Dombroski said. "If the appeal process was used, it could go on for the next ten to twelve years. I don't feel that, emotionally-wise, we would survive."

Jodi Dombroski was clearly fighting to maintain control, but she had words she needed to say. She wondered about the bleak coincidence that her daughter, who had posed as Florida's "Arrive Alive" model in 1971, should now be dead at the hands of a member of the very agency that had sponsored the program.

"How sad it is that this deranged murderer could tarnish the slate of the honorable officers that serve this country and try to do their best to protect us, not destroy us," she told reporters. "Let him start his punishment. He'll live with it, day by day. Our whole family has suffered because we all loved her dearly. And all our friends will pray that each day he's not going to forget how he made her suffer. That each moment of his life he'll wish he was dead."

Sandy Harris was not in the courtroom. She gave a brief statement on the phone to reporters. "It was what he deserved," she said. "Does anyone deserve the death penalty? Life is worse than the death penalty. If I killed someone, I wouldn't want to live my life in jail."

Sandy had taken her children to see Tim in jail two days before—but only so they might understand why their father never came to see them anymore. She hoped never to have to see him again, and that she could forget him.

Tim Harris had come within a hair's breadth of getting the death penalty; that was the only reason his legal advisors had agreed to the plea bargain. He had no right to appeal, and he would have to serve, under Florida law, at least twenty-five years in prison before he could become eligible for parole.

Within hours of hearing himself sentenced to life in prison Tim Harris was transported from the Indian River County Jail to the Orlando Receiving Center, where he would be processed and assigned to the prison where he would live out, quite possibly, the rest of his life.

Shortly thereafter he was sent to the Baker Correctional Institution in Olustee, Florida. Trooper Timothy Scott Harris had become Inmate Timothy Scott Harris, 139009.

Afterword

At the Baker facility Tim Harris joined 1,600 other inmates. He was assigned as a clerk for a math and GED teacher. He joined the prison Jaycees and began to go to church, something he told reporters he had not done before he was sentenced to prison.

DeeLisa Davis visited him faithfully for the first six months of his incarceration. Sandy did not—nor did she answer the letters Tim sent. He would not be easily dissuaded. He still wrote to both DeeLisa and Sandy, assuring them both that he loved them.

On March 12, 1991, Tim Harris carried out his last act for the Florida State Patrol. He was transferred from prison to Fort Pierce so that he could testify as a witness for the State in a case where a drunk driver in a panel truck collided with a car, killing two people and injuring three others. It was, in fact, the case in which the little black boy was killed in 1989. He was not permitted to wear his uniform, but for part of a day Tim Harris was once again a "trooper" on the witness stand—and not a prisoner.

And then he was returned to Baker.

Cut off from his children, Tim Harris had finally become the complete father, wanting nothing more than a chance to be part of their lives. He sent them questionnaires about their lives—asking about everything from their favorite foods to what made them afraid to what they thought, dreamed, felt, and yearned for. He asked Sandy to help the children fill out their answers. One questionnaire, sent to seven-year-old Timmy, had 148 questions—some with many sections—for the little boy to answer.

Sandy tried to comply, but Timmy and Jennifer grew tired and frustrated. They wondered why they had to spend hours revealing every detail of their worlds. Even as children they recognized the invasion of their private, secret selves. Harris's curiosity was voracious—*invasive*.

One nine-page letter sent to Timmy asked, among other questions, "What animal scares you the most? What kind of jelly do you like on your toast? If you caught a fish, would you let it go—or eat it? Are you afraid of sharks? Do you like caramel-coated apples?"

In a sense, it was almost as if Tim Harris was trying to be a little boy again, perhaps trying to relive a childhood by picking at Timmy's brain.

"Have you ever shot a bow and arrow? Have you ever shot a gun? Do you like grilled cheese sandwiches? Do hurricanes scare you? Have you ever gotten seasick? Do you believe in ghosts? What's the name of a famous ghost? When you take your lunch to school, what does Mom put in your lunch box? Do you have a girlfriend? What's her name? Name some things that your mom does that you are glad she does for you. How many times a day do you tell your mom you love her? What's one thing that you would like to do that you don't get to do—or are not allowed to do? And why?"

Tim Harris asked his son to list seven things that scared him and seven things that made him happy. He asked for six examples of things that Sandy did for him that made him glad. He asked, "Have you ever seen a bad car accident?" and "What does a shrimp look like?"

Few adults could have handled so many questions. One seven-year-old boy certainly could not.

Tim's handwriting on his traffic tickets had been scrawling and almost illegible. His letters to his children, and subsequently, the legal documents he filed —acting as his own attorney—were printed as precisely and neatly as if done in a calligrapher's hand.

In the end, Tim Harris's whole purpose in life seemed to be to force his ex-wife, by court order if necessary, to bend to his will and come to visit him in prison with Jennifer and Timmy.

Tim Harris had agreed to a plea bargain that would save his life. He broke that promise in 1991 when he requested an evidentiary hearing on his allegations that his attorneys had not adequately represented him when he pleaded no contest. Assistant State Attorney Lynn Park did not object to the hearing. "There are some allegations he's made that will require testimony from his attorneys," Park commented.

It would be a convoluted hearing legally. Public Defender Philip Yacucci and Chief Assistant Public Defender Clifford Barnes would be on the other side, testifying for the State. Tim Harris alleged that an insanity defense was tossed out three weeks before trial because his psychologist didn't have time to render an opinion. He also claimed he was erroneously told that he would only have to serve half of the minimum mandatory twenty-five years of his sentence.

Both the State *and* his own former lawyers said he knew full well that he would give up his right to appeal when he pleaded no contest. Tim wanted Stuart (Florida) Attorney Robert Udell to be appointed to represent him in his appeal. Udell was the defense attorney in the Ft. Pierce court where Tim Harris had testified in the hit-and-run case.

On June 6, 1991, Tim Harris wrote a letter to the Vero Beach *Press Journal* complaining about the insensitivity of the State Attorney's Office.

After his sentencing, he wrote, he had requested a public disclosure file in reference to his case. It was sent to him.

> There were numerous documents that I never saw until I received the files. . . . The State Attorney's Office saw fit to send me a picture of the victim in my case. I think it was very distasteful and served no purpose. Why did they send it? If it was to remind me of the victim, I am reminded of it every minute of my life. . . . Is this not a common practice that the State sends a person a picture of his victim? They seem to forget that there are a number of victims in this case. . . .
>
> I believe in punishment for a wrong. It's true that nothing will bring back an innocent person. I'm not like some. I do care and I do have feelings. I'm not the "cold-blooded murderer" that some people want to make me. . . .
>
> Prison is bad enough. I think the picture idea is cruel. . . . I'm being punished in the worst way. Please don't make it worse.

Tim had never wanted to see a picture of Lorraine Hendricks's body; he had stayed away from the median strip and kept his dog away until she was found. He had walked out of his interrogation session with McIlwain and Williams when they started to show him a photograph. His letter to the *Press Journal* enraged readers.

Lori Brenton of Vero Beach wrote:

Poor Tim Harris. He receives a photo of the victim . . . and feels it is "cruel treatment." I did feel sympathy when I read his letter; unfortunately, it wasn't for him, but for his victim and her family. Wake up, Tim! That life you took will never again have the opportunity to look at anything . . . never see another sunset or the smile on a child's face. . . .

You are right about one thing; if they do it for one, they should do it for all. Every murderer should be forced to look at his victim and imagine the dreams and hopes he ended. . . .

Mary Ann Layman and Linda Furrows agreed.

Our hearts go out to him, sitting in an air-conditioned cell . . . Hopefully he had eaten dinner before he saw pictures of his victim. . . . Did Lorraine Hendricks's death have a purpose? Did she have a chance? Harris doesn't deserve to live. . . .

"Good grief, poor Tim Harris," wrote Rindy Reardon.

He murdered an innocent woman and wants everyone to feel badly because he was sent a picture of the victim—that same picture that is boldly etched in the minds of her family and friends.

And he says prison is bad enough—that is just really heartbreaking, isn't it? Well, it makes me want to throw up. . . .

Clearly, Tim Harris still didn't get it.

* * *

On Tuesday, December 17, 1991, Judge Vocelle quashed Tim's motion to have his murder conviction overturned. Earlier Tim had told reporters that being a cop in prison wasn't as dangerous as he thought it would be, and that he hadn't needed any special protection from the state. He said that being unable to see his kids and his dog, Shadow, was far more depressing than he had expected. "It's tough," he said. "It's no fun, for sure. But I'm making it."

Judge Vocelle's ruling didn't make Tim any more cheerful. As he was led away, Major Frank Dombroski stood and shouted, "Harris, may you rot in hell!"

Tim Harris went back to prison to continue serving his twenty-five years.

He was not, however, finished with his legal manueverings. Tim sued to have his divorce modified so that he would have more contact with his children. He asked the court to grant him at least two phone calls a month to his children; letters from his children to him in prison; partial parental responsibilities for "catastrophic events," including notification of the children's medical problems; access to their school and medical records; visits with the children in prison. He asked that either his family or court officials bring the children to see him for their birthdays and on Christmas.

In his letter to Judge Vocelle Tim said, "I came from a family where my father and mother divorced when I was young. I don't know a father like a son should know a father. . . . It does have an effect on you in the long run." No one would ever know exactly what Tim Harris's childhood had been like; he had never said, and he was not specific at this point.

Even though Tim had gone for months without contacting his children; even though the calls he made—collect—to Sandy had been to talk to *her;* even though he sent Sandy a very expensive angel doll with one teardrop on her cheek for Christmas, and no presents at all for his children, he was granted his request to see them. The only hitch was that he had to provide money to transport Timmy and Jennifer to Baker. And Tim Harris had no money. (He succeeded in early 1994 in getting a judge to order Sandy to bring his children to prison to see him, at her expense.)

On February 16, 1992, Rick Hendricks filed a wrongful death suit on behalf of Lorraine Hendricks —against the State of Florida and the Department of Highway Safety and Motor Vehicles (which oversees the Florida Highway Patrol). Seeking damages "in excess of $5,000," Hendricks asserted that the FHP "failed to discover the fact that [Harris] had been asked to resign from another agency for improper conduct, and that [Harris] had exhibited a pattern of socially deviant behavior demonstrating that he was psychologically unfit to be a highway trooper assigned to road patrol duty."

That suit was heard in the last week of February, 1994. Once again Lorraine and Katherine Hendricks played together, but this time they were only moving shadows on a videoscreen as jurors in Courtroom D of the Indian River County Courthouse watched silently while the little girl and her mother laughed into the lens of the camcorder.

Rick Hendricks testified about Katherine's uncanny reaction as he began to tell her the sad news about her mother. She had interrupted him and said, "My mom's not coming home, is she?"

When he had to say that was true, Katherine was silent for a few seconds, and then she began to cry and say, "I won't live without Mama. I won't live without Mama. . . ."

Attorneys for Lorraine's and Katherine's estates elicited information from an expert witness that the estates had lost between $588,153 and $898,000 in projected wages and household support when Lorraine was murdered. This, of course, did not—*could not*—include the emotional losses, which were incalculable. However, lawyers for the Hendricks family were asking $3 million for Katherine's pain, suffering, and loss of parental companionship.

Lt. Andrew Morris of the Florida Highway Patrol testified that he had taken "what steps I felt necessary" after Don Dappen brought Tim's inappropriate behavior in December, 1989, to his attention. "I brought the conduct to his [Tim's] attention and told him he may be disciplined by the department for that type of conduct."

For the Hendricks family to win, they would have to prove that the state was liable and had been able to foresee what Tim Harris was going to do. Quite literally, the six jurors would have to believe that the Florida Highway Patrol's failure to act was a cause of Lorraine Hendricks's murder.

On February 25, 1994, the jurors found that the FHP was not liable for having Trooper Tim Harris on road patrol the day he strangled Lorraine. It took them less than ninety minutes of deliberation.

FHP Lt. Jim Howell felt the verdict was fair. "I just think that under the totality of the circumstances, this was not a foreseeable act. We could not have foreseen what happened." He emphasized, however, that his department felt a great deal of sympathy toward the Hendricks family, that the FHP, too, had been "betrayed" by the actions of its former trooper.

Tim Harris remains incarcerated at the Baker Correctional Institution. He is reportedly a model prisoner who sometimes teaches in the prison school. For most of his life he had tried to *own* both people and things.

But in the end, Tim Harris owns nothing at all.

Rick Hendricks has remarried; Katherine will be ten years old this year, and she has a loving stepmother. She visits her maternal grandmother, Jodi Dombroski, often.

Major Frank Dombroski died in September, 1993, after a long battle with cancer. He and Jodi had become active in a new Florida victims' rights group: STOP (STOP Turning Out Prisoners). They handed out scores of postcards addressed to Florida Governor Lawton Chiles that said "I'm mad as hell about crime, and I'm not going to take it anymore. Please stop the release of violent criminals." Jodi Dombroski volunteers at the Veterans' Hospital where her husband died. It fills some of her days and helps her show her gratitude for the wonderful care given her husband; it does not take away the memories of what she has lost.

Mike Raleigh works, as he always has, fourteen-hour days as he produces shows all over the United States.

The man who loved Lorraine at first sight, the man she loved almost as quickly, has never forgotten her. He loves her still.

Ruth Straley, who worked with Lorraine Hendricks in the wonderful days of 1989 and the first months of 1990 in Jacksonville, has moved to Europe, and Lorraine's dear friend, Carol, has moved to Washington State. Life, as it will, has gone on, but I encountered no one who can speak about Lorraine without tears.

Flicka, Lorraine's beloved horse, died a year before Lorraine herself did.

Sandy Harris remarried on New Year's Eve, 1993. She and her children will live far away from Indian River County.

Don Dappen still works for the Vero Beach Police Department.

The Wessendorfs still live in Fellsmere in the winter and New York State in the summer.

Phil Williams has realized his longtime ambition to become a polygraph operator. Like Rick McIlwain, he attended the National Training Center of Polygraph Science in New York City, and he now heads the Indian River County Sheriff's Office Internal Affairs Unit and is an expert at giving lie-detector examinations. He is currently working on his master's degree.

The murder of Carol Orcutt in Clay County, Florida, remains unsolved, four years after the day that she was found. Lt. Jimm Redmond of the Clay County Sheriff's Office, working with Phil Williams, was able to establish that there was no way Tim Harris could have been in the area of her murder at the time she died. Redmond welcomes any new information on the case.

At the time of her murder Lorraine was thrilled to have been assigned to oversee the Micanopy Fall Festival in North Florida. The Micanopy Merchants' Association had met with her several weeks before her last, fatal, trip to Fort Lauderdale and hired Lorelei Promotions to produce the entire festival. Lorraine's enthusiasm was contagious, and many of the association members were excited about the festival for the first time in years.

Lorraine never got to see her plans come to fruition, but she had done such a superlative job at laying the groundwork that Ruth Straley was able to take over the project and see it through so that it would go off smoothly on schedule.

The Sixteenth Micanopy Fall Festival was a great success, and it was dedicated to the memory of Lorraine Hendricks.

"We have chosen to dedicate this festival to her memory so she can be remembered publicly for her accomplishments and the special feeling about life and living that she left behind with everyone whose life she touched—if even for a very short while."

Lorraine Hendricks was many things to many people. She was the pigtailed marathon runner, the fine lady in the satin gown and pearls, the cook who spent days cooking Polish Easter dinner, the self-assured and confident businesswoman, the daughter who made her parents proud, the beloved of one man, the daredevil athlete, the listener who became a mentor for frightened women who didn't think they could make it in this world, the animal lover. Probably, most of all, she was Katherine's mother.

Irony so often touches all of our lives. And it was so with Lorraine Hendricks. When Jodi Dombroski searched through all the pictures that she had saved to remember different phases of her daughter's life, she came across the one from Lori's days as a model. Lori had been so young and so very beautiful when she had posed in 1971 as part of a safe driving campaign for the Florida Highway Patrol.

Lori smiled as she held up a license plate that read "Arrive Alive!"

Black Christmas

This story *is one of many that I never wanted to write. I wanted to turn my head and walk away. It is too sad and too blindly senseless. If crazed, cruel murder could destroy these victims, then should we not all be afraid? The answer is "Of course." But then we must balance that by knowing that our lives would be stunted and boxed in if we lived daily with fear and anxiety. Somewhere in the middle there has to be an answer. Cautious awareness that there are those with skewed minds who march to bleakly perverted drummers can help us to stay a little safer. None of us can assume that every knock on our door is a threat. None of us should trust completely that each knock is powered by the hand of a friend. All of us could benefit by becoming more familiar with the arcane forces that empower humans like the oddly clear-eyed killer in this case.*

No one ever deserves *to be murdered. However, we often read about homicide victims who seem to have programmed themselves for violent death—the woman who goes home with a stranger from a bar, the careless hitchhiker (and, yes, the careless driver who picks up hitchhiking strangers), the drunk who flashes a roll of bills—those who do not take care. We are not like that, we say. It is more comfortable for us to suggest that the victim is partially responsible for his own fate.*

"Well, that would never happen to me," we say confidently. "I don't go to those places," or "See what happens when you don't use common sense."

It takes the inexplicable slaughter of innocents to knock away the crutch of smugness—"My God!" we realize. "If it could happen to them, it could happen to me. . . ."

Charles and Annie Goldmark and their sons—Derek, twelve, and Colin, ten—seemed the least likely family to encounter a killer. Although Charles, forty-one, was a partner in a successful law firm, he didn't practice criminal law. He was a civil attorney dealing with comparatively dull points of law, civil suits, an occasional divorce case, maybe, but nothing that inspired the need for vengeance by the litigants involved. He was brilliant, thoughtful, and kind. Annie (pronounced Ann-*ee*) was a lovely woman at forty-three. She was sparkling and vivacious. Because she was a native of France, Annie often flew with her sons to her homeland during summer vacations so they would understand her roots as well as their father's.

The Goldmarks epitomized what was good about the American family. First above everything, the four of them loved one another and their friends devotedly. They were involved in the concerns of their community, and they were successful—not only financially, but in the more ephemeral things of life. They lived a healthy life, and they were consummate nature lovers, often taking advantage of all that the Northwest had to offer.

Annie was beautiful; Charles was handsome. The little boys were delightful, bright children. Derek was only twelve, but already he played a skilled game of bridge. Ten-year-old Colin sang in the school choir at The Bush School, the private school both boys attended. They were the furthest thing in the world, though, from being snobby rich kids. Their heritage was one of public service and concern for those less fortunate; it was instilled in their genes. The Goldmarks were not unlike the Kennedy family in the days of Camelot.

Charles Goldmark had long been active in Democratic politics. He served as the party's legal counsel in Washington State and led Senator Gary Hart's presidential campaign in Washington State when Hart seemed to be the great hope of the Democratic party, the next "Kennedy" in the White House.

In essence, each of the four Goldmarks had infinite potential to change the world around them, to make it a better place for those citizens who had fallen through the cracks of life.

Although the Goldmarks seemed to have a secure future as 1984 drew to a close, and the promise of a long, good life, Charles had once known the emotional pain of being slandered and ostracized. Long before he met Annie, Charles's family was subjected to cruel and exaggerated publicity.

The story of the smear campaign against his father, Washington State Senator John Goldmark, and his mother, Sally, was so outrageous and convoluted that it became the subject of a book by U.S. District Court Judge William L. Dwyer: *The Goldmark Case: An American Libel Trial.* Dwyer's book was a tribute to Sally and John Goldmark, who had stood firmly behind what they knew was right even though they risked being destroyed.

What happened to John and Sally Goldmark had a

direct bearing on what happened to their son, Charles, and his family many, many years later. And all of it was based on lies, mistakes, half truths, misconceptions, and hate. When the first domino fell, all of the others toppled, creating havoc and death.

Charles's mother, Sally, was a native of New York, born to German immigrant parents. When she entered school in World War I she was quickly shunned because she spoke German. As a very young child she felt the sharp bite of prejudice. She was a vibrant, sensitive child with an IQ in the genius range. She would never forget how it felt to be singled out for torment for something for which she was in no way responsible. Her given name was Irma Ringe, but, when she was old enough she changed the German-sounding Irma to the more American name Sally.

All her life Sally Ringe Goldmark was devoted to helping people; she was particularly drawn to the underdog. After only one year of medical school the Great Depression of the 1930s forced Sally to give up her dream of becoming a doctor. She moved to Washington, D.C., where she worked for the National Youth Administration. It was the era of Franklin D. Roosevelt, and she was caught up in the excitement of the "New Deal." There *was* a way, she saw, to help those less fortunate. When the Work Projects Administration (W.P.A.) was formed in 1935, she saw that jobs were being found for hundreds of thousands of desperate men who had been broken by the Depression, and she realized the power of politics.

Sally Ringe aligned herself for brief periods with any number of causes and groups, always looking for the right channel to help mankind.

At the beginning of the Second World War Sally met a young attorney—John Goldmark. They got married, and John went off to war to serve with bravery and distinction in the U.S. Navy. When the war was over he and Sally struck out for the West, even though Sally had always been a city girl. She went willingly wherever her young husband would be happy. John and Sally Goldmark were about to fulfill their dream of adventure and country living, far from hustle of the East Coast.

In 1947 Charles Goldmark's parents settled on a wheat and cattle ranch on the Colville Indian Reservation in north central Washington State. The ranch flourished, and so did their two sons, Charles and Peter. Yellowed newspaper clippings show the Goldmark boys posing proudly on their ranch. The Goldmarks had become so much a part of the West that it was hard to imagine their origins in the East. The Okanogan country was the best of all possible worlds in which to raise two sons.

In 1956 John Goldmark was elected to the Washington Senate, where he would serve for many years. He was defeated in the mid-1960s after a rumor-filled campaign. Someone in the opposition party had discovered that Sally Ringe Goldmark had once belonged to the Communist Party. Although McCarthyism had reached its peak in the mid to late 1950s, Senator Joseph McCarthy's hearings had frightened and sensitized people to the threat of communists. Many careers were destroyed, often unjustly.

It was true. Sally Ringe had been a member of the Communist Party—for about as long as it took to blink an eye. It had been a long time before, when she was hardly more than a girl, filled as so many young people were in the twenties and thirties with sometimes misdirected fervor in their efforts to help mankind. Sally had quickly become disenchanted with the Communist Party. Her name remained someplace on the yellowing rosters of early communist followers. It was more than enough to provide fodder for the candidate running against her husband decades later. Far more devastating than John Goldmark's defeat at the polls was the damage done to his family's reputation. The rumors grew and became more scurrilous with each telling. This family, who had done so much for others, suffered mightily. The idyllic ranch life Charles and Peter Goldmark had always known was tainted now.

Those who took the trouble to seek truth at the source understood. But others believed the rumors that Sally Goldmark was, at the very least, a lifelong devotee of communism and therefore dangerous. Her name was on "their" lists; that meant she was one of "them." Too many forgot who Sally Goldmark really was and painted her with the black brush of vicious rumor.

The Goldmarks sued, charging libel. They won, but John Goldmark's political career was already smashed. In 1965 they moved from their beloved ranch to Seattle, where John Goldmark practiced law. Sally, her heart still in the vast Okanogan country, gave a family inheritance to the Omak town library so that they might commission an artist to carve the massive library doors. Books and people had always been her loves, a devotion handed down to her sons and her grandchildren.

John Goldmark died in 1979, and Sally lived on for six years. When she died she left behind letters filled with her memories of the Goldmarks' wonderful years of ranch life in the Okanogan. One paragraph was to take on macabre meaning in light of the tragedy of Christmas Eve, 1985. Sally wrote, "There is a great thing in the mechanism that pulsates in every beast and human, a heart that pushes out the juice and heat. It needs feeding, but it creates spirit, and the human angle is a joke, the kid, the banter, which lightens the spirit and warms the heart."

She could not have known about a man whose heart also demanded feeding, but feeding of quite another sort. Where Charles and Peter Goldmark had had it all—or as much as John and Sally could give their beloved sons—this man, this killer with a face like a mask, had had virtually nothing in life. Or at least it seemed that way to him, and he was always searching; while he searched he let hate suffuse him and burn away whatever conscience he once might have had.

When Sally Goldmark died on May 31, 1985, old friends and new mourned her, as did her sons, their wives, and her grandchildren. Only later would someone say, "Thank God Sally died before it happened; she couldn't have borne the grief."

Perhaps so. Barely six months later a disaster of cataclysmic proportions would strike her beloved family.

In December of 1985 the Seattle Homicide Unit was made up of fifteen detectives, three sergeants, a lieutenant, and a captain—all of whom would have preferred not to work on Christmas Eve. For as long as anyone could remember, there had always been approximately fifty to sixty murders a year in Seattle—not a particularly high rate per capita for a city whose environs were home to a million people. So far in 1985 the toll stood at fifty-five; the detectives who investigated murder were hoping it wouldn't climb any higher in the last week of the year. But they also knew that family beefs often exploded into violence during the holidays.

Some families were never meant to get as close to one another as the distance across the Christmas tree.

Detective Hank Gruber, who was also a graphic artist, made the murder charts each year. The 1985 chart was tacked to the wall in the captain's office. With his perfect, precise printing Gruber listed date, victim, sex, age, cause of death, location, and, hopefully, the name of the person charged with the crime. There was very little room left at the bottom of the chart for any additions.

Sergeant Jerry Yates's night crew of detectives was slated to work until midnight on December 24th, and the officers were pleased to find everything blessedly quiet during the early evening. Not a squawk on the phone, nothing from radio—not even a family fight. If they could just make it to the witching hour, they could go home and celebrate Christmas the way civilians did. After midnight Detective Sergeant Joe Sanford and Detectives Hank Gruber and Rudy Sutlovich had volunteered to be on standby to cover any calls that might come in between 12 and 7:30 a.m., when the Homicide Unit offices were closed. In fact, filled with holiday spirit, Sanford decided that Gruber and Sutlovich would start early—at 9 p.m.

It remained quiet on Christmas Eve on the fifth floor of the Public Safety Building through 7, 8, 9 p.m. Finally Sergeant Yates told his men to go home and have dinner with their families. They turned off the lights and locked the office door; if something *should* happen, radio would call standby detectives.

"I got a call from Joe Sanford at 9:30," Hank Gruber remembers the beginning of Seattle Police Case 85-551331. For the Homicide Unit it would be H85-365. "Standby had started earlier than we'd gambled on—Joe had a murder. I said, 'What is it?'

And he said 'Well, from what I can gather, it was some kind of a Christmas party, and it sounds like somebody got in an argument and they started shooting, and they've got some people in Harborview [King County's hospital]—and one is deceased. We can handle it. You and I can just check it out, see what gives.'"

Reports often come in that way. Not garbled, exactly, but piecemeal. Sergeant Sanford sent Hank Gruber to the address furnished to try to get a fix on what had happened.

"I really expected to go up there and find it was some family beef, arguing how to carve the turkey or something," Gruber says wryly, remembering. "When I got up there, of course, I saw that we had something entirely different—and I needed help. Joe ended up calling Rudy in. And later we had to call a whole lot of the guys in."

The address given was on 36th Avenue in the Madrona District of Seattle overlooking Lake Washington. It was a good address in an upper-middle-class neighborhood. There was a breathtaking view of the huge lake from the rear windows of all the houses on the street. The home was like so many built in the 1930s in Seattle; it was a modified Norman cottage with two stories on the street which became three floors at the back as the yard fell away. Hank Gruber saw the police patrol units parked in front and lights on inside the house. Colored Christmas tree lights glowed in the front window.

Patrol Officer Dane Bean, the first officer at the scene, briefed the detective on what he knew so far. The call for help had come in from friends of the Charles Goldmark family. They had come to the house that evening to attend a Christmas party, but no one had answered their knocks. Puzzled and a little worried, they had gone home and telephoned the Goldmarks.

"Nobody answered," Bean said, "so they came back over. They thought they heard someone calling out or crying very faintly inside. They had a key and went in."

What the Goldmarks' friends had found was beyond anything they could have imagined. All Bean knew for sure was that everyone inside had been injured. He thought there was one fatality.

"The aid car took the man and the boys in," Bean explained. "The woman is upstairs. We haven't moved her—or anything in the room."

Gruber stepped into the home. There was something unreal about this; this home simply didn't look like the scene of a homicide. Everything was immaculate. The house was decorated festively for Christmas. There were stockings hung on the fireplace and a poinsettia plant on the coffee table near the tree. In the dining alcove there was a table impeccably set with fine china and red napkins, with a centerpiece made of candles and holly. Places were set for ten people.

The kitchen bar was crowded with candles, chips and dip, hors d'oeuvres. Gruber sniffed and turned toward the kitchen. The oven was still on; the burners had been turned down to simmer while pots of food cooked. Everything smelled wonderful; nothing had even begun to burn. Where was the cook who had prepared all this? She had to have stepped away from her kitchen only a little while ago.

A *party*. That's what the neighbors had said to Dane Bean. They were going to celebrate Christmas Eve at a festive dinner. Gruber sighed and carefully switched the burners and oven to off.

The name Goldmark didn't mean anything special

to him; Hank Gruber was a New Yorker, a transplant into the Northwest, and he was not up on Seattle history. He had long since learned that a clean and classy house was certainly no guarantee that domestic violence wouldn't occur, but his gut feeling said no. This didn't look like a domestic violence call.

Besides, Bean said the husband was injured to the point of unconsciousness, too, and the friends who'd called the police insisted this was a happy family. A happy, loving family. No way could this be a papa-kills-mama case.

Gruber's glance at the dining room and kitchen had taken only twenty seconds at most. Now he moved toward the stairs.

Rudy Sutlovich arrived just then and followed him up. The house was very still.

On Christmas Eve, 1985, they climbed the stairs to the home's top floor, walking softly on the thick beige carpeting, still feeling somehow that they were intruding. The detectives had only to walk across a narrow hall to be in the master bedroom, a huge room that measured 15 feet by 19 feet. They stood just inside the doorway, silent for a moment, taking it all in.

The room was a little cluttered with the last-minute rush of Christmas. There were wrapping paper, ribbons and seals, boxes covered with shiny blue paper, other presents waiting to be wrapped. There was a damp towel at the entrance to the master bath, either carelessly or hurriedly dropped.

Hank Gruber looked toward the bay window with its curving window seat, and his chest tightened. He forced his eyes down to the rug and saw that it was spattered in spots and drenched in other places with both bright red and partially drying dark red fluid. The little boys had been there, Bean was saying.

The woman lay on her side, her hands pulled behind her, her slender wrists handcuffed. Even in death she was beautiful. Her robe had been pulled off her shoulders, leaving her partially nude. That didn't necessarily indicate sexual attack; the robe would have slipped as her hands were yanked backward.

The detectives could see that she had suffered a deep stab wound to her chest, a fatal wound.

This would be Annie Goldmark—a beautiful woman who looked to be a decade younger than they had been told she was. Someone had dealt terrible crushing blows to her skull, apparently as she lay helplessly manacled. She lay with her feet pointing toward an antique organ and her head toward the bed.

The probable murder weapons still rested beside her—a steam iron with its plastic handle broken off by great force, the plate bloodstained, with hairs caught in it. A long, narrow knife was there, too, a kitchen knife. It looked as if the killer had found his weapons in his victims' own home.

One of the patrol officers produced a ring of handcuff keys, and he tested them until one fit the cuffs on Annie's wrists. The officer slipped them off and slid them carefully into a plastic bag to be checked for fingerprints. A gold bracelet still encircled Annie Goldmark's wrist, and an expensive diamond ring remained undisturbed on her finger.

The investigators stepped carefully past the debris left by the Seattle Fire Department's Medic One crew: bandages, hypodermic needles and plastic tubing, packets of dextrose solution emptied of their fluid. Fourteen paramedics and fire personnel had rushed to the Goldmark home. It was apparent that the fire department medics had fought desperately to save the injured.

For both medics and cops the rule is always, "First of all, protect life."

The Seattle Fire Department has been a front runner in emergency medical care. If any paramedic team would be able to save the Goldmark family, Medic One was it. They had raced time and stanched blood from terrible wounds to save as many lives as they could on what had become a bleak and tragic Christmas Eve.

The Seattle detectives didn't know how Charles Goldmark and his sons were doing, but here in this lovely room there was no life left to protect. Dr. Corinne Fligner, from the King County Medical Examiner's Office, examined Annie Goldmark's body. She found that her left ear had been lacerated and that there was a deep puncture wound just behind the ear, in the neck, as well as the chest wound.

Annie's body was removed by the M.E.'s office, and the investigators were alone in the pleasant bedroom that had become an abattoir.

Bean pointed to a large bloodied spot in the entrance of the room. "The man was there when we got here, with his legs pointing toward the stairway."

Hank Gruber and Rudy Sutlovich could tell that the victims had all been down on the floor when they were struck with whatever object had been used to bludgeon them—probably the steam iron. "We could see that from the blood spray pattern," Gruber explained. "So it wasn't like people were running around and trying to get away; they were hit when they were down, helpless."

Rudy Sutlovich looked at the spot where the children had lain and saw a trace of brain tissue. He glanced at Gruber and saw something in his partner's eyes. They were both thinking the same thing. There was every chance the kids wouldn't make it—or maybe worse, that they'd survive terribly brain-damaged. Had the parents seen their children being bludgeoned? Or had the kids had to watch as their mother and father were attacked?

The investigators didn't have to think about that now; they were grateful that they had work to do. The first major puzzle was who had done this and why. And the second was how one person could get control of four people. Perhaps there had been more than one killer.

The detectives peered into the bathroom. The tub was wet; there were more wet towels on the floor, and fresh clothing—a woman's party outfit—was laid out on the bed. Annie Goldmark had obviously just taken a shower and was preparing to get dressed when the intruder—or intruders—grabbed her and handcuffed her.

The patrol officers said that Charles Goldmark had been fully dressed. His neighbors had already managed to cut the handcuffs off his wrists by the time the police arrived. Colin and Derek had also been fully clothed, but someone had yanked their sweaters up around their shoulders and necks to restrain them.

All four Goldmarks had suffered severe battering wounds to the head. Someone had to have been in the grip of rage to carry out such a frenzied, brutal attack.

But *why?*

By 10:45 that night, Sutlovich, Gruber, and Sanford were joined in their investigation by Detectives Sonny Davis, Duane Homan, and Jim Yoshida. Teams of investigators would be either at the crime scene or at the hospital until six or seven on Christmas morning, gathering evidence, bagging it, labeling it, asking questions. They wouldn't be asking questions of the three surviving victims, however; they were comatose and in critical condition.

Detectives had assured themselves early on that there was no forced entry. One of the Goldmarks had to have let the killer in. Searching through the house, the police found the path of exit. The back door in the basement was standing wide open. It had a lock that was dead-bolted on both sides. No one could get in or *out* without a key.

"We assumed the killer had taken the keys," Gruber recalled. "We didn't know how many cars the victims had at that point, so we wondered if the killer might have left in one of their vehicles."

But then they found signs that someone had tried unsuccessfully to get into the detached garage. Unless he found a car on the street he would have had to slip away on foot through the sloping backyard. That was the likeliest possibility. He would have had little time between the attacks and the arrival of the first of the Goldmark's invited guests. He would have been a fool to appear at the front of the house. Indeed, he was probably going out the basement door as friends pounded on the front door.

Dr. Michael Copass, head of the Medic One program, told Detectives Jim Yoshida and Duane Homan that Charles Goldmark had not only been battered on the head; someone had deliberately inserted a thin knife into the brain itself, through the skull fractures made by the iron. The little boys had both been battered and stabbed in the head. They were in extremely critical condition.

The investigators wondered if the killer had been someone they all knew; he seemed to have gone to great lengths to assure himself that even the children would not be able to speak and identify him.

Or *her*. Nobody knew at that point whether they were looking for a man, a woman, or several people.

Back at the Goldmark home Sutlovich and Gruber took *everything* from the bedroom that might conceivably be helpful. "It's kind of an interesting thing," Gruber explains. "Before you figure out the crime, it's hard to know what's important and what isn't—so you end up taking things, and you really don't know why . . . You just say, 'Well, we'll take it—and see if it matters.' So one of the things we found was a handkerchief near her—kind of bloodied up—and we found some handkerchiefs and paper towels over where the kids were, too. It just didn't make sense at the time. What's with the handkerchiefs? They surely weren't able to hold them to their own wounds—and why would the killer do that? We found out later that they were soaked with chloroform. The lab brought it out—in blood studies and from the handkerchief— but by the time we got there you couldn't smell it. That would explain why the victims were down and why they didn't fight."

Indeed it would. Had someone chloroformed the Goldmarks to subdue them and then bludgeoned and knifed them when they were unconscious? If so, it was small comfort to those who loved them. They would not have known what was happening to them.

The most difficult thing of all for the detectives to try to get a handle on was a motive. The place had not been ransacked. The Goldmarks had two computers, several television sets, antique guns on the wall, presents under the Christmas tree, paintings, jewelry, objects d'art, stereo equipment, all the things that any professional burglar would have taken. But nothing had been touched. The only thing the investigators found that pointed to robbery was Charles Goldmark's wallet. It lay on the bedroom floor, and all the credit cards were fanned out on a shelf, as if someone had riffled through them, searching for particular cards. The detectives couldn't tell which, if any, cards were missing. They would have to check later with friends or family members to see what cards Goldmark had.

While evidence was being gathered Sonny Davis, Duane Homan, and Jim Yoshida talked with the friends of the victims, who had gathered anxiously on the ninth floor of Harborview Hospital.

Everyone was so shaken by the shock of Annie's murder and the attacks on her husband and children that detectives had been hesitant to ask much about the Goldmarks' background. Now Homan and Yoshida (who were referred to at Seattle Homicide as "Ho" and "Yo") realized how well-known the victims were. Chief of Police Patrick Fitzsimmons was there in the hospital waiting room, and so was Bill Dwyer, who had written the book about the elder Goldmarks, and Jim Wickwire, an internationally famous mountain climber and one of nine partners in Goldmark's law firm.

Jim Wickwire explained that Charles Goldmark's clients were strictly civil litigants—as was the whole firm's practice. Charles had represented Seattle's historic Pike Place Market, the Seattle Art Museum, and the Flight Museum. There had been absolutely no hassles, no resentments, no threats—nothing—in Goldmark's caseload.

One friend, Janet Lilly,* said she was a very close friend of Annie's. They talked every day, either in person or by phone. They had stored Christmas presents at each other's homes to keep them away from snoopy children, and they had planned to exchange them on Christmas Day. Lilly had talked to

Annie several times on December 24th, the last time at twenty minutes to six.

Lilly said that the Goldmarks had two cars at present—a BMW and an Alpha Romeo. They also owned a Volkswagen Rabbit, but Charles's sister-in-law had borrowed it to drive back to eastern Washington when she missed a flight.

"Chuck was in a wonderful mood, very festive," Janet Lilly said as she recalled the afternoon of Christmas Eve. "Annie always cooked a traditional meal for Christmas Eve, and she was probably going to put on her traditional Swedish gown, as she always did."

Lilly shook her head at the question of marital problems. No, she was positive Chuck and Annie were happy together. If not, she would have known about it.

Homan and Yoshida talked next to Allie Chambers.* She had gone to help Annie at noon that day, and they had set the table together. "I left at a quarter to five to run over to my house and change clothes for dinner—that was to be at seven. Chuck was wearing a red velour shirt and Levi's, and Annie was wearing jeans, a red sweater, blue turtleneck, and a blue apron. She was going to change into her Scandinavian dress after she took a shower."

An hour and fifteen minutes after Allie Chambers left she had returned with her family. She had been a little surprised to find that the porch light was off and that only the kitchen light was on inside. They knocked and then banged and rattled the door—but no one came.

"I thought they were playing a joke on us or something," she said sadly, "so we sat at the outside picnic table on the deck waiting for them. We finally left a note and went on home."

Once home, Allie phoned the Goldmarks and found the line was busy. Puzzled and beginning to be worried, the Chamberses returned to the Goldmarks' twenty minutes later. Allie Chambers thought she heard a faint sound through the peephole in the front door. She called to her husband, Leif.* Frankly worried, the couple went to mutual friends—the Ben Walkers*—who had a key to the Goldmark house.

With that key they had opened the front door. They followed the sounds to the upstairs master bedroom and, horrified, found their friends on the floor.

Leif Chambers had heard Charles Goldmark calling "Leif . . . Leif . . . hurts . . . hurting . . ." He was trembling and complaining about the handcuffs, and, in shock themselves, Walker and Chambers could think only of getting those handcuffs off.

The telephone in the residence was dead. Chambers and Walker worked with tin snips and a hacksaw to cut the cuffs off of Charles Goldmark. As they worked they saw that someone had tossed a blanket over the little boys—as if even the killer could not bear to look upon what he had done to them.

Two patrolmen had ridden in the ambulance with Charles Goldmark on the slight chance that he might be able to identify his family's attacker. Detective Sonny Davis continued still to sit beside Goldmark's bed at the hospital, but he was either silent or incoherent.

One of the Goldmark boys was undergoing a CAT scan, and the other was in the operating room.

At Homan's and Yoshida's request, Ben Walker and Allie Chambers searched their memories for anything unusual that might have happened in the neighborhood during the hour before the party. All they could come up with was that they had seen a 1975 green

Datsun pickup truck drive by the Goldmark house several times. There were two men in it, and they were laughing.

The ninth floor waiting room was jammed with people, and everyone tried to help the detectives. Almost all of Charles Goldmark's law partners were there. None of them could recall that Chuck Goldmark had an enemy. The only thing they could think of that might have sparked animosity was that the firm had many applicants for jobs. The partners often sent rejection letters on the firm's stationery and signed their own names.

Canvasses of the 36th Avenue neighborhood elicited information from a woman who lived next door. She had opened her door to a stranger earlier that evening. The man had carried a white box, and he slurred his words as he asked for "Charles . . . somebody." She had told him she didn't recognize the name.

She remembered the "delivery man," though. It was his eyes that stayed with her. The man was tall, dark-haired, and he'd had light eyes, strangely penetrating—almost crazy eyes. She described the man to Detective Al Smalley, and the sketch he drew was chilling to look at. It was the eyes that made it so. They were blank, inscrutable—but unforgettable.

Ordinarily, someone delivering packages would be easy to trace. But it was Christmastime; everybody on the street was receiving package deliveries. The investigators found a number of packages in the victims' home, but no plain white package.

Nobody on the Goldmarks' street had the heart to celebrate Christmas. Silently, neighbors walked up and left flowers on the doorstep of the house where nobody lived anymore. A little shrine grew there. Vases full of flowers stirring in the rainy wind. But a sad, macabre shrine it was, bordered with yellow plastic ribbons that signified police barriers not to be crossed.

The word from the hospital wasn't good. The three surviving members of the family were not expected to live. Brains so insulted by bludgeoning and knives swelled against the hard plates of the skull, doing more damage, even though physicians had operated to remove sections of the skull to allow more room. And infection was a constant danger. Charles and Colin and Derek could neither hear nor speak.

The Seattle homicide detectives working the case were quick to admit they were in trouble. They had no evidence at the scene that was going to help them— unless they came up with a suspect to link it to. The handcuffs had been brought to the victims' home; the weapons were already there. They had isolated a single fingerprint, but it wasn't any good unless they had prints to compare it to. AFIS—Automated Fingerprint Identification System—was still a few years away. The killer had apparently worn gloves for most of the time he carried out his ghastly work. This appeared to have been a stranger-to-stranger crime, the hardest kind to solve.

And they still had no motive. They would need help from the public. Or a confession. Or some luck.

In Seattle's Broadway District, however—a few miles west of the Goldmarks' house—things *were* happening.

Max Stingley* was a highly educated black man who lived in an apartment in the Broadway District. He was a kindhearted man who had been known to help somebody down on his luck, and Christmastime is a bad time to be down and out. When Stingley heard a knock on his door he was a little surprised to find a man he knew only as David. He knew David slightly as a member of a group he belonged to called the Fox Club.*

The Fox Club was a rather loose organization. It was basically a discussion group whose purpose was "promotion of the strict adherence to the Constitution of the United States." As far as Stingley had been able to tell, the Fox Club was a peaceful enough organization, although its members felt that their rights as citizens were steadily being taken away from them because officials weren't sticking to the Constitution. It was not a militant group; it was a rather homogeneous bunch of people who liked to get together in a restaurant over cups of coffee and discuss political philosophy.

Stingley confided that he was a bit wary of the members, however. He sensed they weren't fond of Jews, and he wondered if blacks might be next.

But here was this kid—David, the one who lived with the lady doctor, Suzanne Perreau*—at his door, saying he had been wandering the streets for seventy-two hours, and that he was cold and needed a place to crash. Stingley had reluctantly invited him in.

David had always been pale with dark circles under his eyes, but on Christmas night he had really looked wasted. Stingley was tired himself and told his impromptu guest that he was going to bed. When he left, David was sitting on the couch in the living room.

It was what Stingley found on the coffee table before dawn the next morning that made him nervous enough to call the police—even though he wasn't sure what it meant. He had seen the kid scribbling on a tablet the night before, but he couldn't figure out if the scrawled words were supposed to be true or some kind of creative writing. Whatever it was, it made the hairs stand up on the back of his neck.

TO WHOM IT MAY CONCERN, I AM THE PERSON YOU ARE LOOKING FOR IN THE GOLDMARK CASE.

I KNOW WHAT I DID WAS A VERY TERRIBLE THING. THAT IS WHY I AM AS YOU SEE ME NOW.

I WANT IT PERFECTLY UNDERSTOOD THAT NO ONE ELSE HAD ANYTHING WHATSOEVER TO DO WITH WHAT I DID. I WENT TO GREAT LENGTHS TO MAKE SURE OF THAT.

THE PERSON THAT I LIVE WITH DOESN'T EVEN KNOW THAT I AM WANTED ON A DIFFERENT CHARGE. SHE RE-CIEVED [sic] A COUPLE OF MESSAGES ON HER MACHINE, BUT I ERASED THEM BEFORE SHE GOT TO THEM.

I DID NOT USE THE RIFLE THAT I PURCHASED A FEW WEEKS AGO. INSTEAD, I FOOLED THEM WITH A TOY PISTOL WHICH YOU WILL FIND IN THE STORAGE LOCKER. I THREW THE RIFLE AWAY A COUPLE OF WEEKS AGO.

AGAIN, I WANT IT UNDERSTOOD THAT NO ONE KNEW ANYTHING ABOUT THIS, SO PLEASE DO NOT CAUSE ANY UNNESESSARY [sic] SUFFERING TO INNOCENT PEOPLE. I THINK THAT I'VE ALREADY DONE ENOUGH.

I GUESS I SHOULD TELL YOU WHY I DID WHAT I DID. THAT WAY, YOU WON'T HAVE TO ASK OTHER PEOPLE ABOUT IT.

MY LIFE IS A MESS. IT HAS BEEN SINCE MY WIFE LEFT. SUE HAD BEEN TRYING TO HELP ME STRAIGHTEN IT OUT BUT . . .

That was all. Either David had been working on a rough draft and decided to start again when he woke up, or he really didn't want to reveal exactly *why* he had done what he had done.

Max Stingley had never heard the name Goldmark. What with the holiday and all, he hadn't read a paper for a couple of days or had the TV news on. He read the note again, glanced at David, who was still asleep, and puttered about making coffee while he decided what he should do. The man he knew only as David was definitely acting weird.

His guest woke up and was sitting on the couch watching television when Stingley said he was going out to get a pack of cigarettes. Stingley crossed the darkened street to a club he belonged to at 11th and Union. Still troubled, he asked a few tv early birds there if they had heard about some shooting or something having to do with a Goldmark.

They looked at him, astounded. Everybody in Seattle must surely know about the Goldmark attack by now. Where the heck had Stingley been, they asked. Somebody held up the front page of the morning *Post-Intelligencer* for December 26. The name Goldmark was spread all over it.

Stingley felt sick. The note he had found on the table in his apartment wasn't fiction at all. He had just slept through the night with a probable killer in his apartment.

Rudy Sutlovich had arrived to work the day shift in Homicide shortly after 7 a.m. on December 26. There was no one there except the two secretaries. The phone rang, and Sutlovich reached for it; it was Elizabeth Eddy, the chief radio dispatcher. "I've got a citizen on the 911 line who says his name is Max Stingley—he's at 11th and Union. Says he's got a guy watching TV in his apartment who says he killed the Goldmarks. What should I do?"

"Get a uniform up there," Sutlovich said urgently, pulling his coat back on. "I'm leaving right now."

Sutlovich ran for the police garage; Gruber coordinated with Dispatch. Sonny Davis, and Sutlovich headed up the hill toward Broadway. By the time they reached Boren and Madison they could hear sirens, and the radio picked up sounds of a foot chase nearby.

"You don't suppose that's our man, do you?" Sutlovich kidded Davis.

Davis shrugged. "No way. That would be too easy."

But it was.

Stingley had been talking to the uniformed officers in front of his club when his guest happened to glance out the window and see the conference. David deduced correctly that they were talking about him. He realized that Max Stingley must have found the note he had been trying to write.

David didn't wait around for the officers to come knocking on the door. He ran out of the apartment building and headed north on 11th Avenue. Stingley saw him and pointed him out to the officers. Patrolmen R. P. Cuncan and Peter Hogan raced after the tall, slender man. Feet pounding, they ran north on 11th, halfway around the block, and then south on Broadway, where the two officers began to close the gap. They saw the suspect had a vial of something in his hand. They watched him lift it to his lips and then toss it away.

In the next instant they had him, and they forced him to the ground and handcuffed him. Just at that moment Rudy Sutlovich and Sonny Davis drove up.

Sutlovich walked over to where the cuffed suspect lay, all the fight seemingly gone out of him. Hunkering down from his considerable height, Sutlovich looked for the first time into the face of the man who gave his name as David Lewis Rice. Sutlovich advised him of his rights under Miranda.

"Why did you run from the officers?" Sutlovich asked.

"I don't want to answer that."

Rice was young, only twenty-seven. He had straight black hair, a luxuriant mustache, and a neat beard. He might have been considered handsome, despite his pasty complexion, but there was something odd about him. His movements and his speech were stilted; he seemed almost like a store mannequin—not real.

"It was his eyes," Sutlovich recalled.

"I looked in those eyes, and I remembered the picture Al Smalley drew from the Goldmarks' neighbor's description. It was as if I were looking into the eyes in that picture. She said she'd never forget those eyes, and I could see why. They were very distinct—faraway, yes—vacant."

Rice had not struggled at all once the policemen caught him. They crawled into the Dempsey Dumpster to retrieve the vial he had tossed there in his flight and asked him what it was.

"Nicotine," Rice replied. "Liquid nicotine."

Could nicotine kill you? Sonny Davis and Rudy Sutlovich wondered about that. Rice seemed to be all right. It had probably been some kind of grandstand play.

Sonny Davis took custody of the prisoner and headed back to the homicide offices. Rudy Sutlovich wanted to talk more with Max Stingley.

Stingley said he really didn't know David Rice—that he hadn't even known his last name until a few minutes before. When Sutlovich asked about the note, which seemed now to be a confession, Stingley said he guessed it was back at his apartment.

Fortunately, it was still there, and Sutlovich retrieved it for evidence. Detective Sergeant Don

Cameron, Sonny Davis, and his partner, John Boatman, could use a copy of it in their interrogation of David Rice.

The case was officially assigned to John Boatman and Sonny Davis. It was their task now to try to get a complete confession or, at the very least, some explanation for the baffling attack on the Goldmark family.

David Rice had been advised once again of his rights under Miranda. Indeed, Sonny Davis had him read those rights aloud. The detectives had obtained an attorney for Rice—one of Seattle's veteran defense attorneys, Bill Lanning, had come to headquarters and conferred with the suspect.

Still, Rice said he thought he wanted to tell them his story, attorney or not. Sonny Davis asked Rice if he was ready to do that, and David Rice hesitated, saying he was not sure yet. Asked to empty his pockets, the suspect laid items on the table. Among them were two key rings, rings that each carried handcuff keys that would open the cuffs found on the victims.

Sonny Davis showed the copy of the note from Max Stingley's apartment to David Rice and asked him if he had written it. He acknowledged that he had. Asked if he cared to finish the letter, Rice nodded. Davis gave him a pen and left him alone, but when he returned he saw that Rice had written nothing. He didn't want to write about it; he wanted to *tell* the detectives what had happened in the Goldmark house on Christmas Eve.

It was December 26, 13:07 hours in police lingo, 1:07 p.m. on the clock, when the suspect began to talk, fully aware that a tape recorder was rolling and catching all his words.

It was a backwards kind of case. The investigators

believed that they had the killer in custody, but this
twenty-seven-year-old man with the empty eyes was
not what they had expected. What *had* they expected?
How could anyone know what kind of a killer could
plot the monstrous crime against the Goldmark family?

It was hard to imagine Rice in Charles and Annie
Goldmark's world. He had not robbed them. Why,
then, had he struck them down? He *had* been looking
for them specifically. He had asked for them by name.
But why had he sought them out? And who was he?

David Lewis Rice was born on November 11, 1958.
Armistice Day. He had two older brothers and a sister
who remembered that he had never fit in—almost
from the time he could walk. He had been raised in
Arizona, and he had been a child who was always
alone. His brothers teased him and laughed at him
because he was an easy target.

When David was eleven, his brothers heard a
peculiar thumping sound coming from his room.
When they forced open the door they found him
hanging by the neck, unconscious. He was already
turning blue. They cut him down, and his skin recovered a pink hue as he regained consciousness. His
mother took him to a doctor, but he received no
therapy of any kind.

Things went on as before. David Rice's brothers
were embarrassed to be associated with him because
he was such a klutz. Later one brother rather ruefully
remembered pushing him out of a tree.

"He never fought back."

Surprisingly, David had dated, gotten married, and
fathered a child—but the marriage didn't last. Nothing lasted for him. He had no talent for life or for

getting along with people or for holding a job. He began to feel more and more that the world was against him.

David Rice moved to Seattle in the early 1980s, perhaps to be closer to his brothers, who lived in Washington. Despite the way they had teased him when they were all children, they did care about him, and they urged him to come north. For a time he worked as a welder for a steel company. He was the lead man in his shop, and he made good money. But then the business he worked for went bankrupt, and he, along with the other men he worked with, was shorted on his last paycheck.

The injustice of it all seemed to trigger overwhelming hatred in David Rice.

He became strongly anti-communist in the early spring of 1983. Communism was something he could focus his hate on. Despite his skills as a welder, he couldn't seem to find a job. He lived on the edges of life, subsisting on unemployment and through the kindness of strangers from the summer of 1984 until his arrest. For eighteen months he had roamed Seattle, full of a malign hunger for vengeance. He wasn't really sure what it was he hated. He was angry at the big-business bosses who had fired him and shorted him on his paycheck. But then he hated communists, too, and he didn't seem to understand that he was at cross-purposes.

Literally on the streets in early 1985, David Rice met Dr. Suzanne Perreau, who was a podiatrist. She was several years older than he. Dr. Perreau belonged to the Fox Club, and she introduced David to the group. He was enthusiastic about the club's discussions, although he sometimes seemed to go on too long when he had comments to make, his voice rising and saliva gathering at the corners of his mouth. The Fox Club was tolerant of him, though. He believed, as they did, in the sanctity of the U. S. Constitution.

David Rice was also fascinated with guns, survivalists, explosives, soldiers of fortune, paramilitary activities, and, of course, with the need to fight communist invasion.

At some point after he lost his job Rice read an article that changed his world, and, eventually, the world of many others. He concluded that that article identified Charles Goldmark as a leading communist. It is far more likely that David Rice's mind was not tracking well. The *only* link Charles Goldmark ever had with communism was his mother's short-lived membership in the party more than a dozen years before he was born.

"Do you know the Goldmarks?" Sonny Davis asked him now as they sat in one of the tiny interview rooms in the Homicide Unit.

"Only by history," Rice answered vaguely.

"History from where?"

"Newspaper clippings and so forth . . . In today's paper it mentioned that Charles Goldmark was a prominent figure in the Democratic Party. What it doesn't mention is that he was also a prominent figure in the Communist Party. . . . I had found out that he had been brought before the Senate subcommittee on Un-Americanism . . ."

"This Mr. Goldmark?" Boatman sounded puzzled.

"Right."

Charles Goldmark? Davis asked.

David Rice nodded, as if the detectives were woefully uninformed. "Charles Goldmark . . . nothing had been done. He was at one time the regional director of the American Communist Party."

Rice said he didn't think he had kept any of the articles he had read that had told about his victims' "past." He thought he might have some of his notes.

"How did you know where the Goldmarks lived?" Davis asked.

"A newspaper clipping. It showed that he had just moved into a house on 36th." Rice said he thought he had read that in an issue of the *Seattle Times* sometime in March, 1983.

"You're talking a couple of years ago, then. Has the Goldmark family been on your mind, then, for some period of time?"

"Yeah, I'd say in the last six months."

David Rice said he had to get himself mentally set to do what he planned to do.

"What were you going to do?" Boatman asked.

"I was going to kill the Goldmarks."

Detectives Davis and Boatman and Sergeant Cameron watched the tall, thin man across the interview table, wondering if he really could explain the virtually unexplainable to them.

David Rice's confession took seventy-seven pages when it was transcribed from tape. He told a bizarrely tragic story, shocking even to detectives who had seen and heard all manner of horror.

By mid-1985 Rice decided he had to kill Charles Goldmark. He believed that Goldmark was both a Jew and a Communist. In actual fact, of course, Charles Goldmark was neither. But to David Rice, Goldmark represented the enemy.

Rice's first reason for destroying Goldmark had been political, but he had some "financial reasons," too. "I assumed that he would have an amount of cash on him. I didn't know how much, but it would be enough to get me by."

By Christmastime, 1985, David Rice was in difficult financial straits.

Although Dr. Perreau had allowed him to live with her, she began to doubt her judgment. She began to find David irritating. She returned home one day to find her television set was missing. She asked David where it was, and he said he had taken it.

"Why?" she asked.

"For the money. I pawned it for ten dollars."

The final straw, however, was more serious. In late October Dr. Perreau found a rifle that David had purchased and hidden. She took it out of her apartment and gave it to a friend. She was leaving for Florida for a vacation over Christmas, and she gave David an ultimatum. She told him that he must be completely out of her apartment when she returned from her trip on December 28th.

Unknowing, Dr. Perreau had unleashed hellish forces. David Rice's financial picture was getting worse and worse because he wasn't working. He was spending his days searching for "enemies" in the library, and he had no time to bother with work. Soon he would have no place to go. He blamed the communists.

The answer to all of his problems had seemed simple to him. He would go to Charles Goldmark's home and steal money from him. This would alleviate Rice's precarious financial condition, which he felt was caused by the Goldmarks and people like them.

He would also obtain from Charles Goldmark a list of the other leading people in the Communist Party, because, as Rice explained to the detectives, they weren't, "after all, listed in the phone book."

After that, David Rice said, he would kill Charles Goldmark and his wife. He hated them with a passion, although he had never seen them—although he hadn't researched much about them or asked questions. He didn't dare; he didn't want to raise any eyebrows.

Of necessity, Rice worked alone. He didn't know what the Goldmarks looked like. He didn't know how old they were. He didn't know they had young sons. He knew virtually nothing about them. He knew only that Charles Goldmark was an attorney, and attorneys, he knew, weren't always on "the up and up."

The world had always cheated David Lewis Rice, and he was about to get even.

On Christmas Eve day David had gone to Dr. Perreau's house to water her plants, just as he had promised he would. He was storing some of his belongings there, and he wanted to get his green parka. Its many pockets would make it well-suited for what he planned. He was wearing blue jeans, a red sweater, and a pair of work boots. He also grabbed a pair of white cotton work gloves.

"I took a toy pistol. I had bought the rifle earlier, which I was going to use, but I figured . . . it would just make a lot of noise."

Rice admitted to Davis and Boatman that he had purchased an M-1 carbine from the Central Gun Exchange but said he had thrown it away two weeks before Christmas Eve because it was too big and too bulky. It was hard to carry around. He hadn't planned to shoot them anyway, he said. He said he had wanted it to keep them under his control. He didn't mention the gun Dr. Perreau had given away.

"When was it, then," Davis asked, "you bought the toy pistol?"

"That was Christmas Eve."

"Was it a realistic-looking pistol?"

"Yes . . . probably the closest it would come to would be a detective's special."

"A snub-nosed revolver . . . black?" Davis asked.

"Uh-huh."

"Thirty-eight-type caliber?" Boatman asked.

"Mmm-hmm."

David said he had purchased it at the Toys Galore store on Christmas Eve, paying three dollars for it. He had also bought two pairs of handcuffs at a Big 5 Sporting Goods store—but that had been a long time ago, maybe four months. He had stuffed the gun, the handcuffs, the gloves, two rags, and two bottles of chloroform in the pockets of his green parka and then taken the number seven bus downtown, where he could transfer to a number three that would take him to the Goldmark's neighborhood.

He had only taken two bottles of chloroform and two rags, he explained, because he expected to confront only two people: Mr. and Mrs. Goldmark.

"Is there any way that evening that you prepared yourself with—" Davis asked.

"No, no drugs," Rice cut in. "No alcohol. I was stone sober."

He hadn't needed drugs or alcohol; David Rice had been preparing himself mentally for six months to carry out his plans. Sometimes he hadn't thought that much about the Goldmarks, but inside he had known that it would be only a matter of time until he did what he meant to do. That it happened on Christmas Eve was just a coincidence, he said.

"Did you include Mrs. Goldmark?" John Boatman asked.

"Yes."

"Did that include anybody who was there—who appeared to be a Goldmark?" Davis said.

"Yes."

"How did you know you had to take a certain bus to get to the area where the Goldmarks lived?" Davis asked.

"I had been there twice before. . . . The first time was, I believe, about the first of November. . . . I went there just to see what kind of house it was and just check out the neighborhood."

This, then, was the man who appeared at the front door of the Charles Goldmark residence a half hour before they were to host a Christmas Eve dinner. David Rice was an angry man. A desperate man. A man who, perhaps, viewed the world more than a bit off-center.

When David Rice went to the house in the Madrona District on Christmas Eve he said he had expected to find only a couple, an older couple. He had not expected to find children. Quite clearly, David Rice had read or heard something about the furor—now a quarter of a century in the past—over Sally Goldmark's brief days as a member of the Communist Party, and perhaps of John Goldmark's troubles because of it. And Rice had confabulated and rearranged that information. Detectives listening to him realized that Rice had gone to kill Sally and John Goldmark, who were both long dead.

His careful plans had been wrong from the start. Sally and John Goldmark were not communists; their son Charles was even further removed. David Rice had set out to kill the wrong people for the wrong reasons.

Dressed in his green parka, he had taken the bus to the Goldmarks' home. He carried the toy pistol and the two pairs of chrome-colored handcuffs.

Nobody paid any attention to him. He was another

face in the busy Christmas Eve shopping crowd as he
rode the buses.

Rice said he had no idea what Charles Goldmark or
his wife looked like. He didn't know what kind of cars
they drove. He had returned during the first week of
December, again by bus, hoping to peek in the windows to see what Goldmark looked like, but the house
was dark. He had stayed on the street for an hour or so
to watch the house, but neighborhood kids were
playing outside; he was afraid someone would notice
him, and he left. He did go around to the back of the
residence to see that there was an alley and a garage
there. He saw there was no handle on the garage door
and realized he had no easy entry there. He figured
that it was operated by an electric eye.

As the detectives' questions probed deeper, David
Rice admitted that he had also gone to the building
where Charles Goldmark had his law offices. But he
had never even gone into the reception area. Still,
there was no question that Rice had been stalking
Charles Goldmark—ineffectively, yes, but determinedly.

On Christmas Eve, Rice explained, he had decided
to go ahead and approach Charles Goldmark. Yes, he
had carried an empty white box with him. He had
inadvertently gone to the wrong house first and said
he was from Farwest Cab and had a package for
Charles Goldmark. "The woman told me I had the
wrong house. I just said thanks and left."

The box had been part of his preparation for the
assassination. It was empty. "I wanted to use the box
to get them to open the door."

Even though the three detectives listening were
relieved that they had Annie Goldmark's killer in
custody, and that he was quite willing to confess his

crimes to them, they dreaded hearing what they knew
was coming next. They had seen the results of his visit
in colored crime scene pictures. His odd, stilted voice
continued, filling in the gaps of what had happened
that night.

David Rice recalled that he had walked up to the
Goldmarks' home a few minutes after seven. He
knocked on the door, and a young boy answered it.

"I was surprised, because I assumed that there were
only two—Charles Goldmark and his wife—but I
went ahead and I said, 'I'm from Farwest Cab, and I
have a package to deliver for Charles Goldmark,' and
so he called him. Charles came downstairs."

The little boy had seemed about eight or ten to
Rice. He stood there as his father walked down the
stairs. Rice pulled out the toy pistol he had hidden
behind the box.

"I flashed it in front of him . . . and I grabbed him
[Charles] by the shirt and turned him around and told
him to get down on the floor. . . . The boy ran out. He
ran into the kitchen."

David Rice kicked the front door shut behind him.
Now no one on the street could see in.

He held Charles Goldmark down on the floor just
inside the doorway. Goldmark had been shocked into
immobility at first; he had expected to come down the
stairs and greet his party guests. Instead he had
encountered a man with a gun.

"I told Mr. Goldmark to call his son and he
did . . . and so he came in, and I took them upstairs."

"Why did you decide to go upstairs?" Sonny Davis
asked.

"I asked him, 'Where is your wife?' and he said,
'Upstairs in the shower,' and so I said, 'Let's go
upstairs.'"

Then he marched the man and the boy up the stairs, the realistic-looking gun pointed at their backs. Charles Goldmark, a peaceful, nonviolent man, was undoubtedly thinking frantically about what would be the best way to save his family.

David Rice continued his statement: "He asked, 'Do you want money?' and I said, 'Yes, I can use all you got,' and he said, 'I don't have much. What I have is upstairs,' and so he showed me there was fourteen dollars and some change."

Rice had also spotted a wallet and gone through that. There was no money, only credit cards and a SeaFirst bank card. "I asked him his identification number."

Rice described the upstairs of the Goldmark home perfectly. He recalled the placement of the doors, the bay window, the location of the bathrooms. There was no question that he had been there.

"And we got upstairs and he [Goldmark] said, 'Honey, could you come out here?' and she said, 'What?' and he knocked on the door. He poked his head in the bathroom door and said, 'Put something on and come out here,' and so she put on a robe and came out."

"What color robe was she wearing, David?" Sonny Davis asked.

"It was a striped robe. It had a lot of different colors, red and green."

Rice had ushered the family into the master bedroom. Only then had he noticed there was a second boy.

At this point in the questioning David Rice asked to stop for a while. He had a cup of coffee and a cigarette, and then he began again. He explained that he had stopped because he thought that what he was about to say might be too rough for the detectives to hear. His own voice was flat and void of emotion.

"Okay, when we entered the bedroom I told everybody to get on the floor face-down and had them face away from me so that they couldn't see that it was just a toy pistol. Then I handcuffed Charles and his wife."

He had handcuffed Charles first, with his hands behind his back and his face pressed to the beige carpet. Then he did the same to Annie Goldmark.

"Do you remember Charles's clothing? The best you can," John Boatman asked.

"It was a tan sweater with, I believe . . . a brown shirt. . . . I think he was wearing gray slacks."

David Rice had been confused. He had expected Charles Goldmark and his wife to be much older, and he hadn't expected to find two children there. "I had to stop for a minute. I was getting a little rattled because there were two kids, and so I stopped and thought and . . . then I just figured, 'I'm in it now. I can't stop.' "

Rice described where the Goldmarks had lain, all of them helpless now on the floor of the master bedroom. He had intended to get some "information" from Goldmark, but he found there was no point at which he could ask questions. There had, Rice recalled, been very little conversation. Charles had told him, "I want to tell you that we're expecting company, and they'll be here at 7:30."

It might have scared off an assailant less obsessed with his "mission." It only made David Rice work faster. He said he had poured chloroform on a rag and pressed it to Goldmark's nose until he became unconscious. Then he bent over Annie Goldmark. She jerked her head away from him, but he held her fast, and she, too, passed out. "She didn't like it. It's got a pretty nasty smell to it."

Sonny Davis asked quietly, "Did the children struggle?"

"No. The one with the glasses moved his head a little bit."

Both vials were empty, and the family lay still. Only about ten minutes had passed since Rice had entered the Goldmarks' home. He glanced at his watch and figured he had five or ten minutes before the company arrived.

He realized that he wasn't going to get the information on other "communists" now. He still intended to kill them all. . . .

Sonny Davis proceeded cautiously with the questioning. He and Boatman now had to elicit details they didn't really want to know. "They were there at your 'disposal,' as it were?"

"Right."

"Now . . . now you've got to determine how?"

"Right."

"What went through your mind, and what did you come up with?"

"Well," David Rice answered, "first I went downstairs into the kitchen, and I was looking for a knife. . . . I found a filleting knife. It was in the drawer right next to the island."

"Could you describe what you mean by a filleting knife?" Sonny Davis asked.

"It's a knife that's got a twelve-inch blade. It's about a half-inch wide. It had a white wood handle."

"You still had your gloves on during this?" John Boatman asked.

"Yeah. What I was looking for was a . . . one of those meat hammers."

"Why?" Davis asked.

"I didn't like the idea of using a knife."

"Cutting?"

"Uh-huh."

"You wanted to beat as opposed to cut?"

"Right."

But David Rice had no luck looking for a hammer. He moved from the kitchen to a storage area near the front door, found nothing suitable there, and went down the basement steps. All the while his victims lay bound and unconscious from chloroform upstairs.

"I found an iron . . . a regular clothing iron."

"Okay," Sonny Davis said evenly. "This appeared to suit your purpose."

"Yeah. That's the closest I could find."

Carrying the iron with the blue plastic handle, Rice ran upstairs. He estimated that it had taken him four or five minutes to find his weapons. He felt comfortable with the chloroform. "It works for about fifteen or twenty minutes."

"Had you ever tried it before to know what the effects were?" Sonny Davis asked.

"Yeah, I timed myself."

"On *yourself?*"

"Uh-huh."

When Rice reached the master bedroom he found all four of the Goldmarks still in the same positions, still unconscious.

"Like I said," Rice continued, "I knew I didn't have much time, so I had to get it over with. And so I took the iron, and I hit Mr. Goldmark on the head—on the back of the head. I think I hit him about four or five times."

"Then what?" Davis asked.

"Then I hit Mrs. Goldmark. I hit her on the side of the head, and she started moving. I figured the chloroform was starting to wear off, so I hit her a couple more times, and then she stopped moving."

Stealthy, deadly, David Rice had bent over the children. They were still unconscious. He hit "the child with the glasses" five or six times in the head with the iron, and the other youngster four times.

The listening detectives fought to distance themselves from emotion. They had to get his information if they were going to convict the man in front of them. They could not afford to think of the little boys lying in the midst of Christmas presents and gift wrapping.

"Then I went over and checked Mr. Goldmark. I checked his arteries in his neck—"

"For a pulse?" Davis asked.

"Right. And it was still beating, and I checked Mrs. Goldmark, and hers was still beating, and so I decided to complete the job with the knife, so I inserted the point of the knife into the skull where it had broken from the iron."

Sonny Davis struggled to keep his voice empty of anger or judgment. "This is Mr. or Mrs. now?"

"Mr."

"How many times?"

"Just once, and I kind of stirred it around."

"How far did you put the knife in?" Boatman asked quietly.

"Maybe five inches. It slipped right in."

"Then what?" Sonny Davis asked.

"Then I did the same thing to the other three."

"Stirred it around once to each, the mother and the two children?" Davis asked, hearing his voice tremble despite himself.

"Well, actually, I didn't . . . I didn't find a . . . a place on Mrs. Goldmark, so I entered it into the chest area. . . . I just had to put a little pressure on it."

And so Annie Goldmark died there. The other three

were surely going to die. David Rice had quite literally tried to destroy their brains. It seemed a miracle they still lived at all.

His description of committing what he believed to be four murders was so workmanlike. He hadn't been angry or afraid when he did what he did; he had done it because it needed to be done.

Now David Rice continued in his strangely empty voice, his blank eyes staring. He had seen there was blood on his green jacket and on his blue jeans. His left boot was covered with blood, and he wiped it with a blue T-shirt and stuck the shirt in his pocket. His gloves were covered with blood from stabbing Annie. He stuffed them in his pocket, too. It was time to leave—to get out of there before the partygoers arrived.

It was almost twenty minutes past seven.

He didn't look around for more money; there was no time. He had killed "the communist," and that was his first priority.

"I was looking for the back door, which I did not find for quite a while. It took me about three minutes to find the back door . . . down in the sub-basement. As I was leaving I turned out all the lights."

He went through the steel-covered door in the basement, through another small room, and out a set of glass doors. David Rice was outside.

He was out and down the walkway, turning the knob to open the back gate to the alley. He intended to go back to Dr. Perreau's house. He didn't dare take a bus; he walked. It was a long way, over two miles, but he knew his clothes were too stained with fresh blood to risk taking a bus.

"But about halfway there I realized that I'd forgotten my handcuffs—so I went home and changed clothes and put the stuff down in the basement . . . and went back over there."

"To the house?" Davis asked, surprised.

Incredibly, David Rice *had* returned to the scene of his crime. Rice said he had taken a cab to 26th and Union and then walked back to the Goldmark house, arriving between 8:30 and 9:00. He had thought that the victims might not have been discovered yet. He walked along an ivy-clotted bank across the street from the Goldmark house, watching.

"I heard radios and so forth, and so I just kept walking . . . police radios . . . I didn't see a [police] car. There were a few lights on in the house, though, and I assumed that, you know, that it'd been discovered."

So the killer had walked on by, the detectives inside the house completely unaware that the man who had created this carnage was within fifty feet of them for a moment or so.

"I thought, Well, I'm caught now. . . . They've got my fingerprints on those handcuffs."

Rice remembered that he had made another stop on his way home right after the attack. He had stopped at the SeaFirst Bank cash machine, armed with the ID number Charles Goldmark had given him. He had written it down. David Rice was furious when he realized that Charles Goldmark had tricked him. The number was no good. He walked three or four blocks further and tossed the paper with the number, the credit card, and a set of keys into the ivy of someone's yard.

Davis and Boatman wondered if the items were still there, sodden now with rain and fog. It would be more physical evidence, and the more the better.

The second time David Rice left the Goldmark home he walked back to Suzanne Perreau's empty apartment again. He stopped at a market and bought a tablet (the same tablet he wrote his "confession" on), some soda pop, and a candy bar. But when he got back to Dr. Perreau's residence he saw someone standing in the garage, and he was afraid the police were on to him. "I just turned south and went downtown."

He had never been back to Suzanne's place since. He had stayed with Max Stingley until his arrest.

"What items did you put in the storage shed [at Dr. Perreau's apartment]?" John Boatman asked.

"Let's see—in a paper sack there was my coat, my pants, that shirt, the gloves in with it." The chloroform vials and rags were in a closet inside the apartment. He had placed the toy .38 in a storage locker that belonged to Dr. Perreau. Oddly, he hadn't attempted to throw all those things away in some spot that could not be connected to him. Every bit of the evidence linking David Rice to the inexplicable attack on people he didn't even know was still in the apartment of the woman who had forced him to move out. Perhaps he had left it all there—either deliberately or subliminally—to embarrass her and involve her in his crimes. He had even left the white box he had carried to the Goldmarks, the "delivery" that had gained him entrance into their home.

It was almost three in the afternoon on the day after Christmas. Sonny Davis stared at David Rice. "Okay —we're getting close to wrapping up this session. For the purposes of this interview, do you have any remorse or sorrow or feeling about what you did to the Goldmark family?"

"The children. I—I didn't expect them there, and I wouldn't have been there if they had been."

"You're sorry about the children?"

"Yeah."

"Did it ever occur to you to just say, 'Okay—they're down and out; let me turn on my heel and walk out of this house and forget it'?" Davis asked.

"They had already seen me. It was too late."

Much too late.

Colin Goldmark died two days later on December 28, 1985.

Charles Goldmark died at 9:47 in the morning of January 9, 1986.

Derek Goldmark died on January 30, 1986.

They were all gone, all of them who had made up that sunny, brilliant, kind family.

David Lewis Rice's trial began in May, 1986. He was represented by Tony Savage and Bill Lanning, two of the very finest criminal defense attorneys in Washington State. King County Deputy Prosecutor Bill Downing would represent the State. He was a young —but tough—opponent. The defense sought to prove David Rice insane under the law, and therefore not responsible for his crimes.

Bill Downing stressed the care with which David Rice planned his attacks, the cruel savagery with which he carried them out, and how cleverly he executed his escape. None of Rice's actions before or after his crimes indicated he was legally insane. Bill Downing also read a list of Rice's future victims; the defendant had apparently not intended to stop his killing swath with the Goldmarks.

It was a long and grueling trial, almost a month of testimony. Through it all a pale David Rice sat as calm as death itself. His relatives cried in the gallery. So did friends and relatives who had loved the Goldmarks.

Perhaps the most telling argument of all for conviction was the playing of the tape made of Rice's confession to John Boatman and Sonny Davis on December 26, two days after the murders. On tape David Rice sounded intelligent, coherent, and completely without remorse. His voice filled the courtroom and made listeners shudder.

On June 5, 1986, the jury of six men and six women retired to deliberate. Less than five hours later they were back with a verdict; they had rejected Rice's insanity plea and had found him guilty of four counts of first-degree murder. Rice took the news serenely. However, as he walked to the jail elevator, he told reporters, "The scum lied about everything. He said I lied to save myself when in actuality the lie was to kill myself." (He did not say whether he was referring to Deputy Prosecutor Downing or to his associate, Bob Lasnik.)

In the bifurcated trial, the next phase was to decide whether David Rice would serve life in prison or go to his death.

On June 10 the jury announced that they had agreed that Rice should be put to death. "It's not easy to play God," Jury Foreman Joel Babcock told reporters. "It's a very emotional thing to have to do something like this. Mr. Rice may very well be insane right now, but we're dealing with December 24. I could be insane if I killed four people and sat in a jail cell and thought about it long enough. I think Mr. Rice has some character disorders, but I think the prosecution showed he was able to think about what he was doing and do this step by step by step."

In the meantime, David Rice had once again gulped a mixture of tobacco and water and been rushed to Harborview Medical Center. And once again he showed no ill effects. He would not respond to the news of the death penalty, nor would he speak to his relatives, who had come to comfort him.

Within days, however, David Rice was talking and eating.

On August 15, 1986, he was ordered to be transferred to the Washington State Penitentiary in Walla Walla. The appeal process lay ahead. Everyone expected it would be years before David Rice's death sentence might be carried out.

On 36 Avenue, the lovely home the Goldmarks had shared remained "an open wound" to their neighbors. All the Goldmarks had done was open their own front door on a happy Christmas Eve.

It would not be stretching the truth to say that a political dirty trick designed to discredit Charles Goldmark's father and mother had set the stage for this tragedy. The lies about Sally Ringe Goldmark that had been whispered three decades earlier had ruined her husband's political career. Even when the elder Goldmarks were vindicated, the lies hadn't really died. They had only slumbered. Somewhere in the dusty shelves of the public library David Lewis Rice, full of hate and looking for someone to blame for the shambles his life had become, had seized on an old article. His delusion had grown and burgeoned and eventually become an obsession.

David Rice had actually believed that he was killing *John* Goldmark. John Goldmark had never been a communist. It had all been such a stupid, tragic mistake.

The entire Charles Goldmark family died by mistake. But they are just as dead as if cruel delusion hadn't followed vicious slander.

Charles, Annie, Colin, and Derek Goldmark were never allowed to realize their tremendous potential for good. The Charles and Annie Goldmark Family Foundation was established in their memory, a living foundation to advance the values of democracy, freedom, understanding, and civic participation they believed in.

The tragic story of the Goldmarks' murders did not end in 1986. The man who had destroyed them was still alive. Although David Rice had killed mother and father and two little boys quite calmly, *he* did not want to die. He began to explore the legal avenues of appeal open to him.

His appeal to the U.S. Supreme Court asked that his death penalty sentence be overturned because his execution would violate the constitutional ban on cruel and unusual punishment. Through his attorneys, David Rice claimed to be suffering from "substantial mental illness."

The appeal argued also that he had been denied the right to a fair sentencing because the prosecution team had asked the jurors to put themselves in the shoes of twelve-year-old Derek and ten-year-old Colin Goldmark, and because the jurors had been shown pictures of the boys taken before the attack that killed them.

On June 19, 1989, the Supreme Court rejected those arguments and refused to overturn David Rice's death sentence.

King County Deputy Prosecutor Robert Lasnik, who, with Bill Downing, had won the guilty verdicts against Rice, said he knew that a death date could be set for David Rice—but warned that there were several more pathways for appeal through state and federal courts. He predicted that it might be as long as three years before a final execution date would be set for David Lewis Rice. In truth, it has been longer.

No one had actually been executed in Washington State for almost three decades, anyway. Not since 1963, when Joseph Chester Self was hanged for the murder of a Seattle taxi driver.

That changed, however, on January 5, 1993, when Westly Allan Dodd, a sadistic pedophile, went to the gallows in Walla Walla for the murders of three little boys.

Despite a number of horrendous homicides since David Rice took his place on Death Row in Walla Walla, his name was still familiar to almost everyone in the state, his crimes as crystalline in the minds of those who remembered the black Christmas Eve of 1985 as if they had happened yesterday.

The public was shocked on August 6, 1993, when U.S. District Court Judge Jack Tanner threw out the death penalty that was imposed on David Rice. Tanner ruled that Rice would not die because he had not been in the courtroom when the jury that convicted him pronounced the death sentence.

Appalled, Assistant Attorney General Jack Jones argued, "Rice was not there because he had swallowed several packs of tobacco mixed with water and had been taken to Harborview Medical Center to have his stomach pumped. He did that *twenty minutes before the jury was to announce its decision.* Rice's counsel waived Rice's presence."

The State plans to appeal Judge Tanner's decision, which ruled that David Rice's absence violated his constitutional rights under the Fifth, Sixth, and Twenty-fourth amendments. The attorney general's office accused Tanner of refusing to hear the State's arguments.

If Tanner's decision is upheld, David Rice will face a mandatory sentence of life in prison without possibility of parole.

One Trick Pony

Most of us *believe that there is no such thing as a perfect murder. And we have good reason to; literature down through the ages has told us that. Shakespeare said it in many of his plays: "How easily murder is discovered!" "Truth will come to light; murder cannot be hid long." "Murder, though it have no tongue, will speak."*

Cervantes wrote in Don Quixote *that "Murder will out."*

In the seventeenth century John Webster wrote, "Other sins only speak; murder shrieks out."

Not really. There are, unfortunately, hundreds of perfect murders. Some are never discovered. More are never solved.

Donna Howard's death was listed as accidental in dusty records for a dozen years. But Donna didn't die the way detectives and coroners originally believed she had, and it took the determined efforts of her own sister, Bobbi, to bring belated justice. Bobbi Bennett never gave up until the truth about Donna's death was exposed to light like the underside of a muddy rock turned over in the bright sun. With a singleness of purpose that defied fatigue and despair, Bobbi fought to avenge Donna. Only when she did could she go on with her own life.

This case, I believe, is a classic example that things are not always what they seem to be—particularly when it comes to murder.

The state of Washington is cut in half by the Cascade Mountains; Seattle and its environs are termed "the coast" by eastern Washington residents, even though the actual Pacific coast is many miles away. The west side of the state is moderate and lush, green, often sodden with rain. Eastern Washington has fertile fields, arid desert, the rolling Palouse Hills covered with a sea of wheat, and orchards as far as the eye can see.

Ellensburg and Yakima are in the middle of orchard country, of horse country. You put an apple or cherry twig in irrigated land there and it will take root overnight. Or so it seems.

These are western towns where even the bankers and the grocery store managers usually wear cowboy boots. There are rodeos, horse shows, and county fairs. Just as it does in every medium-sized town in America, an occasional scandal surfaces. Sometimes the scandals are homegrown: a love triangle exploding into deadly violence, or a family fight that ends in death. The shock waves that follow seem to occur only in small towns. Perhaps it is simply that big cities have so much violence that individual crimes don't stand out as much as they do in small towns.

* * *

Donna Bennett was born on Flag Day—June 14, 1932; a few years later, her sister Blodwyn—who would always be called Bobbi—came along. Their parents were older, at least for that era, both over thirty when their girls were born. The Bennetts and their forefathers had lived near Ellensburg at the upper edge of the Yakima Valley for generations. They were horse people—not fancy-schmancy horse people, but genuine cowboys.

Possibly because they had waited longer to have children, Donna and Bobbi's parents adored their two little girls. The Bennett girls were pretty, with shiny brown hair and huge brown eyes. Both Donna and Bobbi were born to ride horses, galloping joyously with the smell of sagebrush and apple blossoms in their nostrils. They grew up together, as close as sisters are meant to be.

Donna was already standing bareback on a horse at the age of three, her balance perfectly attuned to the horse's gait.

When Donna was five she was chosen the "best-dressed junior cowgirl" at the Ellensburg Rodeo parade.

Donna and Bobbi attended Ellensburg High School. Donna was in the class of 1950, and her friends from those days remember her as clearly as if they had seen her only yesterday. She could be very serious and a little straitlaced, but when she was your friend, she was your friend forever. She didn't have a lot of time for after-school activities because she had chores to do on the farm. She usually rode the bus right home after school, and she didn't date much in high school.

But Donna's dad had played the drums, and she did, too—the slender girl marching along in the Bull Dog band, keeping time on the bulky drums. Jean

"Tex" Turner Parsons was the drum majorette, and Fay Griffin Moss and Gail Kelly Sether were flag twirlers. They were Donna Bennett's best friends. Fay and Donna had known each other since fifth grade. They would stay close for all of her life.

All through high school and for years afterward Donna and Bobbi rode their horses in parades. "They rode in the Ellensburg Rodeo—and in the other parades," Fay Moss remembers. "They were never in the royal court, though. I think it's because their family wasn't rich—and that's what it took to get in the court. But they were so classy, sitting straight in their saddles. They were *real* cowgirls."

When she was eighteen and graduating from Ellensburg High School a local newspaper picked Donna as the graduate with the prettiest eyes. It was true; she had huge doe-like eyes.

Donna and all her closest friends exchanged pictures. On the one she gave to "Tex" Turner she wrote, "Hi Tex, I can't forget all the good times we've had. Parties and the jokes on our band trips. I wish you all the luck and happiness in [the] future and be good!! Love and Kizzes, Donna."

Summertimes and after she had graduated high school, Donna performed as a trick rider at rodeos all over eastern Washington. She was wonderfully talented. Beautiful and slender, Donna wore bright satin shirts in rainbow colors, with sequined embroidery and pearl studs, tight pants, boots, and cowboy hats. Her picture brightened up many a county fair poster.

But Donna wasn't just pretty; she was a superb equestrienne. An action photo from those days in the fifties shows Donna standing *atop* Bobbi's white steed, Dana, her perfect body leaning tautly into the wind, her arms flung out exultantly as she performs a stunt called "The Hippodrome." Bobbi is on the horse, too, her feet hooked into the stirrups as she drapes herself *backwards* down over Dana's hindquarters, so close to the ground and the horse's hooves that her long hair actually trails along the ground of the arena.

Both Bennett girls were as confident with horses as most people would be with a puppy. They were alternately atop, underneath, dragging, and cavorting as the horse trotted so fast that the wind whipped their hair. They were exquisitely coordinated, in their glory.

But they weren't daredevils. They knew that horses could be skittish, and they took no chances. "Donna knew that you never put your head down to work on a horse's hooves," Fay says. "That you *back* up to a horse and present your least vulnerable part."

Donna figured she would meet a cowboy one day and settle down. That was her world, and she met dozens of handsome young men at the rodeos. But another kind of man came along, and Donna Bennett was attracted to him in spite of herself, and in spite of her friends' and family's reservations. She met Noyes Russell Howard at Yakima Valley Community College and began dating him sporadically.

Russ Howard was handsome then—not a big man, but he had a good, compactly muscled build. He was about five feet nine—two inches or so taller than Donna. He combed his thick hair into a wave in front. The best thing about Russ was his gift of gab; he was a riot at parties. You could never predict what Russ would do next.

"He was fun, and he was crazy," Fay Moss remembers. "I could see how she could be attracted to him."

Donna and Russ dated off and on. For a while in 1954 Donna and Fay moved to Seattle and lived

together in a little apartment on Republican Street—
on what would become the site of the 1962 World's
Fair. Donna got a job as sales clerk at Best's Apparel
in downtown Seattle. By the time Best's became the
flagship store of Nordstrom's, Donna had moved back
over the mountains. Her picture often appeared on
fashion pages in the *Yakima Herald*. She was so
photogenic that department stores often asked her to
pose, wearing their newest lines.

After college Russ worked in a number of jobs—
selling shoes at first. Eventually he worked, in one
capacity or another, with seeds, sometimes as a salesman for a seed company in the Yakima Valley and
later as a seed inspector for the State Department of
Agriculture. He was only two years older than Donna,
but far more worldly. When they met Russ was
already a pretty good drinker, and that put Donna off.
She didn't drink at all and didn't want to raise a
family with liquor in the home. She was young; she
thought he would change his bad habits in time.

When Russ proposed Donna hesitated. But she kept
going out with him, and it was soon obvious that the
quiet rodeo rider was in love with the glib party guy.
They were very different, but often opposites *do*
attract. Donna finally said yes, and though she delayed
the wedding a few times, Donna finally married Russ
Howard as the fifties eased into the sixties. She was
almost thirty; all of her friends had been married for
years.

Donna's family smiled determinedly at the wedding, but they worried. Donna's friends could see that
she wanted desperately to make a go of her marriage,
and that she ached for a secure home in which to have
children. Apparently it took her a long time to feel
secure; Donna Howard was into her thirties before

her two daughters, Lisa and Marilyn, were born. Even though things weren't perfect and Russ was drinking, she wanted so much to have children.

Donna's family, well-known and respected in the valley, helped the young couple buy a home and some acreage on Galloway Road a few miles northwest of Yakima on the Naches River. Yakima is only about forty miles south of Ellensburg, so Donna still saw her family often. There was room for a stable; Donna couldn't imagine living without a horse or two.

Russ's job with the State of Washington meant he had to be on the road a good deal. That gave him the opportunity to imbibe away from his wife's disappointed eyes. It also gave him the chance to date other women. He would one day refer rather obliquely to his wife's "changing sexual needs" as the impetus that "drove" him into affairs with at least eight other women. It was an easy and ambiguous excuse for him, and Donna never had a chance to tell her side of the story.

Did Donna know that Russ was cheating on her? Probably. But she was loyal, and she was a very private person. Many women would have run crying to friends or, in Donna's case, to family. But for years Donna Howard kept her problems to herself. Her pride wouldn't let her admit how hellish her marriage had become.

Why any man would want to cheat on Donna Bennett Howard was a puzzle in itself. She was warm and friendly, and her family came first with her. Into her late thirties and early forties she remained a startlingly beautiful woman. She was as slender as she had been during her days as a rodeo queen, her face unlined, her eyes as lovely as ever, and her hair free of gray strands. Russ, on the other hand, had begun to show the effects of years of hard drinking. His face was seamed with deep wrinkles. But he had taken up weight-lifting, and that made him as strong as a man twice his size. He was still a barrel of laughs at a party or in a bar, however—and it was true that he had little difficulty attracting women.

The class of 1950 of Ellensburg High School stayed in close touch. Originally there had been 107 in that graduating class. Although their numbers dwindled, at least half of them showed up at the class reunions they held every five years.

"Donna only came once," "Tex" Parsons says. "And she came alone. I think we all knew that she was afraid that Russ might get drunk and embarrass her. As much as she wanted to come to our reunions, she missed most of them."

"Tex" and Gene Parsons, who had moved to the Seattle area after they got married, stopped by to visit the Howards once when they were in Yakima for a Toastmasters convention. Russ seemed the same as he always had—maybe a little bit cockier. Gene Parsons, who stands well over six feet, found Russ something of a swaggering show-off. "He had several guns, and he took me out on the porch to show me what a marksman he was," Parsons recalls. "He would toss aspirin into the air—ordinary aspirin tablets—and then blast them to pieces before they fell. He was good, and he must have been practicing a lot. It never rains over in Yakima, and his yard was sprinkled with all those little white bits of aspirin. Must have been a thousand or more of them."

Donna Howard apparently tried every means she could think of to save her marriage. She prevailed upon Russ to go to an alcoholic treatment center. He went, but he began to drink again after he was back home. Feeling that his friends exacerbated his drinking problem, Donna put her foot down and barred them from her home, and that irritated Russ. She herself joined Al-Anon (the group for families of problem drinkers), and she talked almost daily with members of the group, seeking some way to help Russ stay sober. When nothing seemed to work she went so far as to consult an attorney about a divorce. But she changed her mind. She worried that she couldn't support her daughters alone, and she really wanted them to have a father as well as a mother.

If there was one thing that the Howards were both concerned with, it was their daughters. The little girls were eight and ten, and Russ and Donna loved them.

Even so, his children were not enough to keep Russ Howard home much. Donna never knew where he was for sure. Once she was injured in a car accident, and nobody could find Russ for hours to tell him she had been hurt.

When Russ was in town he was a frequent patron at the bar at the Yakima VFW Club. The bartender there had been the attraction for a year or more. She was a cute little blonde with a sprinkling of freckles across the bridge of her nose and just the beginning edges of hardness. Her name was Sunny Riley,* and she was about a dozen years younger than Donna.

Sunny and Russ Howard had been involved in a sizzling affair for a year. Sunny liked the same characteristics in Russ that had drawn Donna to him twenty years earlier: he was fun, he was exciting, and he made her laugh. She wanted to marry him. But of course, he was already married. Sunny turned the screws a little. She simply told him that if he didn't get a divorce, he'd better not expect her to wait around; she was going to date other men.

By December, 1974, Donna Howard could no longer hide the strain of living in a house torn apart.

Here it was the Christmas season, and her family was living a sham. Russ was hardly ever home; he'd slacked off the alcohol treatment and gone on as before.

Donna had tried so hard to do whatever Russ seemed to want, hoping that they could get along better. One of the things he had wanted was to buy a new house. Donna hadn't wanted to move, but she'd gone along with it. They bought a house on Tieton Drive, and they would be moving in January. It seemed ridiculous when the marriage was so shaky, but she thought a new house *might* shed a happier light on the marriage—kind of a geographical remedy to a seemingly insoluble situation.

In mid-December Russ got home very late one night, and he was drunk. An argument ensued, and he hauled off and belted Donna twice in the head, practically knocking her out. That scared her. When her head stopped spinning she called the sheriff's office and filed a report. Donna told the officer responding that she was going to see her lawyer the next day, that she would be filing for divorce.

Russ hitting her was the deciding factor. Her lawyer was worried about Donna. He had advised her to file many times before, but Donna had always backed out. Now she was determined to divorce Russ and seek sole custody of her two daughters. She told Bobbi that she was resolute. "I was positive in my heart," Bobbi remembered, "that she was going ahead and getting the divorce."

Fay Moss suspected things had come to a breaking point, too. "Donna was always the kind that never complained. *She* was the one who would always go up to the rest of us, look us square in the eye, and say, 'How are you? How are the kids?' and she really wanted to know. But this one time in late December I said to her, 'Donna, how are *you, really?*' She just broke down and cried and responded, 'Not good. Just not good.'"

Russ Howard was between the proverbial rock and a hard place. If he didn't divorce Donna, Sunny was going to dump him. If Donna divorced him—as she was threatening to do—he might lose his kids, and the equity in their new home as well. Since the original down payment for the old house had come from Donna's family, he suspected a judge would award Donna the new house.

Perhaps to punctuate that she, too, meant what she said, Sunny had broken up with Russ as 1974 turned into 1975. Both women in Russ's life were fed up.

What he really wanted were his kids, the new house, and Sunny. On January 9, 1975, Russ Howard had a long talk with Sunny, and he confided an idea he had. She didn't really believe him; she thought it was the liquor talking.

On that same January 9th Donna's friend Fay Moss was visiting in Ellensburg. "I was talking to a friend who went to Yakima often, and I said, 'Ellie, call Donna. She *really* needs a friend right now.'"

Fay remembered her phone conversation with Donna Howard in December, and it had left her with anxiety over her old friend. Donna had cried during that call, and Donna *never* cried. "She had told me that she was sorry that she hadn't been able to make it over to Seattle to visit. Then she said, 'I'm changing a few things in 1975. We're moving to Selah on January first. This should prove very interesting. I'll let you know more.'"

Fay Moss didn't think the real changes in Donna's life had anything to do with the new house. She knew

Donna, and Donna was talking about something that would mean far more upheaval in her life than simply changing addresses. It had something to do with her marriage. Fay worried about Donna all day on January 9th, and she made up her mind to drive on down to Yakima and see her the next day. "But I didn't. A winter storm blew in, and the roads were so bad that I turned around and came home. When I got home I learned that Donna was dead."

Donna Howard was forty-two years old when she died on January 10, 1975. It happened so quickly; it was 9:27 on that bitter, icy morning in Yakima, Washington, when Russ found her. Emergency medical technicians pronounced her dead at 9:47.

How ironic that Donna Howard of all people should die in a stable, when she had loved horses since before she could walk. It just didn't make sense. It would take almost a dozen years before it did.

Donna and Russ and the girls hadn't quite finished moving everything out of the house on Galloway Road. Russ and Donna took their girls to school, and then they headed back to the old house. They passed some of their neighbors, and Russ and Donna waved.

Russ told the medics that they had put on a pot of coffee, and a little later he went into town to the hardware store to buy a mailbox for their new house. Then he stopped at a doughnut shop and picked up a dozen fresh doughnuts, explaining that he was taking them back to share with Donna. He talked to a number of people at the hardware store and the doughnut shop that morning. He had even written a check at the hardware store. Always talkative, Russ had seemed particularly gregarious.

His call for help came in just minutes before 9:30. A woman had been injured out on Route 8, Box 741. A

fire department medic responded along with Yakima
County Sheriff's Office Patrolmen Jerry Hofsos and
Ron Ward.

A worried Russ Howard led them out toward the
loafing shed where the family's two horses were kept.
He explained that he and Donna were doing some
last-minute moving and repairs. He had gone into
town to get some supplies they needed, and he'd
thought he would surprise Donna with some fresh
doughnuts. But she hadn't been in the house when he
got back, nor had she responded to his shouts. He
figured Donna was over at the neighbors' house
because she often visited there—but they hadn't seen
her either. He felt as if he had wasted precious
minutes looking in the wrong place.

When Russ trudged through the deep snow out to
the barn area he had found Donna. She lay in the
loafing shed, just as she still was—except for the quilt,
which he'd placed over her. The fire department
medic knelt beside her and removed the quilt.

Donna Howard lay on her back with her left arm
raised, her face turned to the left. Her right hand was
pinned palm down beneath her right buttock. The
medic felt for a pulse in the carotid artery in the neck.
There was none. Donna Howard's eyes were slightly
open, but the pupils were already fixed and dilated.
Her body was warm, but she was dead.

The immediate cause of death seemed to stem from
some manner of head injury; there was blood streak-
ing Donna's forehead, running back into her thick
brown hair, which was virtually soaked with blood
from some terrible head wound. Mere inches from her
head one wall of the two-sided shed had thick scarlet
stains, as if someone had taken a paint brush and
daubed on two swaths. Almost directly opposite and a

foot or so above Donna's left elbow one swath was horizontal, the other vertical.

Donna wore bell-bottom jeans, rubber galoshes much too big for her feet (unzipped), a white sweater, a dark quilted jacket (open), and gloves. Her sweater was pulled up, exposing flesh at her waist. Her jeans were wrinkled oddly, too, pulled up slightly toward her knees. Her clothing looked almost as if someone had dragged her by her feet. Her galoshes nudged a salt block placed there earlier for her two horses.

"I found her like this," Russ Howard explained. "I covered her with a quilt, and I called for the medics." He had not moved her at all, he said, fearful of injuring her further.

The fire department and the responding deputies had, of course, called detectives for backup. In all cases of violent death—accidental or deliberate— detectives must investigate. Detective Sergeant Bob Langdale and Detective Ray Ochs responded to the scene to assist in the initial probe.

The sheriff's men took pictures of the scene, but that was all. The barn and the house were a good distance apart. There was nothing in the house that seemed out of place. There wasn't much to photograph. The cause of death seemed obvious: one of Donna Howard's beloved horses had spooked and kicked her in the back of the head. She had lain there until Russ returned.

Pictures remaining in police files show a pretty woman with a lithe, perfect figure lying stretched out on the icy ground of the loafing shed. Over toward the slatted open side there is a plaid quilt and a Bekins Movers' blanket. Beyond, a blizzard has kicked up, and the snow and sky meet in never-ending white.

Neighbors rushed to comfort the bereaved widower, who blamed himself for not being home when Donna needed him. "One of her horses must have kicked her," he said. He couldn't describe his feelings. "I don't know how you describe something like that. I felt a combination of grief and rage, not knowing where to vent the rage."

One of the first things Russ did after Donna's body was removed was to contact Sunny Riley. He told her that Donna was dead, and he explained the events of the morning. Sunny was appalled, even terrified by what he related. But Sunny still loved Russ despite what he had told her. She kept her knowledge to herself.

Donna's family was stunned by the news of the tragedy. That Donna should be killed by the very animal she loved was incomprehensible to them. She had been around horses her whole life; she talked to them in some unspoken language, and she trusted them more than she trusted most people. Moreover, she was no neophyte who didn't know how to approach horses.

Dr. Richard Muzzall, the Yakima County coroner and a local surgeon who had gone to Ellensburg High School with Donna, performed her autopsy on January 11th. Although he was a board-certified surgeon, Muzzall had no special training in forensic pathology. He noted the back of the skull where it had been shattered and found the damage consistent with a blow from a horse's hoof. He also found a second fracture of the skull, on the upper right side, a small ovoid (oval-shaped) depressed fracture. That puzzled him, given what Russ Howard had told him about the accident. Muzzall was not as sure about the cause of that wound as he was about the occipital fractures, and he made a note to go to the loafing shed and find out what had caused that.

When he went back to the horse shed Muzzall spotted three stacked railroad ties that made up part of the wall adjacent to where Donna Howard's body was found. The top tie had been broken off raggedly at some time and had a sharp, jagged piece of wood protruding. That might have caused the small single fracture.

Muzzall deduced that Donna had been bending over, cleaning a horse's hoof, and that she had been kicked by one of the horse's other hooves, knocked headlong into the tie, and then propelled backward, her head sliding across the side of the shed, leaving the two bloody swipes. She had finally come to rest flat on her back with her legs stretched out. That scenario might explain how her skull was fractured both in the back and on the top, and why the smaller top fracture's shape bore no resemblance to a horse's foot size.

Muzzall's postmortem report was only a page long, and the conclusion was death from multiple skull fractures due to horse kick. He noted the two areas of fracture and a third finding—a bruise on the webbing between the thumb and forefinger of the right hand. That bruise bore the imprint of the fabric of the glove Donna had worn. At the bottom of the autopsy report the summary diagnosis listed the fabric-pattern bruise as having been found on the *left* hand. A minor oversight, but one that would have been *very* important to a forensic pathologist.

A bruise in the webbing between the thumb and the forefinger is a classic defense wound. What part of a horse could have given Donna Howard such a bruise? And why hadn't Muzzall proofread the autopsy report?

Outside of major metropolitan areas there are few trained forensic pathologists, and even the best some-

times disagree with one another on a close call.
Indeed, in many rural and thinly populated areas
coroners are not even required to be physicians.
Muzzall had drawn his conclusions from the information available at the time and with the training that he
had. Later several forensic pathologists would agree
with him; others would not.

Neither Detectives Langdale and Ochs nor Yakima
County Prosecuting Attorney Jeff Sullivan could come
up with enough probable cause to arrest anyone for
killing Donna Howard. It was, they were forced to
conclude, a tragic and ironic accident.

Donna was buried, and Russ Howard and his
daughters pulled their lives together, living in the new
house. There wasn't much insurance on Donna's
life—only $17,000—but Russ would receive social
security benefits for the minor children.

Only Donna's family could not accept the cause of
death on the death certificate. Nothing added up. One
might attribute the family's doubts to grief and denial.
And yet . . .

Bobbi Bennett sought—and found—refuge in her
religion, but her growing faith only heightened her
conviction that it was her duty to Donna to see that
the real killer was punished. Bobbi knew how unhappy Donna had been, knew of her decision to divorce
Russ, and knew that he had physically attacked her
sister less than a month earlier—an attack so violent
that Donna had been left almost unconscious. Bobbi
Bennett was convinced that Russ Howard had killed
Donna, but she had no idea in the world how to prove
it.

With her family's backing, Bobbi hired a private
detective.

One of the startling pieces of intelligence the private

investigator reported was that a young woman named Sunny Riley was living with Russ and his daughters. Donna was barely in her grave when Sunny moved in during February. Ostensibly she had been hired as a baby-sitter to care for the girls. Since Russ was a traveling seed salesman, it made sense that he had to have household help, but Donna's family was suspicious. The private investigator pretended to be a real estate agent and talked with Sunny. There was no question that she was living in Russ's home full-time. And she didn't strike him as the baby-sitter type.

Four months later, in June—the month when Donna would have celebrated her forty-third birthday —Russ Howard and Sunny Riley were married, ending the arguments among townspeople over whether Sunny was a baby-sitter or a girlfriend.

There were reasons that the June wedding was not as romantic as it might have been. Sunny Riley was a woman tortured by conflicting emotions. She *did* still love Russ no matter what her suspicions were, and she had wanted to marry him for a long time. But she was frightened, too. Russ had confided things to her that she wished she had never heard. Whatever he might or might not have done, Sunny was absolutely convinced that she was just as responsible under the law as he was. Indeed, Russ often reminded her of her complicity, and she believed him when he said she would be in terrible trouble, too, if she ever revealed what he had told her.

She had been afraid to marry him and afraid *not* to marry him. She had gone along with the wedding plans, she would say later, because she kept hoping something or someone would intervene before she and Russ made it to the altar. For his part, Russ was quite aware that a man's wife cannot be forced to testify against him in a court of law.

No one intervened, of course, and the wedding went off without a hitch. Sunny did her best to block her fears out of her mind; at times she was able to completely submerge her doubts. Once they were married Russ didn't seem to worry much at all about the law. He seemed quite secure. The coroner had agreed with his version of Donna's death, and so had the prosecutor and the sheriff. Let the past bury the past.

But Donna's sister Bobbi was not about to let that happen. She knew nothing about how to investigate a murder when she began her quest, but she read voraciously, and she soon gleaned a great deal of information. One afternoon while she was sitting in a beauty parlor chair she read about Thomas Noguchi, then chief medical examiner of Los Angeles County.

Bobbi Bennett got in touch with Noguchi and asked him and an associate to review Donna's case. After doing that they agreed that it at least warranted a more complete autopsy.

Yakima County D.A. Jeff Sullivan agreed to an exhumation order, and a second postmortem examination was performed on Donna Howard's body in late 1976. Forensic pathologist Dr. William Brady— then the Oregon state medical examiner—performed the autopsy with Dr. Bob Bucklin, an ex-assistant medical examiner for Los Angeles County, assisting. Dr. Muzzall, Jeff Sullivan, and Sergeant Langdale observed.

At length Dr. Bucklin concluded that he could not say with *absolute medical certainty* that the damage to her skull had not been caused by the kick of a horse. His inclination, however, was to *disagree* with Dr. Muzzall's findings.

Dr. Brady prefaced his written report with the

comment that pathological conclusions must take into account what was known to have been at the scene of a death—i.e., common sense combined with autopsy findings. A badly fractured skull and horses would tend to go together; unless other circumstances were known, Brady said he could not say what had caused the damage to Donna Howard's skull.

The lack of a definitive decision on the part of either pathologist was a crushing disappointment for Donna's sister. She had fought so hard to get the exhumation order and the second postmortem examination. It had been agonizing to go through, too—and now it seemed all for nothing.

For D.A. Jeff Sullivan there was still not enough probable cause to issue an arrest warrant charging anyone with murder. For the second time he declined to prosecute.

The world moved on. Donna Howard was dead, and that's the way it was—to everyone but Donna's family. Her parents grew older, their will to live weakened by the loss of their beloved daughter. Donna's father would not live to see the end of the case.

Bobbi Bennett, however, never gave up. She read. She phoned. She wrote letters to anyone who might help her avenge Donna's death. "Some people might say it took over my life," she would recall later. "I made up my mind that I was not going to let her go until they did something."

Over the years Donna's family would spend thousands of dollars on the case, a case everyone else seemed to consider closed.

The marriage between Sunny and Russ Howard was a bumpy one. Perhaps it was inevitable that it would be. Sunny had fallen in love with Russ because he was fun, and she loved fun. But there was little hilarity once they were married; Sunny was scared and guilty about what she knew, Russ was gone a lot, and he continued to drink a great deal. For all intents and purposes the marriage ended in 1978.

Sunny left Russ and ran off with another man. But Sunny was adept at picking the wrong men. She found herself in an abusive relationship. Periodically things got so bad that Russ looked good, and she would phone him and beg him to come and rescue her. He would pick her up, bring her back, and help her get set up in an apartment or in his house. Until 1979 Sunny and Russ had some manner of a relationship, however tenuous.

Donna Howard had been dead for almost five years, but Sunny's conscience still bothered her. If her niggling doubts hadn't gone away by then, she figured they weren't going to. In early July, 1980, Sunny went to a Yakima County deputy sheriff, an old friend from high school, and asked him a hypothetical question: "If I knew information about somebody that was going to be murdered, and then they were, and somebody told me more things—and I never said anything—would I be in trouble, too?"

Her deputy friend stared at her quizzically for a few moments, and then he assured her that *she* would not be the focal point of a sheriff's probe.

Sunny replied that in that case, she had some things to say. However, she told him that if she *did* get charged with a crime, she was going to deny everything. Her friend took her down to the county detectives, who took a taped statement from her.

Bob Langdale had retired, but Ray Ochs was still in the detective unit, and Jerry Hofsos had moved up from patrol. What Sunny Riley had to tell them was riveting, to say the least.

* * *

Sunny began by reviewing late December, 1974. She said Russ Howard had told her that he planned to kill his wife. He had told her he was going to lure Donna out to the barn of their old house on the pretext of making some repairs that had to be done before the new tenants moved in. It would be only natural, he had said, for him to have a hammer with him. Then he planned to strike Donna with the side of his hammer because he thought that would make a wound resembling a horse's shoe. His alibi would be that he had been in town at the time Donna died. He would go to town right after the crime, and he would make sure people in town remembered him.

On the day Donna died Russ had told Sunny he'd done it—but he said it had been more difficult to kill his wife than he expected. He confided that he'd had to hit Donna in the head three times before she died. The rest of his plan had been carried out just as he had outlined it to Sunny earlier.

The information that Sunny gave might well have been enough to indict Russ Howard for the murder of his wife. There were some problems, though; the things he had told her before marriage would be admissible in a court of law, but the confidences after marriage probably would not be. And then there was the fact that Sunny had gone right ahead and *married* a man she believed to be a murderer. A jury might wonder about that and find her a less than credible witness.

A polygraph exam administered by an expert from the Washington State Patrol indicated that Sunny Riley was telling the truth.

The Yakima County Prosecutor's Office continued to mull over whether to charge Russ Howard. So much of the original physical evidence was gone. Donna's bloodstained clothing, the quilt, the Bekins blanket had all been destroyed. The loafing shed had been repainted, obliterating the blood smears there. No investigator had ever found a hammer or, for that matter, even looked for one.

The railroad tie that Dr. Muzzall believed to be the instrument that made the oval fracture in the victim's skull was now anchored in cement, part of a fence. No one had ever searched the barn or the house thoroughly for signs of violence; it hadn't seemed important back in 1975 when the autopsy decreed accidental death.

Now it was too late.

Sunny ran scared. She moved around from place to place, fearful of reprisal from Russ. She moved to California with a new man and waited for word from Yakima authorities. Impatient now, she couldn't wait for Russ to be arrested. But months passed, and nothing happened—at least nothing she could see.

The case was already more than five years old, and authorities were doing their best to make it as solid as possible before they moved on it. They figured Russ Howard wasn't going anyplace.

It was 1981. Sunny was worried, and she was drinking. A few more drinks and Sunny was not only worried, she was angry, too. Russ had her furniture. She called him one night and suggested that they get married again. She pointed out that he was going to be charged with murder sooner or later, and if they were married, she couldn't testify against him. Sunny figured this might make him give back her furniture. After the trial was over they could split up again, she reasoned.

The next day Sunny was sober, and she changed her mind about the plan that had seemed so good the night before. Russ had rejected her proposal anyway. But she had tipped him off that something might be happening that he didn't know about. Still, he didn't move from the Yakima area. He didn't seem the least bit worried.

Russ Howard continued to have bad luck with women in his life. In the early 1980s he was living sporadically with a new woman and working part-time at a local tavern. One afternoon the couple came home together and talked for a few moments with Russ's daughters and a friend of theirs who was visiting.

Russ left a little while later to go to work at the tavern, and his girlfriend went upstairs, apparently to take a nap.

A few minutes later the three teenagers heard a loud noise upstairs. They went up to investigate and found the woman dead on the bed, shot in the stomach. She clutched a gun in her hand.

The nearly hysterical girls called Russ at work, and he rushed home, managing to arrive even before the police did. When the police got there they found Russ standing next to the dead woman, the gun in his hand.

The bartender at the tavern told investigators that Russ had been there when the phone call came in from his daughters. His most recent girlfriend's death was ruled a suicide.

This was the situation when two of the Washington State justice system's most prominent figures entered the case. A special investigative unit of the State Attorney General's Office was mandated by a new law in 1981 to conduct independent inquiries into criminal cases around the state, to offer assistance to counties, and indeed to prosecute in some instances. (At the request or with the concurrence of the governor or the county prosecutor.) It was to be basically a two-man operation, but those two men were quite probably the equal of a half-dozen less-skilled investigators and prosecutors. Greg Canova would head the unit as senior assistant state attorney general, and his sole investigator would be Bob Keppel, late of the King County Police's Major Crimes Unit.

Greg Canova worked as a deputy prosecutor in the King County Prosecutor's Office from 1974 to 1981, ending up as the senior deputy criminal prosecutor in that office. Canova was brilliant, honest, and persistent. He rarely lost a case, and he garnered respect from both conservative and liberal factions. Greg Canova had helped draft Washington State's new capital punishment law. Tall and handsome, with a luxuriant mustache, a quick legal mind, and a deep, confident voice that served him well in the courtroom, Canova had been so successful a prosecutor that he was already something of a legend at thirty-five. Canova candidly attributed some of his wins to luck. "Luck plays a part. In the past I've won some cases I probably should have lost and lost some I figured to win. You can never be sure with juries.

"I always go in thinking I can win. If you don't think you can prove guilt beyond a reasonable doubt, then you shouldn't ever file a case."

The other half of the new team—Bob Keppel, Canova's investigator—is one of the smartest detectives this reporter ever knew, respected all over America for his intellectual approach to investigation. A former track star, Bob Keppel was a young homicide detective in the King County Police Department with only one case under his belt when he found himself plunged into one of the biggest cases of his—or any other homicide detective's—career: the "Ted Murders" that began in the Northwest in 1974 and ended in Florida in 1978.

("Ted" turned out to be Ted Bundy, who died in the

electric chair in Starke, Florida, on January 24, 1989. Just a day before he died, Bundy, who was suspected of murdering anywhere from twenty-five to three hundred young women all over America, confessed some of those murders to Bob Keppel. He viewed Keppel as his intellectual equal, and the two had jousted many times. Indeed, many experts suspect that Bundy's offer to "advise" Bob Keppel and several F.B.I. special agents on how to second-guess serial killers was the basis for *Silence of the Lambs*. Keppel let Bundy *think* he was a respected advisor—just to keep dialogue open between them.

In 1975, using what now seems to be an archaic computer system, Keppel narrowed a field of 3,500 suspects in the "Ted Murders" to only five, and Ted Bundy was one of those five. Keppel's methods were right on target when Bundy was arrested for similar crimes against pretty dark-haired women in the Salt Lake City area. The rest is, of course, criminal history.)

With the expertise he gained in being one of the lead detectives in the "Ted Task Force," Bob Keppel has been called upon by probers in dozens of serial murder investigations in this country. When Canova recruited Keppel away from the King County police, he knew what he was doing. Even so, he had to lend Bob Keppel back to the Green River Task Force for two years.

Greg Canova and Bob Keppel were just what Donna Howard's family had needed for a long, long time; they had become disheartened by years of butting their heads into bureaucratic brick walls. Bobbi Bennett would not give up until someone was convicted for what she believed to be Donna's murder.

Bobbi carried her campaign to reopen the investigation into Donna's death to the governor's office, and her arguments were cogent and persuasive. Then-Governor John Spellman asked the Attorney General's Office (specifically Canova's unit) to look into the Howard investigation in late 1981.

At that time it was a moot point. Canova *had* no investigators. In March, 1982, Bob Keppel came aboard, and the probe began in earnest. Keppel would practically wear a groove in the I-90 Freeway across the mountains to Yakima, interviewing and re-interviewing. He talked to the original detectives, and to Ray Ochs and Jerry Hofsos, who were more than eager to continue the probe. He questioned the paramedic who had been at the scene of Donna's death. He found neighbors and hardware store employees, and perhaps most important, Keppel questioned Sunny Riley.

Meticulously Bob Keppel reconstructed a case that was already seven years old and seemed to be as dead as the victim. In truth, it was about to have a whole new life.

The problem, Greg Canova felt, had begun with the first autopsy. The report was only one page long, and that page stated that the wrong hand bore the defense bruising. Moreover, it had not been a complete autopsy because her death was deemed accidental. The investigating stopped, any physical evidence was tainted or obliterated, the body was buried, and the case collapsed like a straw fence in a windstorm.

What Greg Canova and Bob Keppel *did* have was a witness who had passed the lie detector test with no signs whatsoever of deception. Sunny Riley had come forward even though she was scared to death of being implicated. She was a woman whose life-style had changed from hedonistic to responsible. Sunny knew she would probably face some uncomfortable questions from Russ Howard's attorneys—if this case ever got as far as a courtroom—but she was prepared to answer them.

Bob Keppel's efforts to talk with Russ Howard himself were met with scorn. "I was amused," Howard said later. "I never dreamed it would get this far, that anybody would take Sunny seriously."

Howard confided to reporters that he felt he had antagonized Greg Canova and Bob Keppel by "laughing at them."

Not so. He only intrigued them more.

The physical evidence came down to a few precious items that remained. There were the pictures taken by investigating officers that icy morning of January 10, 1975. Blow-ups of the photographs and the recall of the Yakima deputies who were there indicated that there had been absolutely no hair, blood, or human tissue on the sharp end of the railroad tie. Some experts felt that since the ovoid fracture was a depressed fracture, the instrument causing it would have pierced the brain itself, however briefly, and probably come away with blood and tissue residue, and probably some hairs from the victim's head.

Beyond that, Dr. Muzzall's re-creation had Donna Howard kneeling to clean off her horse's hoof. If that was true, why didn't the pictures show dirt or snow on the knees of her jeans? In the photographs the knee portion of her jeans was clean.

Greg Canova and Bob Keppel had a picture in their minds now of how and why the murder had occurred. Russ Howard had wanted out of his marriage and had wanted to keep his children and his financial assets. So, as he had told Sunny, he had, indeed, managed to get Donna out to the loafing shed on some ruse. There he had struck his wife once with the flat of the hammer, expecting her to go down. But Donna had fought him, fending off the hammer with her right hand, protecting her head. The force of the hammer's blows against the webbing between her thumb and forefinger had been so strong that it was not only bruised, but the actual weave of her glove was imprinted on her flesh. Twice more Russ had crashed the hammer against Donna's head.

Then he would have dragged her body along the frozen ground on the Bekins blanket, arranging the corpse in the loafing shed where the two horses were. If Donna Howard had been kicked and simply fallen back, her shirt and jeans would not have been pulled up as they were in the pictures. That rumpling was exactly what would happen if someone had pulled her by her feet.

Donna's body was warm when the sheriff's men and the paramedic arrived, covered tenderly with a quilt. Russ had probably done that deliberately—to keep her warm while he was in town creating his alibi. Either that, or he had gone to town first and returned to carry out the rest of his plan.

The problem for Greg Canova and Bob Keppel in 1982 was how they were going to prove their theory of what happened in 1975 to a jury's satisfaction.

The main piece of physical evidence was Donna Howard's skull. Cleaned and dry and reconstructed, it would be examined now by some of the most expert forensic pathologists in the country.

Dr. Donald Reay, chief of the King County Medical Examiner's Office, examined the skull in July, 1982, and agreed that the damage did not seem to be from a horse's hoof. The back of the skull, maybe—it had been shattered in nineteen pieces, and all manner of force could have done that. However, the much smaller ovoid fracture on the top right side of the skull was very unusual. An oval piece of bone had been broken clean through and forced through the skull against where the brain had been.

The skull was sent next to the Smithsonian Institution, where it was examined by a chief forensic anthropologist. He thought that the top single fracture looked as if it had been caused by a hammer. However, he said, "There's someone who knows a lot more about this kind of injury than even I do—and that's Clyde Snow."

Clyde Collins Snow, Ph.D., forensic anthropology consultant and something of a legend. Big, gray-haired, and deceptively casual, Snow lives in Norman, Oklahoma, but he is rarely there. He may be in South America working over skeletons or in the Philippines reconstructing skulls of massacre victims. He is a witty and jovial man whose manner belies the grimmer aspects of his profession. Snow can tell all manner of things from a skull.

Dr. Snow is not averse to checking out his findings with other experts, and in this case Snow showed Donna Howard's skull to Dr. Bob Kirschner of the Cook County (Chicago) Medical Examiner's Office, to Kirschner's associates, and to Dr. Fred Jordan of the Oklahoma State Medical Examiner's Office. They all agreed with Snow's conclusion that the small oval fracture had been caused by a hammer. Kirschner particularly pointed out that he felt the wood from the railroad tie would have left splinters in the wound, and the wound would have left tissue on the railroad tie.

When Clyde Snow reported his initial findings to Bob Keppel he commented, "This case shines like a herring left too long in the hot sun." That was Clyde Snow's way of saying things were not as they had been reported to be.

After a meticulous examination of Donna Howard's skull Dr. Snow sent a letter to Bob Keppel and Greg Canova. Donna Howard had not had a thin skull, easily shattered. Rather his exam had shown it to be slightly thicker than normal.

Snow noted, too, that the wood of the railroad tie would have been far too soft to have done the damage found in the ovoid fracture. "The fracture was caused by an object of high density with a flat face and a circular upper margin."

Snow continued, "The critical feature of the cranium is the depressed fracture of the right fronto-parietal region. It is a classic example of a 'fracture à la signature' of a hammer. To me, this finding reduces the arguments about the remainder of the injuries to academic quibbling. Whether it was the first or last blow, or whether there was one, two, or three blows is of little significance. . . . Of course, one might speculate that a horse kicked the victim and then administered the coup de grace with a hammer. I don't know about Washington horses, but Oklahoma horses have not shown that degree of dexterity. . . ."

Snow felt that the back blow (probably two blows, according to what Russ Howard had allegedly told Sunny) had been delivered while the victim was still standing, and from the rear, where she could not see it coming. The depressed frontal fracture had occurred when she was lying on her back with her head turned to the left. The killer would have been standing over the victim at that point, and she could well have tried to cover her head with her hand.

Snow's findings made a gruesome and pathetic mind picture.

Photographs of the blood patterns on the loafing shed wall were blown up to 11 x 14 prints and sent to Lt. Rod Englert of the Multnomah County Sheriff's

Office in Portland, Oregon. Englert is one of the most respected experts in the United States on blood patterns. He spends much of his time traveling to testify in homicide trials and has presented over three hundred seminars on blood spatter analysis. Lt. Englert teaches detectives how to determine myriad facts from the silent testimony of blood—if blood is "high velocity" (gunshot wounds), "medium velocity," or "low velocity." Among the concepts he teaches are "bloodstain transfer" and "blood swipe." In both of the latter, bloody objects come into contact with a surface not previously contaminated with blood and leave distinctive patterns.

Englert examined the pictures of Donna Howard's body and the loafing shed and weighed the blood patterns he saw with the story told by Russ Howard and with the reconstruction of the "accident" by Dr. Muzzall.

Lt. Englert's opinion was that Donna's death simply could not have happened the way Muzzall had perceived. Donna Howard's curly brown hair had been sodden with blood from the head wounds. But *had* she been kicked, had she bounced off the jagged railroad tie and then fallen backward, the blood patterns would have been higher, more diffuse, and well beyond the body. The pictures didn't show that.

Instead, the two thick, bloody swaths in the picture looked as if they had been left as someone was lowering and re-positioning a body on the ground. Donna's hair, so heavy with wet blood, would have left exactly those marks photographed on the wall: one swipe up and down and another side to side. The laws of motion would not have allowed Donna Howard to have been kicked into the railroad tie with enough force to penetrate her skull and then let her fall back so gently that her hair left those two solid stains on the white wall a foot away. A powerful kick from a horse would have sprayed blood in a diffuse pattern all over that wall.

The layman would never have thought of that. A surgeon, trained for other kinds of medicine, might not have seen what Rod Englert saw.

Donna Howard might not have known what was about to happen to her. One would hope she was not frightened by the steps behind her as she concentrated on something in the barn. The first blow might have knocked her unconscious as her skull shattered, and the second might have come hard upon the first. Perhaps she fell neatly on an already-spread Bekins blanket, only to be smashed once more on the top of her head because she still breathed. Perhaps she was still able to use one hand to try to block the hammer coming down.

No one would ever know that except for Donna and her killer.

On November 8, 1984, the Washington State Attorney General's Office charged Noyes Russell Howard, fifty-four, with first-degree murder in the death of his first wife almost nine years earlier. Attorneys Susan Hahn and Wes Raber were appointed to defend him.

But the murder case was to be kept from the courtroom even longer. Challenges were made in pre-trial hearings asking who was going to pay for the defense, challenges that were ultimately appealed to the State Supreme Court. Eventually the state and not Yakima County was found liable for the cost of Russ Howard's defense since it was the state that had filed the murder charges.

In 1986 Washington's state legislature appropriated $50,000 to pay for Russ Howard's defense.

The trial finally began on October 13, 1986, in

Superior Court Judge James Gavin's courtroom. Greg Canova was the sole prosecutor, and most of the State's witnesses would be experts in forensic science.

The only civilian witness Canova called was Sunny Riley. She made an excellent witness as she testified for hours. Yes, she had been told by Russ before the murder that he planned to kill Donna with a hammer and make it look as though a horse had kicked her. And yes, he had called her on the day of the murder and told her he had done it. The courtroom was hushed as Sunny related that Russ had complained it had taken him three blows with the hammer to do the job. Sunny said she hadn't wanted to believe it was true, and when she did allow herself to believe it she said she thought that something would happen to prevent her from actually marrying Russ. Yes, she acknowledged softly, part of her had still loved him even then.

In the end Sunny said she could not live with the thought that Donna Howard's murder had never been discovered.

Each side had its forensic pathology witnesses because the burden of the case rested ultimately on one small skull, its battered occiput reconstructed from nineteen shattered pieces.

It was hard going all the way. The defense would not even stipulate that the skull in evidence belonged to Donna Howard.

The forensic pathologists and anthropologists for the State agreed that the massive crushing at the back of Donna's skull *might* have been caused by a hammer, but that the fracture in the front of the skull *definitely* had been.

The defense team called Dr. Muzzall (then practicing in Alaska), Dr. William Brady, and Cyril Wacht, a world-famous forensic pathologist from Pittsburgh. They disagreed with the absolute statements the State's doctors had made. "Our position was," Defense Attorney Susan Hahn said, "[the injury] does look like a hammer [caused it]. But that's not the only thing that could cause that kind of injury, and the explanation that was originally given was still the best explanation."

Greg Canova questioned Dr. Muzzall carefully about the original autopsy. He asked Muzzall to step down from the witness stand and demonstrate just how the injuries could have occurred given the original autopsy's scenario. Greg Canova argued that a contortionist could not have gone through the sequence that Donna Howard's body was alleged to have completed. Dr. Muzzall resolutely disagreed, and maintained his original stance.

Seventeen days after the trial began the jury retired to deliberate. They went out on the evening of October 30, 1986, and returned in the early afternoon on Halloween. It took them eight hours to find Russ Howard guilty of premeditated first-degree murder.

"I had a feeling the jury wanted to find a way to find the man innocent," the jury foreman commented later. "Then there was the feeling, as one juror said, 'I know he did it, but . . .' We talked about what would follow that 'but.' There was nothing there."

Judge Gavin sentenced Howard to life with a twenty-year minimum term. That would make him eligible for parole in thirteen years and eight months, around the turn of the century—when he was almost seventy. Noyes Russell Howard, fifty-six years old in 1986, continues to maintain his innocence, as do his daughters, and he continues to appeal his conviction.

As this is being written it is January, 1994, almost

two decades since Donna Howard walked out to the stable for the last time. In her case, the wheels of justice ground exceedingly slow—but they *did* grind. Without Bobbi Bennett's determination and dedication, without Greg Canova and Bob Keppel, Donna would have lain unavenged throughout time.

The Computer Error
and the Killer

It is not *"news" when a criminal who should have been locked up for earlier crimes re-offends. It happens so often that we have come to take a kind of ho-hum attitude toward this unfortunate phenomenon of criminology. Still, sometimes there are cases that are so deplorable that we have to shake our heads. How on earth could anyone even have considered letting such prisoners walk free when they have proved over and over that they are more dangerous than the most vicious predatory animals?*

One case keeps running through my mind. This man was a walking bomb; he had been designated criminally insane for seventeen years before his last terrible swath of killing. By his own reckoning, he had wanted to hurt women for thirty years, ever since he was in the third grade. His compulsion to destroy and torture females was not a hidden fantasy; he had acted on it again and again and again. But he was as free as you or I, because of an unbelievable series of "clerical errors." Before he was caught he would wreak incredible damage on a number of women who did not recognize the smoldering dynamite beneath the charming exterior—at least not until it was far too late.

I include this case because I think that it demonstrates how charming and benign the sadistic sociopath can be when he wants to appear that way. Sadly, it also shows what stark tragedy can come of trusting the mask he wears.

When lovely, blond Vonnie Stuth and her husband were married on May 4, 1974, the future looked as bright as a Northwest sunrise. And well it should have. They were very much in love, he had a good job, and Vonnie planned to work as a volunteer case aide at the Youth Service Center in Seattle. Both were youth leaders in the Highland Park United Methodist Church, the church where they were married.

In the summer of 1974 the couple moved into a small house in the Burien area just south of Seattle, and Vonnie settled happily into her role as a housewife. Todd Stuth worked the swing shift at a Seattle foundry, and that meant that they were apart most evenings, but Vonnie's parents and her younger sisters lived nearby, and so did a lot of her friends, so she wasn't lonely.

On Wednesday evening, November 27, 1974, Vonnie was preparing for the Thanksgiving feast the next day. This would be her first Thanksgiving as a married woman. Her contribution to the family gathering was to be a Jell-O salad. She dissolved the Jell-O in boiling water and set the other ingredients out on the kitchen counter while she listened to the television blaring from the living room.

At 10:30 her sister phoned, and the two talked for a while. At one point in their conversation Vonnie mentioned that she had to answer the door. When she came back to the phone she said it had been a man from across the street who wanted to give them a dog. "I told him he'd have to come back tomorrow when Todd is home," she said.

At 11 p.m. Vonnie's stepbrother pulled into the Stuth's driveway to pick up something from a car parked there. He glanced into the house and saw Vonnie on the phone, but he didn't go in to talk with her.

Todd came home at a quarter after one in the morning as usual. He found the door was unlocked, and the television and all the lights were on. He called out to Vonnie, but no one answered. Concerned, he noticed her purse on the desk and the salad preparations, half-done, on the counter. Vonnie had had $150 in her purse, and he could see it was still there. Puzzled, Todd Stuth checked the closet and saw that Vonnie's gray hooded coat was gone.

But there was no note. It was incomprehensible that Vonnie would have gone out so late without leaving him a note. He called relatives and friends to see if she had left on a spur-of-the-moment errand, perhaps to borrow something she needed for Thanksgiving preparations. No one had seen or heard from her.

Vonnie Stuth, nineteen, was simply gone, and there was immediate terror in the hearts of those who knew and loved her.

There were eight other young women who had been reported missing in the Northwest, all of whom had vanished just as inexplicably as the young housewife. The media had been flooded with information on those cases: Lynda Healy, Donna Manson, Susan Rancourt, Roberta Parks, Brenda Ball, Georgeann

Hawkins, Denise Naslund, Janice Ott. Janice's and Denise's skeletons had been found in mid-September.

They were all between eighteen and twenty-two years old, slender, with long hair parted in the middle. All pretty. Vonnie matched the physical characteristics of the missing girls. Brenda Ball and Denise Naslund had both lived in the Burien area; indeed, Vonnie and Denise had known each other in school. And Janice Ott had worked at the Youth Service Center, too. Was it mere coincidence or part of some awful conspiracy?

King County detectives were worried, too. Vonnie's disappearance had all the earmarks of an abduction. Vonnie's family described her as a cautious young woman who always kept her door locked. She wouldn't have opened it to anyone she didn't know.

Todd Stuth spent the next few days either in the homicide unit, talking with King County Police detectives, trying to offer some clue that might help them find her, or in his house, waiting for a call from Vonnie. He was adamant that they had had no quarrel; there had been nothing at all that might have made Vonnie want to run away. "It's weird," the twenty-one-year-old foundry worker said. "She was definitely taken. There's no doubt in my mind. If a nut took your wife, you'd be worried, wouldn't you?"

Assured that there seemed to be no direct links to the other eight girls who had vanished, he tried to agree: "I hope not. Because I don't want my wife dead. I'm not leaving this house until I find out what happened to her."

There was nothing in the Stuth house that indicated a struggle. Detectives found no signs of blood or a scuffle. Nothing. For some reason Vonnie Stuth had unlocked the front door, and something or someone had persuaded or coerced her to leave the house.

The only clue investigators had was Vonnie's comment to her sister about the man from across the street who had offered to give her a dog. But which man? Detectives talked to neighbors, but no one recalled—or admitted—talking to Vonnie on the night before Thanksgiving.

The house directly across the street was empty, recently vacated. Stuth said they hadn't known those tenants well at all. He recalled that a couple approaching middle age had lived there. They had driven a van. One neighbor had seen that van parked in the driveway of the vacated home for about ten minutes on the night Vonnie disappeared.

Detectives checked the vacant house and noted that there was a great deal of trash left behind. Pawing through garbage is one of the more onerous tasks of criminal investigators, but trash can yield a gold mine of information, too. Among other items, the King County detectives found a number of snapshots torn into pieces. When they were fitted together the pictures were of a dark-haired woman, attractive enough to be a model, who was posing nearly nude. Neighbors recognized her as the woman who had lived in the house. Other bits of paper bore the address and name of Gary A. Taylor. Neighbors thought that sounded like the name of the man who lived there.

The Taylors had kept to themselves. No one knew what Taylor did for a living or where he and the woman came from. They had lived in the home only a few months. As far as anyone remembered, they didn't have a dog. Taylor was about thirty-five or forty, maybe a little over six feet tall, with light brown hair graying at the temples. He had worn dark-rimmed glasses.

Of course, they couldn't be sure that *he* was the man who had come to Vonnie's door with a dog. Any stranger could have come to the Stuth's door, pointed to a nearby house, and *pretended* to be a neighbor.

Vonnie hadn't told her sister *who* the neighbor was. She had talked to someone, shut the front door, and come back to the phone. She certainly had not sounded upset. Her stepbrother had seen her safe at eleven, a half hour after that.

But the man could have returned, perhaps even urged Vonnie to come out and look at the puppy so she could describe it to her husband. She had been firm about not going outside on the first visit; could she have been persuaded to do so later? She hadn't screamed. Neighbors were sure they'd heard nothing. But then the neighborhood where they lived was almost directly under the flight path of giant jets just before they landed to the south at Seattle-Tacoma Airport. When the jets roared in for a landing all other sounds were drowned out.

Detective Sergeant Len Randall and Detective Mike Baily worked on the case, which had been officially designated as a missing person case. But they didn't feel it was only a missing person case as the days passed and no word of Vonnie came.

They felt the same frustration they had felt in the cases of the other missing girls. Even if they had a red-hot suspect they would have to handle him with great tact and discretion. There was no corpse to make anyone a homicide suspect. A suspect could cry "harassment" and "false arrest" and play the snowy-white innocent. There was as yet no crime. There was only a missing person, an adult who might have left of her own free will.

Mike Baily and Len Randall located a forwarding address for Gary Taylor and saw that he had moved to an isolated three-acre ranch near Enumclaw, Washington, deep in the southeastern portion of King County. They put out a request for information on Taylor through the NCIC (National Crime Information Center) computer, which programmed all data on wants, warrants, and records of criminals.

It was 1974. Computers were in their infancy, and they were horse-and-buggy, technically, compared to what they can do in 1994.

There were no hits on the name Gary A. Taylor. According to information relayed back to King County, Taylor was not currently wanted in any jurisdiction in America, nor did he have a record that might make him a prime suspect in the Stuth case.

On December 6th the detectives located the isolated farm where the Taylors had moved and talked to Gary Taylor in person. He wasn't exactly delighted to see them, but he seemed agreeable enough. He said he would go back with them to the county police offices in the King County Courthouse in downtown Seattle. There he was routinely informed of his rights under Miranda, and Randall told him he was a suspect in the disappearance of Vonnie Stuth.

Randall and Baily studied the tall man. He was visibly nervous. Beads of sweat stood out on his forehead as he denied having any connection with Vonnie Stuth's disappearance. He didn't even know her, he assured them. Still, both detectives had the gut feeling a good investigator senses when he faces his quarry. This guy was antsy, far more that the normal anxiety they saw in an interview situation. But the days of holding a suspect because it felt right were long gone. They could hold Taylor for a few hours, but there were absolutely no legal precedents that would let them book Gary Taylor into jail. They had no probable cause to arrest him.

Technically, there had been no crime. They had no victim. They had no crime scene. And their check through NCIC had failed to show that Taylor was wanted for even a traffic warrant.

Len Randall drove Gary Taylor back to the little house in the woods near Enumclaw. He elicited a promise that Taylor would come into the homicide unit on Monday, December 9th, to talk further and to take a lie-detector test. Once out of the atmosphere of the detectives' office Gary Taylor became relaxed, even affable, and he assured Randall he would be in on Monday to straighten everything out.

Monday came—but Taylor didn't. He was gone. The house in Enumclaw had been vacated hurriedly, and the whereabouts of the Taylor couple was anybody's guess. Belatedly, King County detectives learned who Gary Addison Taylor really was. And the information that came in from authorities in Michigan left very little hope that Vonnie Stuth would ever come home again.

Somehow there had been a horrendous glitch in the system. Somehow a monster had slipped through an escape hatch and been let free to prowl once again.

Gary Addison Taylor was born in 1936 in Howell, Michigan, a small town between Ann Arbor and Lansing. As in most small midwestern towns, there were few secrets—everybody knew everybody else. Gary lived in Howell with his parents and one brother until he was fifteen. School friends recalled him as a physical fitness enthusiast with a lightning-quick temper, and also as a very talented trumpet player. The only trouble he had with the law in Howell could have been considered a boyish prank: Gary shot out windows in downtown stores with a pellet gun.

In 1951 the Taylor family moved to St. Petersburg, Florida, where they managed a motel. Taylor's first arrest took place on Christmas Eve, 1954, when he was eighteen. He was accused of attacking a thirty-nine-year-old St. Petersburg woman, a theater cashier, with a wrench as she stepped off a bus. He didn't know her. Police said at the time that they believed Gary was responsible for sixteen or seventeen other attacks on women in the area. Mindless, motiveless episodes of violence against females. He was tried on a single charge of assault with intent to murder and acquitted by a jury.

Later Gary Taylor told three Michigan psychiatrists he "felt lucky" that he hadn't killed the theater cashier because he "might have."

Shortly after Gary was acquitted in Florida the Taylors moved back to Michigan—this time to Royal Oak near Detroit, where the elder Taylor opened up a dry goods store. Gary joined the navy.

He lasted eleven months. He was discharged because he complained of chronic migraine headaches.

Gary Taylor had been home in Michigan only a month and a half when he was arrested once again for terrorizing women. With each incident the crimes of which he was suspected grew more ominous. The Detroit papers had been full of headlines about "The Phantom Sniper of Royal Oak." Someone with a rifle had been hunting women as if they were deer.

Gary Taylor's arrest came after a nineteen-year-old woman was shot as she walked home from a bus stop. Police spotted him as he fled, and he was captured following a wild three-hour chase through four Detroit suburbs.

Taylor confessed to shooting the woman, as well as to fifteen other sniping attacks on females. Four of the victims had been wounded; no one had been killed—but that was only through sheer luck. One of the victims was an eleven-year-old girl. Gary Taylor hadn't known any of the girls and women he had shot at; their only crime had been that they were females. He told psychiatrists that he had bought the .22-caliber rifle "expressly for the idea of shooting women." He said he aimed at them above the waist because of impulses he couldn't control. He appeared to have derived terrific pleasure from the shootings. Sexual pleasure.

He admitted that he had had "a compulsion to harm women ever since I was in the third grade." He told examining psychiatrists that he had gone to prostitutes since he was only fifteen and that he had enjoyed seeing the fear on their faces as he beat and robbed them.

Why had he picked women as his targets and his quarry? Why did he hate them so? The psychiatric team was fascinated with this young man who seemed so intelligent but whose affect was so cold. Like the biblical Samson, Gary Taylor explained that he found that women were "a source of weakening him, and possibly all men," and he felt that threat fully justified his shooting at them.

Although a teenage Gary Taylor had struck out at females with sheer brute force or through the sights of a gun, an older Taylor had learned that he had only to put on a kind of mask to make women trust him. He was a handsome young man, tall and muscular, and he enjoyed presenting himself as a nice guy, a witty guy good for laughs; he liked seeing the reaction he got from women. It was a kick for him to play a part, to be an actor on the outside while inside he laughed at them, and worse.

Warming to his subject, he told detectives about the waitresses he had encountered who were "flirty." He explained that he would always smile back at them. "They'd think I might be flirting with them. 'If she only knew what I was thinking, she'd be scared to death because I might be thinking something like, Boy, I'd like to shoot you.' "

After the Royal Oak phantom snipings Gary Taylor was deemed to be psychotic—criminally insane. Dr. Abraham Tauber told a Michigan court that Gary Taylor was "so unreasonably hostile toward women, this makes it very possible that he might very well kill a person—and probably a woman—if he were allowed free in the community."

On March 28, 1957, Taylor was committed to the Ionia State Hospital for the Criminally Insane. He was one day away from his twenty-first birthday.

Some 2,500 miles away, Vonnie Stuth was one week away from her second *birthday.*

In 1960 Gary Addison Taylor was transferred for treatment to the Lafayette Clinic in Detroit. He had apparently shown improvement during his three years in Ionia. At any rate, he was given passes outside the clinic to attend classes in arc welding at the Wolverine Trade School.

Over the years he had learned a lot more than arc welding; he had become the complete sociopath. He had a story for every occasion. He could be anyone he chose to be—and be so most convincingly. His charm was as superficial as the thin glaze of ice on a pond in autumn, but how he made it work for him.

At Christmastime Taylor was allowed to be away from the Lafayette Clinic on temporary leave. He posed as an Internal Revenue Service agent as he knocked on the door of the west side Detroit home of a former beauty queen. Earlier he had watched her and followed her home to see where she lived. Once inside he set down his empty briefcase and raped the woman. Perhaps as an afterthought, he robbed her of $13 on his way out the door.

Gary Addison Taylor was twenty-four that year.

Vonnie Stuth was in kindergarten.

Given more and more freedom because he was apparently doing so well at the Lafayette Clinic, Gary Taylor roamed the Detroit area with ease. His savage obsessions had not changed. Four months later, in April, 1961, he was arrested by Detroit police after he assaulted a rooming house owner and her daughter with an eighteen-inch machete.

As he always did, Taylor had a ruse to get into the homes of his chosen victims. He had rented a room in the victims' house, and of course they let him in when he returned several hours later. This time he attacked them.

When the news of Taylor's arrest broke, a twenty-six-year-old Detroit woman who owned an art import store called police and identified Taylor as the same man who had choked her into unconsciousness in her store in January. She had been horrified to see the smooth connoisseur of paintings and sculpture change into a man filled with rage and lust. In only a second the "mask" had dropped, revealing the monster beneath.

There was a great deal of negative publicity in Michigan about Gary Taylor in 1961, and a resounding response from the public. People asked loudly why he had been transferred out of Ionia in the first place. He was whisked back to the hospital for the criminally insane without ever going to trial in the 1960–61 cases. Then Michigan Attorney General Paul L. Adams launched a three-month investigation into Taylor's transfer to the Lafayette Clinic and concluded that patients should be paroled *only* through court hearings instead of simply being released from mental hospitals in the state.

It would have seemed that premise should always have been followed.

Twice more, in 1966 and in 1967, Gary Taylor and his family requested his release from Ionia through court orders. Both times the requests were turned down on the grounds that he was still dangerously mentally ill.

Like many once-high-profile offenders, Taylor no longer made headlines. The public forgot about him.

In 1970 Taylor was transferred from the prison for the criminally insane in Ionia to the Michigan Center for Forensic Psychiatry in Ypsilanti, a relatively small city between Detroit and Ann Arbor. Without fanfare he was released from inpatient care in July of 1972— with, of course, the stipulation that he return periodically for treatment. Dr. Ames Robey, the center's director, said he believed Taylor was no longer mentally ill and would be dangerous only if he failed to take his medication. Even in therapy Gary Addison Taylor could be convincingly sincere, a man who said all the right things.

Gary Taylor was now thirty-six years old. Vonnie Stuth was seventeen; she had grown to be a beautiful young woman, but she was still safe, still 2,500 miles away from Taylor.

For about a year Gary Taylor returned sporadically for treatment to the forensic psychiatry center in Ypsilanti, but in mid-1973 he stopped showing up for his appointments.

He was not listed as an escaped mental patient for three months, not until November, 1974. And then, to compound the mistake further, through some human error or some temporary aberration of the teletype network that crisscrossed America, Taylor's name was not entered into the national law enforcement communication system.

After more than a year Michigan authorities discovered the mistake and asked that any law enforcement agency in America take Taylor immediately into custody if he was located. This urgent notification to all agencies was *supposed* to have been issued on November 6, 1974, but was not, because of an oversight.

That made *three* tragic oversights.

There would be a fourth. Indeed, Gary Taylor's name was not entered into the nationwide computers until January 13, 1975—seven weeks after Vonnie Stuth vanished.

Would the correct notifications have saved Vonnie? The first three almost certainly would have; if anyone in authority had known Taylor was a walkaway from his treatment, he would have been picked up and locked up. If the November 6, 1974 "urgent" bulletin had been disseminated on time, he might have been arrested in the twenty-one days between the bulletin and the night he encountered Vonnie.

One thing was certain: the last mistake kept county detectives from holding Gary Taylor in jail after they talked to him on December 6. But they had checked the system to see if there were any "wants" on him and found none. By January 13 Vonnie was still missing, and Taylor was nowhere to be found.

Detectives had searched the Enumclaw property where Gary Taylor last lived for some trace of Vonnie. It would have been an ideal spot to hold her captive. Although modern homes fronted the main road on each side of the property, the white frame house Taylor rented sat six hundred feet back on the rugged farm, accessible only by a winding dirt road through a

thick stand of evergreens. There were many outbuild-
ings—a double garage and sheds—all hidden from
the road and from the neighbors' view. Behind the
house the property dropped away a hundred feet or
more, ending in the rushing Newaukum Creek. The
ground was frozen solid in December and January;
there were no obvious gravesites.

Short of digging up the whole three acres—an
almost impossible task in winter—there was no way
for the investigators to be sure Vonnie was there
somewhere. Gary Taylor had moved on in his van and
might well have taken Vonnie, or her body, with him.

He had had hundreds of miles of lonely spots where
he could hide Vonnie.

King County detectives knew that he had gone
south, but they didn't know how far south. They had
managed to trace Taylor to Portland, Oregon. A
woman who said she was his wife, Emily* Taylor, had
rented an apartment there with him from December 6
to December 16. His van was found in Portland,
where it had been repossessed by a finance company.

The van was processed, and a long blond hair,
similar in class and characteristic to Vonnie Stuth's
hair, was found inside. There was no way of knowing
how long it had been there. And there was no way of
proving that it actually *was* her hair.

By the time King County detectives traced him to
Portland, Gary Taylor had left; he was rumored to
have departed Portland in a Ford Pinto, leaving his
wife behind. He was seen in several small Oregon
towns, alone, but he moved on before authorities
could catch up with him. Taylor's wife left Portland in
late January, 1975, and drove the couple's Chrysler to
Tucson, Arizona, where a relative of her husband's
lived.

The house in Tucson was staked out, but Taylor

himself did not appear in Arizona. However, a court-ordered phone tap of calls to the residence in Tucson indicated that calls were coming in from various areas in the Southwest. Gary Taylor was on the move again.

Houston, Texas, special assault detectives were dealing with an elusive sexual predator in March and April of 1975. The four victims were all women managers of large apartment complexes, and they had all been attacked by a man who had shown interest in renting a unit.

The tall, good-looking would-be tenant was described as being quite charming at first, but his charm had quickly vanished when he was alone with a woman in an empty apartment. In each case he had held a chrome nine-shot revolver on the women and demanded sex. But he hadn't raped the captive women. He had been unable to achieve an erection, and he had demanded that they perform fellatio on him.

The female victims all described their attacker as a man in the grip of a white-hot rage. He had shouted terrible things at them, threatened to kill them, and screamed "bitch" at them as if he loathed them.

Two of the Texas victims had been assaulted on March 11th, the other two in late March and early April. One of the Houston women told her attacker that she had multiple sclerosis and managed to pull away from his grasp as he seemed momentarily hesitant. She fell down a stairwell in her flight and screamed as loud as she could. The man fled, leaving behind his chrome revolver. Disappointed police found no prints on it; the suspect had worn black gloves during all the attacks.

There was one more victim in Houston whom detectives felt might be part of the pattern. A smooth-talking man managed to get inside the home of a

pregnant sixteen-year-old housewife. She had been
alone there with her eighteen-month-old baby. After
sexually assaulting her in her house the man ordered
her to go with him to a motel, and she complied,
fearful for her baby's safety. He allowed her to take
the youngster along with them.

This time the attacker was not impotent and succeeded in raping the terrified young mother. The girl
managed to escape when her attacker fell asleep. She
crept out of the room with her baby and took a cab
home, then called the police. She told them that the
man who had raped her seemed very drowsy, and she
thought he was high on drugs. His clothing had
smelled of marijuana.

Houston police rushed to the Ramada Inn but
found the rapist gone. But he had made a mistake, his
normal attention to detail dulled by drugs. He had
registered as "Sarge" Taylor and had given a Michigan
license plate number. Houston checked the number
with NCIC, and this time the proper information had
been programmed.

The plates belonged to Gary Addison Taylor, an
escaped mental patient from Michigan, also wanted in
Seattle for suspicion of homicide in the 1974 disappearance of Vonnie Stuth. The four other Houston
victims identified mug shots of Taylor. They were
positive he was the man who had attacked them.

Once again Gary Taylor was gone. The pressure to
arrest Taylor was tremendous—especially when a
busload of girls and several motorists were fired on by
a sniper with a .22 rifle in Sherman, Texas, on May 16.

A month after the attack on the young mother in the
Ramada Inn Houston police received an anonymous
tip that Gary Addison Taylor was working in a
Houston machine shop. He had learned arc welding

long ago when he was on leave from one of the Detroit clinics; he had also, of course, attacked women after he left class.

The Houston informant whispered that Taylor would be taking a particular route from his job to the duplex he was renting. He was stopped and arrested by police at 3 a.m. on May 20, 1975.

Vonnie Stuth was still missing.

Once Gary Taylor was safely in jail in Texas, Emily Taylor surfaced through her attorney in San Diego. She had much to tell authorities. Her fears and suspicions had grown to the point where she had fled from Taylor, whom she had married three years earlier without knowing his true background.

She told the attorney, Frederick A. Meiser, that she believed her husband had been involved in several murders. Whenever he was drunk, she said, he had talked of killing people. "He would get drunk and say, 'Hey, you know those people. I killed them and buried them outside our house in Michigan.'" Emily Taylor also thought that he had killed Vonnie Stuth and buried her in their yard in Enumclaw.

The Gary Taylors had lived in the hamlet of Onsted, Michigan, near Ann Arbor and Jackson, when he had last reported at the Forensic Center in Ypsilanti. Even as Houston detectives began to unravel cases that might be traced to Taylor in Texas, Washington and Michigan authorities were alerted to the possibility that murder victims might be buried on properties where the Taylors had lived in those two states.

Sheriff Richard Germond of Lenawee County, where the Taylors' Michigan home was located, gathered a search crew on Thursday, May 22, 1975. King County, Washington, authorities were doing the same. Germond's crew worked in the yard of the little house where the Taylors had lived in the early seventies. The home was located twenty miles southeast of Jackson near the Irish Hills. They had been instructed that they would find four bodies. They found only two bodies and a quantity of women's clothing, buried almost underneath the Taylors' former bedroom window. The decomposed bodies were encased in plastic garbage bags and the clothes stuffed into two other bags. A cursory examination of the corpses, which had been buried naked and were bound with electric cords and rope, seemed to indicate the victims had died of gunshot wounds to the head. The remains were transported to Lansing, where forensic pathologists would do postmortem examinations.

A library card in one of the bags was for Lee Fletcher, twenty-four, with a Toledo, Ohio, address. The Ohio city is just south of the Michigan border, and Michigan authorities were aware that two women had been listed as missing from a bar in Toledo since late April, 1974.

The women, both alleged to be prostitutes, had last been seen leaving the bar with a tall man who drove a van with Michigan plates. Lee Fletcher was one of the women. The other was seventeen-year-old Debbie Henneman. A male friend of the two, concerned about their disappearance, spotted a van that matched the description of the one in which the women had left. He checked the license plates and found it registered to Gary A. Taylor. He had gone to Taylor's home and searched for Lee Fletcher and Debbie Henneman but had been unable to find them.

Now, at last, they had been found.

Lenawee County detectives got a search warrant for the house where Gary Taylor and his wife had lived. Their initial search of the home was unremarkable; it was just a house like any other. However, when they

got to the southwest corner of the residence's basement they found a small room that could only have
been a soundproof torture chamber. Even though
more than a year had passed, the investigators found
blood and human tissue on the floor, ceiling, walls,
and pipes.

According to the path of the Taylors' travels that
police all over the country were retracing, the couple
had left Onsted, Michigan, in the spring of 1974 and
traveled west.

In Enumclaw the search for Vonnie Stuth's body
began on Thursday, May 22, and lasted through
Friday and Saturday. Seven King County officers,
forty Search and Rescue Explorer Scouts, several
National Guardsmen and a German shepherd search
dog went over the grounds of Taylor's former home
literally inch by inch.

Wildflowers dotted the grass beneath the cedar trees
now, and rhododendrons and wisteria planted by a
former owner softened the grisly search somehow.
The Newaukum Creek at the back of the farm property ran high along its banks, and birds sang.

Vonnie had been spirited away in the depths of
winter. Now it was spring, and the thaw had softened
the ground. Even so, the searchers ended each day
with no sign of Vonnie. When they had finished a
section they marked it with sticks with strips of plastic
attached. By the third day the backyard was almost
filled with the little sticks and their tiny multicolored
banners fluttering in the wind.

The searchers paused along a dike area between a
small pond and the creek. The underbrush was very
thick, but one of the team detected just the tip of what
appeared to be a shoe protruding from the ground.

Now the Explorer Scouts and non-police personnel

were relieved of their duties, and they moved away. Carefully, meticulously, detectives removed the sandy dirt from the gravesite. A body lay buried fourteen to twenty inches beneath, a body clad in jeans, a gray hooded coat, and small brown ankle-high boots. The body had long blond hair.

On Monday, May 26, the King County Medical Examiner, using dental records, positively identified the remains found buried beside the Newaukum Creek as those of nineteen-year-old Vonnie Stuth. She had died of a gunshot wound to the head and appeared to have been dead for six months. There was no way to determine if she had been sexually assaulted.

Just as a pebble dropped into a still pool makes endless rings in the water, the ramifications of Gary Addison Taylor's urge to kill grew and grew. In Houston, Homicide Detectives Carol Stephenson and Theresa Pierce were asking the suspect about the death of a twenty-one-year-old go-go dancer, Susan Kay Jackson. There was a singular irony in the fact that this man who detested women had his case assigned to two female detectives.

Susan Jackson had disappeared from the Three Thieves Bar, where she worked, on May 14, 1975. Four days later an elderly heart patient, out on his prescribed daily hike, stumbled over her blanket-wrapped body in an isolated area thirty miles from downtown Houston.

Gary Taylor made no pretense of innocence. Yes, he had killed Susan Jackson, he confessed. He said he had picked her up in the bar and taken her to his duplex, where he had suffocated her. He had then wrapped her feet and legs with one garbage bag and her trunk and head with another, swaddled her in a blanket secured by chains, and driven her body to the spot where it was found.

He also confessed to the killing of Vonnie Stuth, and to murdering the two women from Toledo, whose names, he said, he never knew. He did not ask for an attorney, even though he had been told repeatedly that he had the right to one. He signed confessions to the murders but confessed only orally to the sexual attacks in Houston.

Informants told Michigan police that Gary Taylor had bragged of killing yet another woman in that state as well as a man who had worked with him in Ypsilanti. In Ann Arbor Police Chief Walter Krasny and Detective Bernard Price were most interested. They had been investigating the disappearance of thirty-three-year-old Sandra Horwath, a mother of three, who had dated Taylor. Mrs. Horwath, employed by an Ann Arbor building firm, vanished in October of 1973.

The male alleged murder victim surfaced, alive and well, a day later in Garden City, Michigan. He said he had no idea he was the man supposed to be buried along with the three woman. He had known Taylor only casually. Sandra Horwath, however, remained missing.

No one knew how many unsolved murders might be linked to Gary Addison Taylor. In one of his sanity hearings Gary Taylor had told a psychiatrist, Dr. Ivan A. LeCore of the Pontiac, Michigan, State Hospital, that he fantasized about killing a woman skier. "He thought of sniping at women on a ski jump and went so far as to procure a rifle and a telescopic sight, but after a personal trip to a ski jump he decided that he would not do this for some reason or another," Le Core recalled.

Taylor's wife remained secluded in San Diego. She was asked how she could have lived with the suspect and not realized he was a killer. "I tell you he's a very cunning person, and he acts completely sane, and all the time he probably wants to kill."

Houston Detective Carol Stephenson was inclined to agree. She felt that there were more victims than anyone knew about. Taylor denied that there were any crimes other than those he had confessed to, but Stephenson shook her head and added, "I don't feel he would confess to anything he thought we knew nothing about. He was asked that and said he wouldn't."

She described Taylor succinctly as "mean," but also as "very intelligent."

"I feel like he is far and away the most dangerous person I've ever talked to in the fourteen years I've been in this work," she said, adding that he would be charged for the Texas crimes. "His 'irresistible urge' won't hold water in this state."

Detective Stephenson said Taylor had told police in Houston that he had decided to move there in December, 1974, after reading want ads from several papers in major cities to check job opportunities. He was hired by the Houston machine shop two days before Christmas and more than three weeks before he ever actually made national "wanted" networks. He had listed three Michigan men as references. The addresses he gave for the men were nonexistent.

Nobody checked.

Taylor had also listed his father as a reference. In mid-March he asked for a leave of absence to attend his father's funeral in Tucson. His father was alive and well. When he was contacted by a Detroit paper the elder Taylor reportedly said that he had not seen his son in five years and wanted nothing more to do with him.

Gary Taylor was indicted by a Harris County, Texas, grand jury on May 28, 1975, on five counts of sexual crimes: three of aggravated sexual abuse, one of aggravated rape, and one of attempted rape. He was held in lieu of $340,000 bail.

Taylor complained to a Houston judge that city detectives had beaten him and threatened his life at a city park before he signed statements confessing to the murders in Texas. Detective Theresa Pierce denied that either she or Carol Stephenson had beaten Gary Taylor. She said Taylor was not mistreated, and he had never been taken to a park.

On May 29, 1975, Gary Taylor was formally charged with first-degree murder in the death of Vonnie Stuth in an affidavit filed by King County Senior Deputy Prosecutor Phil Killien.

All hope had ended for Vonnie Stuth's family when her body was found on the lonely acreage in Enumclaw after six months of waiting. They had kept the top layer of her wedding cake frozen on the slight chance that she might be home to celebrate her first anniversary on May 4th. There would never be such a celebration, and her mother, Lola Linstad, quietly disposed of the cake.

Memorial services for Vonnie were held on Sunday, June 1, 1975, in the church where she had been married thirteen months before. Lola Linstad, a co-founder of Families and Friends of Victims of Violent Crimes and Missing Persons, remained active in the group. "There was still a job to do. It was important to me that other families, if at all possible, be spared this kind of tragedy."

There was some faint comfort for Vonnie's family.

They knew that she had been dead for a very long time. They had some closure, and they could go on. They did not know, however, how long Gary Taylor had held Vonnie captive after he lured her out of her home to look at a dog. They agonized over that.

"It would have been hard to do," Lola Linstad said when a reporter suggested that Vonnie might have been alive for several days after she was abducted. "She was a fiery girl, and in his confession Taylor said he got her outside to look at a dog he wanted to give her, but when it wasn't in his van she got mad."

Everyone who knew Vonnie Stuth wanted to believe that she had been shot in the back of the head as she broke free of Taylor and ran from him when they arrived at the Enumclaw farm. The fact that she was still dressed when her body was found seemed to substantiate that. When he appeared before King County Superior Court Judge William Goodloe in Seattle, Taylor pleaded guilty to second-degree murder. It was a way for him to escape trials in Texas and Michigan. Deputy Prosecutor Joanne Maida urged the minimum recommendation of life in prison. Judge Goodloe sentenced Gary Addison Taylor to up to life in prison. "If I had the power to do so, I would recommend a *second* term of life."

But he didn't have that power. Actually, the mandatory minimum for second-degree murder was not less than five years in prison. The King County prosecutor recommended that the Washington State Board of Prison Terms and Paroles not parole Taylor for at least fifteen years.

After hearing his sentence Gary Addison Taylor said he wanted to express his "regrets" for Vonnie Stuth's death. He appeared very calm, and he had smiled as he entered the courtroom. After he heard his sentence he shook hands with his attorney. All in all, he had fared well. The King County Prosecutor's Office had little choice but to accept the plea bargain. Taylor had confessed to Vonnie's murder before her body was found. There had been questions about how his confession was obtained, and there was the likelihood that evidence against him would be suppressed. There was also the issue of a speedy trial on the sexual assault cases in Texas, and he might, *incredibly,* have been set free without the plea bargain of second-degree murder.

No one knows why Gary Addison Taylor felt that women were his enemies, Delilahs and Jezebels who drained men of life and strength. Perhaps this man who chose Adolf Hitler as his hero *was* insane.

But for an insane man, he was able to stay away from the scores of detectives who were seeking him for an incredibly long time.

Gary Taylor had admitted to killing four women and assaulting five more, but this was only in his final reign of terror across America. This did not include the myriad attacks on women that had begun when he was in his mid-teens. There *were* some victims that he could not claim—the women who disappeared in Washington and Oregon in 1974. Lynda Healy, Donna Manson, Susan Rancourt, Roberta Parks, Brenda Ball, Georgeann Hawkins, Denise Naslund, and Janice Ott were not murdered by Gary Addison Taylor; they had the terrible misfortune to cross Ted Bundy's path. Both serial killers had been prowling in Washington State in 1974.

Gary Taylor *was* imprisoned in the Washington penitentiary in Walla Walla, but only for eight years. Washington State correctional computers—which are far more sophisticated and dependable than the computers of two decades ago—indicate that Taylor went out of the Washington penal system in 1984 and was transferred to another state. He remains behind bars as this is written. Although his status is reviewed every few years, the earliest possible release date for Gary Taylor is May 17, 2036. If he survives, he will then be a hundred years old and, one would hope, no longer dangerous.

But in 1994 Gary Addison Taylor is fifty-eight years old. If she had been allowed to live, Vonnie Stuth would have been thirty-nine.

Lola Linstad pondered a question I asked her, not out of curiosity, but from my admiration for her strength: "How have you survived? How have you been able to bear losing Vonnie the way you did?"

"Vonnie was such a happy person, and she would have wanted us to be happy," Lola answered. "If we had spent the rest of *our* lives grieving and mourning for her, I know it would have made her so sad. She would have wanted us to go on celebrating Christmas and laughing and living. We will always miss her, but I know we are living as she would have wished us to. . . ."

The Vanishing

Back in the late 1950s, when the author was a Seattle
policewoman, it was something of a rarity to have a
teenager disappear or even run away. In the whole city
of Seattle there were perhaps two or three girls missing
at any given time. In the decades since, the problem of
missing youngsters has, of course, reached epidemic
proportions. Every police department of any size has
dozens of runaways listed on its books.

The vast majority of missing teenagers have left of
their own accord, and while they often become involved
in unsavory situations, most of them are alive and well.
One day most of them will come home, sadder and,
hopefully, wiser. Sometimes, however, there are disappearances so totally unexpected, so inexplicable, that
even seasoned police investigators shake their heads.

Stacy Sparks's disappearance was one of those.

Stacy vanished under the strangest circumstances—
vanished so completely that it was difficult for a
rational mind to understand how it could have happened.

Stacy's story has an ending. No one of us who
searched for her could ever have guessed what that
ending would be. Of all the possibilities, the truth was
one that no one ever considered.

On July 9, 1979, Stacy Sparks's life was not only completely normal, it was filled with happy plans. She had a new job and a steady boyfriend, and she was looking forward to the realization of a longtime dream: Stacy was going to Hawaii. Eighteen years old and a recent high school graduate, Stacy had less reason than most young women to run away voluntarily. And yet something changed the pattern of Stacy's life that long-ago night in June, something that no one who knew and loved her could explain.

By midnight Stacy had disappeared. In fact, both Stacy and her beloved new car seemed to have been swallowed up by the earth itself. Detectives found it hard to believe that her car, at least, had never turned up.

When Stacy awoke on July 9 she was happy. In the weeks and months after she vanished, her mother and stepfather—Peg and Mike Haley—went over and over that day, trying to think of some small signal they might have missed, something to indicate that she had a problem. They came up with nothing at all.

Stacy left their home in the Ballard area of Seattle on her way to have breakfast at Sambo's Restaurant a mile away. Stacy had worked at Sambo's for a long time but had recently taken a job as a waitress at the Little Pebble restaurant at the Shilshole Marina, which was also in Ballard. The Little Pebble was the coffee shop portion of the elegant Windjammer restaurant, and the new job meant more pay and an opportunity in the future for Stacy to be promoted upstairs, where the tips were usually lavish. She liked the new restaurant, and she liked the job.

Stacy worked her daytime shift that Monday, wearing the little nautical outfit the café furnished. She did the uniform proud. At five feet, two inches, her 115 pounds gave her a perfect figure. Her ash-blond hair was streaked with lighter blond from the summer sun, and her brown eyes sparkled. Stacy was vivacious and unfailingly friendly. It was rare to see her without a smile, even when her feet hurt at the end of a long shift.

Stacy finished her shift about six that evening and walked to the car that was her pride and joy. It was a light blue 1978 Plymouth Arrow with four-inch-wide white racing stripes along its sides.

Stacy Sparks drove next to the Ballard apartment of two friends, Kim Turner* and Polly Gunderson.* Polly was due to go to work that evening at the Raintree restaurant and lounge in Lynnwood, a suburb north of Seattle. The three girls chatted while she got ready to leave. Kim and Stacy stopped at Stacy's while she changed into blue jeans and a yellow T-shirt with a large rose appliqued on the front. Stacy loved roses; she always wore a necklace with two carved white roses with gold leaves surrounding them. She slipped into thong sandals.

Stacy and Kim had never been to the Raintree before July 9, but they headed next for the popular spot where their friend worked. Stacy carried a change of clothes with her because she planned to spend the night in West Seattle, where her boyfriend lived.

On the drive to the Raintree Stacy talked enthusiastically about her trip to Hawaii. She already had her round-trip ticket to Honolulu for August 1st. The Hawaiian trip had been a dream for Stacy and the three girlfriends who were going with her since they were fifteen. Now she was working hard to save enough spending money so that she could see and do everything possible in the islands.

At the Raintree Stacy parked her Arrow just outside the main entrance in the crowded parking lot. It was 8:30 p.m.

Stacy's boyfriend, Ron Bates,* had to work late in the auto supply firm where he clerked. She had promised to be at his home in West Seattle at nine so that he could call her and have her pick him up at work.

But when Ron called at nine there was no answer. There is no mystery about that; Stacy had simply dawdled at the Raintree and realized there was no way she could get to West Seattle by 9 p.m. She figured Ron could get home all right.

Ron gave up trying to reach Stacy and, somewhat annoyed, caught a bus for home, figuring she would probably be there by the time he got home. He had promised to take her out to dinner.

Stacy and Kim had several drinks at the Raintree, chatted with their friend, Polly, and talked to some young men at the bar. Sometime around 9:30 Stacy left—alone. She had perhaps five feet to walk to her little blue car in the parking lot. All things being equal, she would have quickly reached the I-5 freeway heading south into Seattle, driven through the downtown section, and then exited at the West Seattle off-ramp and driven west to meet Ron. The drive should not have taken more than half an hour to forty-five minutes, even though it was pouring down rain.

Stacy never got to Ron Bates's home. First he was mad, and then he was worried; he waited up all night for her. Her parents weren't concerned that night or the next day. They hadn't expected Stacy home Monday night, and they assumed that she had gone directly to work at the Little Pebble on Tuesday morning.

But Stacy didn't come home Tuesday night, and a call to Ron Bates brought forth the frightening news that he hadn't seen her at all on Monday night.

Nor had she shown up for work at the Little Pebble on Tuesday.

Stacy's parents contacted everyone they could think of who might have seen her. The last direct contact anyone had had with her was at the Raintree.

On July 12, 1979, Stacy Sparks was officially listed as a missing person, and the file was flagged "suspicious circumstances." It was the beginning of one of the most massive searches that the Seattle police and the Lynnwood police had ever carried out, and the case file would grow over the next months until it consisted of two bulging folders several inches thick. Detective Bud Jelberg, head of the Missing Persons Unit, worked it first, and it was subsequently handled by the Homicide Unit, with Detectives John Boatman and Mike Tando spending untold hours on it. Since she had last been *seen* in Lynnwood, detectives there coordinated their efforts with the Seattle police.

A check on the WASIC (Washington State) computers failed to bring a "hit" on any accident, impounding, or police stop involving Stacy's little blue Plymouth Arrow. The investigators knew she wasn't lying injured and unconscious in any hospital in the state; her car had not been involved in an accident.

Information on Stacy and the missing car was broadcast in every county in Washington, and then to every law enforcement agency in a seven-state area. The hunt became widespread.

Stacy's family was sure of one thing: If anyone had grabbed her, she would not have gone quietly. She was a fighter who would have kicked, screamed, and scratched. However, the walls of the Raintree facing the parking lot were windowless. And the Raintree, which catered to a young crowd, featured disco music at top volume. If the parking lot had been temporarily empty of everyone but Stacy and an attacker, no one inside could have heard her cry for help.

It seemed frighteningly obvious that Stacy Sparks had not left voluntarily. She hadn't picked up her last check from Sambo's, she hadn't touched her savings account, and she would have had no more than $25 in her purse the night she vanished.

Seattle Police Sergeant Craig VandePutte and Detectives Boatman and Tando contacted Kim Turner. She recalled that Stacy had stayed about an hour at the Raintree, leaving about 9:30. They had talked to two Oregon men in their twenties at the bar—Ken Brinks* and Ralph Lawrence.* The men hadn't come on strong or said anything offensive. Stacy had left first—to go to West Seattle to pick up her boyfriend—and Ralph Lawrence had left shortly after. After Stacy and Lawrence had left, Kim had played a game of backgammon with Ken Brinks, and then they had left—but not together.

VandePutte contacted Brinks in Portland. The man, married, admitted that he and Lawrence had talked with Kim and Stacy, and he agreed with Kim's recall of that night. They had talked with the girls but hadn't seen them outside the tavern. Brinks stayed with an aunt when he was in Seattle on business, and Lawrence, who was divorced, stayed at his parents' home. VandePutte felt that Brinks was giving him a straight story. The men had arrived at and left the Raintree in their own cars.

A waitress at the Little Pebble recalled Stacy's last day at work to the detectives: "She was very happy. She was looking forward to spending the evening with her boyfriend."

The waitress described Stacy as a very friendly girl. "She was almost too friendly. She would talk with just anyone, and she wasn't afraid of anyone."

The detectives checked out the alibis of both Ken Brinks and Ralph Lawrence and found that there was no way either man could have abducted Stacy. They were seen by relatives within half an hour of leaving the Raintree. There was simply no way they could have kidnapped Stacy and hidden her car so thoroughly that no one could find it in half an hour.

Both Polly and Kim said that Stacy had had only two or three beers and was not even slightly intoxicated when she left for the drive to West Seattle.

"Would Stacy ever consider picking up a hitchhiker?" Mike Tando asked.

"Yes," Kim said. "She might. She's a really sweet person. She'd pick up a hitchhiker . . . if they looked all right."

It was the only viable theory going. The detectives knew that hitchhikers who look "all right" often turn out to be monsters, but they didn't say that to Polly and Kim.

On July 14th a man came into the homicide offices. He'd seen the papers full of articles about Stacy Sparks, and he had a strange story to tell. "Some guy where I work has been telling this story about something that happened on the night of July 9th. He was driving on I-5 during the evening, and he saw this naked girl lying in the freeway. She was badly injured.

He stopped to help, and so did some others—including a doctor or a nurse or something. It wasn't a car wreck; the girl was just out there in the middle of the freeway up by the Snohomish County line."

Sergeant VandePutte immediately began calling hospital emergency rooms checking for the possible arrival of a "Jane Doe" injured on the freeway on July 9. He came up empty at Seattle's Harborview Hospital, where Seattle Medic One paramedics take their emergency patients, and in the Shoreline district north of Seattle. However, when he called the Sno-Com line in Snohomish County he found that there *had* been such an incident. VandePutte was directed to the paramedic who'd made the run.

"Yeah, we picked her up," the medic recalled. "We got the call at 11:18 p.m. We responded to I-5 northbound at 228th. There was a nude white female, about twenty-one, lying in the road with multiple leg injuries and other trauma. While we were working on her she kept asking. 'What happened to my friend?' "

The injured woman had been taken to Stevens Memorial Hospital and placed in the intensive care unit. It sounded as if the mystery of Stacy Sparks had been solved. However, a check with the hospital brought disappointment. The woman was not Stacy, and she didn't know Stacy. She had been hurt in an accident, and there was absolutely nothing linking her to Stacy Sparks.

On the slight chance that Stacy had somehow managed to fly to Hawaii despite the fact that her ticket was still in her parents' home, detectives contacted the airlines. No one had tried to use the reservation or to change it. There had been no attempt to redeem the ticket.

On July 15, an anonymous caller rambled on and on, saying that Stacy's body was probably at a rest stop on Blewett Pass. The area was searched—to no avail.

Stacy's blue Arrow hadn't turned up on any of the computers, nor had it been located in a search of used car lots.

Police divers couldn't very well search waterways for the little Plymouth without having some idea of where it might have gone in. To get from Lynnwood to West Seattle via I-5 Stacy would have had to cross two bridges: first the University Bridge over the Lake Washington Ship Canal, and then the West Seattle Bridge over the Duwamish Waterway. Helicopters did flyovers in these two areas. If Stacy's car had been in the water, spotters could have discerned it from the air in fifteen to twenty feet of water when it could not be seen any other way, but no pilot or spotter detected the blue car below.

The fact that Stacy's car had vanished as completely as she had was a continuing puzzle. It is always easier to find a car than a hidden body.

Peg and Mike Haley, Stacy's parents, and her friends and relatives distributed hundreds of pictures and flyers describing her and her car to stores, bowling alleys, Laundromats, and other public places all over King and Snohomish counties. Her face was familiar to thousands of people who had never known her— but still there were no early solid reports of sightings. In desperation the Haleys turned to psychics, hoping that there might be a message from the spirit world that could let them know what had become of their daughter.

Some psychics have proved eerily accurate in finding the bodies of crime victims, but others can fill families full of both false hope and deep anxiety.

One Seattle psychic held the earrings that matched

the carved rose necklace Stacy was wearing when she vanished and, according to Peg Haley, described Stacy's purse and its contents—something that he could not have known.

But his "vision" of Stacy was unsettling, to say the least. He "saw" the missing teenager in a deserted cabin near Snoqualmie Pass. He described a candy factory (Swiss type) and a dirt road leading away from it. There is a Swiss chocolate factory outlet near the pass, a very well-known store. The psychic said that three people were involved, one of them a man named Tom who was part Indian. The psychic gave Stacy only three days to live because she was being injected with heroin.

The Haleys could think of three Toms that Stacy knew—one an Indian, the other two part-Indian. One was quickly ruled out, the second was out of the area, and the whereabouts of the third was unknown. Because her parents were so upset by the psychic's visions, King County police units were contacted, and they carried out a fruitless search in the mountain foothill area. Issaquah police—whose jurisdiction covered the cabin location—were alerted, too, but they found no cabin matching the seer's description. Relatives and friends searched the region, too, frantic to find Stacy before her three days ran out. And when all the searching was finished they found not one trace of her in the little mountain foothill town.

The police searchers continued their probe into Stacy's disappearance through more realistic channels. More and more bulletins bearing Stacy's picture were printed and distributed. A clerk at the Washington State Department of Motor Vehicles volunteered to hand-search all vehicle impound forms in the state for one on a blue Plymouth Arrow that might have been missed in the computer checks. It was a tedious task, going through all the impounds back to July 9—but the little Plymouth wasn't there.

A man in his mid-forties, Jeff O'Dell,* called Detectives Mike Tando and John Boatman and said he had talked to Stacy Sparks twice on July 9. He said he was a longtime customer at Sambo's. He said he'd seen Stacy at Sambo's that Monday morning and talked with her then. O'Dell said she had confided in him that she had a boyfriend who was getting serious, but that she was a long way from being ready to settle down. She had invited O'Dell to drop into the Little Pebble sometime.

"Did you?" Boatman asked.

"Yeah, I went over that night for dinner. Stacy waited on me, and then she got off work just as I was leaving. I showed her my new van, and she told me she was going out with friends that evening."

The man had no new information; he only verified what the detectives were hearing again and again— that Stacy Sparks was a cheerful, friendly girl who seemed to have no real problems at all. She had told O'Dell that she wasn't ready to settle down, but she hadn't been so concerned about that that she would run away to avoid marriage. Detectives already knew that she didn't want to get married. Ron Bates had told them that he and Stacy had broken up for a week after he had proposed to her, but they had reconciled when he told her he wouldn't press her for a commitment. The trip to Hawaii was to have been a chance for Stacy to "gain new experiences and a new outlook on life," according to Ron.

Detectives Boatman and Tando had alerted the Canadian customs stations at the northern border of Washington, and they, too, were watching for the missing girl and her car. Had Stacy turned north instead of south on I-5, she would have been at the U.S. border in two hours.

On the off chance that Jeff O'Dell might have had more interest in Stacy than the avuncular affection he proclaimed and that he might even have followed her to the Raintree, the Seattle detectives checked out his movements for the night of July 9th. They found that he had attended an AA meeting with a married couple and that the couple could verify that he was with them continually until hours after Stacy had vanished.

Two of Stacy's former co-workers at Sambo's had left Seattle for California within a day or so of Stacy's disappearance, and the investigators wondered if it was possible that Stacy had joined them. It would have been completely out of character for her to do that, but the timing was perhaps more than coincidental. When the women returned to Seattle they were shocked to hear that Stacy was missing; they hadn't seen her at all.

The public's response to the intensive campaign to find Stacy was overwhelming. One of the more interesting leads came from a woman who lived in Kent, Washington, a small town south of Seattle:

"I was driving on I-5, headed south, on July 9th or 10th. When I was on the southern edge of the downtown section my attention was drawn to a medium blue small car with a girl driving. She looked just like the pictures I've seen of Stacy Sparks. There was a man sitting in the backseat right behind her—thirty-eight to forty, white, dark-haired. The girl kept staring at me, and I stared back. She looked at me for so long that our cars almost nudged each other. Then the man in the back sat forward. He leaned against her, and he stared at me. Our cars were going about sixty miles an hour at the time. I looked at her because she seemed to be staring at me so intensely. When I saw the picture of Stacy on TV tonight I was sure it was her."

This report made sense in light of the theory that Stacy might have either picked up a hitchhiker or been forced into her car by a man waiting in the parking lot of the Raintree. Perhaps she had been trying to get the woman's attention and help by staring so fixedly at her.

On July 19 Detective Deardon of Lynnwood reported that a pair of girls' jeans and women's panties had been found two blocks west of the Raintree. The jeans were Levi's brand with an elastic band made of variegated colors. The jeans were extremely dirty but in good condition. The panties were white with a green floral print.

Detectives asked for a more thorough description of the jeans Stacy had worn when she vanished. Kim Turner didn't know if Stacy had worn panties or not because Stacy hadn't changed clothes in front of her on July 9, but Kim knew her jeans well; she had given them to Stacy. "They were high-waisted, size 30, probably. I don't think they had any elastic band with colored thread. I think they had a strap around the waist which buckled in front."

The jeans found on the dirt road near the Raintree were not Stacy's.

An older couple who had been vacationing called to say that they were positive they had seen a light blue car with a white stripe on July 10 at 5 p.m. near Mud Bay, some seventy miles from Seattle. "It passed us, speeding and wavering erratically. We could only get a partial license number: UCX—."

Stacy's license number was UCX-487!

"Did you notice anyone in the car? Who was driving?" Tando asked.

"We couldn't see. It went by too fast," was the disappointing reply.

A woman from Olympia, Washington, sixty miles south of Seattle, reported that she had seen Stacy's car on Martin Way in that city, which was only ten miles from Mud Bay. "I know it had a UCX prefix, because our car does, too, and I noticed it."

Again she could not identify a driver or any passengers. The sightings—if they were actual sightings—of Stacy's car had all taken place on a route leading south out of Seattle and heading toward the Pacific Ocean.

In the meantime, Seattle detectives gathered items that might help to identify the missing girl if she eventually turned up as a homicide victim. Kim was asked to purchase a pair of jeans identical to those she had given Stacy, and she did that, bringing in a pair of jeans with a belt fastening in front. Stacy had carried her hairbrush in her purse, and it was missing along with her, but strands of her hair were retrieved from a hair dryer's brush attachment. Even as they gathered these identification items Mike Tando and John Boatman hoped that it was still possible that Stacy had left of her own accord.

But they no longer believed that. Everything they'd learned about the missing girl told them she would never have put her family through such agony. Her stepfather, Mike Haley, had resigned his job and was now spending all his time looking for her. On foot, by four-wheel-drive vehicle, and from a private plane he had scanned the acres of wilderness east of the city, trying to spot a glint of blue or a sheaf of blond hair. Stacy's mother, brother, aunts, uncles, grandmother, and dozens of friends spent their days delivering bulletins, asking questions. Always searching. They were trying to raise funds, too, to consult another psychic.

The Haleys contacted Peter Hurkos, the famed Dutch psychic who was living in California. His services, he explained, would cost $6,000. Although the psychics who had tried to help them so far hadn't charged at all, and the Haleys didn't have that kind of money, they thought Hurkos might be able to tell them something more than the clairvoyants they'd consulted in the Seattle area. They determined that somehow they would find the money.

People who cared about Stacy began the Stacy Sparks Search Fund, and high school students fanned out across Ballard, a close-knit, basically Scandinavian community. They collected donations, they had rummage sales—anything to raise the money needed for the psychic whose books detailed his many successful searches.

By the end of July the donations given to help in the search for Stacy reached $3,500. On July 30th—two days before Stacy would have left for her long-planned trip to Hawaii—Peg Haley and Polly Gunderson boarded a plane for Los Angeles. Their mission was to persuade Hurkos to help them for half his usual fee. Stacy's mother had a cashier's check for $2,000 and $1,900 in bills and rolled coins in her purse.

After pondering it for a while Hurkos agreed to help them. He placed a picture of Stacy, turned facedown, on a table, and after concentrating in silence for several minutes he described her. He seemed able to tell Peg Haley things about Stacy and their family that he couldn't have known. In three subsequent sessions he said he had divined that:

—Stacy had been having an affair with a man in his thirties. (Polly Gunderson said that Stacy had referred to such a man, but she had never told Polly his name.)

412

—Stacy had stopped at a gas station on the night of July 9.

—Although Hurkos could not see how, when, or where Stacy had been abducted, he perceived that three men were involved—one of them Stacy's secret lover, a man who was jealous of Ron Bates and resistant to Stacy's trip to Hawaii. Another was a younger white man. The third was probably of Indian descent.

—Two of the men took Stacy away in one car, while the third followed in her blue Arrow. Hurkos thought the missing Plymouth Arrow was hidden in a garage in Tacoma, Washington.

—Stacy had fought and had been subdued by an injection of heroin.

The vision Hurkos saw was similar in many ways to the Seattle psychic's and not a pleasant one; he too felt that Stacy had overdosed on the heroin injection and been dumped in a ditch.

Hurkos furnished Mrs. Haley with a map that showed a Y-shaped road in front of a mountain range with three prominent peaks. Near the bottom of the left corner he drew a small airfield. The gas station at the Y had a trailer parked beside it. There was a residential area near the right foothill of the mountains, and a narrow road veering off from the main road. At the end of this road was a falling-down cabin, its yard filled with junked appliances and an old trailer. Stacy's body, he pointed out, lay in a ditch nearby, covered with leaves. Hurkos circled three areas on a Washington map—all of them near Everett in Snohomish County, just north of King County, and, incidentally, close to the Raintree. He instructed Peg Haley to check the area near Lake Stevens first.

As soon as Peg Haley and Polly Gunderson re-

413

turned from Los Angeles on August 2 their family and friends geared up for another search. They located a pilot in the Lake Stevens area who studied the map for a few seconds and then said he knew the area depicted on the hand-drawn map: "It's Highway 92 leading to Granite Falls!"

The searchers headed into the brush. They worked until dusk and found . . . nothing. The next day it was the same story. For the next three weekends they searched every side road in the Granite Falls area and found no trace of at all of Stacy. They still felt sure that Hurkos held the answer, but the area circled was just too big.

Peter Hurkos had assured Peg Haley that if Stacy wasn't found by October, he would personally come to Seattle and lead them to her. But when Peg phoned him for more information he never returned her calls.

For a long time Stacy Sparks's family went out on searches for her, given new hope each time by psychics who were sure they could "see" her body.

The police, too, thought twice that they had, indeed, found Stacy.

On September 26, 1979, the skeletonized body of a young girl was found off a dirt road in Kent, Washington. Dental records proved it was not Stacy, but Jacqueline Plante, a visitor to Washington from Utah, who had been missing since early June. On December 7th, Bellevue, Washington, police found a skeletonized body in that city, which was much closer to the area cited by psychics. Dental comparisons showed this second tragic victim to be fifteen-year-old Teresa Sterling, a runaway from Georgia. With the discovery of each body Stacy Sparks's family spent anxious days until they learned that neither of the victims was their daughter.

One man was convicted of the murder of Jackie Plante, and another in the killing of Teresa Sterling.

A year later police were no closer to knowing what had happened to Stacy Sparks than they were a day after she vanished. It was not from lack of trying. There simply was no place else to go with the investigation, nothing beyond asking for help from the public. After a while the posters and fliers with her picture became weather-worn and tattered. It was hard to make out what they said:

> Stacy Sparks is five feet two inches tall and weighs between 115 and 120 pounds. Her eyes are deep brown. Her hair is probably blond or its natural light brown. Her birthday is January 25, 1961. Her work experience is principally as a waitress. If she is alive, she may well be in Hawaii.
>
> Stacy's car is pictured on this flier. There are black louvers on the rear hatchback window, and there is a tassel hanging from the rearview mirror. The license number is Washington UCX-487. The VIN number is VIN.7H24U84300830.

Something terrible had happened to Stacy Sparks; that seemed almost certain. It was possible that she had walked away from the lights and laughter in the Raintree tavern on that warm Monday night in July, 1979, out to a dark parking lot where she met someone she couldn't get away from. It was less likely that she picked up a hitchhiker who was not what he seemed. It was doubtful—but possible—that she had undergone a psychic shock that caused amnesia. It was vaguely within the realm of possibility that she chose to leave for reasons of her own.

* * *

There are thousands of young women who vanish every year, and many of them are never found. Stacy Sparks was not to be one of those missing forever. She disappeared on a Monday—July 9, 1979—and she was found on a Monday—September 14, 1981—two years and two months after she vanished. She was where she had been all along, where no one had ever searched.

Seattle, Washington, is flanked to the west by Elliott Bay and to the east by Lake Washington. Until 1940, when the first Lake Washington Floating Bridge was dedicated, there was no way to get to eastern Washington from Seattle without driving *around* the huge lake. Lake Washington is so deep that a standard bridge wouldn't work, and so the very innovative floating bridge was constructed. The Lacey V. Murrow Bridge floated on pontoons and had a bulge in the middle that opened to allow small craft and sailboats to pass through.

The Floating Bridge was nowhere near Stacy Sparks's route from Lynnwood to West Seattle along I-5; she would have had to go exactly opposite the direction of her destination to come anywhere near the bridge that led to Mercer Island and then on to Bellevue along the I-90 freeway.

And she had done just that. For what reason, no one will ever really know.

On Monday, September 14, 1981, the Floating Bridge was closed from midnight on while workmen removed the bulge in the center and replaced it with a straight section. Any number of fatal accidents had been blamed on that bulge, which had caught a number of motorists unaware in the forty years it existed. Workmen for the General Construction Company were hooking cables to the new straight portion of the bridge when they found something snagged on the bulge cables far beneath the surface of Lake Washington.

Lake Washington is very cold and very deep. In its deepest regions the bottom is two hundred feet down. Under the bulge in the bridge the steel cables stretched at least eighty feet into the dark water.

Divers found what was snagging their cables. It was a blue car with white racing stripes. A Plymouth Arrow. At 8:25 a.m. it was winched to the surface by a crane on a barge and taken to the west end of the bridge.

There was a body inside, a body wearing blue jeans, a shirt with a rose, and a necklace with two carved roses. It would take a check of dental records, however, to be certain that this was Stacy Sparks.

The Plymouth Arrow had extreme front-end damage, which included sharp dents in both front wheels. The roof was smashed flat, almost to the top of the seat. The driver would almost certainly have died instantly as the car became airborne, flipped over, and cleared the concrete bridge rail. Water can be as hard as steel on impact.

It was Stacy they had found. The license plate and the VIN (Vehicle Identification Number) matched her missing car. Dental records matched the remains exactly. There was some sense of closure, some relief, finally, for her parents. "I know now that Stacy wasn't murdered," Peg Haley said, "that she wasn't tortured . . . that she didn't suffer."

But the questions remained. They probably always will. Was it raining so hard that Stacy became confused and turned off on a ramp that led to the Floating Bridge? That seems unlikely; she knew the trip to West Seattle by heart.

Had she been more affected by the few beers she drank at the Raintree than anyone realized? Possibly.

But there was the most puzzling element of all. When the Washington State Patrol reconstructed the accident—and they did believe it was an accident—they determined that Stacy had not been headed eastbound *toward* Mercer Island when she hit the bulge at high speed; she had been coming *from* Mercer Island and was heading toward Seattle. Westbound.

One possible answer is that the older man that Stacy had talked about to her friends lived on the Mercer Island side of the bridge, and that she had decided on a sudden whim to go to meet him—instead of meeting her young boyfriend in West Seattle. If Stacy Sparks did take that detour, if she did see the unknown man, had they had an argument? Had she been upset when she raced back across the bridge, her vision blurred by tears and the pelting rain? This was pure conjecture. No one would know that but the man himself—if, indeed, such a man existed.

Kenneth Irwin, the Washington State trooper who investigated the accident two years after it occurred, set an arbitrary time for the crash—2 a.m. on July 10, 1979—mostly because that was when the summer storm was at its peak. And that was the time the bridge had had the least traffic. In truth, no one saw it happen. No one could really know the exact time Stacy lost control of her car.

Irwin estimated that Stacy's car had been traveling well in excess of the forty-five-mile-an-hour speed limit when it failed to negotiate the bulge and jumped the concrete bulkhead on the bridge's north side. It hit nothing above the waterline. That would account for the absence of broken glass or any other debris on the bridge; that was why no one was aware at the time that there had even *been* an accident. But it *was* an accident—not a murder. Had anyone else been in the car with Stacy, he—or she—would have ridden to the bottom of Lake Washington, too. No one could have jumped out before the car cleared the cement railing.

The Arrow, like its namesake, had taken wing for a short, soaring space before it plunged down and down and down into the depths of Lake Washington, crushed like a tin can.

Many homicides are carried out so cleverly that they are written off as accidents. In the case of Stacy Sparks, what had been investigated as a murder was, in truth, only a tragic accident.

The Last Letter

No one who knew them through the decades of their relationship would ever deny that Bill and Jackie were in love. Their years together—and apart—were full of longing and wonder, jealousy and ecstasy. They were, indeed, two people who embodied the kind of emotion we hear about in love songs. Songs of love lost, love regained, and sometimes love destroyed—forever. But popular songs seldom mention a kind of supremely selfish "love" that can hurt innocent people and smear even the most romantic love affair with blood.

This story haunts me. Why? I suppose it is because the ending was so pointless, so totally unnecessary. Quite probably thirty years of happiness were thrown away because one of the partners did not believe in love. And the other believed—and trusted—in love too much. There is an old adage: "Be careful what you wish for—because you just may get it, but your wish will never come about exactly as you planned . . ."

Detectives from the Bellevue, Washington Police Department, of necessity, viewed the "Bill and Jackie" story first as a forensic puzzle. Only later could they allow themselves to delve into the reasons why Bill and

Jackie Brand's romance ended as it did. They had a bit of a head start. One of the principals in the love affair had written their story, possibly believing that theirs was a relationship too momentous not to be shared with the world, possibly feeling the need to explain what was unthinkable.

In 1958 Bill Brand lived in Fairbanks, Alaska, with his wife and small daughters. He was in his early thirties, a tall, sandy-haired man who was handsome in a rugged way that seemed to fit Alaska. He was involved in lumber and construction and was already on his way to a considerable fortune. Brand had had the foresight to see where Alaska was headed and had dug himself a solid foothold in the building supply business there. When Alaska became the forty-ninth state on January 3, 1959, Bill already had it made. The largest state in the union had the smallest population, but it was about to boom, and housing was in great demand. As the years went by Bill Brand would become an extremely wealthy man.

Jackie Lindall* was seventeen, pretty, dark-haired, and slender when she met Bill Brand for the first time. She had moved from her Minnesota home to go to the University of Alaska in 1958, leaving behind small-town life and a large, loving family. She had a sister two years older than she, and two brothers, seven and twelve years younger. Although it was hard for her to travel so far from home, a spirit of adventure burned within Jackie. And Alaska was about as adventurous a spot as Jackie could imagine.

Wherever she went, Alaska—or rather, what it meant to her—would always call her back and back and back.

Her family didn't worry about Jackie as much as they might have because she was going to live with the Brand family instead of in a college dormitory or apartment. She would be a nanny for the little girls and help around the house to pay for her room and board.

Bill Brand apparently found the willowy teenager absolutely enchanting. To a seventeen-year-old a man over thirty must have seemed far removed from her social sphere, and yet it is likely she found him a little exciting; he was dynamic, and much smoother than the college boys she met. Indeed, Jackie may well have had a crush on Bill.

Whatever Jackie's and Bill's relationship may have been in the late 1950s and early 1960s, nothing openly marred the surface of the Brand marriage. Although his work meant he was always busy and often away from home, Bill was a devoted father, and seemingly as devoted a husband. He and his wife had a third baby girl.

After a few years of living with the Brands Jackie graduated from college and returned to Minnesota. Jackie moved out of Bill's life. Or rather, she tried to. Bill Brand always managed to know where Jackie was and what she was doing. He never really let her go.

With her personality, poise, and beauty, Jackie Lindall quickly found a job with Northwest Orient Airlines. Jackie went through flight attendant's training in Minneapolis in 1962. (She was called a stewardess in those days.) Her first home base was in Washington, D.C.—all the way across the country from Bill Brand.

In 1963 Jackie shared an apartment with another stewardess from her training class, and she was caught up with a new social life, dating, and making friends. She refused, however, to date pilots or other airline employees. More experienced stewardesses had warned her that it usually brought only grief. But then, she didn't need to; Jackie met scores of men on every flight. One businessman, Dan Barret,* who flew regularly between Detroit and Washington, introduced her to his roommate in Washington, D.C., Cal Logan.* Jackie fell in love with Cal, and they were soon engaged. For a while she was able to relegate her life in Alaska to her past, and she was excited about her wedding plans.

Only months before her wedding day Cal Logan was killed in an automobile accident. That was the first time violent death wiped out Jackie's plans. Dan Barret had lost his best friend, and Jackie had lost the man she planned to marry. They comforted each other, and it strengthened their platonic friendship. For years Dan was special to Jackie—but she never loved him in a romantic way.

Whatever might have happened between Jackie and Bill back in Fairbanks, it was pivotal in his life. He had never forgotten Jackie, and he missed having her as a part of his life. She was no longer a schoolgirl. She was a grown woman now, and drifting farther and farther away from him. He had no intention of letting that happen. Bill Brand wanted Jackie—possibly he had from the first time he saw her—and he detested the thought that another man might touch her. Even though he remained in his marriage he kept tabs on her, calling her often, questioning her when she wasn't home for his evening calls. Brand comforted himself for a long time, convinced Jackie wouldn't have sex with anyone else because she had such a solid midwestern religious background.

It did not seem to occur to him that an affair with a married man—himself—might be far more alien to her moral upbringing than intimacy with a single man.

Jackie's friendships with the other flight attendants were solid, and she would keep in touch with many of them for the next two decades, just as she remained close to the friends she had grown up with in Minnesota, and with her brothers and sisters and parents. She was a very loving young woman; Jackie was "down-to-earth," according to friends. Despite her tragically short engagement to Cal Logan, most of her close girlfriends had realized even then that Jackie's real longing was for Bill Brand. Few of them would ever actually meet the man Jackie spoke of in such glowing terms.

Jackie compared every man she met to Brand, and none measured up. But instinctively she tried to pull away from the big man she had left behind in Alaska. Although she had probably loved Bill Brand since she was in college, Jackie wanted security. She wanted a home and a husband who could support her without worrying about bills. She had exquisite taste, and she hoped one day to be able to have the home she wanted without considering the cost.

Bill had taught her that. He had told Jackie over and over that *she* was like royalty—that she should never consider riding a bus or streetcar. That was for ordinary women, and she was special. She never believed that part—but subtly, cunningly, Bill had instilled in Jackie an appreciation of and desire for expensive clothes and lovely homes.

After Cal died Jackie began to date often, but in the back of her mind there was always Bill. And Bill was not free to marry her. Bill Brand was not an option for her.

After she had spent a few years in the East, Northwest Airlines transferred Jackie to Seattle. It was a promotion; now she would have a chance to fly to the Orient as well as the States. One of her best friends was transferred with her. They had lived a block apart in Washington, D.C., and they were delighted and surprised to find they had taken apartments just as close in Seattle.

Bill Brand would later claim that Jackie became pregnant in the summer of 1965. He suspected the father was either an Alaska state trooper or an airline pilot. He told people the "pregnancy" was aborted while Jackie was on a flight to Tokyo. The alleged father of that child was rumored to have committed suicide in Anchorage, Alaska. It was all very nebulous. It may have been true; more likely it was a vicious figment of Bill Brand's jealous imagination. Years later, as he looked back upon his life and Jackie's, he saw indiscretions that had never happened, and he hated vehemently anyone he thought might have come between him and Jackie.

Friends who knew Jackie Lindall since kindergarten and others who remember a younger Bill Brand believe the physical affair between Jackie and Bill probably began in the mid-sixties. He was, of course, still married, but his obsession with Jackie had continued undeterred by time or distance.

Although far apart in miles, Alaska and Seattle seem right next door to northwesterners, and commuters fly back and forth all the time. Brand frequently had business in Seattle, or he *made* business in Seattle. Jackie was flying out of Seattle, and he saw her as often as he could, seething with jealousy over her other suitors.

And still he did not plan to divorce his wife or leave his children. He offered Jackie nothing more than an affair. For the ultimately selfish man, it worked out well. Jackie would have her job to fill much of her time, and she would wait for Bill in the meantime. Brand couldn't see that she might need a life beyond that; he liked the thought of her in her Seattle apartment, waiting for his call.

He made vague promises to Jackie from time to time. Someday, perhaps, they *could* be married, but not until his children were grown. He missed Jackie when he was away from her, but he was a very busy man, continuing to build his fortune in Alaska's booming construction era.

For Jackie it wasn't as easy; she wanted a *life.* She could see her twenties passing by with no man who was really her own, and she dreaded spending her life that way. Bill was always showering her with presents —but presents were cold comfort over lonely weekends.

Friends remembering Jackie recall that, of all things, Jackie seemed to need security the most— emotional security and financial security. Bill Brand was not in a position to give her either.

At that point, in the mid-sixties, Jackie probably truly loved Bill Brand. She clung to the same dream every "other woman" has—that someday Bill would be divorced and they would marry. He was even more attractive at forty than he had been when she first moved into his home, and he was quite powerful in the business world, making money hand over fist. As one of Jackie's friends said later, Jackie would have left any man for a chance to marry Bill Brand. "He personified all the things she admired in a man."

Jackie turned down scores of dates to keep her promise to be faithful to Bill.

But finally there were just too many days and too many long nights alone. Maybe Jackie intended to force Bill's hand; maybe not. More likely, in the end she simply couldn't bring herself to break up another woman's home. Jackie met another man, a good man who was free to be with her. Jud Jessup* was divorced and had custody of his two children. Worst of all for Bill Brand, Jessup lived on the East Coast.

By 1967 Jackie was twenty-six, and she had decided to marry Jud and help him raise his youngsters. It was a decision that Bill Brand deplored. He was incredibly vicious when he spoke of Jessup and his children. He could not imagine why Jackie would leave him to raise what he termed "another man's idiots." As he remembered the situation, the events were cunningly rearranged to suit his obsession. It was almost as if he believed that Jackie had been somehow *forced* to marry Jud Jessup, and that Bill had tried vainly to save her.

Bill Brand was a man who kept diaries, marked dates on calendars; writing down his thoughts helped him remember those things that were of great importance to him, both in business and in his relationships. He would one day write a long, long letter, the pages chronicling so many years of his feelings for—and about—Jackie. Many of his recollections were about the many rendezvous the pair had had.

During October, 1967, Jackie and I got together in Anchorage. I was there on business and she was on her way through on a trip to the Orient, and when she arrived, she found that we were staying at the same hotel. So she left word for me to call her. I did, and that night we went to dinner together at the hotel. Luckily, the next day her flight was delayed for twelve hours which gave her the chance to recover and we made plans to meet in Portland on December 12th.

I arranged for a suite at a hotel in Portland for that day, and that evening Jackie flew in from Seattle after having worked a flight from Tokyo that day. She was absolutely exhausted. . . . We went back to the room, she in one [bed] and I in another, and she immediately fell asleep. . . . During dinner that night at the hotel, I told her that I really loved her. There wasn't much of a response to that, but that night she came into the room where I was sleeping and laid down on the bed next to me and asked, "What are we going to do?" I knew that she was to be married, but it wasn't until then that I understood that the date was hard and fast.

Brand would not accept Jackie's marriage to another man.

The next day she turned, put her arms around me and told me that she felt she was in love with me . . . we had decisions to make.

My position was that I would proceed immediately with the business of a divorce because nothing would ever be the same between my wife and I. She objected to that, saying that was nothing for me to do because the girls were too young and their absence would make my life miserable for me. The indignity of aborting her wedding plans and the subsequent explanation to her family were repulsive to her, so much so that she would rather cast her lot with a life of unhappiness. It later developed that the decision was almost disastrous. . . .

Bill Brand had waited too long to be with Jackie. She had simply decided to take her life off hold and marry a man who loved her and was free to do something about it.

She must have had doubts. After a decade of being bound to Bill she must have wondered if she was doing the right thing. Even as she prepared to marry another man, Jackie gave Bill a silver letter opener inscribed "Somewhere, Someday, Somehow." Bill interpreted that to mean they would eventually be together.

Maybe she did mean it that way. Maybe she knew how Bill was hurting over her defection from their relationship, and she wanted to ease his pain. But she still went ahead with her wedding.

"The saddest day of my life took place while I was a continent away," Bill Brand wrote of Jackie's wedding day. "The marriage wasn't going to amount to anything from the beginning."

Despite the fact that she was married to someone else, Bill called Jackie Jessup three times a week. He gloated, "She was in his bed, and I was on his phone talking to her three times a week. . . ."

Jackie's best stewardess friend was married in late 1969, with Jackie as matron of honor. Bill planned to fly to meet her, but at the last minute his business in Fairbanks "went to hell" and he didn't go. He reminisced later, "Jackie felt betrayed. That pack (her new family) had been giving her fits, and she badly needed a renewal of hope."

That was only Bill's perception, and in retrospect at that. Jackie's stepchildren liked her, and would always remember her as "a 'mother' and our friend."

Bill considered Jessup a monster and his children "genetic cripples." They were impediments to his true love for Jackie. He fought constantly to break up her marriage. He urged Jackie to meet him and arranged to fly back to her home on the eastern seaboard to see her. In Bill Brand's mind Jackie was being driven nearly insane by her marriage and her separation from him. In actuality it was quite the other way around.

If Jackie was upset, it was undoubtedly because she was being pulled in two directions. Now that he could not have her, Bill Brand *would* not let go.

In October, 1973, Bill Brand was forty-eight years old. He was admitted to a Seattle clinic for a procedure designed to prevent a stroke. Tests had shown that his left carotid artery—the artery that carries blood to the brain—was ninety percent occluded (blocked). He had episodes of tingling and numbness in his hand and trouble with one eye. There was the very real possibility that his mental functions might also be compromised by the lack of oxygen to his brain. Delicate surgery removed the fatty plug that blocked the vital artery, and he recovered uneventfully.

In the years to come Brand would have frequent checkups and take an vast array of medications—to help him sleep, to relieve depression, and to control ulcers. He was clearly not a happy man; his ailments were those often triggered by anxiety and depression.

How could he be happy? Jackie was married to someone else, and even though so many years had passed he still struggled to find a way to bring her back to him. He called and wrote and sent tapes, cajoling, pleading.

She still cared about him, as much as she fought it. Time after time Bill's campaign to draw her back worked. He sent Jackie money to come to Seattle to

talk with him in April of 1974. He rented a suite at an
expensive hotel; he always got accommodations in the
very best hotels. But he recalled later that Jackie's
visit was not as wonderful as he had expected. Bill was
convinced he had caught her in an assignation with
another man—an airline friend she had known for
years. Bill Brand was becoming shockingly paranoid
in his thinking, at least when it came to Jackie. There
were so many men he suspected of being Jackie's
lovers.

There were not enough hours in the day for Jackie
to have had that many lovers.

One day Bill Brand would document his years with
the woman he loved so possessively in a missive he
called "The Bill and Jackie Letter."

"The reason that I mention this incident," he wrote
many years later, "is because she displayed a vulgar
capability that was so totally foreign to me according
to my moral values."

Bill Brand was so righteous. He saw sin wherever he
looked—if Jackie was involved. In reality, he manu-
factured sin out of whole cloth. Except for her meetings with Bill, Jackie was faithful to her husband.

"The week was memorable," he wrote of the 1974
visit, "and was the foundation for our being together.
There were no hard and fast dates set because things
in Fairbanks needed attention but things in Maryland
were coming apart pretty fast by then and arrangements in Seattle were in order. . . ."

Bill constantly urged Jackie to leave Jessup as soon
as possible and to come to Seattle to live. He would set
her up in an apartment and take care of her completely. Then, in time they would be married.

Jackie Jessup was, as the song goes, "Torn Between
Two Lovers." She was thirty-three years old in 1974,
and whichever man she chose to be with she fully

expected to *stay* with until she died. If she expected to have children of her own, she didn't have that many years left. Bill clearly wasn't going to go away unless she did something convincingly decisive. But did she truly *want* him to go away? She loved Jessup—but not with the fiery passion she felt for Bill. She had been in love with Bill for so long that he was part of who *she* was. And now, for the first time, he was promising that he really would marry her. He tugged at her continually, and finally he pulled her free of her husband.

He wrote proudly in "The Bill and Jackie Letter" that he had convinced her to leave Jessup and her stepchildren, and how "relieved" she was when he instructed her to be in Seattle by November, 1975.

Jackie really had no choice at that point. Jud Jessup had finally discovered Jackie's other love when he found a bunch of cassette tapes with long messages to Jackie from Bill. Not surprisingly, he gathered up his youngsters and left.

"He had gone into a rage and otherwise behaved like a jerk," Brand wrote happily. "He must have realized long before that his days with her were limited. . . ."

Jackie's marriage had lasted a little more than seven years. In reality, it never stood a chance. By sheer force of will Bill Brand had not allowed it to succeed.

Bill Brand was gleeful. He had won. He had his Jackie back. She packed her things and shipped them to Seattle.

"Then she got herself on an airplane and headed to Seattle to arrive here late in the day on November 1st. There was a suite ready for us at the hotel. We needed to stay there until we decided just where in the Seattle area it would be that we wanted to live."

Bill was a bit premature. They would not actually live together for a long time. Bill Brand was still married and living with his family in Fairbanks.

But he had wrenched Jackie free of her marriage, and she was once again waiting for his visits. Now she no longer had her career as a flight attendant to fill her time. Bill could not be with her for Christmas or New Year's, of course; he had his family. He bought her a ticket to fly to Minneapolis to be with her family.

Bill Brand had become her sole support. Jackie was his mistress. She loved him. She was faithful.

On November 14, 1977, Jackie Jessup moved into the apartment where she would live for the next eight years. It was a lovely three-bedroom unit in Bellevue, Washington, one of Seattle's posher bedroom communities. She signed the lease and listed her occupation as a "buyer's assistant" for a Fairbanks, Alaska, corporation. It was, of course, one of Bill Brand's corporations. In reality, Jackie didn't work at all.

She was a quiet tenant, and her landlady soon became familiar with the handsome man who often spent time with Jackie. "It was my observation over these years that Jackie was beautifully courted by Bill Brand," she recalled. "Although I didn't know the Brands socially, I was never aware of any domestic strife between them. I knew Bill Brand as a very gentle man with a gruff exterior."

Bill Brand still nursed his paranoid fantasy that Jackie was not true to him. For all his blustery gloating, he felt deep down that his main attraction for Jackie was his wealth. He believed that she wouldn't stay with him unless he could support her better than any other man. It was a premise that wasn't even remotely true. He was her "prince," her perfect man. She adored him. All Jackie sought was honesty and commitment.

The two things Bill would not give her.

Brand later recalled:

During late February, 1980, Jackie and I had some problems communicating. I wasn't spending enough time in Seattle, and according to her, I wasn't moving fast enough to get things done in Fairbanks so that we could get on with our lives. I was in my office one afternoon when the phone rang. She was on it, asking if I was sitting down because she had just checked into an inn in Fairbanks. The purpose of the visit was to talk and get our stuff together. She stayed overnight and the better part of the next day, and then left for Seattle.

The problem was simple enough. Bill Brand wouldn't make the break with his wife. Even so, he was furiously jealous when he found a rough draft of a letter on one of Jackie's legal tablets. She had written to a man—a friend of one of her brothers—thanking him for buying her dinner when they met accidentally in the airport. This had been the night she returned from her trip to urge Bill to divorce his wife. In the letter she invited the friend, his wife, and his daughter to stay in her apartment in Bellevue if they ever found themselves passing through Seattle.

"I never mentioned anything about it to her," Brand wrote in his "Bill and Jackie Letter"—"but it's another example of her morally loose style of life and her need to have something going on. I have no way of knowing how often he stayed with her, but I do know that she's spectacular enough in bed that any man would rig more than one Seattle trip to be with her if he was invited."

Bill Brand saw shadows of sex everywhere. If Jackie went to the beach with a friend and her husband during the time Bill was home in Fairbanks, he imagined kinky threesomes. He even suspected Jackie of having incestuous relationships with a male member of her family. He perceived her hand touching a man's as she passed a cigarette lighter as an overtly sexual signal.

It was all in Bill's own distorted perception, but frightening in its intensity. As he wrote out his evaluation of Jackie's morals, the skewed convolutions of his thinking show in his tangled prose.

She has always had traces of the hedonistic approach to things such as, "If it feels good and the consequences aren't that bad, do it." Sex to some people is like shaking hands, no more consequential than that. The most disturbing matter to this is that while I have been aware of it, I have never exposed my resentment to her behavior, expecting to be accepted on a normal social and moral level, while, because she isn't going to say anything different, she doesn't, in fact, belong at *any* level. When it's considered the number of men she has had sex with in her lifetime and then demands and receives acceptance of a moral and social level that most people have to earn, there is something very wrong.

There *was* something very wrong. Jackie Jessup had no hint of the rage in her lover. Bill never mentioned his jealousy to her. He never gave her a chance to convince him of her fidelity, of the truth. Jackie didn't realize Bill considered her "morally loose"; she would have been appalled had she known what was really festering in Bill's mind.

Bill Brand finally obtained a divorce and came to Jackie at last a single man.

On April 23, 1982, almost a quarter of a century after they first met, Jackie Jessup and Bill Brand were married. When Jackie married Bill she virtually gave up friends, family, and all outside interests. Jackie's role—a role she accepted gladly—as defined by her bridegroom was to live for Bill, and only for Bill. Their life together, realized after many years of frustration, was supposed to be one long honeymoon; the peak phase of Bill Brand's ecstasy must never be allowed to settle into a pleasant, comfortable marriage. It must be romance, romance, romance.

A devastatingly impossible goal.

Bill finally moved into the Bellevue apartment he had rented for Jackie so many years earlier. He opened a business, Alaska Marketing Industries, and rented an office on 116th N.E. in Bellevue.

It should have been a happy ending. It was anything but.

Bill wanted to know where Jackie was every minute, and who she was talking to. He resented it if she spent too much time with anyone else—even her own family. She had made scores of friends—but Bill was annoyed when they passed through Seattle and called her. If she did arrange a brief lunch with a girlfriend, he paced and grumbled until she came home again. She always seemed to be on edge during those quick meetings, explaining that she had to hurry home. She was too jumpy to enjoy herself.

Bill's pervasive jealousy was ridiculous. Jackie loved him; she never cheated on him. The only thing that could have made her leave her marriage to Bill

Brand would be her death. She had given up so much to be with him, and she appreciated what he had given up for her. A quarter of a century of longing had finally led to their marriage, and she treasured it above anything else.

Barring an accident, however, Jackie Brand wasn't likely to precede Bill in death; she was much younger than he was—forty-three to his fifty-nine—and it was Bill who had a number of health problems.

All things being equal, Jackie would outlive Bill. That was a possibility she had considered and found unimportant when she married Bill in 1982. Whatever time they might have together would be worth the pain of widowhood later.

On February 22, 1985, Bellevue Police Lt. S.M. Bourgette received a phone call from the police dispatcher. They had received a worried call from Regis Caulfield,* Bill Brand's insurance agent. Caulfield had been alerted by another business associate of Brand's, Thomas Donley.* Both men had reason to be concerned; they had each received long identical letters from Brand which also contained his last will and testament. Caulfield had only recently tried to talk Brand out of changing his will. Bill had wanted to exclude Jackie completely and leave everything to his daughters instead. Besides that, Bill Brand had taken out an additional half million dollars worth of insurance.

After they received the bizarre letters from Bill Brand both Donley and Caulfield had attempted to phone his apartment, but no one answered. They had then contacted the apartment house manager. The manager went to the Brand apartment and knocked, and finally Bill Brand, his hair tousled, had come to the door. He assured the manager everything was "fine." The manager hadn't seen Jackie Brand but reported back that nothing was wrong at the apartment.

Not satisfied, Regis Caulfield had driven to Bellevue. It was nearly 4:30 when he got to the Brands' apartment house. Both Jackie's and Bill's cars, a Plymouth Arrow and a Mercury Cougar, were parked outside. He knocked at their door, but no one answered. He went to the manager's office and used the phone there. This time Bill's answering machine picked up his call.

Worried, Caulfield had called the Bellevue Police Department. Both he and Tom Donley had received an odd ten-page typewritten letter, with "Bill and Jackie" scrawled in Brand's handwriting across the top. It was mimeographed, and it was a scalding exposé chronicling the couple's twenty-five-year relationship, but mostly decrying Jackie Brand's lack of morals and her betrayal of Bill. Even to a layman's perception the letter was sick and full of rage. It was as if Bill Brand had attempted to obliterate Jackie with words, revealing the most intimate things about her to virtual strangers.

But what alarmed Caulfield and Donley were not the slurs on Jackie's fidelity. The document had ended, "Inasmuch as my wife has died with me, I direct that she shall be conclusively deemed not to have survived me."

Lt. Bourgette and Patrol Officer Dennis Dingfield arrived at the Northside Apartments at 5:30 p.m. on February 22nd. The day had been gloomy and cloudy, and it was almost full dark out.

Regis Caulfield pointed out the Cougar and Plymouth Arrow parked in the lot. "The first time I looked through the window," Caulfield said, "I saw a glass with some liquor in it—when I came back twenty minutes later, it had been moved. Somebody's in there."

Bourgette and Dingfield noted that the Brands' apartment occupied the entire lower half of the south side of the building. Apprised of the floor plan of the apartment by the manager, they could see light in the kitchen, the dining/living room area, and a back bedroom. And then they saw someone walking around inside. It was a tall man with silver hair.

Dingfield asked the police dispatcher to try to call the apartment and gave both of Brand's numbers. The phone rang, but the man inside didn't answer. The second number was the answering machine. The dispatcher left a message that the police were outside and wanted Brand to come to the door. Bourgette, watching, saw the man inside walk to the machine, rewind it, and listen to the message.

But he did not come to the door. The lights inside were turned off now, save for one in the back bedroom and a stove clock light.

Bourgette called for backup and got a key from the manager. He could still see someone walking around inside the apartment, and then the tall man drinking from a glass.

He could not see a woman.

The Bellevue Police thought they might have a hostage situation, and they quickly surrounded the apartment building. Armed officers covered all its perimeters. Hostage negotiators Tom Wray, Cherie Bay, James Kowalczyk, and E.O. Mott, led by Lt. Mark Ericks, were briefed on the situation.

Thomas Donley, still surprised that he had been designated the executor of Bill Brand's estate, was convinced that Brand's will meant "There will be no tomorrow." Caulfield, the insurance agent, knew very little about Bill Brand. He knew only that Brand was married to a second wife, that he was a "self-made, very hardheaded man" whose huge Alaska business empire had collapsed, and that all he had left were real estate holdings. Brand was described by both informants as an awesome drinker.

They waited. Minutes and hours passed. If Jackie Brand was inside, perhaps unable to get past Bill and come out, they didn't want to rush the apartment and give Brand a chance to carry out the promise in his "will."

Dennis Dingfield had not taken his eyes off the dimly lighted rooms inside the apartment for even a minute. After hours of observation he spotted the man inside crawling on his hands and knees. He would crawl for a while and then either lie or fall down. He appeared to be injured, or perhaps about to pass out from an overdose of some kind. He no longer looked capable of harming anyone. Bourgette called for an aid car.

At the same time, 2126 hours (9:26 p.m.), the TAG (Tactical Arms Group) team advised over police frequencies that there was a Code 4 at the Brand residence. Code 4 meant that everything was stable. It did *not* necessarily mean that everything had turned out well.

And then the TAG team went in. The man inside was standing as they went through the door, but only with great difficulty.

It was Bill Brand. He was alive—but extremely intoxicated.

Dennis Dingfield looked beyond the man frozen in the TAG team's flashlights. Dingfield's breath caught in his throat. Beyond the man, down the hallway, Dingfield spotted someone else, a woman lying motionless on the carpet. There was a dark red circle spread out around her body.

Too late.

Maybe it had been too late four hours earlier when they first surrounded the apartment building. It would have made the police feel better, somehow, to know that.

Dingfield cuffed Brand and led him to a police car to drive him back to headquarters, where E. O. Mott and Tom Wray were waiting to talk to him.

The investigation at the apartment was handed over to the detectives. Sadly, there was no hurry now.

Detective John Hansen had worked some of the more bizarre homicide cases that had begun to proliferate in Bellevue, the sleepy little town of the 1940s that had become one of Washington State's largest cities. Hansen was a stubborn, even dogged, instinctive investigator with flashes of brilliance. Tall and husky, with a voice like a bear, Hansen rarely smiled —unless the conversation turned to hunting dogs or his wife and children. In repose his face was handsome, but closed off; no one ever knew what he was really thinking.

Bill and Jackie Brand and John Hansen moved in different worlds, even though they all lived in Bellevue. Hansen was active in his church and spent whatever time he wasn't on duty with his family.

However, Hansen now began to be intimately acquainted with the tangled story of the Brands' lives, probably *better* acquainted than anyone else ever had. He would be the principal investigator assigned to Case No. 85-B-02260.

Hansen had stood outside the Brand apartment since 6:30. One paramedic from the Bellevue Fire Department had been allowed in to confirm that the woman inside was beyond human help, and then the scene had been sealed. As soon as Bill Brand was taken out Hansen and Detective Gary Felt stepped in.

The woman lay facedown on the hallway carpet. She wore a brown plaid skirt, a yellow silk blouse, and a brown corduroy jacket. She was also wearing high heels, stockings, and black gloves. Her makeup was perfect. A brown and tan comforter, which the fire department medic had lifted from her body, lay at her feet. A shiny briefcase was there, too.

John Hansen touched the calf of one of the woman's legs; the flesh was icy and stiff. The victim had been dead a long time. Hours at the very least.

The dead woman looked as though she had been headed for a trip; a camera on a red strap, a key ring, and a large blue purse rested on the floor beside her. A tweed suitcase was further down the hall. A capped container of tea lay where it had dropped from her hand. Her feet pointed toward the front door. She looked as if she had fallen straight backward, felled instantly by someone or something.

She could not have known she was about to die.

Although a layman might wonder why it was necessary to have permission to investigate what almost surely was a murder, the detectives needed a search warrant to move freely around the apartment. Hansen immediately listed his reasons for a search warrant and obtained one via telephone from District Court Judge Brian Gain. With this in hand Hansen and Detective Gary Felt began to search the apartment.

The apartment was impeccably furnished, as if it had been done by a designer—or by someone with natural talent and a loving hand. The living room was done in shades of red and white, with objets d'art, pillows, and paintings all carrying out the same theme.

Someone had apparently been sleeping on the floral and satin striped couch. There was a rumpled quilt there. A glass of scotch, its ice not yet melted, was leaving a ring on the shiny waxed surface of the teak coffee table. Beside the glass there was a cocked handgun. A .357.

Ironically, the walls of the hallway where Jackie Brand lay dead were hung with gentle pictures of children and fields of flowers. All the furnishings were expensive. All the pictures were of flowers and children and, of course, of Bill and Jackie.

Bill had been proud of his affluence and his expensive tastes; he had discussed that in "The Bill and Jackie Letter" that Regis Caulfield and Tom Conley had turned over to the investigative team. The letter would answer many questions, but it would leave more unanswered. Brand had written of the Bellevue apartment and of the time when Jackie first agreed to live there and wait for him to "take care of things in Fairbanks."

"We found the apartment that suited our needs, leased it, and headed for downtown Seattle to shop for the furniture to furnish it. On one day, we bought for three bedrooms, a devan [sic], patio furniture, and a new car. When we got home, she threw up because we spent so much money."

Bill Brand seemed to have liked to communicate by writing—of one kind or another. The apartment was littered with notes. Felt and Hansen gazed around the apartment and saw them. They were everywhere. Notes from Bill to Jackie hung from door jambs, and fluttered where they were taped on cabinets. Brand had even taped them to the wall above her body.

They were love notes of a sort. Some of them were requests for sex; others were weird affirmations of Brand's devotion to the woman who had apparently been his wife for almost three years, his lover for twenty.

One note dated February 11, 1985—ten days earlier—read: "My weekends are great because of you. Monday comes and that means I have to leave you—I hate that. I can barely wait for the next weekend. That tells you what my life is all about. Love is what you and I are all about and that's what makes us go. I'll see you this noon. Be kinky—wear it to lunch. Bill."

The detectives shook their heads. What had he meant? Probably some Frederick's of Hollywood piece of lingerie he had bought Jackie. If the note had been there ten days, that probably meant that no one but Jackie and Bill ever entered this apartment. They couldn't imagine that she would have left such an explicit note for someone else to read. She must have felt like a prisoner.

Hansen and Felt moved around the apartment. Hansen noted a scuff on the hallway of the kitchen area, just a slight gouge in the plasterboard, probably a bullet ricochet. He saw an ashtray and a calendar on the dining room table. Bending to read, he felt the hairs rise on the back of his neck. The last entry on the calendar was penciled neatly into the block for February 21st. Yesterday.

"Jackie passed away at 13:10 hrs."

There was a half-empty bottle of Johnnie Walker Red Label scotch and an empty bottle of Bulloch scotch in the kitchen, and at the other end of the counter a long row of vitamin bottles next to a pack of Winstons. That must have been Jackie Brand's choice.

A last cigarette, a Winston, was stubbed out in a crystal ashtray, its filter scarlet with fresh lipstick.

Liquor, cigarettes, and vitamins. Everything in this place was a contradiction. Guns, flowers, blood, love notes.

Trying to look at it all rationally and with as little emotion as possible, John Hansen deduced what had probably happened. For whatever grotesque reason, Bill Brand had shot his wife in the back of the head as she was walking ahead of him toward the front door. The cup of tea in her hand indicated she had been totally oblivious to the danger behind her.

After she was dead Brand had apparently calmly jotted down the time of her death on his calendar, as if he were marking some business appointment.

Then he would have hit the scotch, trying, perhaps, to get the courage to shoot himself, too. He had indicated in the letters he sent out that they would *both* be dead by the time the letters reached their destinations. The .357 Magnum six-shot revolver was cocked and ready there on the coffee table, with three cylinder chambers empty.

Deputy Medical Examiner Corinne Fligner checked for the wounds of entry and exit. She determined that two .357 slugs had struck Jackie's head; one on the right side had entered between her ear and the top of the head and penetrated her brain. A fatal wound. At the back of the victim's skull a shot had simply grazed Jackie's head.

Barring an eyewitness, it is impossible to reconstruct *exactly* how any homicide occurs—but John Hansen could almost visualize what had happened here.

The location of the wound at the rear of the head—plus the gun debris that surrounded it—

indicated that this was the first wound, fired from a short distance away. The shooter would have been just behind Jackie in the hall. This bullet appeared to have deflected off the back of her skull and lodged in the hallway ceiling directly ahead of her.

The direction of fire of the fatal wound was different. Its path went from front to back, right to left and very slightly downward.

When the first shot was fired and it grazed Jackie Brand's head its force would probably have spun her around to face the man with the gun. Her Bill.

The second bullet was fired from farther away but had pierced her brain, killing her instantly. Would she have had time to form a thought? Had she looked into her killer's eyes when she spun around?

No one would ever know.

At Bellevue police headquarters Detectives E. O. Mott and Tom Wray observed Bill Brand. His face was flushed, and he appeared intoxicated. He wore a white dress shirt with blue pin stripes, buttoned at the cuffs and tucked into his dark blue slacks. His clothing had clearly cost a great deal; the labels showed the garments had been purchased at Seattle's best stores. He was shoeless, but he wore dark socks.

Alone with the detectives in the interview room, Brand suddenly began talking about football and the Seattle Seahawks as if nothing unusual had happened at all. More likely, he didn't want to remember the tableau he had left behind in the apartment he shared with Jackie.

Mott introduced himself and Wray and waited for directions from Lt. Mark Ericks before they proceeded. The guy seemed so drunk, they wondered if they would be able to get any sense out of him. Ericks and John Hansen called from the crime scene to ask that Bill Brand's hands be "bagged" and that he remain handcuffed until a neutron activation analysis test could be performed to determine if he had indeed fired the .357. They also asked that a nitrate test be done to see what would show up on swabbings of his hands, and that a breathalyzer reading be taken before Wray and Mott proceeded with any questioning.

Gary Felt had advised Brand of his rights under Miranda before he was driven away from his apartment. However, when Brand suddenly blurted to Mott and Wray that he had shot his "beautiful wife," both detectives tried again to advise him of his rights to be absolutely sure that he understood.

Brand commented that he understood his rights but said he was quite willing to talk and answer questions. He said he was sorry for shooting his wife. He had shot her, he recalled, about noon the day before. She had been headed for the front door, and he was following her when he shot her twice. She had fallen to the floor, and he had left her there.

"Why did you kill her?" Mott asked quietly.

Brand did not answer directly.

"He only indicated that she was a very beautiful woman and that I wouldn't understand things about her, nor would I understand things about him," Mott wrote in his report.

"I got nothing to hide," Brand blurted. "I murdered my wife. I shot the most beautiful woman in the world."

And then he had begun to drink scotch.

Bill Brand was still drunk, twice as drunk as required in order to be considered legally drunk in the State of Washington. His blood alcohol was .20; his breathalyzer was .19.

He rambled on about killing his "beautiful wife," interspersing his memories of Jackie Brand's murder with a chillingly calm discussion of football. He shook his head back and forth, and his eyes filled with tears. He acknowledged that he was intoxicated and promised he would give a written statement when he sobered up—"tomorrow."

Brand stared at Detective Tom Wray and blurted that Wray looked just like a Seattle Seahawks football star. Then he sat silent for long minutes, tears welling up and beading at the corners of his eyes. Brand finally looked up at Wray and said, "I murdered my wife about twenty-four hours ago. I just got bombed —Johnnie Walker Red. . . . I used a .38 or a .357 and shot [pointing his left index finger under his chin]. I loaded five rounds—.38s, I think. There are three left, the gun's on the table, you know. . . . Who were those guys who barged into my home?"

Brand confided to Wray that he had kept drinking because that was the only way he could sleep. He had slept on the couch, waking up every three hours or so and drinking more.

"I can't believe I really messed things up. She didn't deserve this. . . ."

Bill Brand was coming down from his alcoholic binge, and he began to confront the horror of what he had done.

None of the detectives yet knew why.

Back at the Brands' apartment Hansen and Felt, along with Ericks, Oliver, and a police photographer, worked until almost four in the morning gathering evidence.

Gary Felt found a single spent bullet lying on the ceiling light trim, just beyond where it had passed through the wall. They had to saw a square of plasterboard free to get at that one. Ericks discovered a small lead fragment on the hallway carpet. They knew that Brand had blown a .19 on the breathalyzer—that he had been legally intoxicated when he was arrested. But had he been intoxicated thirty-three hours earlier when Jackie Brand died?

The tenant who lived in the apartment above the Brands told Hansen and Felt that she had heard a "thud-like sound, like someone had dropped something heavy" the day before, confirming that Jackie had been dead more than twenty-four hours when police entered her home.

John Hansen realized he would have to work this case backwards. He knew who the murderer was; the killer had been waiting for the police. And the evidence they had gathered during the long night after Bill Brand was arrested only served to confirm what had happened. The question was why. Why on earth had Bill Brand shot his "beautiful wife" in the back of the head?

Some of the answers began to come in from a dozen or more people who had received "The Bill and Jackie Letter." With each passing day that monstrous document showed up in more and more mailboxes across the country. Bill Brand had spewed out his jealousy and suspicion, so long repressed, in the ugly letter, and then he had sent it to everyone he could think of that Jackie had known—her family, her friends, even men he suspected had cuckolded him. It was not enough that he had killed Jackie; he had wanted to destroy her image, too. He had tried to wipe away every trace of the real, loving woman. Most of those who received the letter were horrified and sickened. Some were disgusted. Some—who had barely known Jackie Brand—were merely bewildered.

In talking with her relatives and friends, John Hansen found nothing to substantiate Jackie's alleged infidelities. Rather, friends who had received the letter gave statements that were just the opposite. Whenever they had come to Seattle and tried to spend some time with Jackie, her ex-stewardess friends said, she was always looking at her watch, anxious to get back to Bill. On the very rare occasions when they did meet Bill he was pleasant enough, but disinterested, obviously bored with their company.

"Jackie told me Bill unplugged their phone—so they wouldn't be bothered by outsiders," one woman remarked.

Bill had cloistered Jackie, keeping her just for himself, but she hadn't seemed to mind it. Hansen didn't find one witness who could remember that Jackie ever complained about her husband's suffocating affection. She still loved him. Nor could Hansen find anyone who believed Jackie had cheated on Bill Brand.

Two of Jackie's girlfriends had spoken to her a day or so before she died, and she had told them that Bill was going to fly to Alaska on the 21st—and that she would be taking him to the airport. That made sense. The suitcase found next to Jackie's body was packed with men's clothing.

Hansen read "The Bill and Jackie Letter" again and again. It was apparent, even with Brand's exaggerations, that the two had been a part of each other's lives for a long, long time.

They had, indeed, finally been married. Happy ever after.

It wasn't going to be easy for Hansen to ferret out what had gone wrong. Sobered up in jail, Bill Brand declined to talk. He would only say—as if John Hansen could give him some answers—"I'd just like to understand why it all happened."

Hansen was silent, and the room seemed to hum

with tension. If anyone should know why it happened, it was the man in jail coveralls, the man who had known Jackie for almost three decades. But Bill Brand just shook his head as if he, too, was bewildered. Perhaps he was. Perhaps he was beginning to try to save his own skin.

Finally Brand sighed and said, "I'll be able to sort it all out in a few hours." And then he said he wanted an attorney. John Hansen ended the interview.

As John Hansen interviewed Jackie's friends and Bill Brand's business associates he was told that Brand had once been extremely wealthy in Fairbanks. At some point, however, his fortune had begun to slide. He had suffered severe business reversals in the late seventies when high interest rates began to cripple the construction business. Bill Brand had finally been forced to file for three separate bankruptcies—a personal bankruptcy due to his guarantees to his bank and supplier debts on behalf of his companies, and two business bankruptcies. Along with his own financial disaster, Brand's first wife sacrificed most of her holdings to settle Brand's debts.

From 1977 on, Bill Brand had suffered continual financial reverses. His vast fortune dwindled. The Alaskan oil pipeline had gone on line in 1975, and Brand had counted on a natural gas pipeline to follow. It never happened, though, and interest rates kept climbing.

Amid the ashes of what had once been a thriving business Bill divorced his first wife, moved to Seattle, married Jackie, and began a business that was scarcely more than a front to conceal his growing desperation. He had begun with high hopes that he could earn a good living again by helping Washington businesses that wanted to branch out into Alaska. He still had savvy; he still had contacts. But the only real money Brand had coming in was from leases he held in Alaska.

Jackie had no idea how bad things were. Bill had always showered her with jewelry and presents, and he worried that she would leave him if she found out how close he was to financial disaster. So he didn't tell her. Even though he wasn't doing any business at all, he left their apartment each day, carrying a briefcase. At the office he phoned friends or read magazines. Sometimes he chatted with people in neighboring offices. In truth, Bill simply marked time until he could rush home to Jackie.

If only he had confided in her, she would have understood.

Jackie knew they were living off his prior investments, but Bill had always had so much money, she assumed he had a stake that would see them through any hard times.

But failure bred failure. Bill Brand, stressed to the breaking point by his business losses, by the fact that he had almost reached the limit on his many credit cards, by his overriding fear that he would lose Jackie, became impotent.

Although she had seldom confided in anyone about her marriage, Jackie did mention Bill's sexual problems to one of her two Seattle friends. She also said it was no big deal. "I like so many other things about my Bill that it really does not matter to me."

One friend told John Hansen that Jackie Brand had always struck her as a woman so straight and puritanical that she was "almost sexless," and that she couldn't imagine Jackie in the role of the harlot Brand described in his final letter. No, she assured Hansen, a husband who could no longer make love wouldn't have been the end of the world for Jackie. Not at all.

But it had been for Brand. He had consulted sex therapists, trying to regain his potency. Hansen found a desk planner in Brand's office that went back two years, and its pages were full of coded notations about business meetings and about sex. He had listed both his failures and his successes. Bill Brand had been obsessed with his sexual performance. Perhaps in an attempt to prove himself, he had been unfaithful to Jackie, even during the times in his marriage when he had accused *her* of cheating on him.

Bill Brand's sexual notations and the derogatory notes about Jackie were all written in red ink. Every sexual encounter, however brief, had been noted in Brand's books. There were also a number of references to pornographic movies Brand had seen, right down to the titles and the dates he had viewed them.

Along with all of this Hansen read through medical records that showed that Bill Brand had consulted physicians more and more frequently, worried about his eyes, his lungs, his heart, his blood pressure. The business and sexual performance strain Brand felt had quite clearly converted into physical symptoms. Beyond that, there was the very real possibility that Brand *was* falling apart physically. He overindulged in everything; that had worked when he was younger, but he was almost sixty, and his body was failing him.

It was easier now for Hansen to see what had gone wrong. Bill Brand had feared he was losing those things that *he* perceived Jackie wanted from him— money and sexual performance. He was no longer the vigorous young man she remembered from 1958.

Brand had been gripped in a nightmarish midlife crisis blown all out of proportion. Despite all the years they had been involved with each other, Brand clearly hadn't known Jackie at all. He didn't know his wife well enough to trust her with his pain. And she obviously had known virtually nothing about what was going on in his head.

Something had to happen, some explosion, some end to it.

And tragically, something had.

John Hansen met another of Jackie's friends a week after Jackie died. This friend had known Jackie, she said, since they grew up together in Minnesota. She said she had not approved when Jackie married Bill. He had been overly possessive, and rude and overbearing toward her family and friends.

"I realized I could not enjoy Jackie's company when Bill was around. I resorted to meeting her for lunch or talking with her on the phone. But if you called and left a message for her with him, he wouldn't pass it on."

Jackie had called her friend at 5:00 p.m. on either the 19th or 20th of February to say that Bill was flying to Fairbanks on Thursday for business and wouldn't be back until Sunday. Jackie had invited her friend over to the Bellevue apartment for dinner, but the woman said she had other plans. They had agreed to meet at a restaurant for lunch the following week.

Instead of having dinner with Jackie Brand in her apartment on February 22, the friend had received "The Bill and Jackie Letter" by Priority Mail and read it with growing horror.

Two of Jackie's other friends said that they had always felt that Bill treated his wife tenderly. One friend had last seen Jackie only six days before she died. During this last meeting she had been a little surprised when Jackie commented, "I would like to have had somebody more handsome, but you know, Bill is so good to me."

It had been almost as if Jackie was trying to

convince herself that she *had* made the right choice when she committed her life to Bill Brand.

This friend received the letter on the 22nd, too. "When I read it I knew instinctively that Jackie was dead; I immediately called their house, starting at 6:25. I left messages on the tape machine, but never got an answer. . . ."

February 21, 1985, had been Bill Brand's cutoff day. He had told Jackie he would be flying to Fairbanks. He bought a ticket, but he never really expected to fly to Alaska that day. He had hoped against improbable hope that he would make a deal, extend a lease, do *something* so that Jackie wouldn't know they were flat broke. If nothing happened by the 21st, they would both have to die. To Bill Brand it was that simple.

Nothing happened. All Brand's money was gone. He couldn't even charge a meal on a credit card. Jackie didn't know. He had lived a lie for so long that Bill was able on this one last day to paste a serene look on his face so that she *wouldn't* know. He mailed his hate-filled letters, a dozen or more of them.

There was no turning back now.

When Thursday morning came they both dressed. Jackie packed Bill's bag, stubbed out her cigarette, grabbed a cup of tea for the ride to the airport, and walked down the hall ahead of Bill on her way to drive him to SeaTac Airport.

Bill raised the gun. He fired. Jackie spun around, a look of pain and shock on her face, and Bill thought for one crazy second that she might be having one of her headaches. She had terrible headaches. He fired again.

And Jackie died. She never knew that Bill had no

more money. For a man who had failed at so many things, Bill Brand had managed to succeed in this one tragic effort. This one useless, senseless act of cruelty.

Bill's note to his executor was succinct. He wrote that he had supported Jackie since November 1, 1975.

It was Brand money that purchased all the furniture and appliances that are in the apartment. That includes a Maytag washer and dryer and a Sears freezer. . . . Also, I brought to the marriage a Unigard policy. . . . At the time we were married, I made my wife beneficiary, but on the 12th of December, I signed the enclosed change of beneficiary statement. . . .

I should make clear to you . . . that my wife never adopted the Jessup children which will severely limit any claims they might think they have for any of her possessions. . . .

Bill had never accepted Jackie's stepchildren. He saw them, too, as interlopers, and he wanted to be sure they got nothing. He wanted his body cremated and sent to relatives. He left Jackie's remains to her family.

Bill Brand would have preferred that Jackie's family received nothing more. But John Hansen made a decision to give the victim's family the few pieces of gold jewelry that the medical examiner had removed from her body. That was all they would have left of her—that and the despicably savage letter from Bill.

It was over.

But of course, it really wasn't. Bill Brand had had the courage to kill the woman he claimed to love beyond life itself, but he had not had the courage to commit suicide.

John Henry Browne, his defense attorney, had Bill

Brand examined by a psychiatrist to see if he had been, under the law, responsible for his actions on February 21, 1985.

Brand's diagnosis was that he was in the grip of a major clinical depression and that his responses were indicative of a narcissistic personality disorder. The former was understandable, given the circumstances; the latter had probably been a part of Bill Brand his whole life. The narcissist focuses always on himself. He is not crazy, either legally or medically; he simply cannot empathize with other human beings. He expects special favors and views those around him as extensions of himself—his to summon or to send away at will. Jackie's main job was to admire Bill and offer him unconditional support. As all narcissists do, Bill alternately overidealized and devalued her.

Jackie made Bill whole. He owned her, and he could not let her find out that he was a failure. "Unconsciously," his examiner wrote, "his need to kill her represented his need to protect himself from her harsh judgment. His life . . . was dominated by her attentions and approval, from which he sustained his major—if not his sole—emotional support."

No one would ever say that Jackie had not done her best to make Bill Brand happy. She shut herself away from everyone but Bill. It wasn't enough. Nothing ever could have been.

Bill Brand had a profound personality disorder, and he was depressed—but he was not crazy. His examiner, a physician from the University of Washington School of Medicine, determined that Bill Brand had indeed been aware of his actions when he shot his wife in the head, and that he had had the ability to distinguish right from wrong. He could not hope to plead innocent by reason of insanity.

Bill Brand was convicted of second-degree murder

in King County Superior Court Judge Jim Bates's courtroom in February, 1986. Sentencing was delayed as Defense Attorney John Henry Browne argued that medical tests had revealed a degree of brain damage. It was a defense that might have worked six or eight years later, when medical experts understood how devastating steroids could be to both the physical and mental health of men who took them. Bill Brand, panicked by impotence, had been taking steroids. He had also been taking Halcyon pills to sleep. The synergesic (cumulative) effect of combining those drugs—not to mention his excessive use of alcohol and other medications he was taking—might well have heightened the paranoia he felt over losing Jackie.

It would have been an interesting courtroom battle. Crimes committed while someone is under the influence of so-called recreational drugs and/or alcohol do not usually go unpunished. A "diminished capacity" defense doesn't usually work because the defendant has *chosen* to render himself less than capable. Might an insanity plea have convinced a jury, given the new information that has come out on steroids? Perhaps. But then there was the whole quarter of a century of background of Bill Brand's possessive hold over Jackie—a thread going back to the days when he was young and alert and vigorous.

At any rate, John Henry Browne, who is one of Seattle's most sought-after defense attorneys, did not yet have the final decision on the negative effects of steroids to argue with in 1986.

In the late summer of 1986 Bill Brand was sentenced to thirteen years in prison. Due to his increasingly poor health and diminishing mental capacity his sentence was appealed, and he was released on October 11, 1991. He was suffering from chronic obstructive pulmonary disease, better known as emphysema.

In the summer of 1993 Bill Brand, now sixty-eight, was admitted to the Veterans Administration Medical Center in Seattle. He died there at ten minutes past eleven in the evening on July 16th. Brand's death certificate listed him as a widower, and he was indeed that. Jackie had been dead for eight years.

Jackie had told him long before that they would ultimately be together. And they were—but for such a bitterly short time.

"Somewhere, Someday, Somehow" had come and gone.

EVERYTHING SHE EVER WANTED

Ann Rule

Jointed in a romantic love that most people only ever dream about, Pat Taylor's marriage to Tom Allanson was all she ever wanted. Both came from fine Southern families, and both longed to recreate for themselves a plantation where they would raise horses, grow roses, and move with grace and style in the highest social circles of Atlanta: in short, to be the Scarlett O'Hara and Rhett Butler of their time.

But scarcely two months later, their perfect world had erupted into family hatreds, terror, bloodshed and murder. The beautiful estate was mysteriously burned to the ground and Tom Allanson stood accused of the brutal slaying of his own mother and father. Before the terrifying truth about the perpetrator was revealed, other innocent victims were to suffer attempts on their lives as intricate family loyalties and cruel, obsessive jealousies were played out.

EVERYTHING SHE EVER WANTED
is a compelling study of a systematic, remorseless sociopath. Former Seattle policewoman and bestselling true-crime writer Ann Rule's meticulous recounting of heedless ambition and selfish passion alternately arouses and chills the senses.

'Ann Rule is the undisputed master crime writer of the eighties and nineties – no one does it better'
John Saul

THE STRANGER BESIDE ME

Revised and Updated Edition

Ann Rule

Ann Rule was a writer working on the biggest story of her life, tacking down a brutal mass-murderer. Little did she know that the young man who was her close friend was the savage slayer she was hunting.

Ted Bundy was everyone's picture of a natural 'winner' – handsome, charming, brilliant in law school, successful with women, on the verge of a dazzling career. On January 24, 1989 Ted Bundy was executed for the murders of three young women; he had also confessed to taking the lives of at least thirty-five more young women from coast to coast.

This is his story – the story of his magnetic power, his unholy compulsion, his demonic double life, and his string of helpless victims. It was written by a woman who thought she knew Ted Bundy, until she began to put all the evidence together, and the whole terrifying picture emerged from the dark depths.

'The most fascinating killer in modern American history ... Ann Rule has an extraordinary angle that makes *The Stranger Beside Me* as dramatic and chilling as a bedroom window shattering at midnight' – *New York Times*

Warner Books now offers an exciting range of quality titles by both established and new authors. All of the books in this series are available from:

Little, Brown and Company (UK),
P.O. Box 11,
Falmouth,
Cornwall TR10 9EN.

Alternatively you may fax your order to the above address. Fax No. 01326 317444.

Payments can be made as follows: cheque, postal order (payable to Little, Brown and Company) or by credit cards, Visa/Access. Do not send cash or currency. UK customers and B.F.P.O.: please send a cheque or postal order (no currency) and allow £1.00 for postage and packing for the first book, plus 50p for the second book, plus 30p for each additional book up to a maximum charge of £3.00 (7 books plus).

Overseas customers including Ireland, please allow £2.00 for postage and packing for the first book, plus £1.00 for the second book, plus 50p for each additional book.

NAME (Block Letters) ....

....

ADDRESS ....

....

....

☐ I enclose my remittance for ....

☐ I wish to pay by Access/Visa Card

Number ☐☐☐☐☐☐☐☐☐☐☐☐☐☐☐☐☐☐

Card Expiry Date ☐☐☐☐